HOW TO STUDY IN COLLEGE

FOURTH EDITION

How to Study in College

WALTER PAUK

Director, Reading Research Center
Cornell University

Houghton Mifflin Company • Boston
Dallas Geneva, Illinois Palo Alto Princeton, New Jersey

Printed in the U.S.A.

Library of Congress Catalog Card Number: 88-81354

ISBN: 0-395-43409-2

Cover painting by Masoud Yasami. Courtesy of the Elaine Horwitch Galleries, Scottsdale, Arizona. © 1988 Masoud Yasami.

Photo Credits

Part 1: Hazel Hankin/Stock, Boston.
Part 2: Franklin Wing/Stock, Boston.
Part 3: Franklin Wing/Stock, Boston.
Part 4: Ed Carlin/The Picture Cube.
Part 5: John Blaustein/Woodfin Camp
Part 6: Mark Antman/The Image Works

ABCDEFGHIJ-KR-9543210/898

Contents

PART III Your Notes

10 Thinking Visually 209

PART IV Tests and Examinations

11 Preparing for Exams 237

12 Answering True-False, Multiple-Choice, and Matching Questions 263

13 Answering Sentence-Completion and Short-Answer Questions 283

14 Answering Essay Questions 291

PART V Your Vocabulary and Reading Ability

15 Improving Your Vocabulary 307

16 Improving Your Reading Speed 331

17 Ten Techniques for Improving Your Reading Comprehension 345

To the Instructor

OF THE FOURTH EDITION

How to Study in College is based on the belief that what students want and need is straightforward, practical instruction on how to tackle and overcome the special difficulties they face in college. They want something they can readily understand and apply, and something that works. During the last thirty five years, I have seen the study techniques presented in this book work for thousands of students at universities and two-year colleges alike.

The techniques presented in *How to Study in College* are the product of extensive experience based on accepted educational and learning theory. Theory is never presented, however, without specific instruction on how to apply it—after all, the person who needs penicillin is seldom cured by learning the history of antibiotics! In making this book a practical tool, I have relied heavily on visual examples. For example, students are shown various sample schedules for controlling their time. They are shown facsimiles of lecture notes. They are shown how and how not to mark the books they study, to take notes on their reading, and to answer questions on examinations. Thus they learn by vivid example to apply the principles of contemporary research in learning and education.

Because it is so crucial that students learn, I am wholeheartedly against techniques that stress memorization. Such techniques fill the mind with "knowledge" that melts away after a test and leaves everything to be done over again. The techniques presented here result in real learning, and real learning lasts.

Finally, no textbook, no matter how up-to-date, is truly useful if it is boring, confusing, or excessively difficult to read. I have therefore written and edited to achieve a conversational tone, to make reading seem like a person-to-person chat. Research into how we learn continues to uncover fascinating new possibilities for enhancing the tasks of both students and teachers. The Fourth Edition makes extensive use of the results and implications of this research.

What's New in the Fourth Edition?

Chapter 1, "Preparing for Academic Success," now introduces the student to campus resources and services and discusses the special difficulties of older students.

As a further refinement on the twin skills of listening and notetaking, this edition devotes a chapter to strengthening listening habits and a chapter on note taking.

Information on concept mapping is combined with updated material on understanding visual materials, making Chapter 10, "Thinking Visually," unique in the classroom.

Unique in study skills texts, Chapter 21, "Learning with the Computer" introduces the student to the uses of computers they are likely to encounter in college. The chapter helps the student overcome initial misgivings by debunking myths about the computer, by describing the basic computer applications and their uses, and by detailing the particular uses to which educational software can be put.

To improve an instructor's ability to test student comprehension, a new battery of in-depth test questions has been added to the Instructor's Manual. These questions can help stimulate class discussion or assist a student in self-study situations.

Three chapters on vocabulary study have been condensed into a single chapter, presenting the various methods in a more streamlined unit.

Three chapters on taking notes from the textbook have been condensed into two chapters.

Chapters on studying foreign languages and mathematics have been updated and moved from the Instructor's Manual into the Special Skills section of the text in response to increasing enrollments in these areas.

Every chapter in the book is now more extensively cross-referenced with chapters that present related material.

Acknowledgments

Warm and sincere words of thanks go to those who are deeply and permanently linked to this book: Professor Marvin D. Glock; Ian D. Elliot; and the late Henry F. Thoma.

My sincere thanks also go to the contributors of material in previous editions: Professor Harrison A. Geiselmann of Cornell University; Professor Kenneth A. Greisen of Cornell University; Jane E. Hardy of Cornell University; Professor William G. Moulton of Princeton University; Professor James A.

Wood of the University of Texas at El Paso; and Dr. Nancy V. Wood, now Director of Study Skills and Tutorial Services, the University of Texas at El Paso, but then a graduate teaching assistant in the Cornell Reading and Study Skills Program, for certain materials she originally prepared for that program.

I am also very pleased that a valued colleague, Professor H. Dean Sutphin of Cornell University, has contributed his chapter on learning with the computer. Professors Mike Radis and Ron Williams of The Pennsylvania State University prepared the in-depth questions for further study and discussion that appear in the Instructor's Manual of this edition, and Professor Carol Kanar of Valencia Community College assisted with the updating and revision of Chapter 1; I thank them for their assistance. Ross James Quirie Owens remains a valued friend and contributor. His talents are particularly noticeable in the mini-overviews that precede and the quizzes that end each chapter.

I would also like to thank the reviewers of the text and manuscript for their many fine suggestions:

Delores A. Austin	*University of California, Santa Barbara*
Karen Bozeman-Gross	*Robert Morris College*
Barbara J. Clennon	*North Hennepin Community College*
Barbara R. Davis	*Georgia State University*
Thomas Deschaine	*Grand Rapids Junior College*
Ken Dulin	*University of Wisconsin at Madison*
Marilyn Eanet	*Rhode Island College*
John Elder	*Sinclair Community College*
Sara Davis Fine	*Enterprise State Junior College*
Carol C. Kanar	*Valencia Community College*
Theodore Kaul	*Ohio State University*
Edie Kochenour	*University of Utah*
Susan Steger Farmer	*William R. Harper College*
Nancy L. Matte	*Arizona State University*
Joyce McClemore	*Savannah State College*

Hilda G. McRaney	*Hinds Junior College*
Jim Mullen	*Bloomsburg University*
Joan Pallante	*College Misericordia*
Mike Radis	*The Pennsylvania State University*
Carolyn B. Robbins	*Lewis and Clark Community College*
Carole Steadman	*Tacoma Community College*
Juanita Stock	*Haywood Community College*
Edward Wightman	*Hudson Valley Community College*
Richard Wilkerson	*Ernest Holmes College*
Brenda R. Williams	*University of Hartford*
Ron Williams	*The Pennsylvania State University*
Donna Wood	*State Technical Institute*
John Zehnder	*Modesto Junior College*

Finally, I am eternally grateful to my many students, who have taught me much, so that I may pass on a little to others.

W.P.

To the Student

How did Helen Keller learn to read and communicate, in spite of being blind and unable to hear? Why did Abraham Lincoln walk twenty miles to borrow a book? How did Booker T. Washington, born in slavery, travel five hundred miles to a high school where he could get the education he craved? Each was motivated by the will to learn. Each so desired learning for its own sake that he or she allowed few things to interfere with that goal.

Perhaps you know people like Keller, Lincoln, or Washington. Perhaps you are such a person yourself. If you are, you have already discovered that the desire to learn can give you the strength to start projects, see them through during difficult spots, and finish them with satisfaction. In college, you are likely to find that the will to learn—perhaps more than any other single factor—will help you the most, particularly when you falter from time to time. On a cold winter morning, it's far easier to get out of bed if you want to ace a mid-term than if you don't really care about your performance!

By the same token, it's much easier to require a difficult task of yourself if you have some confidence you'll succeed at it. After all, even the most motivated person is likely to lose hope if his or her attempts to succeed at a particular task are continually frustrated. There's an old adage about this that's really true: "We do best at the things we like, and like them because we do them well." If you haven't become a successful student yet, maybe it's because you've been frustrated by your lack of success in the past. If so, success—even a small success—is likely to strengthen your will to learn.

What This Book Can Do for You

Whether you feel confident or nervous about your chances of succeeding as a student—and most of us feel a healthy dose of both—this book can help you. In it you will learn a variety of practical ways to strengthen your chances at succeeding. In theory there is no limit to learning and no limit to how you can improve your natural abilities with the material you study. By reading and applying the study skills techniques presented here, you will quickly begin to improve as a student, making your college experience a rich and rewarding one.

You will find many ideas, tips, and systems presented in this book, but you should not try to follow them all. Instead, select and then try those you believe will help you the most. To discover the ideas that suit you best, follow this procedure. First, make sure that you comprehend the idea *and* that you also see the reason or principle behind it. Second, consider how the idea would fit in with the way you already do things. Third, give the idea a try to see if it works before you adopt it. In short, use this book as a collection of ideas from which you can select what you need both for immediate and future use, according to your particular needs and personality.

How to Read Each Chapter

On the first page of each chapter you'll find a mini-overview, almost like a menu. Read it first to whet your appetite for the content of the chapter. Then read the entire chapter thoughtfully—in one sitting if you can—and read the chapter summary carefully. Then, with the understanding you've gained from the summary, go back and re-read any part of the chapter that particularly interests you. Make notes on any techniques or ideas you want to remember.

How to Use End-of-Chapter Questions

The end-of-chapter questions are designed to teach, not test; you'll find no trick questions and no traps to lead you to an incorrect answer. Take each question at face value and answer it to the best of your ability. When you answer a question incorrectly, take this as an opportunity to re-read the pertinent portion of the chapter. By re-reading and rethinking the question and answer, you will greatly strengthen your understanding of the entire concept.

A Final Thought

To state in one sentence what I try to do in this book, I'll rely on the words of Ralph Waldo Emerson: "The best service one person can render another person is to help him help himself."

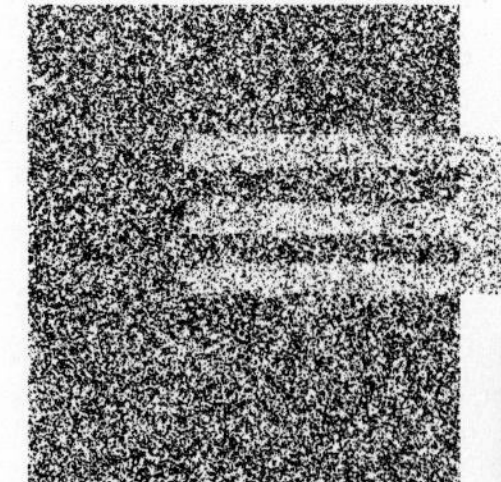

PART I

Your Goals

CHAPTER 1

Preparing for Academic Success

Just go to the mirror and look at yourself today
And see what the person in the mirror has to say.
It isn't your father, mother, husband, or wife
Whose stern and final judgment upon you must pass.
The person whose verdict counts most in your life
Is the person staring back from the looking glass.

Anonymous

Most of us place a premium on succeeding. Success is important for personal growth and, later on, for professional growth. In college, academic success is most at stake. Learning to succeed here will help lay the groundwork for success in the future. This chapter introduces you to the fundamentals of academic success. In it we'll discuss

- Which student are you?
- Getting familiar with college resources
- Understanding your style
- Trying new ways
- Study skills: the great equalizer

with emphasis on

- Independent learning

and finally

- The power of study skills

hether you are a recent high school graduate attending college for the first time, an older student seeking a career change, or a returning student pursuing a goal or a dream, you are about to experience major changes in your life and in the lives of those closest to you. Whether you commute to school or live on campus, whether you are enrolled in a two-year or four-year institution, attending college will be rewarding at times and frustrating at times.

WHICH STUDENT ARE YOU?

Recent high school graduates have the special problem of making the transition from high school to college. If you are one of these students, you are probably missing your friends who went to other colleges or took jobs. You are probably confused by all the things you are expected to know, such as your college's requirements and deadlines. Or maybe you are feeling overwhelmed by what seems an impossible workload compared to that in high school, where you hardly had to study at all to make good grades. You are probably concerned about the difficulty of making friends on a campus where people of various ages, nationalities, cultures, and ethnic, racial, regional, and social groups are members of the student population. You may be afraid to approach instructors or professors who don't yet know your name, who have offices and secretaries, and who seem very busy. Perhaps you are worried that you won't be able to meet your parents' expectations. You may even be doubting your own abilities, imagining that everyone around you is smarter and better prepared to succeed in college than you are. Where do *you* go for help?

Older students may have special problems of readjusting to school life. They may have worked and raised a family and now may have the burden of simultaneously juggling home, school, and job responsibilities. If you are one of these students, you may worry that your family will feel left out while you go to classes or struggle with homework. You may worry that they won't understand when you have to ask them to do more of the chores or to leave you alone so you can study. You may be concerned that your job will suffer because of the time you spend at college, or that your studies will suffer because of the time you spend at work. Perhaps you are annoyed by college requirements that seem pointless and time-consuming to a person who, unlike a recent high school graduate, has achieved independence and has set definite goals. On the other hand, perhaps you've been away from school so long that course descriptions don't mean much to you, and you don't know what courses to take. As a result, you're spending too much time making what should be quick decisions. Maybe you are a woman, divorced, forced into the job market though you have little experience and few skills. You are attending college out of necessity and must succeed if you are to compete for good-paying jobs. Or perhaps, like many older students, you are intimidated by the presence of what seem to be so many bright, young people whose education is more recent than yours. Where do *you* go for help?

No matter what kind of student you are, one or more of the student services your college offers can help you meet your needs. Your adjustment to college life will be easier if you know where to turn for answers to questions and solutions to problems. Even if you are a student who has been in college for a while, you may not be aware of all the help your college provides. The following is a list of resources available at most colleges. Use this list as a starting point to get to know your college and its services, and take the first step toward academic success.

GETTING FAMILIAR WITH COLLEGE RESOURCES

College Catalogue. General information about your college's requirements, policies, programs, and services appears in the college catalogue. Make sure you have a copy, and use it often during the first weeks of classes to remind yourself of requirements and deadlines to be met. In the catalogue you will find courses listed by department or by subject area and descriptions of course content. This information can help you plan your schedule of future courses. Whenever you have a problem, check the catalogue's index to see if there is a listing that may help you.

Student Handbook. The Student Handbook will give you information on your school's procedures, regulations, and code of conduct. It may also describe the school's requirements for good academic standing and graduation. (Your department may have more specific requirements; you should check there or consult your academic adviser for details.) It's a good idea to read the student handbook to familiarize yourself with your school's codes and policies.

Admissions or Registrar's Office. You can get answers to questions concerning grades, transcripts, and college requirements in the admissions or registrar's office. Application, admission to college, and registration for courses begin in this office. All your records are kept here, and at the end of each term you will receive a grade report from this office.

Office of Financial Affairs. You can get answers to questions concerning scholarships, loans, and grants from the financial affairs office. You will come here to pay fees and fines and to pick up your checks if you are on a work-study grant or program. If you decide to take a part-time job on campus for which you must qualify on the basis of your financial status, you will fill out application forms in this office.

Career Development and Placement Office. You might go to the career development and placement office if you want help deciding on a major or choosing a career goal. People in this office can administer various interest, personality, and skills-assessment tests to help you determine the kind of work for which you are best suited. They can help you find jobs on and off campus. Some career development centers sponsor on-campus recruitment by businesses that send people to interview prospective graduates and aid them in submitting applications and résumés. Upon graduation, you can file a résumé in the placement office if you want your college's help in landing your first job.

Academic Advisement Office or Counseling Department. Academic and guidance counselors can help you with everything from choosing the right course to solving personal or other problems that are preventing you from meeting your educational goals. The academic advisement office or counseling department may be part of the admissions office, or it may be a separate department. In many colleges, students are assigned to an adviser or counselor who follows their progress throughout their college careers. If you have such a counselor, he or she may become a friend to whom you can turn for help.

Student Health Center. If you become ill, you can go to the health center and a doctor will see you. The health center may have a pharmacy and may provide a limited amount of hospital care. Some mental health services may be available through the student health center, through the office of a school psychologist or psychiatrist, or through a peer counseling group. When mental health problems are beyond the scope of what the college can handle, someone in the health center may refer students to an agency outside the college.

A residential college is more likely than a commuter college to have a student health center. If your college does not have one, someone at the college will contact a family member or some other person responsible for you in case of an emergency.

Student Government Association. Working with the dean of students, the student government association sponsors student activities such as intramural events, dances, special-interest organizations and clubs, and other social and academic events that may be of interest to you. Joining a club or taking part in campus events can be a way for you to meet other students who share your interests. In addition, your student government may publish a weekly bulletin that keeps you informed about campus life or a student handbook that summarizes college requirements and resources.

Student Publications. The college newspaper or literary magazine offers contributors unique opportunities for self-expression and provides readers with information and entertainment. Serving on the editorial staff of one of these publications may also fulfill some journalism or English requirements.

Learning Lab or Skills Center. You may turn to the learning lab or skills center for help in improving your study skills, reading abilities, writing techniques, or math skills. You may get tutorial help here either from student tutors or from instructional assistants. The center may provide an open lab where you can go on your own to study, or a counselor may require you to spend time in a reading, writing, or math lab because of your performance on a college skills assessment test. Or perhaps you'll come here to learn how to use a word processor or other computer program. For whatever reason, if you find yourself in a learning lab or skills center, consider it an opportunity to gain the skills you need to succeed in increasingly demanding college courses.

Special Student Services. Veterans and handicapped, learning-disabled, minority, international, and economically disadvantaged students may need the special assistance of a trained support group to meet their educational goals. Ask your counselor or adviser about these services if you think you qualify for them. Your college may offer other special services. For example, suppose you want help finding an off-campus residence. Look in the index of your college catalogue under "housing" to find the page number and section in the catalogue where your questions might be answered.

Undergraduate Athletics Office. A listing of the college's athletic programs and events will be available in the undergraduate athletics office. This is the office to visit if you are interested in participating in intramural or varsity sports or if you want to know how to get tickets for the next football or basketball game.

Resident Assistant. If you are an on-campus student unfamiliar with campus services, the resident assistant, or RA, can give you advice. RAs are almost always students; they frequently live down the hall from you and can be a great source of information about campus services. Although RAs are not as professionally qualified as people who staff the counseling center or other campus offices, they have been through the process you're undergoing, and they probably know where you need to go and what you need to do in order to adjust. An RA will often function as a referral service, directing you to the campus office best suited to your situation. He or she may also be someone in whom you can confide.

UNDERSTANDING YOUR STYLE

Besides trying to understand what the college requires of you, you may also be wondering how *you* will adapt to college. Understanding yourself and what you need to study well is important. You can start to understand yourself by identifying your strengths and weaknesses, likes and dislikes. Identifying your own pattern will help you zero in on the study skills techniques that will help you most.

The list below will help you identify your basic learning style or styles. Circle the letter that best matches your style. Keep your responses in mind as you read this book.

Learning Styles Self-Assessment

1. I study better (a) by myself; (b) in groups; (c) a combination of the two.
2. I remember best when (a) I've *heard* something; (b) I've *read* or *seen* something; or (c) I've *done* something more active, like problem-solving.
3. I think I'm better with (a) facts, such as names or dates; (b) concepts, ideas, or themes; or (c) about the same with both.
4. I learn better when I read (a) slowly; (b) quickly; (c) it doesn't seem to matter in terms of what I remember.
5. I study more efficiently in (a) one solid study period; (b) small blocks of time.
6. I work (a) well; (b) poorly under pressure.
7. I work (a) quickly, for short periods of time; (b) at a steady, slower pace for longer periods of time.

8. I (a) do; (b) do not learn best in a structured setting, such as a classroom or laboratory setting.
9. I think that the greatest strength in my learning style is ____________.
10. I think that the greatest weakness in my learning style is ____________.

Now that you've identified your style, take a couple of minutes to look at your skills. The list below presents some common statements students make about different aspects of studying. Circle the response in each sentence that best describes you and your study habits. Then use the page numbers that follow each item for additional self-study.

Study Skills Self-Assessment

1. I have/don't have enough time for sleep. I do/don't get so wound up about school that I can't sleep. (pp. 17–36 and pp. 81–83)
2. I can/can't set aside reasonable periods of time for studying. (pp. 37–67)
3. I think/don't think it's necessary for me to make a personal schedule. (pp. 41–53)
4. Noise distracts/doesn't distract me during study. (pp. 76–77)
5. I have/don't have difficulty concentrating. (pp. 77–79 and pp. 85–90)
6. I have/don't have difficulty remembering what I've read. (pp. 91–118)
7. I do/don't have trouble remembering the content of a lecture. (pp. 91–118 and pp. 121–133)
8. My mind does/doesn't wander during lectures and group discussions. (pp. 121–133)
9. My notes are/aren't disorganized. (pp. 135–161)
10. I follow/don't follow textbook material while I'm reading. (pp. 163–234)
11. I feel I could/could not use improvement in taking tests. (pp. 237–303)
12. Learning new vocabulary is/isn't a problem for me. (pp. 307–329)
13. I have/don't have any special difficulty with researching and writing essays and longer papers. (pp. 363–388)
14. I have/don't have any special difficulty with studying math. (pp. 389–408)
15. I have/don't have difficulty learning foreign languages. (pp. 409–430)
16. I have/don't have experience with computers. (pp. 431–447)

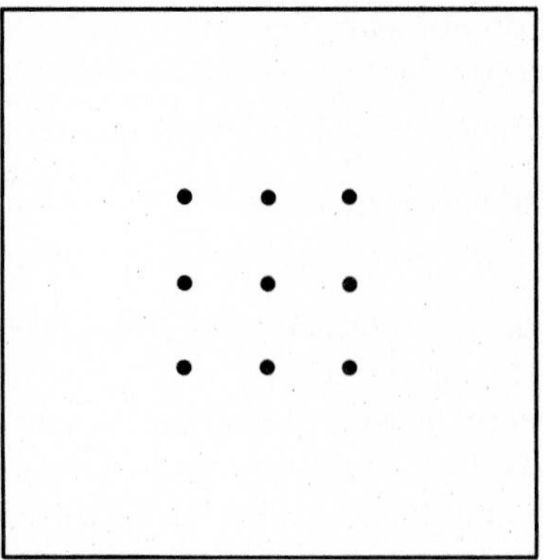

FIGURE 1.1 The Nine-Dot Problem
Try to connect these dots by drawing four straight lines without taking your pencil from the paper and without retracing any lines. The solution appears on page 12.

TRYING NEW WAYS

Now that you've identified your learning style and study habits, you may have one of a couple of thoughts in mind. You may be thinking, "It's true, I'm a sprinter who works like mad for a while and then slacks off, and that's the way I've always been. How can I possibly change?" Or you may believe that studying all night is an effective way of coping with a tight schedule and that you have no intention of changing to a more regular method. These ways of thinking probably feel comfortable, but they may have created blind spots in your view of studying. To get a sense of how blind spots may limit you, try to solve the problem shown in Figure 1.1. Chances are that a blind spot will prevent you from solving it. Once you see the solution, however, you'll say, "How easy! Why didn't I think of this tactic myself?"

STUDY SKILLS: THE GREAT EQUALIZER

If you use the study skills explained in this book, you should become as strong a student as the average hard-working student. After all, there is just so much to know about any assignment. By working hard and applying these skills, you will be able to reach the theoretical 100 percent mark. That's what mastery means. Of course, one student may master an assignment in half the time it takes another, just as it takes some people eight minutes to run a mile while others do it in four. The primary goal of this book is to help you run the full distance. The book will also help you learn to reduce the amount of time you need to complete that distance. These techniques are designed to help you do the very best you can with the abilities you have. The goal of study skills is independent learning.

INDEPENDENT LEARNING

"No one can teach you, but you may learn." Even the greatest words of wisdom will remain mere words unless you internalize them. Later in life, you will remember the names of courses you took in college—algebra, world history, business, Spanish, English—but you will not recall what you "learned" unless you have internalized the subject matter.

Good study skills will not only allow you to learn material thoroughly and permanently, they will also reduce your dependence on your teachers. If you must look to someone else for an "interpretation" or an "explanation," you cannot be an intellectually free person. To become an independent student, you must have the desire and the courage to open a textbook and to read it, study it, and think about it. Then you must be able to say in class the next day, or write in a paper a week or so later, "I believe this author is saying . . ."

THE POWER OF STUDY SKILLS

The decision to use study skills rests with you. Only you can decide which, if any, of the study skills described in this book will work for you. Studies have shown that effective students have solid, consistent work and study habits. Alex Main of the University of Strathclyde, Scotland, has noted that the effective student

- Has a regular study schedule
- Usually works at the same times each day
- Works mostly in a regular study place
- Works for short periods with frequent rest breaks
- Reviews notes soon after a lecture
- Does not leave work until the last minute
- Does not get easily distracted
- Does not need exams for motivation[1]

[1]Alex Main, *Encouraging Effective Learning* (Edinburgh: Scottish Academic Press, 1980), p. 2.

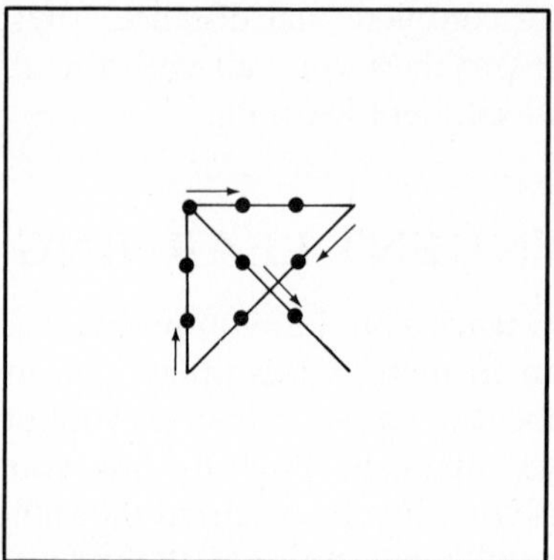

FIGURE 1.2 Answer to the Nine-Dot Problem
Begin at the top left corner and follow the arrows.

However, when Main questioned new undergraduates, he found that

- Forty percent of all students have no regular work schedule
- One-third of all students tend to put off work and leave too much for the last minute
- Almost half of all students get easily distracted when studying
- A similar proportion lose interest when things get too difficult
- More than a third need exams to make them study[2]

In another survey, students were asked to account for their success or lack of success. Thirty-three percent of the successful students attributed their success to study habits, and 25 percent of the unsuccessful students believed their *lack* of good study habits was the probable cause of their failure.

"All right," you may say, "but how do I go about getting good study habits before the first paper is assigned or before midterms? How do I achieve academic success if I don't even know how?" Those are good questions, and as you read Chapter 2 and later chapters, you'll be able to answer them.

SUMMARY

Why is the transition to college toughest for recent high school graduates?

Although the adjustment is difficult for everyone, recent high school graduates often enter college with the greatest trepidation. Among

[2]Ibid.

their concerns are leaving old friends and making new ones; deciphering college requirements and deadlines; dealing with a seemingly insurmountable workload; facing intimidating instructors and professors; coping with the pressure of parental expectations; and getting used to being surrounded by students who seem smarter and better adjusted than they.

What are some of the problems that older students face?

Unlike recent high school graduates, older students have to readjust to the academic environment while juggling the concerns of school, job, and family. If you've been out of school for a while, the regimentation of college life may seem restrictive and pointless on the one hand and confusing and time-consuming on the other. You may feel additional pressure if you view your return to academic life as a kind of sink or swim proposition designed to enhance your job-related skills. Or perhaps you are intimidated by your youthful classmates, who seem brighter and more attuned to college ways than you are.

Is there a simple solution to these problems?

Although the solutions to your problems may not always be simple, there is a wealth of resources and services from which you can receive help. The first step toward adjusting to college life and achieving academic success is to get to know your college and its services.

Is the office of financial affairs just for students who need financial aid?

No. In addition to dealing with financial aid, the office of financial affairs often collects various fees and fines. If you are interested in getting a part-time or work-study job, you would fill out an application in the financial affairs office.

Should I go to the career development and placement office before I'm ready to graduate?

Yes. It is important to decide on a career goal and to select a major early, so that you can tailor your course schedule to suit your specific needs. People in the career development and placement office can administer a variety of tests that may help you make your decision. In addition, they can tell you about potential job opportunities both on and off campus.

What does the academic advisement office or counseling department do?	People in those departments help students deal with problems, both academic and personal. A staff of counselors is ready to help you with everything from choosing the right course to coping with stress. In some colleges, you may be assigned to your own academic adviser or counselor.
Why should I go to the learning lab or skills center?	The learning lab or skills center exists to help students who want to improve their academic or study skills. If a particular class is giving you trouble, you can usually get tutorial help there. In addition, some learning labs now provide mini-courses on various computer and word-processing software.
What does the resident assistant do?	If you live in a dormitory or other on-campus housing, you probably have a resident assistant, or RA. RAs are usually upperclassmen who know the ropes and can help you adjust to campus life. They can give you a student's perspective on professors and courses, and they can lend a sympathetic ear when you're feeling down or overwhelmed.
What is the goal of study skills?	Learning and applying wise study habits can allow you to reduce your dependence on your teachers. Ultimately good study habits can help you become an independent thinker.
What are some of the characteristics of an effective student?	The effective student 1) has a regular study schedule; 2) usually works at the same times each day; 3) works mostly in a regular study place; 4) works for short periods with frequent rest breaks; 5) reviews notes soon after a lecture; 6) does not leave work until the last minute; 7) does not get easily distracted; and 8) does not need exams for motivation.

HAVE YOU MISSED SOMETHING?

1. *Sentence completion.* Complete the following sentences with one of the three words listed below each sentence.

a. A vast majority of new college students feel insecure about their

____.

age abilities friends

b. The greatest concern of older college students is probably the added

____.

cost homework responsibility

2. *Matching.* In each blank space in the left column, write the number preceding the phrase in the right column that matches the left item best.

_____ a. Parents	1. Serves as a good starting point for locating college services
_____ b. Professors	2. May be developed or improved at the learning lab
_____ c. Workload	3. Increases noticeably from high school to college
_____ d. Catalogue	4. A source of additional pressure for young college students
_____ e. Courses	5. Listed in the college catalogue
_____ f. Transcripts	6. Usually obtained through the admissions or registrar's office
_____ g. Skills	7. Often eligible for special student services
_____ h. Veterans	8. Can seem busy and aloof to a new college student

3. *True-false.* Write *T* beside the *true* statements and *F* beside the *false* statements.

_____ a. Some older students return to college in order to make a career change.

_____ b. For the most part, attending college is rewarding only when you live on campus.

_____ c. Recent high school graduates and older students have identical concerns about attending college.

_____ d. Students, young and old, are often intimidated by the apparent intelligence of their peers.

_____ e. A student health center is more likely to be found at residential colleges than at commuter colleges.

_____ f. A college's existence depends on the students it serves.

4. *College requirements.* Write "yes" next to possible sources of information about college requirements.

_____ a. College catalogue

_____ b. Admissions office

_____ c. Resident assistant

_____ d. Health center

_____ e. Student government

_____ f. Office of financial affairs

5. *Multiple choice.* Choose the word that completes the following sentence most accurately, and circle the letter that precedes it.

The learning lab or skills center is *least* likely to provide you with assistance that is

a. remedial
b. tutorial
c. financial
d. occupational

CHAPTER 2

Understanding Your Emotional and Physical Needs

If the only tool you have is a hammer, you tend to treat everything as if it were a nail.

Abraham Maslow (1908–1970), American humanistic psychologist who formulated the theory of self-actualization

Good mental and physical conditioning is vital to your success in college. Your mind has to be in good shape to handle the challenges posed by your instructors, textbooks, and fellow students, as well as the stress and tension you are certain to feel as you strive to complete assignments on time and maintain a decent grade-point average. A healthy body will brighten your mental outlook and help you deal calmly and effectively with your coursework and with other people. This chapter covers both aspects of conditioning, presenting specific information on

- The nature of stress
- Good habits to relieve stress
- Specific ways to handle stress
- Type A behavior and your health
- Relaxing your tensions away
- Safeguarding your health

and finally

- Social behavior and academic success

Most of us worry too much, criticize too much, get angry too often, and become too tense. When you mix such strong negative feelings with studying, you become inefficient both as a student and as a human being. You worry about low grades and about all the work you have to do. You are likely to spend so much time worrying that you can't get the work done, and as a result you worry still more.

The college years are unique because they offer you the opportunity to focus your time and energy on becoming the person you want to be. To make the most of this opportunity, you need to take control of your life. It is important for you to understand your emotional and physical needs and to attend to them.

THE NATURE OF STRESS

Stress, according to Hans Selye, M.D. (1907–1982), a pioneer in the study of stress, is

> the spice of life or the kiss of death—depending on how we cope with it. Stress gives us the means to express our talents and energies and pursue happiness; it can also cause exhaustion and illness, nervous breakdowns, heart attacks, accidents. Strictly speaking, stress is simply the body's non-specific response to any demand made on it. . . .
>
> Fundamentally, it is not the quality or intensity of the events that counts. What matters is not what happens to us, but the way we take it.[1]

Other researchers, extending Selye's work, now distinguish between *stressors* and *stress. Stressors* are the situations, people, and events that make demands on you. *Stress* itself is your response to those demands.[2] Stressors you are likely to encounter at college include anticipating and taking exams, learning to get along with roommates or teammates, commuting to and from college, adjusting to multiple demands of family and school work, and the need to participate in class. How your body responds to these and other stressors in part determines how much stress you feel.

Many researchers believe that stress reactions to situations and events can have physical, psychological, and behavioral results.[3] Because of an unresolved conflict, at first you may feel tired or dragged-out. Then you may feel anxious, confused, or uncertain. Eventually you may notice that your behavior toward other people is changing because of the stress you feel.

---

[1]Hans Selye, "How to Master Stress," *Parents* 52 (November 1977), p. 25.

[2]Douglas A. Bernstein, Edward J. Roy, Thomas K. Srull, and Christopher D. Wickens, *Psychology* (Boston: Houghton Mifflin, 1988), p. 472.

[3]Ibid., p. 479.

It's important for you to realize that *feeling* that college is stressful is normal. Look around you. It's safe to say that most of the people with whom you interact are experiencing the effects of the stressors in their lives. You might ask, "If everyone experiences stress, then isn't stress inescapable? I'm sure I'll probably feel 'stressed out' in college, but there's nothing that can be done about it."

In fact, there are several strategies that can help you through stressful situations. Some situations are inherently more stressful than others. For you, speaking in a small-group setting may be more stressful than taking an exam. For your best friend, however, just the opposite may be the case. Regardless of the stressful situation you find yourself in, you can use the tips and tactics described in the remainder of this chapter to minimize stress and make yourself more productive and healthy besides.

GOOD HABITS TO RELIEVE STRESS

Habit plays a crucial role in our lives. If you eliminate bad habits and develop good ones, you will have taken an important step toward relieving stress. Here are eight habits that are worth developing.

1. Do your very best on all the tasks that you undertake. Consider, of course, the relative importance of each task and the time available to complete it.

2. When you complete a task, evaluate the strengths and weaknesses of your performance. After you have made this assessment, wipe your mental slate clean, and turn to another task or take a break.

3. Never fall victim to the "broken-record syndrome." Do not allow yourself to get stuck in a mental groove, replaying past events and punishing yourself with thoughts of what you should have done.

4. After you complete a task, release yourself from stress by going out to play tennis, paddle ball, or squash, or by jogging, walking, or engaging in some other activity that will establish a good, strong break between tasks. In short, take a break of some sort.

5. Avoid situations—other than your coursework—that you know will produce a high level of stress.

6. Be *overprepared* for tests, class discussions, and speeches. You'll still feel anxious, but once you concentrate on what you're saying or writing, your anxiety and tension will disappear.

7. If you feel guilty about taking time to relax, then do this: Before taking time off, work hard at your assignments so that you'll feel you've *earned* the right to a rest or a change of pace.

8. The greatest producer of stress in college is probably procrastination—that is, putting off until tomorrow the things you should do today. Students often seek exotic ways to cope with procrastination without realizing that the means are already within their grasp. The means are self-discipline and self-organization. Remember: You can take charge of your own life, and here is one way to do it. Every night before you go to bed, list on a 3 × 5 card, in order of importance, "things to do tomorrow." Then tomorrow, without any hesitation, do each task in the order listed, and draw a line through each completed task. This system will give you a sense of great accomplishment and, best of all, will let you sleep soundly every night.

SPECIFIC WAYS TO HANDLE STRESS

Sometimes, in spite of your best efforts, you will fall victim to stress. The National Association for Mental Health recommends ten simple, specific actions that may help you when that happens.[4] Remember as you read and visualize them that success will not come from a half-hearted effort, nor will it come overnight. You will need determination, persistence, and sensitivity. The results, however, will be worth your best effort, whether yours is an occasional mild upset or a problem that is more lasting and severe.

Talk It Out

Bertrand Russell (1872–1970), a famous British philosopher, once observed, "Worry is like a rocking horse. It keeps you going, but gets you nowhere." When something worries you, talk it out. Don't bottle it up. Talking to a friend will bring the worry into the open, where it can be dealt with rationally. If a problem persists, don't be afraid to seek the help of others. Resident tutors, resident counselors, the health services, and peer advisers and counselors can be of assistance. Different colleges have different names for these important services. Find out what your college has so that if the need arises you can act.

Escape for a While

Sometimes, when things go wrong, it helps to escape from the painful problem for a while, to lose yourself in a book or a game or to take a brief walk for a change of scene. Making yourself stand there and suffer is a form of self-punishment, not a way to solve a problem. It is realistic and healthy

[4]Reprinted by permission of the National Association for Mental Health, Inc. Eleven Things You Can Do. *How to Deal with Your Tensions.* (with some adaptations.)

to escape punishment long enough to recover your breath and balance, but be prepared to deal with your difficulty when you are more composed.

Work Off Your Anger

If you feel yourself using anger as a general way of behaving, remember that although anger may give you a temporary sense of righteousness or power, it will probably leave you feeling foolish and sorry in the end. If you feel like lashing out at someone who has provoked you, let it wait until tomorrow. Meanwhile, do something physical. Play a game of tennis or squash; take a brisk walk or even a good hot shower. Remember: Your body and mind work together.

The following true story, told by the sales manager of a large Cadillac dealership, illustrates how anger interferes with rational thought. Year after year, one customer always beat the sales manager into an unprofitable deal. One day, the customer revealed his secret for getting those good deals. He said, "Every time we'd talk, I'd purposely make you angry. Then you couldn't think straight, and in frustration you'd agree to my terms."

To make this powerful principle of psychology work for you, put on an act of supreme calmness. Miraculously, you'll gain instant and genuine inner calmness. If you act happy, you'll be happy. If you act calm, you'll be calm.

Give In Occasionally

If you frequently find yourself quarreling with people and feeling obstinate and defiant, remember that that's how frustrated children behave. Stand your ground about what you know is right, but do so calmly and make allowance for the fact that you could be wrong.

Here is a practical way to avoid a stark confrontation. No matter how sure you are of a fact or idea, put yourself in a nonthreatening position. Say, "I may be wrong, but as I see it . . . ," or "Don't you think that? . . ." If you had instead said, "I believe that . . . ," you would have put yourself into a combative corner; and if your listener had confronted you by saying, "I don't agree with you," then you would have felt forced to disagree.

Do Something for Others

If you feel yourself worrying about yourself all the time, try doing something for somebody else. Unselfish behavior will take the steam out of your own worries and give you a fine feeling of having done well.

Here are two ways that you can help someone who is worried. First, let the person know that you are interested. Second, be a good listener. People with worries need someone with whom they can share their trouble. Don't criticize or give advice; just listen and show that you care.

Take One Thing at a Time

For stressed-out students, an ordinary workload may sometimes seem unbearable. The load seems so great that tackling any part of it—even the things that you most need to do—is more than you can bear to contemplate. When you reach this sorry state, remember that it is a temporary condition and that you *can* work your way out of it. The surest way to do this is to identify a few of the most urgent tasks and pitch into them, one at a time, setting aside all the rest for the time being. Once you have disposed of these, you'll see that the remainder is not such a horrible mess after all.

Don't Be Too Hard on Yourself

Some students expect too much from themselves and are in a constant state of worry and anxiety because they think they are not achieving as much as they should. They try to achieve perfection in everything. Admirable as this ideal is, it is an open invitation to failure. No one can be perfect in everything. Identify the things you do well, and then devote your major effort to them. They are likely to be things that you like to do and that give you the most satisfaction. For the things you don't do so well, give them your best effort, but don't take yourself to task if you don't achieve top honors or break records.

Give the Other Person a Break

When you are under stress, you may feel that you have to "get there first," to edge out the other person, even if the goal is as trivial as getting ahead in a cafeteria line. When everything becomes a contest, somebody is bound to get hurt—either physically, as on the highway, or emotionally, in the endeavor to lead a full life. You need not be this way. Competition *is* contagious, but so is cooperation. When you give the other person a break, you often make things easier for yourself. When people no longer feel that you are a threat to them, they stop being a threat to you.

Make Yourself Available

Many of us have the feeling that we are being left out, slighted, neglected, rejected. You may imagine that other students feel that way about you when in reality they are eager for you to make the first move. Instead of shrinking away and withdrawing, it is much healthier and more practical to make yourself available—to make some overtures instead of always waiting to be asked. Of course, the opposite of withdrawal—pushing yourself forward—is equally futile. It is often misinterpreted and may lead to real rejection. There is a middle ground. Try to find it.

Schedule Time for Recreation

Many students drive themselves so hard that they do not allow time for recreation, which is essential for good physical and mental health. You should include in your schedule definite hours for some form of exercise—playing tennis or squash with a friend; participation in a team sport such as basketball, volleyball, or softball; jogging, walking, swimming, hiking, skiing.

In a recent study that used college students as subjects, swimming and jogging emerged as highly effective stress-reducing techniques. Swimmers and joggers reported decreases in tension, anxiety, depression, anger, and confusion, and an increase in vigor after exercise. Joggers and swimmers gain physical as well as psychological benefits: an increase in cardiovascular performance, an increase in muscle strength and endurance, improved physical appearance, enhanced self-esteem, and reduced blood pressure.[5]

TYPE A BEHAVIOR AND YOUR HEALTH

In 1974, in *Type A Behavior and Your Heart,* Meyer Friedman, M.D., and Ray H. Rosenman, M.D., described for the general public a specific behavior pattern closely linked to coronary heart disease. They named this behavior pattern Type A and contrasted it with a different pattern, which they named Type B.

People who exhibit Type A behavior are aggressive, competitive, impatient, and assertive. They are tense, always trying to accomplish more in less time, and easily aroused to anger. Success is very important to them. They have difficulty relaxing.

People who exhibit the opposite, or Type B, behavior are rarely impatient or angry and do not feel a chronic sense of urgency. Type B individuals are more relaxed, easygoing, and readily satisfied. They are less concerned with achievement and the need to acquire more things.

In the United States, about 50 percent of the population exhibits Type A behavior, about 40 percent Type B. About 10 percent exhibits a combination of each. To see whether you are inclined toward Type A behavior, answer yes

[5]Bonnie G. Berger, "Use of Jogging and Swimming as Stress-Reduction Techniques," *Human Stress,* vol. 1 (New York: AMS Press, 1986), pp. 169–90.

or no to the following questions. Keep in mind, however, that this quiz is not a clinical analysis. It is usually given in conjunction with an interview by a trained clinician, and a person's actual behavior is more important than the answers to the questions. For an accurate assessment, you would have to undergo more rigorous testing.

1. I like to do things quickly, such as eating, walking, talking. __X__ Yes _____ No
2. I am hard-driving and feel very competitive about almost everything, and don't really trust most people. _____ Yes __X__ No
3. When others take too long to get to the point, I usually jump in and finish their sentences to speed things up. __X__ Yes _____ No
4. I like to be precisely on time and get irritated at delays or when others are late for appointments. __X__ Yes _____ No
5. I often do two things at once, such as opening the mail while on the phone, or reading or watching TV while eating. __X__ Yes _____ No
6. I often think of other things when people talk to me. __X__ Yes _____ No
7. I hate being interrupted and get irritated waiting in lines or when slow drivers hold me up. __X__ Yes _____ No
8. I usually bring conversations around to what interests me. __X__ Yes _____ No
9. I am very aggressive about getting what I want. _____ Yes __X__ No
10. Compared to my friends I easily lose my temper and usually show it. _____ Yes __X__ No

To score: Give one point to either a Yes or No answer. About 4 Yes answers is average; higher Yes scores indicate [a Type A behavior pattern], especially for Yes to Questions 1, 2, 4, 7, and 10.

Rosenman, R. H., "Do You Have Type 'A' Behavior?," *Health and Fitness '87* (New York: Newsweek), June 22, 1987, pp. S–12 & S–13. Reprinted by permission of Newsweek.

The behavior patterns you develop in college are most likely the ones you'll have in your business, professional, and personal life. If you think that you have some Type A habits, begin now to change your behavior. Your objective is not to change yourself into a Type B; rather, it is to *reduce* the excessive behaviors that are linked to heart attacks. Continue to manage your time, but allow more time for leisure, rather than for accomplishing things that aren't really necessary. Here are some things you can do to modify specific behavioral patterns.

1. **Excessive Competitiveness.** Take every opportunity to be genuinely unselfish. The mellow, comforting feeling will add years to your life.
2. **Constant Impatience.** Fuming while you stand in line will change stress into distress. Convert waiting in line into an opportunity by whipping out your pocket dictionary and reading it. There's adventure, wonder, and knowledge on every page.
3. **Chronic Sense of Urgency.** Go to bed an hour earlier and get up an hour sooner to get a head start on the day. A leisurely breakfast will set a leisurely tone for the rest of the day, and you'll feel in control.
4. **Insecurity.** Don't talk about your past successes. When your accomplishments are discovered naturally, people will have a higher regard for you because you didn't brag about them.
5. **Aggressiveness.** Have you ever been caught in the wrong line of traffic and had to move over into another jam-packed lane? Remember how grateful you felt when some considerate soul let you move in? When you do the same for someone else, you will feel even better!
6. **Hostility and Irritability.** When you find yourself being antagonistic, unfriendly, sarcastic, and disagreeable, try to stifle this corrosive behavior and do something that is friendly, warm, and generous. Help others in little ways such as by holding open a door. Smile more, and cheerfully and sincerely say things like "good morning" and "how are you?"
7. **Concern About Accomplishments.** Realize that your friends will like you because of the kind of person you are, not because of your accomplishments or your possessions. Work hard, but don't make the acquisition of possessions and superachievement your life's only goals.

RELAXING YOUR TENSIONS AWAY

A smile on your face will not only make you happy, it will also relax you. Being mentally and physically relaxed is exactly what you need for success in your academic life. A relaxed mind receives classroom lectures and discussions clearly, free from the internal static caused by tension and worry. Ideas received clearly in the first place have a better chance of sticking in your memory.

Memory does not work well under conditions of tension and strain. Consider a tip-of-the-tongue situation: You're sure you know a certain person's name (you can almost say it), but the name keeps eluding you. Then, when you stop tensing and straining and begin talking about something else, the name bobs up like a cork.

We all have ups and downs. Despite your best efforts, you might find yourself on the tense side, especially when you are studying for an important exam or are about to take one. Here are three sure-fire relaxation methods and one tension preventer.

The Count-of-Three Method

Just before an exam, just before an interview, or just before a dental appointment, your palms are sweating, your body is tense, and your breath is short and shallow. Here's what to do (count slowly and calmly through each step):

1. Inhale slowly through your nose while silently counting to three.
2. Hold your breath for the count of three.
3. Exhale slowly through your nose while silently counting to three.
4. With your breath out, count to three.
5. Repeat the cycle (steps 1 to 4) several times. (Once you have the rhythm, you need not continue counting; but maintain the same timing and the same pauses.)

The Doctors' Method

Medical science has come up with a breathing exercise to reduce blood pressure. Breathe in until your lungs can hold no more, and then take in a quick extra gasp of air through your mouth. Breathe out slowly and evenly. Repeat this seven times. What works for high blood pressure also works for high exam anxiety. You can quietly practice this exercise while studying for your exams and during an exam.

The Optimum-Rest Method

Five minutes in the position of optimum rest is the equivalent of hours of sleep, says Professor Richard Parks, who has worked as a director with hundreds of students and actors.[6] If you have a lot of studying to do but find yourself tense, tired, and tempted to take a nap, here's a substitute for sleeping:

---

[6]Richard Parks, *How to Overcome Stage Fright* (Fremont, Calif.: F-P Press, 1979), p. 57. Thanks to Professor Parks for the ideas for both the method and the figure.

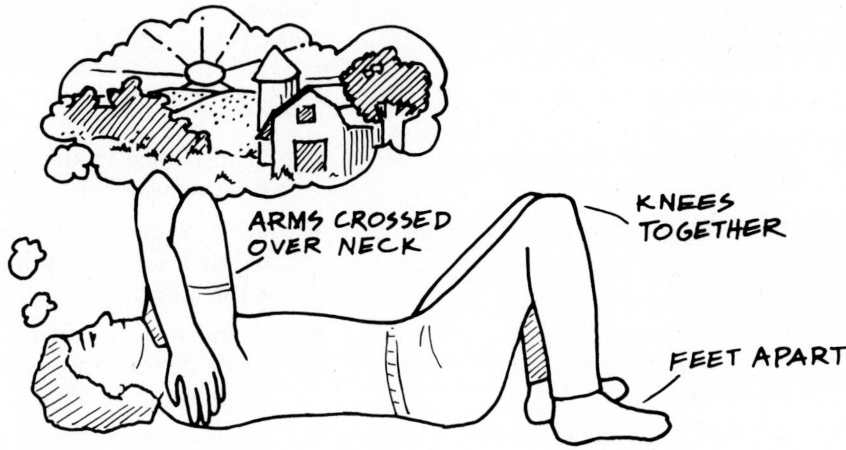

FIGURE 2.1 The Optimum-Rest Position

1. Lie flat on your back on the floor (use a rug or pad).
2. Raise your knees, keeping your feet flat on the floor.
3. Separate your feet to about 18 inches (about shoulder width).
4. Point your toes in and your heels out.
5. Allow your knees to come together in a relaxed way.
6. Cross your arms so that your hands hang limply alongside your neck.
7. Close your eyes; relax your mind; and imagine your favorite serene, quiet scene. You should look somewhat like the individual shown in Figure 2.1.

The Believe-in-You Method

You can use the Count-of-Three, Doctors', and Optimum-Rest methods to treat tension. It is better, of course, to prevent tension before it starts. Psychologist S. C. Kobasa says that when you are facing a stressful situation, you can prevent overreaction and aggravation simply by *believing that you are in control and that you can find a solution to any problem or crisis.*[7] The secret is not to make negative self-statements. For example:

[7]S. C. Kobasa, "Stressful Life Events, Personality, and Health: An Inquiry into Hardiness," *Journal of Personality and Social Psychology* 37 (1979): 1–11.

Negative: Don't Think This	*Positive: Think This*
• Three exams in two days is more than I can handle.	• I've survived worse things than this. I'll just do the best I can.
• This time there's no escape.	• I'll just hang in there. There's always a way out.
• Can't do these math problems.	• I'll work them as far as I can, and then see the T.A. first thing in the morning.
• Don't know how to start this research paper. Never could write.	• I'll make a list of ten titles or topics, then see the instructor in the morning for ideas.
• Can't make heads or tails out of this chapter. I'll just forget it.	• I'll go as far as I can, identify what it is I don't understand, and then see the T.A. or instructor immediately.

Use your head, not your emotions, when problems pop up in front of you like space invaders.

SAFEGUARDING YOUR HEALTH

Before you came to college, you had already formed many habits. Now that you are a college student, you are likely to drop some, modify some, add some, and retain some. Take a minute to think about the consequences of the habits that affect your health. If you believe they're good for the long pull, keep them. If not, consider changing them.

In a study of seven important health habits performed by the Human Population Laboratory of Alameda County, California, 6,928 adults were chosen as a cross section of the general population. The habits studied and the conclusions drawn from the research were these:

Habit	*Conclusion*
1. Smoking	Never smoke.
2. Exercise	Engage in some physical activity daily.
3. Alcohol	Use alcohol very moderately or not at all.

4. Sleep	Get from seven to eight hours of sleep regularly.
5. Weight	Maintain the proper weight.
6. Breakfast	Always eat a balanced breakfast.
7. Snacking	Do not eat between meals.

The results of the study were startling. Women who followed six or seven of these conclusions lived more than *seven years longer* than women who followed from none to three. Men who followed six or seven of these conclusions lived more than *eleven years longer* than men who followed from none to three.

Those seven conclusions are so easy to follow that you might wonder who would value life so little as not to follow them. You might think that no person would trade a year of life for any amount of money; yet, for no money at all, many people may be shortening their lives by consuming too much caffeine and coffee, smoking, and drinking too many alcoholic beverages.

Caffeine and Coffee

Caffeine will keep you awake at night. Many people are sensitive to caffeine. If you are one of them, even a cup of coffee toward evening will keep you from falling asleep easily. Laboratory studies show that from 200 to 500 milligrams of caffeine per day may produce headaches, nervousness, and gastrointestinal disturbances in some people. Coffee is not the only substance that contains caffeine. The amounts of caffeine in coffee, tea, soft drinks, chocolate, and nonprescription drugs are shown in Table 2.1.

Coffee apparently may do more damage than simply keeping you awake. Coffee has been linked to diabetes, heart attack, and cancer of the colon, urinary tract, and stomach. In addition, Harvard University researchers have found a statistical link between coffee and cancer of the pancreas, which is virtually incurable. After admitting that the pancreatic link needs further study, Dr. Brian MacMahon, the leader of the Harvard research team and a three-cup-a-day man himself, nevertheless stopped drinking coffee.

Smoking

When asked how long it takes for a cigarette to harm you, one California doctor answered, "About three seconds." In just *three seconds,* your heart pounds an extra fifteen beats per minute, raising your blood pressure about twenty points.

TABLE 2.1 Caffeine in Foods and Drugs

Foods and beverages	Per serving
Brewed coffee, 6-oz cup	100–150 mg
Instant coffee, 6-oz cup	86–99 mg
Decaffeinated coffee, 6-oz cup	2–4 mg
Tea, 6-oz cup	60–75 mg
Cocoa, 6-oz cup	5–10 mg
Colas and Dr Pepper, 12-oz	32–65 mg
Milk chocolate, 1 oz	6 mg
Bittersweet chocolate, 1 oz	20 mg
Baking chocolate, 1 oz	35 mg
Prescription drugs	**Per tablet**
Cafergot and Migralam	100 mg
Migral	50 mg
Fiorinal, Esgic, and Apectol	40 mg
Darvon Compound and Soma Compound	32 mg
Over-the-counter drugs	**Per tablet**
Vivarin	200 mg
NoDoz	100 mg
PreMens	66 mg
Excedrin	65 mg
A.P.C.'s, Anacin, Cope, Vanquish, Goody's headache powders, Empirin Compound, Midol, Easy-Mens, Sinapils	32 mg
Triaminicin and Coryban-D	30 mg
Dristan	16 mg
Neo-Synephrine Compounds, Cenegisic	15 mg

Around 26 percent of American adults smoke. If you are a member of this minority group, consider these facts[8] and draw your own conclusions:

1. Smoking is the leading cause of preventable death in the United States.
2. The Centers for Disease Control estimate that in 1984, 320,500 deaths from heart disease, lung cancer, and other illnesses were linked to smoking.
3. Millions of people all over the world are disabled by heart or lung diseases as a result of smoking.

[8]See "Tobacco's Toll," *Newsweek,* November 9, 1987, p. 62; and "Smoking Raises Female Heart Attack Risk," *Science News,* November 28, 1987, p. 341.

4. Men and women who smoke the same number of cigarettes have about the same chance of developing coronary artery disease.
5. Cigarette smoking is the single most avoidable risk factor for heart attacks in young and middle-aged women.

Alcohol

You are aware of the misery that alcohol abuse brings to individuals, families, and society. You know too about the damage alcohol can do to the user's body and mind.

Here are some facts about alcohol:

1. Research shows that alcohol increases the likelihood of cancer of the mouth, esophagus, larynx, and stomach.
2. Alcohol causes diseases of the stomach, intestines, liver, and nervous system.
3. Even in small amounts, alcohol interferes with the functioning of nerves and muscles.
4. Alcohol impairs speech, vision, coordination, balance, and judgment.
5. Alcohol is involved in many accidents, especially traffic accidents. Drunk drivers are 25 times more likely to be in an accident than are sober drivers.

One last point: When the alcohol in your blood courses through your brain, the alcohol kills off thousands of your brain cells, which are irreplaceable.

SOCIAL BEHAVIOR AND ACADEMIC SUCCESS

Your ability to get along with others can affect your academic performance. For example, the lingering effect of having said the wrong thing, even innocently, can interfere with your concentration and peace of mind, both of which are necessary for effective studying and learning. Here is some advice from Ann Landers. Learning and abiding by her list of dos and don'ts can be as valuable as any course you will take in college.

> 1. Keep skid chains on your tongue. Say less than you think. Cultivate a pleasant voice. How you say it is often more important than what you say.
> 2. Make few promises and keep them faithfully, no matter what the cost.
> 3. Never let an opportunity pass to give a well-deserved compliment.

4. If criticism is needed, do it tactfully. Don't use a sledgehammer when a fly swatter will do the job.
5. Be interested in others—their work, their homes and families. Let everyone you meet feel that you regard him as a person of importance.
6. Don't burden or depress those around you by dwelling on your minor aches and pains and small disappointments. Everyone has something in his life that is not exactly as he would like it to be.
7. Discuss, don't argue. It is the mark of a superior mind to be able to disagree without being disagreeable.
8. Let your virtues, if you have any, speak for themselves. Be constructive. Don't indulge in gossip. It is a waste of time and can be destructive. People who throw mudballs always manage to end up getting a little on themselves.
9. Be respectful of the feelings of others. Wit and humor at the expense of a friend is rarely worth the small laugh, and it may hurt more than you know.
10. Pay no attention to derogatory remarks about you. The person who carried the message may not be the world's most accurate reporter. Simply live so that nobody will believe him. Insecurity (or a stomachache, a toothache or a headache) is often at the root of most backbiting.
11. Do your best to forget about the "rewards." If you deserve credit, someone will "remember." Success is much sweeter that way.
12. Keep in mind that the true measure of an individual is how he treats a person who can do him absolutely no good.

SUMMARY

Is stress inescapable?

Everyone feels stress at some time or other. As a new college student, you are likely to find the transition from high school or from your job stressful. Even after you have become familiar with your campus and have made new friends, you will feel stress caused by deadlines, the need to handle a heavy load of coursework, and your desire to maintain a respectable grade-point average.

How can stress be relieved?

Relieving stress is often a matter of breaking bad habits and developing good ones. You can start by doing the best you can in everything you do. When you finish a task, figure out what you did wrong and what you did right and then move on. Learn from experience, but don't fall victim to the "broken-record syndrome." Relax by engaging in recreational activities: Take a break of some sort. Avoid high-stress situations. When you can't avoid a high-stress situation—such as an exam, for instance—compensate by being overprepared. If you ever feel guilty about taking a break, work hard right up until the time you call it quits and you'll feel as though your rest is well deserved. Finally, keep procrastination out of your life.

How do I combat procrastination?

Fighting procrastination requires self-discipline and self-organization. You can start by listing the things you plan to do the following day on a 3×5 card just before you go to sleep each night.

What is Type A behavior?

People who exhibit Type A behavior are aggressive, impatient, competitive, and assertive. Type A behavior is closely linked to high blood pressure and heart attacks. About half of the people in the United States exhibit Type A behavior.

What is Type B behavior?

Type B behavior is marked by an easygoing attitude. Type B individuals are relaxed and readily satisfied and do not feel a chronic sense of urgency.

Can I change from Type A to Type B?

Not really. To a certain extent, you are born either Type A or Type B. What you can do is try to reduce some of the excessive behaviors associated with the Type A personality and thus reduce your risk of heart attack.

Specifically, what should I do?

Try to be less competitive. Try to be more patient. Learn to take breaks. Do not feel that you have to accomplish everything all at once. Don't dwell on your past successes. Go out of your way to be kind to other people. Instead of giving your customary snappy put-down, bite your tongue or say something helpful and pleasant. Try to internalize the idea that people worth caring about will like you, or not like you, because of the sort of person you are, not because of your grades or your worldly possessions.

What are some bad habits that need to be eliminated?

Smoking at all, drinking any more than a moderate amount of alcohol, overeating, and snacking between meals have all been found to have a detrimental effect on health.

Are these the only bad habits I should worry about?

No. Another bad habit appears to be heavy coffee drinking and consuming large amounts of caffeine. Coffee has been linked to diabetes, heart attack, and numerous forms of cancer. Caffeine, which is present in chocolate, soft drinks, and nonprescription drugs as well as in coffee and tea, may produce headaches, nervousness, and gastrointestinal problems.

What are some good habits that I need to develop?

Regular exercise, getting sufficient sleep, and eating a balanced breakfast all have the potential to prolong your life.

What other factors can affect academic success?

In college you will commune with people as well as with textbooks. Because how you are treated by others can affect your emotional well-being and because your emotions affect your academic performance, it is important for you to develop a pattern of behavior that makes it easy for you to get along with others.

HAVE YOU MISSED SOMETHING?

1. *Sentence completion.* Complete the following sentences with one of the three words listed below each sentence.

   a. The body's response to demands that are made on it is known as ____________________.

      stress   tension   deviation

b. The desire to attain perfection in all that you do usually leads to ____________________.

failure success cooperation

c. People who exhibit Type A behavior are often ________________.

assertive relaxed athletic

2. *Matching.* In each blank space in the left column, write the number preceding the phrase in the right column that matches the left item best.

____ a. Broken-record syndrome	1. Impairs speech, vision, and thought
____ b. 3 × 5 card	2. Essential for good physical and emotional health
____ c. Recreation	3. A relaxation technique
____ d. Memory	4. A demanding situation such as a midterm examination
____ e. Coffee	5. Linked to diabetes, heart attack, and cancer
____ f. Stressor	6. Doesn't work well under conditions of tension and strain
____ g. Alcohol	7. Simple tool to prevent procrastination
____ h. Doctors' Method	8. Tendency to relive the past

3. *True-false.* Write *T* beside the *true* statements and *F* beside the *false* statements.

____ a. Self-discipline and self-organization can help you lick procrastination.

____ b. If you keep your worries to yourself, they'll usually go away.

____ c. The caffeine in chocolate is less harmful than the caffeine in coffee.

____ d. Swimmers and joggers are likely to feel depressed after exercising.

____ e. Tension and strain adversely affect your ability to remember.

____ f. People who exhibit Type B behavior are excitable and short-tempered.

4. *Tension releasers.* Write "yes" next to the items that are tension releasers.

_____ a. Escape for a while.

_____ b. Tell someone off.

_____ c. Give in occasionally.

_____ d. Do several things at once.

_____ e. Offer criticism freely.

_____ f. Don't be too hard on yourself.

_____ g. Make yourself available.

5. *Multiple choice.* Choose the phrase that completes the following sentence most accurately, and circle the letter that precedes it.

The greatest single producer of stress in college is probably

a. cigarette smoking
b. essay exams
c. procrastination
d. competition

CHAPTER 3

Controlling Your Time

YESTERDAY is a canceled check.
TOMORROW is a promissory note.
TODAY is ready cash. Use it!

Anonymous

Time flies, but that's no reason for you to go through each day simply "winging it." Through conscientious use of time and common-sense planning, you can make the most of your day. This chapter ticks off the important elements of time management, including

- Mastering time
- Scheduling time to gain time
- Principles of scheduling
- Types of schedules
- Scheduling for students with jobs
- Tips for saving time

and finally

- Getting things done

Your success or failure in college depends directly on your use of time. If you use it wisely, you'll prosper. If you use it poorly, you'll fail in the job you came to do. The management of time is the number-one skill to master in college.

Anyone who has paid $30 an hour (50 cents a minute) for a plumber, knows that time means money. Actually, time is worth far more than money. Time is life itself, and no price can be put on that. The preciousness of time has never been evoked more convincingly and more succinctly than in the final words of Elizabeth I (1533–1603), queen of England:

> All my possessions for a moment of time.

MASTERING TIME

If you want to take control of your life, you must take control of your time. Golda Meir, a schoolteacher in Milwaukee, went on to become prime minister of Israel. Her success was due in part to how she dealt with time. She said, "I must govern the clock, not be governed by it." In order to be the master of time instead of its slave, you must have a *goal,* you must have a *plan,* and you must *take action.*

Formulating a Goal

Nothing will fortify your inner self more than setting personal goals. To succeed in almost anything, you must have a goal. You have to know what you want to be before you can become it, and if you don't know where you're going, you won't get there. Goal setting is not kid stuff. It's student power! It's adult power!

Successful people in all walks of life realize the importance of setting goals. Businesspeople put their goals in writing. They have to show their weekly, monthly, and yearly goals to their immediate supervisors. Even the president of a corporation has to write goals and submit them to the board of directors. Setting goals is almost instinctive behavior. Pioneers heading west painted "California or Bust" on their covered wagons. This slogan was not a magic carpet whisking them across the continent, but it was a constant reminder of their goal.

You *must* express your goal in writing, on a sheet of paper. Your goal should be more specific and less general than simply getting a college education. You need to formulate a clear notion of not only *what* you want in college and life but also *why* you want it. Writing is important. The act of writing will help you clarify your thoughts.

No matter what you want to become—a computer programmer, sales manager, a civil engineer, a teacher, a dentist, a journalist—put your goal in writing and work to achieve it. As a college student you will have to weather some very rough days, and at times things may seem to be falling apart. That's when you'll need a lifeline to hold onto. Focusing on your goal can give you the perspective and strength you need to keep going.

Making a Plan

A plan is the route or approach you want to take in order to reach your goal. A record sheet such as the one shown in Figure 3.1 will help you devise your plan.

On a separate sheet of paper jot down all that comes to mind regarding your goal. Summarize these jottings in a brief statement, and transfer that statement to block 1 in Figure 3.1.

Keeping your goal in mind, on a separate sheet jot down the steps that you must take to reach your goal. Select from your jottings the steps that lead directly to your goal, and list them in block 2 in Figure 3.1.

On another separate sheet list positive factors that will help you accomplish your goal. It helps a lot to know what's working for you. Once you've identified these factors, add them to block 3.

You need to face reality, so think about the problems and obstacles that you have to overcome to reach your goal. List them in block 4.

With your record sheet in hand, take the next step of talking to your academic adviser as well as to a counselor in the career center. Don't underestimate the value of thinking about, writing about, and discussing your goal and plan. Get as much discussion and feedback as you can; then modify your plan if necessary. You will end up with a plan for your future that is realistic and attainable.

Taking Action

Among the saddest words in life are "It might have been." If you take no action, your goals and plans will amount to nothing. Taking action, however, is more easily said than done. In order to take action, you will need a large dose of self-discipline. Adapting to military discipline might even be easier than imposing discipline on yourself, yet self-discipline is what you must have if you are to take the action required to implement your plans. For instance, let's say your particular goal is to excel in your biology course. You think you

1	2
My Goal	Positive Factors
	1.
	2.
	3.
	4.
	5.
	6.
	7.

3	4
Steps Leading to My Goal	Obstacles
1.	1.
2.	2.
3.	3.
4.	4.
5.	5.
6.	6.
7.	7.

FIGURE 3.1 Record Sheet for Planning

may have trouble with some of the terms and concepts, so you've decided to seek the assistance of a department tutor. The department identifies the tutor for you, and now it's up to you to contact him or her. If you procrastinate here, all the time and thinking that went into your plan will have been wasted. Taking action simply means taking those steps necessary to complete your plan. When you identify a task, you must go ahead and do it.

SCHEDULING TIME TO GAIN TIME

Lee Iacocca, president of Chrysler Corporation, who became internationally famous as the man who saved the company from almost certain bankruptcy in 1981, made this observation: "I'm constantly amazed by the number of people who can't seem to control their own schedules." The way we use time—or waste it—is largely a matter of habit. It is not easy to change old habits, but if they are bad habits, they put a ceiling on achievement. For example, a professional baseball player with a poor batting stance can become a good hitter, up to a point. Unless he improves his stance, however, progress behind that point is doubtful. To change and begin almost all over again—to break a bad habit and make a good one—takes determination and will, but the decision to change brings the chance for success. If you find that you need more time for all your studies and other activities, consider scheduling your time in order to gain time.

Where Does All the Time Go?

In an effort to find out specifically how he spent his time, a student kept a diary of his daily activities for one week. He found that his "ten-minute" coffee break was nearer forty minutes. Figure 3.2 shows one page of his diary and contains an analysis that demonstrates how the student could avoid dribbling away minutes and save hours for both recreation and study. A time log, or daily diary, is a valuable tool for getting control of time. Without a time log, you really don't know how you are spending your time. Try keeping one for a week or two.

Reasons for Scheduling

How much spare time do you have every day? The student whose activities record appears in Figure 3.2 would probably answer, "None. There are not enough hours in the day for all the things I have to do." That's the way things may seem to you too, but it's not necessarily the way they are.

Time		Time Used	Activity - Description
Start	End		
7:45	8:15	:30	Dress
8:15	8:40	:25	Breakfast
8:40	9:00	:20	Nothing
9:00	10:00	1:00	Psychology - Lecture
10:00	10:40	:40	Coffee - Talking
10:40	11:00	:20	Nothing
11:00	12:00	1:00	Economics - Lecture
12:00	12:45	:45	Lunch
12:45	2:00	1:15	Reading - Magazine
2:00	4:00	2:00	Biology Lab
4:00	5:30	1:30	Recreation - Volleyball
5:30	6:00	:30	Nothing
6:00	7:00	1:00	Dinner
7:00	8:00	1:00	Nap
8:00	8:50	:50	Study - Statistics
8:50	9:20	:30	Break
9:20	10:00	:40	Study - Statistics
10:00	10:50	:50	Chat with Bob
10:50	11:30	:40	Study - Accounting
11:30	11:45	:15	Ready for bed
11:45	7:45	8:00	Sleep.

Paste 3 X 5 cards on mirror: laws of economics; psychological terms; statistical formulas. Study while brushing teeth, etc.

Look over textbook assignment and previous lecture notes to establish continuity for today's psychology lecture.

Break too long and too soon after breakfast. Work on psychology notes just taken; also look over economics assignment.

Rework the lecture notes on economics while still fresh in mind. Also, look over biology assignment to recall the objective of the coming lab.

Use this time to read a magazine or newspaper.

Not a good idea. Better finish work, then get a good night's sleep.

Break is too long.

Good as a reward if basic work is done.

Insufficient time allotted, but better than no time.

While brushing teeth, study the 3 X 5 cards. Replace cards that have been mastered with new ones.

FIGURE 3.2 Record of One Day's Activities and Suggestions for Making Better Use of Time

TABLE 3.1 Time Spent by Students in a Typical Week

Activity	Hours Spent
Sleep	49.3
Study	19.8
Classes and labs	18.7
Meals	10.7
Total	98.5

Source: Arthur A. Dole, "College Students Report on the Use of Time," *The Personnel and Guidance Journal* 37 (May 1959), p. 635. Copyright American Association for Counseling and Development. Reprinted by permission of American Association for Counseling and Development.

Table 3.1 shows how students at one university spent time in four main activities during a typical week. The students spent 98.5 hours sleeping, studying, attending classes and labs, and eating their meals. When you subtract that total from 168 (the number of hours in a week), you have 69.5 hours unaccounted for—almost ten hours a day.

You can gain extra time in only two ways: (1) by doing a job in less time than usual, (2) by using small blocks of time that you usually waste. The first way requires you to study more efficiently, and this book provides a great many techniques to help you do just that. The second way requires you to schedule your time, and this chapter offers a number of suggestions.

Although some people believe it's a waste of time to make a schedule, planning actually *saves* time and energy. Sure, it takes time to schedule your time, but the time you spend making a schedule is returned to you several times over when you work—and relax—according to your schedule. Spending a little time to make a schedule saves a lot of time that you would otherwise waste.

Some people feel that maintaining a schedule will make robots or slaves of them. Just the opposite is true. The people you see dashing madly from class to library to gym, or eating a junk-food lunch on the run, are slaves to time because they are not in control of their time. The student who schedules time, who decides how it will be used, is the master of time rather than its slave.

Some people won't schedule their time because they want to be "flexible." But a disorganized person wastes so much time that there really isn't any time left to be flexible with. Scheduling, however, frees up time for a variety of activities, and flexibility can certainly be built into a schedule.

Scheduling actually gives you more time, makes you the master of your time, and provides the flexibility that *you* want. Here are some additional benefits of scheduling.

1. ***Gets you started.*** You know how hard it is to get started. Often a well-planned schedule can be the external force that gives you a needed shove.
2. ***Prevents avoidance of disliked subjects.*** The mind can play tricks. Without actually deciding to do so, you can keep yourself from doing something you don't like by occupying yourself with favorite subjects.
3. ***Monitors the slackening-off process.*** By apportioning time properly, you can keep yourself from slackening off as the semester wears on.
4. ***Eliminates the wrong type of cramming.*** If cramming just before exams is to be effective, the original studying and learning must take place day by day.
5. ***Makes studying enjoyable.*** When done without the pressure of time, studying and learning can be intensely interesting.
6. ***Promotes cumulative review.*** Sandwiching in short review periods is the best way to retain knowledge as well as to prepare for exams. It is less fatiguing and more effective to review a subject in four *distributed* thirty-minute sessions than in a single *massed* two-hour session.
7. ***Frees the mind.*** To keep from forgetting details, you may think and rethink them. This often leads to a tense feeling of pressure and confusion. Putting things to do on paper takes them off the mental treadmill.
8. ***Controls the study break.*** Rewarding yourself with a ten-minute break when you finish a scheduled block of study helps minimize clock watching. During short breaks, stand up, walk around, or just stare out the window, but keep in mind the subject you're studying. Then you won't need a warm-up period when you resume studying.
9. ***Keeps you from overlooking recreation.*** Physical and social activities are needed for a well-balanced personality, good health, and efficient study. On the other hand, allowing extracurricular activities to outweigh studies probably accounts for more failures in college than anything else.
10. ***Helps raise your recreational efficiency.*** One of the saddest wastes of time and pleasure is to mix study time and recreation time—that is, when studying, to keep thinking how nice it would be to be playing some game; and when playing, to think about all the studying that needs to be done.
11. ***Regulates daily living.*** Without a plan to guide you, assignments are bound to pile up. When they do, you lose control, and your daily living

is thrown into chaos. With a schedule, even weekends and holidays can be free from worry.

PRINCIPLES OF SCHEDULING

Just as there are basic rules for driving a car, no matter how long or short a trip you are taking, so there are basic rules for making a study schedule. The following list includes general principles that apply to all study schedules.

1. ***Eliminate dead hours.*** Make each block of one hour a productive unit. Some of the most important lessons of our lives are learned in less time.
2. ***Use daylight hours.*** Research shows that each hour used for study during the day is equal to one and a half hours at night.
3. ***Study before recitation-type classes.*** For a course in which you recite and discuss, it is an advantage to study just before class. The material will be fresh in your mind.
4. ***Study after lecture-type classes.*** For a lecture course, retention and understanding are aided by a review of your lecture notes immediately after class.
5. ***List according to priorities.*** By putting first things first, you are sure to get the most important things done on time.
6. ***Avoid too much detail.*** Packing a weekly schedule with too many details is a waste of time for two reasons. The time you take to make such a schedule could be better used in studying a subject directly. The chances of your following such a schedule are very slim.
7. ***Know your sleep pattern.*** We all have daily cycles of sleepiness and alertness. If your work, classes, and circumstances permit, sleep when you're sleepy and study when you're naturally alert.
8. ***Discover how long to study.*** The rule of thumb that you should study two hours for every hour in class is a rough guide at best. The time required varies from student to student and from subject to subject. Start out allowing two hours of study for every hour in class, but adjust the hours according to your experience, as you find out how long you need to master each assignment.
9. ***Plan blocks of time.*** Optimum efficiency is reached by planning in blocks of one hour: fifty minutes to study and ten minutes for a break.
10. ***Allow time for sleep.*** Your need for eight hours of sleep every night is supported by medical evidence. Make no mistake about it: The quality of your education depends on sufficient sleep.

11. ***Eat well-balanced meals.*** Take time for good meals. Living on greasy foods or a low-protein diet most of the time is no way to treat your body and brain. Dietary deficiencies result in irritability, fatigue, and lack of pep.
12. ***Double your time estimates, and start long jobs ahead of time.*** Most people tend to underestimate the amount of time they need for a project. To avoid discovering the hard way that you cannot bang out a 1500-word paper in three hours the evening before it is due, start ridiculously early, thus allowing yourself more time.
13. ***Don't pack your schedule too tightly.*** Be precise, but leave room for last-minute problems that require your time.
14. ***Make a plan for living, not merely for studying.*** After all, life, even in college, is many-sided, and its many sides must be recognized.

TYPES OF SCHEDULES

It is important to choose the type of schedule that fits your circumstances best. Some students work best with a detailed schedule; others work best with a brief list of things to do. Circumstances also influence the type of schedule you should make. There are on-campus students, commuting students, married students, employed students, night-class students, and part-time students, and each has different scheduling requirements. You should *adapt* the principles of schedule building to your personal circumstances, rather than *adopt* some ideal model that fits hardly anybody, let alone you.

The schedule for *you* is the schedule that *works.* With time and experience, you can refine your schedule until it is an almost perfect fit for your situation.

Master Schedule

Any plan to schedule your time and activities must have at its core a master schedule—that is, a fixed schedule of activities. A master schedule needs to be drawn up only once each semester, unless changes occur in your basic program. Figure 3.3 shows a useful format.

First, fill in all required school activities, such as courses, classes, and laboratory periods. Then add other regular activities, such as a part-time job, commuting time, sports, and regular meetings. Next, add housekeeping chores, sleeping, and eating. When your fixed activities have been accounted for, the blank spaces on the chart are available for weekly or day-by-day planning. Here are some suggestions on how to use some of the time periods represented by the blank spaces in Figure 3.3.

	Mon.	Tues.	Wed.	Thurs.	Fri.	Sat.	Sun.
7-8	← Dress and Breakfast →						
8-9	History		History		History	Dress + Breakfast	
9-10		Phy. Ed		Phy Ed.		Phy Ed.	Dress + Breakfast
10-11		Chem.		Chem.		Chem.	
11-12	French		French		French		
12-1	← Lunch →						
1-2	Math	Film making	Math	Film making	Math		
2-3				↑			
3-4				Chem. lab.			
4-5	English		English	↓	English		
5-6							
6-7	← Dinner →						
7-8							
8-9							
9-10							
10-11							
11-12	← Sleep →						

FIGURE 3.3 A Master Schedule

Monday/Wednesday/Friday

9–10 A.M.	Use the free period after history (a lecture course) to study lecture notes.
10–11	Since French (at 11) is a recitation course, prepare by studying during the free period that precedes class.
2–3 P.M.	In math class (1–2) problems are usually discussed and worked out on the blackboard. Take very brief notes on both discussion and blackboard work. Then, because math problems can quickly become "cold," use the free period (2–3) to go over the work covered in class during the preceding hour.
3–4	English (4–5) is often a discussion period. Use the free hour to study and warm up in advance.
7–8	Evening study time begins. Start with English, your last class, so that any notes you have taken can be reviewed before forgetting takes place.
8–9	Study French, giving priority to the notes and assignments of the day.

Such a master schedule, on a 5 × 8 card taped over your desk or carried in your notebook, unclutters your mind. More important, it enables you to visualize the blank boxes as actual blocks of time into which you may fit necessary activities. With the master schedule as your base, you can devise any type of schedule that fits your unique combination of courses, your part-time or full-time job, and your personality.

Detailed Weekly Schedule

Some people work best when they are guided by a weekly schedule that is an expansion of the master schedule. If the demands on your time are both heavy and predictable, you may need a detailed weekly schedule. This kind of schedule needs to be made out only once, early in the semester. A sample weekly schedule is shown in Figure 3.4. The lists that follow indicate how the principles of scheduling were used to set it up.

Monday Through Friday/Saturday

7–8 A.M.	Avoid the frantic dash and the gobbled (or skipped) breakfast by getting up on time.
12–1 P.M.	Take a full, leisurely hour for lunch.
5–6	Relax before dinner—your reward for a day of conscientious work.

Time	Mon.	Tues.	Wed.	Thurs.	Fri.	Sat.	Sun.
7-8	Dress and Breakfast						Church, Recreation, Conversation, Recreational Reading
8-9	History	Study Chem.	History	Study Chem.	History	Study Chem.	
9-10	Study History	Phy. Ed.	Study History	Phy. Ed.	Study History	Phy. Ed.	
10-11	Study French	Chem.	Study French	Chem.	Study French	Chem.	
11-12	French	Study Chem.	French	Study Chem.	French	Study Chem.	
12-1	Lunch						
1-2	Math	Film-Making	Math	Film Making	Math	Recreation, Conversation, Special Projects, Reading, Extra Work on Difficult Subjects, Thorough Review.	
2-3	Study Math	Library: Paper	Study Math	Chem. Lab.	Study Math		
3-4	Study English	"	Study English		Study English		
4-5	English	"	English		English		
5-6	Recreation						
6-7	Dinner						
7-8	Study English	Study Math	Study English	Study Math	Study English		English Paper
8-9	Study French	Study History	Study French	Study History	Study French		English Paper
9-10	Review English	Review French	Review History	Review Math	Review Chem.		Study History
10-11	Recreational Reading						
11-12	Conversation, Sleep						

FIGURE 3.4 A Detailed Weekly Schedule Based on a Master Schedule

7–9 Keep up with current notes and assignments by systematic studying.

9–10 To forestall cramming at quiz and examination times, give some time every day to a review of previous assignments and ground covered to date.

10 A cease-study time of 10 P.M. is an incentive to work hard during the day and early evening.

10–12 Devote some time every day to reading books that truly interest you. Recreational reading and conversation help you unwind for a good night's sleep.

Tuesday/Thursday/Saturday

8–9 A.M. Since chemistry (10–11) is your hard subject, build your morning study program around it. An hour's study before class will make the class period more meaningful.

11–12 Another hour's study immediately after chemistry class will help you remember the work covered in class and move more readily to the next assignment.

Special

Tuesday 2–5 P.M., library: paper

Sunday 7–9 P.M., English paper
For some assignments you will need to schedule blocks of time to do research or to develop and follow up ideas.

Saturday From noon on, Saturday is left unscheduled—for recreation, for special projects to which you must devote a concentrated period of time, for extra work on difficult subjects, for thorough review.

Sunday This is your day until evening. Study history before you go to bed, because it is the first class you'll have on Monday morning.

Assignment-oriented Weekly Schedule

Another type of weekly schedule is based primarily on assignments, rather than on available time. It is a supplement to the master schedule and can be used whenever you face unusual or long-term assignments. Because it schedules specific assignments, it covers only one specific week.

Figure 3.5 shows a weekly assignment schedule. The format is simple: Draw a horizontal line to divide a lined sheet of paper approximately in half. In the top half list your subjects, assignments, estimated study times, and due

Subject	Assignment	Estimated Time	Date Due	Time Due
Electronics	Chap. V - 32 pp. - Read	2 hr.	Mon. 13th	8:00
English	Paper to Write	18 hr.	Mon. 20th	9:00
Math	Problems on pp. 110–111	3 hr.	Tues. 14th	10:00
Industrial Safety	Make shop layouts	8 hr.	Fri. 17th	11:00
Graphics	Drawing of TV components	6 hr.	Fri. 17th	1:00
Electronics	Chap. VI - 40 pp. - Read	2½ hr.	Weds. 22nd	8:00

Day	Assignment	Morning	Afternoon	Evening
Sun.	Electronics - Read Chap. V English - Find a Topic			7:30 - 9:30 9:30 - 10:30
Mon.	English - Gather Notes Math - Problems		2:00 - 6:00	7:00 - 10:00
Tues.	English - Gather Notes Industrial Safety	8:00 - 10:00	3:00 - 6:00	7:00 - 10:00
Wed.	English - First Draft Graphics		2:00 - 6:00	7:00 - 10:00
Thurs.	Industrial Safety English - Paper Graphics	8:00 - 10:00	3:00 - 6:00	7:00 - 10:00
Fri.	English - Final Copy Electronics		2:00 - 6:00	7:00 - 9:30
Sat.				

FIGURE 3.5 A Weekly Schedule Based on Assignments
To provide a time dimension, this schedule is being made out on Saturday, November 11, for the coming week.

dates. Then, using the due dates and estimated times as control factors, check your master schedule for hours available. Choose enough hours to do each job, and write them on the appropriate line on the bottom half of the weekly schedule sheet. *Stick to your schedule.* Give study hours top priority. As long as you do, your remaining free hours will be really free.

FOR MONDAY

8-9	Psychology - Review Chapter V and lecture notes
9-10	Psychology lecture
10-11	Economics lecture
11-12	Economics - fix up notes, begin Chapter VII
1-2	Campus store - Pick up paper and binder, pen, lead, calculator
2-5	Engineering - work on assignment
5-6	Exercise - Tennis court with Joan.
7-10	Accounting and Math

Review: Just before class is a good time to review the high points of chapters previously studied. Also review the previous lecture for continuity.

Fix up notes: The very best time to fix up lecture notes, and review them simultaneously, is immediately after the lecture.

After lunch: This is a good time to give yourself a semi-break from academic work and do some necessary errands.

2-5 block: This is a valuable block of time during which you should be able to read the assignment and work out the assigned problems without losing continuity.

Exercise: After an entire day with the books, some exercise and a shower will help to put an edge on your appetite, as well as making a definite break between study during the day and study during the evening.

After dinner: Both subjects need unbroken time for efficient production. Use the block of three hours to do a balanced amount of work for each, depending on the assignments.

Breaks: Breaks are not listed. You judge for yourself when a break is best for you. Also, the break should be taken when you arrive at a good stopping point.

FIGURE 3.6 A Daily Schedule

Daily Schedule

You will probably want to have a daily schedule that you can carry around with you. A 3 × 5 card is just the right size. It will fit perfectly into your shirt pocket or shoulder bag and will be at hand when you need it. Every evening before leaving your desk, look at your master schedule to determine your free hours and courses for the next day. Then jot down on the card a plan for the next day: the subjects you plan to study, the errands, appointments, physical exercise, recreation, and any other activities you want to do, and the time you allot for each. The five minutes you spend are important for two reasons. First, you will have a written record to which you can refer, and this will unclutter your mind. Second, you will have mentally thought through your day, thus putting into action a psychological clock that will help keep you on schedule.

Notice in Figure 3.6 that the daily schedule is organized on the basis of blocks of time, rather than fragments of time. By assigning a block of time to each topic or activity, you will ensure that you work at peak efficiency.

Scheduling Long-Term Assignments

Most assignments are not portioned out in bite-size, day-by-day units. Some assignments span a week, some a month, some (research papers and projects) an entire semester. Although it pays to study every day, you must also do some long-term planning.

You are likely to have one or two long-term assignments at all times, and you may get confused if you have too many separate schedules. It is best to keep a record of the full assignments and their due dates in your notebook for each subject. Get started on these assignments early by allotting some time to each of them on your daily schedules. If you still have trouble remembering to do them, you may need to make out a weekly assignment schedule like the one shown in Figure 3.5.

SCHEDULING FOR STUDENTS WITH JOBS

If you have a full-time or part-time job, you probably have less time and less energy for studying than regular full-time students; consequently, you must use your time and energy very carefully. A full-time student can use big blocks of uninterrupted time for studying, but you must find ways to use scattered pieces of time.

If you are a working student, your daily study schedule should simply be a list of things to do, in the order of priority. Figure 3.7 shows a typical daily list for a working student. To be successful, you should have a sense of urgency about referring to your list and studying whenever an opportunity presents itself. Cross off the tasks you complete. Assigning specific times is likely to lead only to frustration. Your study materials should be in a form that permits you to carry them about for use whenever you have some spare time.

Preparing Notes for Study on the Run

To take advantage of moments of spare time, your study materials must be readily available. One way to make them available is to write or type notes on small cards; another way is to record notes on cassettes.

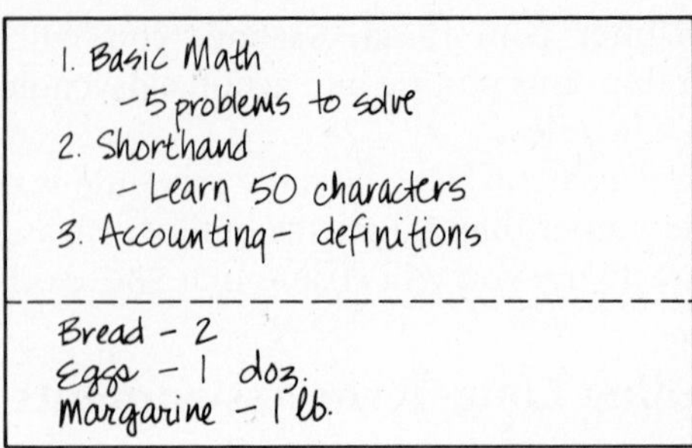

FIGURE 3.7 A Things-to-Do Schedule for a Working Student

After reading an assignment or attending a lecture, select from it only the information that you believe is important enough to master. Using your own words, write or type this information on 3 × 5 or 5 × 8 cards. You can then record the same notes, or a portion of them, on cassettes. If you have time for only one of these, use the cards.

How to Study on the Run

Here are some ways to study during time periods that are ordinarily only half-used.

1. Attach small metal or plastic clips near mirrors and on walls, at eye level. Place a note card in each clip. While shaving or combing your hair, or while washing dishes, you can read the notes on the cards. Cards placed in clips can be easily changed; pasting or taping cards to walls is not as practical.
2. To vary the routine and to use your sense of hearing, listen to a cassette or two while going through your morning routine.
3. When you drive to work, listen to several cassettes instead of to music on the car radio. If you have only cards, recite aloud from memory (not verbatim) some of the ideas, formulas, or definitions that are on the cards. After you stop driving, read the cards to check your accuracy.
4. As you walk from the parking lot to your place of work, flip through several of your note cards or listen to a cassette.
5. At lunch, while eating a sandwich in your place of work, do a problem or two in math, or, if you prefer, listen to a cassette.

Knowing how to study on the run will enable you to devote more time to your family, job, and school without scrimping on sleep.

TIPS FOR SAVING TIME

You have twenty-four hours of time every day. You get no more and no less, whether you're rich or poor, stingy or spendthrift, deserving or undeserving. You cannot buy or manufacture more time. There are, however, three ways to accomplish more within the hours you have: (1) by using the mini-size study skills explained in this section; (2) by using the self-discipline strategies explained in this section; and (3) by using the time you once wasted.

Mini-Size Study Skills

Bundle-of-Sticks Technique. A father once tied a bundle of small, thin sticks together with a strand of twine. Handing the bundle to his youngest son, he said, "Son, break these sticks in half." The boy used his hands and knees but could not break the bundle. Sadly, he handed it back to his father. Without a word, the father untied the twine and, using only his fingers, snapped each stick, one by one.

When one of your assignments is long and seems overwhelming, unbundle it and divide it into small, manageable units—units that you can start on immediately. For example, when you're assigned a research paper to write, spring into action immediately by breaking the assignment into small, practical units, and do one or two of them per day:

1. Choose a topic. Remind yourself to choose a topic in which you are interested.
2. Narrow the topic; in fact, make three or four significant narrowings.
3. Look in the *Readers' Guide to Periodical Literature* to see how much current information there is on your topic.
4. Sharpen the focus of the topic to make sure you are answering a question.
5. Buy a stack of 3 × 5 cards or slips of paper for recording your bibliography and notes.
6. Look in the card catalogue, and make bibliographical notes.
7. Look in the reference sections, and make notes.
8. Look in the periodical sections, and make notes.
9. Take separate notes for the bibliography and for detailed information for your paper.
10. Etc. (For more detailed information on researching and writing papers, see Chapter 18 of this book, or follow the steps described in any good book on writing papers.)

Right from the beginning, remind yourself that you do not intend to plunge into the main job of writing the paper. After you have divided the assignment, begin your work in the first free study period of the same day, while the full concept is still fresh in your mind. Once underway, the paper will practically write itself.

The secret of the Bundle-of-Sticks Technique is to make the pieces the right size so that each is easy to do. "Divide and conquer" applies to assignments just as it does to military tactics.

Setting a Time Limit for Each Task. According to Parkinson's Law: Work expands to fill the time available for its completion.[1] To be sure you don't run out of time before you've finished a project, work Parkinson's Law in reverse: For each task, set a deadline that you will find difficult to meet, and then work hard to meet that deadline.

Each time you achieve your goal, reward yourself with a pleasant activity (any behavior that is followed by something pleasant tends to be reinforced and is more likely to happen again). Take a break. Briefly chat with a friend. Get a drink of water. Walk around the room. You may want to keep a special snack, such as a jar of peanuts, in the bottom drawer of your desk, to be opened only as a reward. Lee Iacocca used this principle in college and even as a child:

> As a little kid I had learned how to do my homework right after school so that I could play after supper. By the time I got to college, . . . I used to tell myself: "I'm going to give this my best shot for the next three hours. And when those three hours are up, I'll set this work aside and go to the movies."[2]

Remember these two additional principles:

1. If you fail to meet a deadline, don't punish yourself harshly by, for example, not going to a football game. Your punishment is sufficient if you deprive yourself of the peanuts in your desk. It is *positive* reinforcement that is powerful in effecting a change in behavior.
2. Reward yourself for your small successes, not only for your major ones.

The Pareto Principle.[3] Named after Vilfredo Pareto (1848–1923), an Italian economist and sociologist, the Pareto Principle states that the truly

---

[1]C. Northcote Parkinson, *Parkinson's Law and Other Studies in Administration* (Boston: Houghton Mifflin, 1957).

[2]Lee Iacocca, with William Novak, *Iacocca: An Autobiography* (New York: Bantam Books, 1984), p. 20.

[3]Edwin C. Bliss, excerpted from GETTING THINGS DONE: The ABC's of Time Management. Copyright © 1976 Edwin C. Bliss. Reprinted with the permission of Charles Scribner's Sons, an imprint of Macmillan Publishing Co.

important items in any given group constitute only a small number of the total items in that group. This principle is also known as the 80/20 rule.

For example, in almost any sales force, 80 percent of the business is brought in by 20 percent of the salespeople. In any committee, 80 percent of the ideas come from 20 percent of the members. In a classroom, 80 percent of the teacher's time is taken up by 20 percent of the students.

In any list of things to do, 80 percent of the importance resides in 20 percent of the list. In a list of ten items, 80 percent of the list's value lies in 2 items, which constitute 20 percent of the list. Because of Pareto's Principle, in your lists of things to do always put the most important items first. Then, if you accomplish only the first few items, you will have accomplished the most important tasks on the list.

Keep the Pareto Principle in mind whenever you make up a list or a schedule or must decide which subject to study first. Apply the principle by listing first things first.

Concentrating Your Time and Efforts. Some students jump from subject to subject when they study, scattering their time and efforts. They touch many assignments but finish none. When you focus the sun's rays onto a piece of paper, the rays will burn a hole; unfocused rays, like scattered time and effort, make no impression at all. Pause, make a plan, and then take action. Remember that action without planning won't get you very far.

Planning Ahead. You must not try to play things by ear. No football coach would field a team without a game plan, and no student should try to face a school day without an academic game plan. If you do not have one, other people's actions will determine what you do, and your time will be wasted. By having a plan of your own, you will be able to use your time to achieve *your* goals.

Using a Month-at-a-Glance Calendar. Buy or make—but use—a calendar that shows the entire month on one page. For precise control, you need to see what assignments are due and when at a glance. A page per week won't do. Above all, don't use a page for each day, because assignments hidden from view in next week's pages are out of sight and out of mind.

Taking Study Breaks. Which is better: sticking with a two-hour assignment until you have finished it or breaking the assignment into half-hour periods separated by five-minute breaks? Breaking up a long assignment is better, for several reasons:

1. Study breaks keep you from getting tired and bored.
2. You work harder and concentrate better in short spurts.

3. Five-minute breaks are great motivators.
4. During the rest periods, the material you studied has a chance to sink in.

However, just as some runners need a long time to warm up, some students take a long time to get into a long assignment. If such students broke long assignments into half-hour periods, they would need warming up at the end of every half hour. Such students should study for a full fifty minutes or longer before taking a ten-minute break. It is better for them to be like marathon runners, finishing the long assignment in one continuous stretch.

Before you take a break, review your underlinings and jottings. This will help the facts sink into your long-term memory. Just before a break is also a good time to reread a particularly difficult problem or passage. This gets your mind working on the problem while you rest.

Beating the Sleepy Feeling. While studying, if you get sleepy before your scheduled sleep time, *don't* take a nap. Instead, pick up your textbook, stand up, and pace the floor, reading aloud as you do. The sleepy feeling will pass. When you go to bed at your scheduled time, you'll be able to fall asleep.

Writing Notes to Yourself. When you reach the end of a study session, write a note telling yourself where to begin during your next study period. You'll be surprised at how much time this practice will save you each day, and you'll enjoy the boost that such a note provides.

Self-Discipline Strategies

A "yes" answer to any of the following questions is a sure sign of poor planning and poor self-discipline:

1. Did you have to cram for an exam?
2. Did you have to stay up most of the night to finish a term or research paper?
3. Did you have to give up your recreational time?
4. Did you have to miss a basketball or a football game in order to study?
5. Did you have to excuse yourself from going to a good movie with friends?

If you answered "yes" to any of them, take out a sheet of paper and write down why you had this problem; then list specific ways that you could have avoided the problem and ways that you can prevent it from happening again. By taking this action, you show that you are in control of your life.

Here are some other strategies to bolster your self-discipline.

Deciding to Change Your Behavior. Old habits are difficult to break and new ones difficult to make, but you can do it if you follow these rules:

1. ***Develop a strong determination.*** If you want to make or break a habit, your determination must be powerful enough to carry you over rough spots. Every day you succeed, the success of your plan is made more certain.
2. ***Never, ever make an exception.*** Making an exception is like dropping a carefully wound ball of string: "A single slip undoes more than a great many turns will wind again."[4] Never willingly lose a battle.
3. ***Take every opportunity to put your good habit to work.*** Always practice behavior that you want to come naturally.

Listing Tasks According to Their Importance. Do you list your priorities according to importance or according to urgency? Should tomorrow's quiz head your list, or should you do some work on that long-range research paper that could make or break your final grade? If your priority lists reflect urgency instead of importance, you have a problem: You began working on such tasks too late, and as time runs out, you must rush frantically to meet your deadline. As a result, you shove aside your heavyweight research paper to make room for a quiz. Avoid this situation. Start early, and work steadily.

Understanding the Relationship Between Time and Goals. There is a direct relationship between goals and time. When you have a goal firmly in mind, you will think of objectives rather than activities. You will make better decisions, speak and write more forcefully, and treat time as a precious commodity. You will be as serious about time as Ben Franklin, who said, "Time is the stuff of which life is made," and you will avoid falling victim to the four great robbers of time:

1. Laziness: "I don't feel like doing it now."
2. Sidetracks: "I'll wash my hair and then I'll begin working."
3. Procrastination: "Sure, I'll do it later."
4. Daydreaming: "Some day I'll amaze them."

Concentrating on One Task at a Time. Nothing can help you use time more productively than concentration. Many students never become proficient concentrators because they try to do too many things at once. All your

[4]William James, *Psychology* (New York: Holt, 1893), p. 145.

tasks may be important, but you can do only one at a time. To start the time-saving process, you must decide which one task is most important. Push all else aside. Set a realistic deadline, and then work on this task until you have completed it. When you have finished, reward yourself with a five-minute break.

Avoiding Procrastination. "Nothing [is] so fatiguing as the eternal hanging on of an uncompleted task."[5] These words by William James (1842–1910), distinguished American psychologist, strike at the heart of us all. Every one of us has had many bouts with procrastination.

If a task that you are doing is about three-quarters finished and is finishable, finish it no matter how tired you are. If you delay completion until tomorrow, you'll need extra time to overcome inertia, reread what you have done, pick up your train of thought, and recapture yesterday's momentum.

Make it a habit to save both time and energy by doing a needed task immediately or at the first free opportunity. By doing so, you prove that you are in control of your life.

Obeying the Alarm Clock. Once you have decided on a time to get up, don't ignore the decision when the alarm goes off. Without stretching, yawning, or groaning, make your feet hit the floor immediately. Five minutes later, you'll be glad you did.

Striving for Excellence. In *Getting Things Done,* Edwin C. Bliss writes: "There is a difference between striving for excellence and striving for perfection. The first is attainable, gratifying, and healthy. The second is unattainable and frustrating. It's also a terrible waste of time."[6] If you strive for perfection, you will waste time and energy that you could put to good use elsewhere. Trivial errors in your papers, for example, could be corrected neatly in ink; they do not necessitate retyping. In sum, do the best you can; then go on to the next task.

Acknowledging That Everyone Makes Mistakes. Because we all make many errors in judgment, the words "Everyone makes mistakes" help us preserve our self-image and self-confidence and keep us from giving up on ourselves. Do not use this expression to excuse mistakes that were easily avoidable, however. Try to understand how and why you erred so that you can prevent a reoccurrence. Once you have come to terms with a mistake, put it

---

[5]William James, *The Selected Letters of William James.* Ed. with an introduction by Elizabeth Hardwick (New York: Farrar, Straus & Cudahy, 1960, 1961), p. 125.
[6]Bliss, p. 79.

behind you and concentrate on using the precious minutes of today for today's living.

Having Courage. You need personal courage to follow a good schedule because when you do so, you'll leave some students behind—perhaps some who are your friends. You may feel some loneliness, but you can take pride in the fact that you are controlling your life and achieving your goals.

Using Time Once Wasted

Getting a Head Start. If possible, finalize your class schedule before classes start, so that you can plan the days and weeks that lie ahead. Buy your textbooks early, before the campus store runs out of stock. Being without a textbook for even a little while can throw your study schedule off-balance. Before the first session of each class, visit the building and room where the class is to be held, so that you will know exactly where to go on the hectic, first day.

Carrying Pocket Work. Always carry some work you can do while you are waiting in lines and in places such as bus stations and air terminals, while you are sitting down to rest, while you are eating alone, and so forth. Never be without pocket work such as 3 × 5 cards carrying key words, key concepts, or formulas; a few pages photocopied from an important part of your textbook; or a paperback book. Also carry a few blank cards for jotting down brilliant ideas that occur to you.

Spare-Time Thinking. Use your spare time to think. While you're walking *from* a class, try to recall the main points of the lecture you just heard. If you're walking *to* a class, try to recall the main points of the lecture you heard at the last meeting of the class. At other times—when you're jogging, for example—try to think up interesting topics and titles for your next paper.

Using Your Subconscious. At one time or another, you have awakened during the night with a bright idea or a solution to a problem that you had been thinking about before bedtime. Your subconscious works while your conscious mind is resting in sleep. If you want to capture the ideas or solutions produced by your subconscious, you should write them down as soon as you wake up; otherwise, they'll be lost. Many creative people know this and keep a pad and pencil near their beds. For example, Nobel Prize winner Albert Szent-Györgyi said, "I go to sleep thinking about my problems all the time, and my brain must continue to think about them when I sleep because

I wake up, sometimes in the middle of the night, with answers to questions that have been eluding me all day."[7]

At Stanford University, Dr. William Dement and his colleagues studied the phenomenon of problem solving in dreams. Five hundred students were given the following two problems to solve at two different and separate times. Try to solve these problems before looking at the answers that follow.

> *Problem 1:* The letters O,T,T,F,F . . . form the beginning of an infinite sequence. Find a simple rule for determining any or all successive letters. According to your rule, what would be the next two letters of the sequence?
>
> *Problem 2:* Consider the letters H,I,J,K,L,M,N,O. The solution to this problem is one word. What is this word?[8]

The students were instructed to read the problem fifteen minutes before going to bed. The correct solutions appeared in the dreams of nine students.

In Problem 1, the letters in the sequence are the first letters of *one, two, three, four,* and *five.* The next two letters in the sequence are therefore S, S.

In Problem 2, the solution is the word *water.* The sequence of letters runs from *H* to *O,* and H_2O is the chemical formula for water.

Working During Prime Time. There's a certain time of day when you do most of your best work. If you work best from 6 to 8 A.M., set up an early-to-bed and early-to-rise schedule. Remember to schedule your one or two highest-priority assignments for your prime time. Work on other assignments at other times.

GETTING THINGS DONE

A schedule represents a plan. Just as the buzz of an alarm clock is a signal to get up, so sitting down at your desk should be a signal to begin to study. If you make a habit of getting started immediately and then studying vigorously, you will accomplish a great deal, and your feeling of satisfaction will make it easy for you to get started next time.

This vigorous, aggressive approach must become your way of life in the classroom, the laboratory, the library, and elsewhere. Get what you came for! During a lecture, for example, be alert and work hard to capture the lecturer's ideas and get them down on paper.

---

[7]Originally published in SOME MUST WATCH WHILE SOME MUST SLEEP by William C. Dement as a volume in The Portable Stanford series published by the Stanford Alumni Association. Copyright © 1972. Reprinted by permission of the Stanford Alumni Association.

[8]Ibid., pp. 99–100.

In the library, some students wander aimlessly or spend most of their time looking around and watching other students coming and going. If your purpose is to gather data for your research paper, then go to the card catalogue, gather your references, find the books, begin reading and taking notes. Get something done according to plan.

The intelligent use of time is a large part of academic success. Schedule your time wisely, and be sure to follow your plan.

SUMMARY

What's the number-one skill that I need to master in college?

Time management heads the list of skills that you need to learn. It can mean the difference between success and failure in college.

Where does all the time go? I don't feel as though I'm wasting much time, yet I never seem to have enough.

Wasting time becomes such a habit that you don't realize you're wasting it. One excellent way to keep track of where your time goes is with a time log, in which you keep a precise record of how you spend your time, right down to the minute. If you're like most students, you'll be able to reclaim hours of wasted time.

Won't making a schedule consume more time than it saves?

Making a schedule is not busywork. Taking the time to write up a schedule is like making an investment but, unlike the case with most investments, the returns are almost guaranteed. If you spend a few minutes to draw up a schedule, you'll save far more time than you spent scheduling, you'll feel more relaxed, and you'll get more done.

What is the master schedule?

The master schedule is a day-by-day, hour-by-hour breakdown of your typical week. The master schedule should feature the immovables of your semester—the things that aren't going to change from week to week, such as meals, sleep, a job (if you have one), and classes. Once these "obligations" have been filled in, the master schedule should provide you with an excellent illustration of the time you have available.

What is the detailed weekly schedule?

The detailed weekly schedule picks up where the master schedule leaves off. In addition to showing your semester-long obligations, it shows how you intend to use each block of free time. To make a detailed weekly schedule, photocopy your master schedule several times and use it as the foundation for your weekly schedule.

How does the assignment-oriented weekly schedule differ from the detailed weekly schedule?

Instead of being divided up by blocks of time, the assignment-oriented schedule is split into individual assignments. All the information it contains can fit on a single sheet of paper. The top half of the sheet contains a list of your assignments, the time you estimate that each will take, and the date and time due for each. The bottom half of the sheet contains the days of the week, along with the assignments, and splits each day into morning, afternoon, and evening. You write in the day you plan to work on the assignment and the time of day that you want to work on it.

What is the daily schedule?

The daily schedule can usually be squeezed onto a 3 × 5 card. It lists the things you plan to do each day and the time you plan to spend on each. A written record that you carry around with you is an excellent reminder and a great motivator.

How does scheduling differ for students who have jobs?

A working student must use time far more efficiently than a full-time student. Because working students lack the luxury of large blocks of free time, the daily schedule of a working student should simply be a list of things to do, ordered by priority but not limited by time. The tasks can then be crossed off the list whenever free time presents itself.

What is the mini-size study skill called the Bundle-of-Sticks Technique?

Just as a bundle of sticks is easy to break when you break one stick at a time, a large assignment becomes less threatening if you divide it into manageable tasks and work on each task separately.

Why should I set a time limit for my tasks?

The purpose of this mini-size study skill is to prevent you from spending too much time on any one aspect of a project. According to Parkinson's Law, work expands to fill the time available for its completion. You should reverse Parkinson's Law by setting deadlines that you will have difficulty meeting and then reward yourself for meeting them.

What is the Pareto Principle?

Also known as the 80/20 rule, the Pareto Principle tells us a very interesting fact about the tasks we set for ourselves. In any list of things to do, 80 percent of the list's value resides in 20 percent of the items on the list. What that means in concrete terms is that you need to identify the most important tasks to be accomplished. Following the Pareto Principle is a mini-size study skill that will prevent you from spending too much time on relatively unimportant tasks and ignoring the crucial ones.

Are study breaks a good idea?

They can be, and getting the most out of them is an enjoyable mini-size study skill. A short break—five minutes for every half hour of work—gives you a rest, allows you to work in short, efficient spurts, creates motivation that carries you over until the next break, and, most important, gives your brain some time to let new knowledge sink in.

Are there any little tricks of the trade that can help me save time?

Yes. There are five ways to use time that you once wasted. (1) *Get a head start.* Plan your class schedule, buy your books, and locate your classrooms in advance. That way, when the semester begins, you'll be spending time on work instead of on preparations. (2) *Carry pocket work.* If you have some work with you, while the rest of the world is waiting in line and getting more impatient by the minute, you'll be relaxing and accomplishing things as well. (3) *Think in your spare time.* Instead of daydreaming between classes, use that time for real thinking. If you're leaving a class, give some thought to the lecture you just heard. If you're on your way to a class, recall the key points from the last lecture. (4) *Use your subconscious.* Your subconscious is working even when you're asleep. If you wake up with an inspired idea, write it down instead of letting it slip away. (5) *Work during your prime time.* There is a time of day when you do your best work. Use that time to work on high-priority assignments.

HAVE YOU MISSED SOMETHING?

1. *Sentence completion.* Complete the following sentences with one of the three words listed below each sentence.

a. In order to take control of your life, you must take control of your ______________________.

personality principles time

b. How we spend or waste time is largely a matter of ____________.

habit procrastination priority

2. *Matching.* In each blank space in the left column, write the number preceding the phrase in the right column that matches the left item best.

_____ a. Procrastination
_____ b. Parkinson's Law
_____ c. Pareto Principle
_____ d. Perfection
_____ e. Planning
_____ f. Priorities

1. A saver of time and energy
2. Unattainable and frustrating goal
3. One of the four great robbers of time
4. Work expands to fill the time available for its completion
5. Should reflect importance rather than urgency
6. Also known as the 80/20 rule

3. *True-false.* Write *T* beside the *true* statements and *F* beside the *false* statements.

_____ a. The master schedule should be updated daily.

_____ b. It's best to study notes from a lecture course immediately after class.

_____ c. A leisurely breakfast can start a productive day.

_____ d. Your goal will be the same whether you put it in writing or keep it in your head.

_____ e. A month-at-a-glance calendar is recommended for optimum time management.

_____ f. All assignments should be broken up into half-hour study sessions.

4. *Study breaks.* Write "yes" next to the advantages of study breaks.

_____ a. Prevent you from getting tired or bored

_____ b. Give you a chance to take a refreshing nap

_____ c. Help you work harder and concentrate better

_____ d. Divide hour-long study sessions into four or five bite-sized pieces

_____ e. Provide motivation during the work period

_____ f. Allow work to sink in

5. *Multiple choice.* Choose the phrase that completes the following sentence most accurately, and circle the letter that precedes it.

Of the three steps toward success, action is the

a. easiest to achieve but the most important.
b. hardest to achieve but the least important.
c. hardest to achieve as well as the most important.
d. easiest to achieve as well as the least important.

PART

II

Your Memory

CHAPTER 4

Concentrating to Learn

Consider the postage stamp. It secures success through its ability to stick to one thing until it gets there.

Josh Billings (1818–85), pen name of Henry Wheeler Shaw, American humorist

The pitcher wants the perfect fastball; the student wants the clearest thought. Both need concentration, yet both will come up empty if they seek out concentration directly. Concentration is elusive. This chapter helps you learn to concentrate. It discusses

- Combating external distractions
- Combating internal distractions
- Concentration techniques
- The food-body-mind connection
- Getting enough sleep
- Combating insomnia
- Combating boredom

and finally

- Improving concentration while reading

oncentration is thinking. During our waking hours we are, with varying degrees of intensity, thinking all the time. We never run out of things to think and worry about. Thoughts and ideas bang, rattle, and knock on the door of our consciousness, trying to gain entry.

Concentration is not a product or a process; rather it is a by-product. Concentration happens only when we don't think about concentration. For example, if you were thinking deeply about the principle of magnetism and suddenly realized that you were concentrating, then, at that moment of realization, you would have broken your concentration on the subject of magnetism.

What do you see in Figure 4.1? Your visual focus will probably shift every few seconds, so that you first see a goblet, then two profiles, and then the goblet again. It is difficult to focus visually on one of the images and ignore the other. Similarly, it is hard for your mind to focus on one idea at a time, but people who *can* focus exclusively on the task before them have a much better chance of completing the task more quickly and accurately than those who divide their attention even when they don't mean to do so.

Concentration is key in physical tasks as well as mental tasks. Watch a good bowler as she takes her position and then gathers and concentrates all her thinking on knocking down the pins at the end of the alley. Watch a professional quarterback concentrating only on getting a pass to an open receiver, in spite of the opposing linemen rushing at him from several directions. That's concentration!

Imagine reading your textbook so intensely that you speak out to the

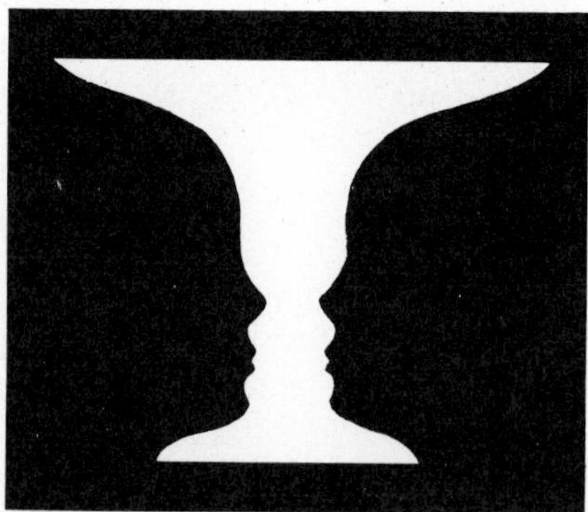

FIGURE 4.1 A Goblet or Two Profiles?

author: "That's not proof enough," or "Other writers explain it differently," or "I never thought about the problem that way before." That's concentration!

Trouble in concentrating may come from external and internal distractions, fatigue, sleepiness, or lack of interest in the work to be done. Once recognized, each of these causes of poor concentration can be overcome.

COMBATING EXTERNAL DISTRACTIONS

Anything outside of you that disrupts your concentration is an external distraction. College study halls and libraries are full of external distractions, ranging from blue eyes to banging doors. You must select and equip your place of study carefully.

A Place to Study

You need a definite and permanent place of study. Place your desk against a wall—never in front of a window. To avoid sharp contrasts of light and dark, which can cause eye fatigue, place a light-colored blotter (not a green one) on your desk top. If the wall is dark, nail or tack a light-colored square of cardboard to fill the area behind your desk.

Psychologists emphasize that a conditioning effect is created between the desk and you: If you nap or daydream a lot while sitting at the desk, then the desk can act as a cue for napping or daydreaming. To avoid this type of negative conditioning, use your desk only for studying. When you want to nap or daydream, leave the desk and nap or daydream elsewhere.

Your place of study should be your workshop, a place where you feel secure and comfortable. Such a place will not distract you.

Equipment for Studying

Get yourself a comfortable, well-cushioned chair. Whether you stay awake or fall asleep does not depend on your chair; it depends on your method of study, your attitude and self-discipline, the light, and the room temperature.

A practical piece of equipment is a book stand that you place on your desk to hold the book in a tilted position with the pages held down. Such a stand can make you feel ready to study, and this feeling alone is worth many times the price of the stand. The stand allows you some physical freedom. It eliminates the strain of continually holding the book open and the need for you to find something heavy enough to hold the book open while you make notes. It permits you to sit back with your arms folded, to contemplate and reflect on the meaning of what you are reading. Also, tilting a book about 30 degrees toward your eyes makes reading easier. The type on the page of a book flat on your desk is foreshortened because of your angle of vision; seeing and reading are thus more difficult.

Other basic equipment includes an up-to-date dictionary, a calculator, a clock, a calendar, paper, notebooks, paper clips, tape, rubber bands, pencils, pens, erasers, and note cards. Keep your desk well stocked so that you don't have to make unplanned emergency trips to obtain necessities.

Lighting

Good lighting makes for good studying. By contrast, poor lighting makes for eyestrain, general tension, headaches, and sleepiness—irritations that interfere with concentration. If you study under good light, but your eyes still bother you, have them examined by an ophthalmologist. Clear and comfortable vision is essential to good studying.

Provide your area of study with enough properly placed light of good quality. The Better Light Better Sight Bureau in New York has made some specific recommendations.

Enough Light. If you are using one lamp, use a light bulb of at least 250 watts. You may use the "top step" of a three-way 50-200-250-watt bulb or the total wattage of two or more bulbs. According to the Better Light Better Sight Bureau, two lamps are better than one. If you use two lamps, position them as shown in Figure 4.2, and put a 150-watt bulb in each.

You may decide to use fluorescent lighting. Fluorescent tubes produce from three to four times more light than an incandescent light bulb of the same wattage. A fluorescent tube has a constant flicker, but in a double-tube lamp the two tubes are synchronized and the visual flicker is eliminated.

For seeing comfort, select lamps that will provide well-diffused light. A diffusing element under the lamp shade will soften the light and reduce glare from shiny surfaces. The element can be a glass or plastic bowl that surrounds the light bulb, or it can be a diffusing disk across the bottom of the shade. If the shadows cast by your lamps are soft, and if there is little glare from shiny surfaces, your lamps are equipped with an effective diffuser.

Proper Lamp Shades. Researchers found an 81 percent loss of clear vision in a group of students studying by an unshaded light bulb. Glare must be eliminated!

Your lamp shades should be open at the top to provide upward lighting, which helps reduce sharp differences between lighting on the desk and its

two lamps
are better than one

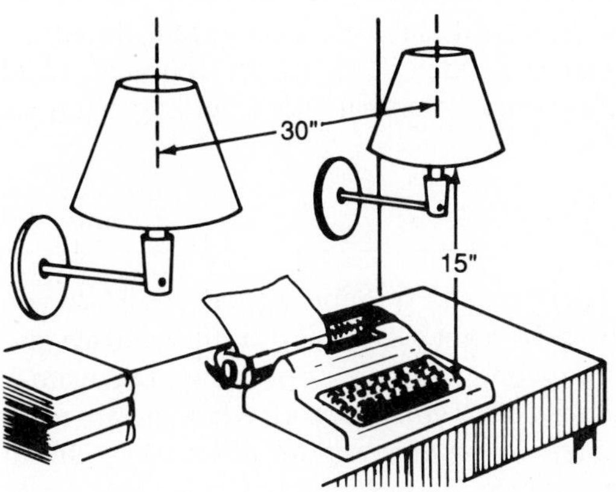

- 150-watt bulb in each lamp
- Diffusing element under the shades
- Fairly dense or opaque shade, light-colored
- Light-colored, non-glossy desk top or blotter
- Light-colored back-wall, or tack-board

FIGURE 4.2 Two-Lamp System of Lighting
Source: How to Make Homework Lighter! *Better Light Better Sight Bureau, 750 Third Avenue, New York, NY 10017.*

surroundings. They should be wide enough at the bottom (a diameter of at least 16 inches) to permit light to spread over the entire working area. Shades should be deep enough to conceal the light bulb from view when you are either seated or standing. They should have a white or near-white lining to reflect as much light as possible and be sufficiently dense or opaque to prevent glaring bulb brightness from shining through the material of the shade.

Proper Placement of Lamps. When your lamps are properly placed, the light is close to the task; no glare bounces up into your eyes, and no shadows fall across your work. Never try to read or work in your own shadow. If you are writing or drawing, the light should come from the side opposite your working hand, so that your hand doesn't cast a shadow on your work. Have the light as close to the task as possible but not so close you can see up under the shade, because it may be uncomfortably bright.

You can use other lights in the room to avoid uncomfortable differences in brightness. General room lighting helps make your desk lighting comfortable.

Noise

If you need a quiet spot for efficient study, do your utmost to find one. If the library is the right place for you, then always go there. Nothing is more wasteful than going over the same paragraph again and again because there is too much noise for you to absorb what you are reading. Noise in your living quarters is one of the most serious obstacles to effective study.

Some students rationalize that it takes too much time to walk to the library. But two or three hours of efficient study in quiet surroundings does more good than ten hours in near bedlam. Many students find the walk to the library refreshing, and report that they can even concentrate on their studies and get something done as they walk.

One sure way to avoid being trapped in a noisy dormitory is to study in the library from the *first* day of classes. Find a quiet spot in the library free from distractions.

Background Music

Many students use music from a radio or stereo as a background for studying. Does background music help the learning process or interfere with it?

A review of thirteen experiments on the effect of music on learning ability yielded the following results:

1. In seven experiments, groups *without* music in the background achieved higher scores on a quiz than groups *with* music.
2. In five experiments involving some groups *with* and some groups *without* music in the background, tests showed that there were no significant differences in achievement.
3. In one experiment in which a bell was struck intermittently, a group of college students taking a thirty-minute intelligence test gained *slightly.*

> *The most intelligent students in the group, however, made the most mistakes with the bell striking.*

The box score for background music is one win (not really by music, but by the bell), five ties, and seven losses. A very poor record!

Turn off your radio or stereo. When you are studying, music is *noise.* Some students report that all through high school they studied successfully with music in the background. Success in passing high school courses, however, is no proof that the background music does not interfere. These students should be asked how much better they could have done without music. How much more could they have learned during the same period?

By exerting extra energy when the music is playing, you may be able to keep your mind on your studies 75 percent of the time, and the music will capture only 25 percent of your attention. But your mind and body will be bombarded by the sound waves 100 percent of the time. Such bombardment is physically tiring. Why ask for problems when you are studying? Concentration is already hard to achieve.

COMBATING INTERNAL DISTRACTIONS

Internal distractions are distractions that you yourself create: indecision, daydreams, personal problems, anxiety, forgetfulness, and unrealistic goals. Because they come from within you, you have the power to eliminate or at least control them.

Here are some suggestions for eliminating or minimizing internal distractions. They have worked for many students.

1. *Plan ahead.* Indecision about when to study and which subject to study is a great waster of time. It is also a sure way to create a negative attitude toward studying. You can hurdle this psychological barrier by planning ahead.

2. *Don't daydream.* One of the worst time wasters is daydreaming. Daydreaming is a way of escaping from hard work. Pleasant as it is, it uses up time in which you could be working toward your goals. Establish the positive habit of plunging directly and efficiently into your work—a habit that will stand you in good stead all your life.

3. *Deal with your personal problems.* We all must develop ways of dealing with personal problems that distract us from our work. Worrying does not solve problems; positive action does. If a problem intrudes on your thoughts while you are studying, write it out on a sheet of paper and deal with it when you have finished your work. Then, after you have completed your work, attack the problem directly. If you cannot solve it yourself, get the help of friends or counselors. Decide on a plan of action, and follow it.

4. *Deal with anxiety caused by a course.* Every semester, you are likely to have one course that bothers you for some reason or other. It is surprising how quickly an initial uneasy feeling becomes general anxiety that interferes with all your studies. One way to dispel such anxiety is to talk the matter over with the instructor of the course or with another instructor or with your counselor.

For example, one student first told her counselor that she liked her political science instructor and the course. Four weeks later, however, she said, "The instructor is unorganized; and, in his lectures, he doesn't stick to the topic." About five minutes later, almost as an afterthought, the real reason for her discontent surfaced: "He wants everyone to lead a class discussion." Then she added, "I'll be home for the holidays, but I won't enjoy a minute of it thinking about having to get up in front of the class as soon as I get back." Almost to herself, she ended by saying, "Maybe I'll drop the course."

Realizing that students with no formal training in speaking may find such a venture traumatic, the counselor suggested, "Go to the instructor, and sincerely lay your cards on the table."

Two weeks later, the student told her counselor of her meeting with the instructor: "He said he understood my fear, and he let me write a paper on my topic instead."

5. *Set realistic goals.* Set realistic study goals. If you have hardly been studying at all, it is not realistic to announce suddenly: "Tonight I plan to study for six hours." Chances are that the required effort will be too much for you, and you will only experience another failure. To succeed, change your habits gradually. If you were to study for only two hours on that first evening, you would have a far better chance of achieving your goal.

6. *Use a reminder list.* To avoid worrying about the possibility of missing personal appointments, write them down on your daily schedule (see Figure 3.6, page 52). If an appointment is several days away, write it on your month-at-a-glance calendar. Having made a written reminder, you will no longer have to clutter your mind with these details.

CONCENTRATION TECHNIQUES

Here is a list of techniques that have helped students concentrate. Try one or two at a time to see whether they work for you.

1. *Have a positive attitude.* Try to view studying as an opportunity to learn, rather than as an unpleasant task to complete. Because you may be spending a great deal of time in your room, do not make it a prison; consider your room a sanctuary. Remember: You are always free to take a well-earned break.

2. *Use the spider technique.* A vibrating tuning fork held close to a spider's web sets up vibrations in the web. After the spider makes a few hurried investigations and finds no fly in the web, it learns to ignore the vibrations. The next time you are studying in the library and the door opens, don't look up. Controlling your impulse to look up will disturb your concentration the first few times. But very soon, like the spider, you'll learn to ignore these external disturbances.

3. *Ignore noise around you.* There will always be some noise around you. Avoid disturbances if you can, but do your best to ignore the noise you cannot avoid. By all means do not let yourself become annoyed. The internal irritation that you create has a more devastating effect on your concentration than the external noises themselves.

4. *Make sure you have everything.* Before sitting down to study, make sure you have everything you need: sharp pencils, fresh paper and cards, necessary books. Then stay in your chair until you have studied a half an hour or so.

5. *Use the no-room principle.* Imagine that the pathways of your mind are completely filled with thoughts about the subject in front of you. Then your mind will have no room for extraneous thoughts, and they will be turned away.

6. *Use the checkmark technique.* Have a sheet of paper handy by your book. When you catch yourself not concentrating, put a checkmark on the sheet. The mere act of doing this will remind you to get back to work. Students report that when they first tried this system, they accumulated as many as twenty checkmarks per textbook page; but after one or two weeks, they were down to one or two checkmarks per page.

7. *Don't rely on will power!* Will power alone can't make you concentrate. You will be breaking concentration whenever you remind yourself, "I must use will power to concentrate!"

8. *Don't fight hunger.* Hunger is such a basic and persistent state that there is no sense trying to overcome it. Give in! Feed yourself; then go back to work.

THE FOOD-BODY-MIND CONNECTION

What you eat and when you eat are crucial to your success as a student. Eating a healthy breakfast in the morning and maintaining an adequate level of blood sugar in your body throughout the day are key to how you concentrate, how you take notes in class, and how vigorously you do your homework.

Keep Your Blood-Sugar Level Up

Every cell in your body receives its food from glucose (blood sugar), which is transported by your blood. The level of glucose in your blood determines the amount of energy you have or don't have. When you feel dragged out and find it hard to think, your blood sugar is probably low. When this happens, do not try the quick fix of a candy bar. Candy will make you feel better for a short while, but you'll quickly feel even more tired and you'll find it even harder to think.

When too much sugar suddenly enters your bloodstream, an alarm triggers your pancreas to send out a flood of insulin to neutralize the sugar. The pancreas usually overreacts, and in no time at all your blood-sugar level is drastically reduced, usually below the point at which it was before you ate the candy bar.

A good way to maintain the proper level of blood sugar is to eat some protein every day. Protein is digested slowly, and the glucose derived from the digested protein is absorbed into the blood stream steadily and thus does not cause the pancreas to overreact and produce too much insulin. The glucose carried by the blood gets to every cell, where it is converted to energy.

Because your body cannot store protein, you must provide it with a new supply every day. According to nutritional chemists, you should consume some protein at breakfast. If you *start* the day feeling tired because of low blood sugar, you'll feel tired all day long, even if you try to make up for the deficiency by eating protein at lunch.

Eat a Healthful Breakfast

Do not skip breakfast, even if you are not hungry. Eating a nutritious breakfast will improve your physical and mental performance. A 10-year study of seven thousand people in California showed that people who often skip breakfast do not live as long as people who eat breakfast almost every day. Another study showed that students who had no breakfast were listless and had trouble concentrating—and you know that without concentration there can be no learning.

Many of us are in a hurry in the morning and don't want to spend a lot of time preparing food. Consequently, most of us opt for ready-to-eat cereals. Here are your best bets according to *Consumer Reports*.[1] Special K supplies the

[1] "Ready-to-Eat Cereals," *Consumer Reports* 51 (October 1986): 628–37.

most protein. One ounce supplies 6 grams. Add one-half cup of milk and you get a total of 10 grams of fairly complete protein—nearly twice the protein of one large egg. One ounce of Life cereal supplies 5 grams of protein. The following cereals supply 4 grams per ounce: All-Bran, Cheerios, Quaker 100% Natural Cereal, and Raisin Life. Remember: One-half cup of milk supplies an additional 4 grams of protein.

A good alternative to cold cereal is Quick Oats, which cooks in only one minute. One ounce gives you 5 grams of protein. A half-cup of milk adds four more protein grams.

Wheat germ is a good supplement to hot or cold cereal. Two tablespoons of wheat germ sprinkled on top add 6 grams of protein.[2]

You probably know that eggs are also a great source of protein. Unfortunately, they are also high in cholesterol. Cholesterol causes fatty deposits to adhere to the walls of arteries. Eventually, the arteries become blocked, preventing an adequate supply of blood from reaching the tissues. Since one large egg contains 252 milligrams of cholesterol,[3] cardiologists recommend that you eat no more than two eggs per week.[4] If you like eggs, but want to restrict your cholesterol intake, discard the yolks, poach the egg whites, and serve the egg whites on toast. Egg whites have no cholesterol.

GETTING ENOUGH SLEEP

People used to believe that eight or nine hours of sleep were necessary for an adult to feel well-rested. Recent research indicates, however, that the amount of sleep needed varies considerably among people. According to one study, some people need only five or six hours of sleep a night, while others may need as many as nine or ten.[5] Each person's requirements usually remain the same. Such findings indicate that each person's individual requirements are more important than an absolute amount of sleep. If you get six hours of sleep a night and still feel rested and well during the day, then that period of sleep is sufficient for you.

Each individual has a natural sleep rhythm. Your internal biological clock signals the time for sleep. Full alertness during the day is possible only when your sleep phase coincides with the hours you spend in bed. When this occurs, your sleep will be long, deep, and probably continuous. During the

---

[2]Carol Hupping et al., *Hints, Tips & Everyday Wisdom* (Emmaus, Pa.: Rodale Press, 1985), p. 280.

[3]Jane Brody, *The New York Times Guide to Personal Health* (New York: Times Books, 1982), p. 26.

[4]Anthony J. Sattilaro, *Living Well Naturally* (Boston: Houghton Mifflin, 1984), p. 19.

[5]J. Clausen, E. Sersen, and A. Lidsky, "Variability of Sleep Measures in Normal Subjects," *Psychophysiology* 11 (1974): 509–516.

daytime, you will be zestful and energetic. You will not become sleepy after lunch, or fall asleep in class, or struggle to stay awake until dinner. You'll be able to concentrate and take pleasure in your work all day long.

However, if your sleepy phase and time in bed are not synchronous, sleep deprivation is inevitable. You'll know you are experiencing it because you'll keep falling asleep in the daytime or you'll feel very drowsy. Other indicators of sleep deprivation are the following: Your classes seem boring. Your mind wanders. You are unable to take notes or your notes are just fragments. Getting started is hard. You put off studying. You are losing interest and feeling dull. You are concentrating poorly. You have no enthusiasm. Your judgment is impaired.

Factors that affect the quality of your sleep include the following:

1. *Environment for sleeping.* The room in which you sleep should be quiet, dark, and secure. Use your bedroom only for sleeping. Don't eat or read in bed.
2. *Regularity.* Go to bed and get up at the same time each day. Regularity is the single most important rule. Be a lark: Get sleepy early and wake up early. Avoid daytime naps.
3. *Duration of sleep.* Sleep the number of hours you feel you need on a regular basis.
4. *General health.* Optimal nighttime sleep and optimal daytime alertness result from regular exercise, proper diet, and regular timing of meals.
5. *Drugs.* Alcohol, sleeping pills, caffeine (see Table 2.1, on page 30, for sources of caffeine in your diet), and amphetamines damage the sleep mechanism.

Naturally, the sleepy feeling occurs in us all, even if we are regularly getting enough sleep. In order to get your work done, you may occasionally be forced to fight the sleepy feeling. One way to fight sleepiness is to take frequent five-minute breaks. Another way is to pace the floor slowly while you read a book or recite a lesson. Still another is to schedule recreation or academic assignments involving physical activity (such as rearranging your lecture and reading notes, writing in key words, formulating questions, or doing errands that you have been accumulating) at hours when you ordinarily find it hard to study.

Many students give in to the urge to sleep and rationalize that when they awake they will be refreshed. Few students report this happy result, however. Rather, they awake to a pile of undone work. It is far better to combat the desire to sleep, get the work done, and go to bed at your usual time with a clear conscience.

Optimum sleep promotes not only a more alert, energetic, zestful life but also, according to some studies, a longer life. If you're not concentrating, if you're dozing off in class and at your desk, if you're feeling dragged out, then you may not be getting enough sleep. Take steps to put yourself back on the right track.

COMBATING INSOMNIA

In a recent study, 6 percent of adult men and 14 percent of adult women said they experienced insomnia often or fairly often. This means that about 10 million adult Americans toss and turn before dropping off to sleep. Another study estimated 25 to 30 million suffer from insomnia.

If you carry unpleasant arguments, defeats, and disappointments in your thoughts, playing and replaying the episodes over and over again (the broken-record syndrome discussed in Chapter 2), you will have trouble falling asleep. According to Hans Selye, internationally recognized stress specialist,

> Hormones produced during acute stress will circulate in your blood and will keep you awake just as a tablet of ephedrine (chemically related to adrenaline) would. Your insomnia, thus, has a chemical basis, which cannot easily be talked away after it has developed; and at night in bed it is too late to prevent it from developing.[6]

To avoid insomnia, you should avoid exceedingly stressful situations. However, if you are in bed and can't sleep, try the power of positive thinking. A positive person sees a glass as half full, not half empty.

You can open the door of your mind to whatever thoughts you want. Admit only the positive ones; eliminate negative self-talk. Whenever you have a negative thought, make up a positive one to counteract it. Thomas J. Coates and Carl E. Thoresen suggest the following:[7]

Nonhelpful Thoughts (Negative)	*Helpful Thoughts (Positive)*
• "I've been lying here for an hour already. I'm going to be totally wiped out tomorrow."	• "That's okay. I'm getting rest and it's very peaceful. If I continue to relax, I'll fall asleep soon."
• "Oh brother. Here it is 3:30 A.M. and I'm awake. I bet I'll never get back to sleep."	• "I'll get back to sleep if I just stay calm and don't worry about it."

---

[6]Hans Selye, *The Stress of Life* (New York: McGraw-Hill, 1956), p. 271.
[7]Thomas J. Coates and Carl E. Thoresen, *How to Sleep Better* (Englewood Cliffs, N.J.: Prentice-Hall, 1977), pp. 78, 80.

COMBATING BOREDOM

It is almost impossible to develop mental fatigue by studying, even by studying hard. You get "tired" readily enough, but this happens because you are bored with the subject or because the subject is difficult and not particularly interesting, not because bodily wastes are accumulating in your brain or muscles. You may push away a textbook with the comment, "I'm exhausted! I can't read another word," and then casually pick up a magazine or newspaper and read avidly, without any signs of fatigue.

Here are some suggestions that will help you take a more kindly attitude toward a boring or difficult subject.

1. *Try small group sessions.* Find two or three other students who will meet with you to discuss briefly each assignment in the particular subject that is boring to you. During the give-and-take of the discussion you are bound to learn a great deal, and the subject may come alive or the enthusiasm of some of the members might rub off on you. Once you begin to know something about the subject, your interest level will rise. The only prerequisite for a group meeting is that all members do their homework. Only then can each person become an active contributor as well as a receiver.

2. *Get some individual tutoring.* When you see that you are having trouble, find a classmate who is mastering the subject and arrange, for a modest fee, to be tutored. The tutor will probably be able to get you on your own in a short time. Another possibility is to find out whether your college has a central office where arrangements can be made for tutoring between outstanding students and students needing some special help.

3. *Read alternative textbooks.* The writing in some textbooks is more difficult to grasp than in others. Often the style of the author causes the difficulty, not the difficulty of the topic itself. In the library you will find many books in which other authors discuss the very same topics. After you have read an alternative book, however, it is important to go back to your regular textbook to read the assigned chapters. You will understand them then.

4. *Use workbooks and programmed instructional materials.* There are many supplementary materials on which to practice and learn. These materials force you to take action. In programmed materials, especially, each step is a small problem that has to be solved on the basis of information presented in the previous steps. The ongoing sequence of problem solving forces you to concentrate and remember previous steps. Your solutions are immediately compared with the correct answers. In this way, wrong solutions are straightened out in your mind before they become embedded, and correct solutions are reinforced. Ask your instructor or the teaching assistant in your particular course whether such materials are available. Also, inquire at your college library, at the reading and study skills center, or at the college tutorial center.

IMPROVING CONCENTRATION WHILE READING

Use self-talk to gain and maintain concentration while reading. The surest way to gain and maintain concentration while you read is by having a lively conversation with the author. (Get to know the author by first reading the preface and the introduction of the book.) The conversation usually consists of general and specific questions as well as a stream of talking-to-yourself comments made silently or audibly. Through this conversation, you'll become personally involved in your own learning. Furthermore, this conversation, fostering alertness and concentration, will lead to a higher level of comprehension. The following textbook material and accompanying comments is an example of how to keep a stream of meaningful questions and comments going while you read.

Textbook Material[8]	**Reader's Comments and Questions**
Chapter title: MAGNETISM	"Oh, magnetism! Always wanted to know something about magnetism."
"The first magnetic materials discovered were in the form of mineral deposits found in Magnesia in Asia Minor."	"Magnesia! So that's how the words *magnet* and *magnetism* came about. Didn't know that."
"The Chinese, in about the first century A.D., discovered that when a magnet is suspended by a string, it will align itself in a north-south direction."	"Why this alignment?" "What's magnetism anyway?"
"It is found that if two north poles are brought near to one another they repel each other. Two south poles also repel each other, but a north pole and a south pole attract each other."	"Curious! I wonder why *like* poles repel and *unlike* attract each other?"
"In this chapter we will find that the study of magnetism cannot be divorced from that of electrical currents."	"I wonder what's the relation between electricity and magnetism?"

Reading a textbook in this conversational manner can be not only enjoyable but also productive. This is only the first step in textbook reading, however.

[8]Textbook material is from Jerry S. Faughn and Karl F. Kuhn, *Physics for People Who Think They Don't Like Physics* (Philadelphia: W. B. Saunders, 1976), pp. 280–81.

In this step, do *not* underline, highlight, or write in the margins. Keep the margins clean and clear for a better and higher-level use, which is explained and illustrated in Chapter 10.

SUMMARY

What is concentration?	Concentration is thinking. Concentration happens only when you're not thinking about it. As soon as you think you're concentrating, you're no longer concentrating.
What causes breaks in concentration?	External and internal distractions, physical and mental fatigue, and boredom may keep you from concentrating.
What are external distractions?	Anything outside of you that disrupts your concentration is an external distraction. Noise, bad light, music, even an unsharpened pencil are all external distractions.
How do I combat external distractions?	First of all, you need a good place to study. Generally, that's going to be a quiet spot with a desk or table that contains all the materials you need (like sharpened pencils) and none of the diversions you don't need (like pictures, knickknacks, and food).
How important is good light for concentration?	You need a minimum of 250 watts of good-quality shaded or diffused light. The light should come from the side opposite your working hand without creating glare or shadows. Poor light or glare can strain your eyes and, by tiring you out faster than usual, destroy your concentration.
Is it possible to find a place to study that isn't noisy?	If you head for the library, you are likely to find a quiet spot. Walk or drive to the library instead of trying to tune out the noises that are typical at home or in a dorm room.
Does background music interfere with studying?	Yes. Music is noise. Any outside sound, no matter how pleasant, lessens your ability to concentrate. Use music as a reward after you've finished studying and not before.

What are internal distractions?	Internal distractions come from inside yourself. Basically, internal distractions are any thoughts or feelings that interfere with the task at hand. Indecision, daydreams, personal problems, and anxiety are all internal distractions.
How can I eliminate internal distractions?	The best way to eliminate almost any internal distraction is to deal with it directly. If you're indecisive, plan ahead. If you've got a personal problem that won't go away, write it down on paper; get it out of your mind and in print. Then when you've finished your studies, you can tend to it. If you're a daydreamer, make a point of not daydreaming. If you're anxious about a course, talk to the instructor and get your concerns out of your mind and onto the table.
Are there any tricks or techniques for aiding concentration?	Yes. Have a positive attitude. Use the spider technique. Ignore noise around you. Make sure you have everything you need for studying. Use the no-room principle. Use the checkmark technique. Don't rely on will power. Don't fight hunger.
What's the food-body-mind connection?	It's a chain that starts with what you eat and winds up with how well you concentrate. Too much sugar in your diet can cause your body to overreact. Often, as a result, you wind up feeling dragged out. When that's the case, you're going to have a tough time concentrating. One way to counteract the negative effects of too much sugar, but maintain the energy level that sugar can produce, is to add protein to your diet.
How else can I improve my diet?	Start each day with a well-balanced breakfast.
What's a good, protein-rich breakfast food?	Eggs are a great source of protein, but they contain an unusually high amount of cholesterol. One-ounce servings of ready-to-eat cereals such as Special K, Life, and Cheerios

supply between 4 and 6 grams of protein. One-half cup milk adds another 4 grams.

How much sleep do I need?	Studies indicate that most people need between five and nine hours of sleep per night. Generally speaking, you can tell if you're getting enough sleep by how tired or dragged out you feel during the day.
When is the best time to sleep?	Everyone has an internal biological clock that signals the best time for sleep. Each day you have a sleepy phase and an alert phase. Full alertness during the day is possible only when your sleepy phase corresponds with the hours you spend in bed. During the day and during study time, fight sleepiness.
Are naps a good idea?	No. They play havoc with your sleep pattern. Furthermore, if you give in and take a nap before bedtime, you'll wake up with the same amount of work and less time to do it in.
Any other facts about sleep?	It's important to develop a regular sleeping pattern. If you go to sleep at the same time every night, your body will become used to the pattern you set. As a result, you'll be at your most alert each morning when you wake up. If you vary your sleeping pattern, you run the risk of feeling drowsy when you should be alert, and vice versa.
What can I do about boredom?	There are a number of ways to beat boredom. You can try studying in groups. Often the enthusiasm of one group member will rub off on the rest. You can get individual tutoring. Boredom may stem from a lack of success. A good tutor can help to get you back on the right track. You might also try reading an alternative textbook. In some cases it is the style of the author that's boring you, not the subject itself. You can use workbooks or other programmed materials. They work like mini-quizzes to help keep both your concentration and your interest level high.

Is there a special technique to aid concentration while I am reading?	Yes. Talk back to your textbook. As you read a chapter, strike up a lively conversation with the author. The conversation gets you thinking, forces you to take an active part in your reading, and, best of all, does wonders for your comprehension.

HAVE YOU MISSED SOMETHING?

1. *Sentence completion.* Complete the following sentences with one of the three words listed below each sentence.

a. A good example of an internal distraction is a ________________.

problem noise roommate

b. Recent research shows that the effects of sleep loss are __________.

harmless pathological cumulative

c. We have a tendency to confuse fatigue with ________________.

illness boredom hunger

2. *Matching.* In each blank space in the left column, write the number preceding the phrase in the right column that matches the left item best.

_____ a. Book stand	1. Feeds every cell in your body
_____ b. Insulin	2. Simple device that promotes readiness to study
_____ c. Spider technique	3. A good source of protein
_____ d. Glucose	4. Often confused with mental fatigue
_____ e. Boredom	5. Method of ignoring external distractions
_____ f. Checkmark technique	6. May result from stressful situations
_____ g. Wheat germ	7. Reduces the body's blood-sugar level
_____ h. Insomnia	8. Provides a gentle reminder to get back to work

3. *True-false.* Write *T* beside the *true* statements and *F* beside the *false* statements.

_____ a. Poor lighting can produce eyestrain and sleepiness.

_____ b. Hunger should always be resisted during study time.

_____ c. The smell of pizza is an internal distraction.

_____ d. It's a good idea to begin studying in the library on the very first day of classes.

_____ e. Background music is an aid to concentration.

_____ f. Unrealistic goals are an internal distraction.

4. *Fighting sleepiness.* Write "yes" next to the recommended ways to stay alert.

_____ a. Take frequent five-minute breaks.

_____ b. Drink coffee or other caffeinated beverages.

_____ c. Pace the floor while reading or reciting.

_____ d. Take a brief but restful nap in the middle of the day.

_____ e. Do assignments that require no physical activity.

_____ f. Schedule recreation for your "tired times."

5. *Multiple choice.* Choose the phrase that completes the following sentence most accurately, and circle the letter that precedes it.

Concentration can be gained and maintained through self-talk, which involves having a conversation with

a. the author of your textbook
b. your instructor
c. your roommate
d. all the above

CHAPTER 5

Forgetting and Remembering

Those who cannot remember the past are condemned to repeat it!

George Santayana (1863–1952), Spanish-born American philosopher

Believe it or not, you will have forgotten most of this chapter before the day is out. Forgetting is an unstoppable process unless you take immediate action to arrest it. In the following pages, you'll learn ways to combat the devastating effects of forgetfulness so that this chapter, as well as countless other chapters and lectures, does not fall victim to learning's greatest enemy. This chapter discusses

- Reading, listening, and forgetting
- Pseudo-forgetting
- Theories about forgetting
- Principles of deep cognitive processing
- Remembering with mnemonics

and finally

- Commercial memory courses

ithout memory, there would be no learning. Without memory, every experience, no matter how common, would be a brand new experience.

Although the human brain does record and store experiences, it does not automatically recall prior experiences. The recalling is up to us.

READING, LISTENING, AND FORGETTING

Hundreds of research studies tell the same story: When you learn something new, the greatest amount of forgetting takes place during the first day. In one experiment, people who read a textbook chapter forgot 46 percent of what they had read after one day, 79 percent after fourteen days, and 81 percent after twenty-eight days. Converted into percentages, these data indicate that you remember 54 percent after one day, 21 percent after two weeks, and 19 percent after a month.

Remembering what you have heard is even more difficult than remembering what you have read. While you read, you can slow down, pause, reflect, and reread. Furthermore, you have the advantage of seeing the words (visual memory). When you are listening, you usually have just one chance to catch the words that are spoken.

In another experiment, researchers secretly recorded a seminar held by the members of the Cambridge Psychological Society.[1] Two weeks later, the members were asked to write down all they could recall of the seminar. The average proportion of specific points correctly recalled by each member was 8.4 percent. Happenings were reported that never took place; casual remarks were greatly expanded; points were reported that had only been hinted at. This group of psychologists forgot 91.6 percent of the specific points made in their seminar.

The results of this experiment show the limitations of memory. This experiment tells us that if we want to remember what really went on in a meeting or a classroom lecture, we had better take notes.

PSEUDO-FORGETTING

Whenever you cannot remember a name, telephone number, fact, idea, or even a joke, you probably say, "I forgot." Yet forgetting may not have anything to do with your problem. "I forgot" is a convenient, socially accepted explanation for these lapses. There are two kinds of so-called forgetting that are not really forgetting at all.

[1]See Ian M. L. Hunter, *Memory: Facts and Fallacies* (Baltimore: Penguin, 1957), p. 83.

"You Never Had It" Forgetting

It is inaccurate to say "I forgot" about something when you never did have it in your memory. You wouldn't expect to pull a $100 bill out of your wallet if you had not put one there in the first place. Similarly, you should not expect to remember a name that was so mumbled during an introduction that you never heard it clearly. Nevertheless, you might later say, "I was introduced to him ten minutes ago, but I have forgotten his name already," when the truth is that you never had the name in your memory. The same is true of things you have briefly read in your textbook and briefly heard in a classroom lecture, without really grasping them, understanding them, and then making an effort to commit them to memory. If you can't repeat them, it's not because you've forgotten them but because you never really knew them.

"Mental Blur" Forgetting

Mental blurs result from grossly incomplete learning. You read a chapter straight through but don't have time to go back to take notes. Next morning, when a question is asked in class, the best you can say to the instructor is, "I read it only last night, but I forget most of it. I guess I have a poor memory."

You are wrong about having a poor memory. Although you read and understood the words in the chapter, you did not stop to put the words together into ideas. Instead of isolating the eight or ten important ideas in the chapter, you just saw a continuous string of words. If you point a camera at the distant hills and rapidly swing the camera to photograph all the hills while you click the shutter, all you'll get is a blur. Your quick reading of the chapter, without stopping to get a separate mental picture of each idea, produced a mental blur of the entire chapter.

If an idea or fact is to be retained in your memory, it must be impressed on your mind clearly and crisply at least once. Some sort of mark, chemical change, or neural trace must be laid down in your brain. You cannot retain something that is not there in the first place.

THEORIES ABOUT FORGETTING

Scientists don't know for sure why we forget, but they have some interesting theories. Each theory contains some truth, and knowing how these theories work might help you combat forgetting.

Fading of the Memory Trace: Fading Theory

According to the fading theory, the trace or mark left in the brain by a fact or idea is like a path across a field. If you don't continue to walk over the path, grass will grow up and obliterate it. A similar fading process happens in the brain, obliterating a fact or idea that you had learned. If you don't use it, you'll lose it.

Stored It, but Can't Find It: Retrieval Theory

Some psychologists believe that a fact or idea once thoroughly learned remains in the memory for life. According to the retrieval theory, you may forget a fact or idea not because a trace or mark has faded but because you can't find, or retrieve, it in the vast storehouse of your mind. This theory suggests that organizing whatever you learn is very important.

Fighting for a Place in the Sun: Interference Theory

Psychologists like the interference theory mainly because it is easy to demonstrate in laboratory experiments. According to this theory, old facts and ideas cause us to forget new facts and ideas (forward interference), and new facts and ideas cause us to forget old facts and ideas (backward interference). The memory is a battlefield on which old and new facts and ideas fight for attention and survival. Some win and some lose.

Caught in a Crossfire: Interactive Interference Theory

Imagine that you have learned three facts at three different times. For example:

Oldest: Pike's Peak gold rush took place in 1851.

Middle: California gold rush (Sutter's Mill) took place in 1849.

Newest: Klondike gold rush took place in 1897.

According to interactive interference theory, you'll lose the middle fact rapidly, because it will be bombarded by both the oldest learning and the newest learning. To complicate things, the middle fact, fighting for survival, will do its best to bombard both the newest and oldest learning (fighting both frontal and rear attacks). In the course of this fighting, the middle fact, while going down in defeat, will inflict some damage (forgetting) to both the oldest and the newest learning.

Avoiding Disliked Subjects: Reactive Interference Theory

Reactive interference arises from negative feelings or attitudes toward a disliked subject. Such feelings not only make understanding difficult but also make the material difficult to remember.

Because a disliked subject is usually a required subject, you must learn the material to pass the course. To cope with reactive interference, study the subject in sprints. Work actively with paper and pencil in a disciplined effort for fifty minutes; then take a well-deserved ten-minute break. The rest period will allow the annoyance generated by the task to subside and disappear.

Choosing to Forget: Motivation Theory

You forget some things that you want to forget—the names of people you dislike, embarrassing situations, poor investments. Conversely, you choose to remember things that are pleasant. The lesson here: You have the power to influence both remembering and forgetting.

PRINCIPLES OF DEEP COGNITIVE PROCESSING

Powerful forces of forgetting are constantly attacking from the front, the back, and the flanks to scatter, to fragment, to erode knowledge. The winner of the battle, however, is not always the negative forces of forgetting. You have the ability not only to stop the onslaught but also to roll back the attack. Your weapon is deep cognitive processing.

In plain language, deep cognitive processing means *deep thinking.* It is this deep thinking that is the key to a strong, clear, long-lasting memory trace. Deep thinking in effect chisels a memory trace in stone.

To achieve a long-lasting memory of a fact encountered in your textbook, for example, you must seriously and whole-heartedly take three steps:

1. *Understand* the fact thoroughly so that you can explain it in your own words. Like an orator, try to explain it aloud to yourself. If you succeed, you have mastered the fact.
2. *Analyze* the fact by pausing to view it from all sides, all approaches, all implications. Think of yourself as a scientist in this step.
3. *Relate* the fact to all the pertinent information already stored in your memory. Like a spider, weave a neat, systematic web that strongly fastens the fact to the foundations of knowledge that are already permanent structures in your memory.

As a result of these three steps, the fact has no fuzzy edges; it is an entity that is cleanly etched in your memory. The fact is no longer a flat, one-dimensional, on-the-textbook-page assemblage of words; it is full-bodied. The fact is not free-floating; it is fastened to and interrelated with other facts in your memory.

Ten principles of deep cognitive processing will help you *understand, analyze,* and *relate* the facts and ideas presented in your textbooks and in classroom lectures.

Motivated Interest

Psychologists agree that to learn something thoroughly, you must have an *interest* in the material you are studying. It is almost impossible to remember anything that does not interest you in the first place. When you *are* interested, however, you are motivated to learn.

Charles W. Eliot, president of Harvard for forty years, each year learned the names of all the students and faculty members. He did this because in the past he had been terribly embarrassed by his inability to remember the name of one of his colleagues and had promised himself that he would never suffer that embarrassment again.

A basketball coach at Cornell University recalled that as a student at DePauw University he found physics uninteresting until he encountered material dealing with angles, trajectory, and force. He immediately applied this information to the caroming of basketballs off the backboard. Because of his new-found interest, he was able to raise his grade from a C to an A by the end of the semester.

If you could study every one of your subjects with motivated interest, you would not have to worry about your final grades. When you are naturally interested in a subject, you have no problem. If, however, you are not naturally interested, try to combat boredom by artificially creating interest (see Chapter 4). Once you begin to learn something about a new subject, the chances are great that you will find it genuinely interesting. Use the power of interest to work *for* you, not against you.

Selectivity

Hermann Ebbinghaus (1850–1909), a German psychologist who investigated memory and forgetting for over twenty years, counted the number of trials required to learn a series of six nonsense syllables (such as *bik, luf, tur, pem, nif,* and *wox*). He then counted the number of trials required to learn a series of twelve such syllables. He found that the number of trials required to memorize the twelve syllables was *fifteen* times greater than the number required for the learning of the six syllables.[2] So, for example, if it took you one minute to memorize six syllables, it would take you fifteen minutes to memorize twelve syllables.

You might be inclined to assume that you would need only twice as long to learn twelve syllables as you would need to learn six, but that is not how memory works. Interference theory and interactive interference theory, discussed earlier in this chapter, account for the great increase in effort and time needed to memorize longer lists of syllables. In effect, every new fact or idea must fight with old facts and ideas for a place in your memory.

Although Ebbinghaus dealt only with nonsense syllables, his research teaches a valuable lesson that can be applied to both textbook and lecture material: In order to remember, you must condense and summarize. Pick out the main ideas from your lecture and textbook notes. Once you have identified the essential points, you should be able to memorize them in a manageable amount of time.

Reducing pages of notes down to a handful of main ideas is often easier said than done. If you need a foolproof method of consolidating and summarizing your notes, consider the poker-chip technique.[3]

In the game of poker, the blue chips are worth the most, followed by the red chips and then the white chips. By analogy, the most important ideas in any message are the blue chips. Subordinate to the blue-chip ideas are the red-chip ideas, and subordinate to the red-chip ideas are the white-chip ideas, which may be considered details.

Around a poker table, you'll usually find each player with four or five blue chips, eight or ten red chips, and a large stack of white chips. In the same way, a writer usually has only a few blue-chip ideas, a few more red-chip ideas, and many more white-chip details. When you are summarizing, your job as a student is to find the blue-chip ideas. Mark them with a capital B, the red-chip ideas with R, and the white-chip details with W. Then gather up in your summary all the blue-chip ideas. Use the red-chip ideas and the white-chip details only where necessary to support the main ideas.

The poker-chip technique makes main ideas easy to remember. The main ideas act as strong magnets, holding together the subordinate ideas and the supporting details not included in the summary. The exclusion of red-chip and white-chip ideas from the summary does not automatically wipe them out of your memory. You *will* remember them.

---

[2]See R. D. Williams and G. W. Knox, "A Survey of Dynamic Principles Governing Memory," *Journal of General Psychology* 30 (April 1944): 167–79.
[3]See John O. Morris, *Make Yourself Clear!* (New York: McGraw-Hill, 1972), p. 13.

Intention to Remember

If you do not intend to remember, little worthwhile learning can take place. You have probably experienced the truth of this principle without realizing it. For example, many of you have helped a child memorize a poem or a speech by correcting his errors and prompting him when he forgot his lines. After spending as much time on the poem or speech as the child, you knew hardly any of it, but he had mastered it. He *intended* to remember; you did not.

Your mental attitude has a surprising effect on your memory. In a carefully designed study, H. H. Remmers and M. N. Thisted worked with students who learned material with the intention of retaining it for only one day, as for an exam.[4] The retention rate of these students at the end of two weeks was lower than that of students who were determined to remember the material for a two-week period.

The intention to remember is well demonstrated by waiters in restaurants. They exhibit a remarkably good memory for what customers order, up to the moment they have paid their bills. Then the waiters jettison the entire transaction from their mind so that they can give full attention to the next customer. Just as they intend to remember, so can they intend to forget.

The intention to forget to make room for new material was described by Hans Selye:

> It seems that to some extent *newly learned facts occupy the place of previously learned or subsequently learnable ones.* Consequently there is a limit to how much you can burden your memory; and trying to remember too many things is certainly one of the major sources of psychologic stress. I make a conscious effort to forget immediately all that is unimportant and to jot down data of possible value (even at the price of having to prepare complex files). Thus I manage to keep my memory free for facts which are truly essential to me. I think this technique can help anyone to accomplish the greatest simplicity compatible with the degree of complexity of his intellectual life.[5]

Intending to learn is a positive attitude that triggers several subsidiary attitudes, such as paying attention, getting a fact right the first time, and striving to understand.

Attention. Attention is the mental state of giving yourself fully to the task at hand. Unfortunately, inattention is common in readers of textbooks. When an idea in the book starts your mind wandering, then your eyes move along the printed lines but you don't comprehend them at all.

---

[4]H. H. Remmers and M. N. Thisted, "The Effect of Temporal Set on Learning," *Journal of Applied Psychology* 16 (June 1932): 257–68.
[5]Hans Selye, *The Stress of Life* (New York: McGraw-Hill, 1956), p. 269.

Getting It Right the First Time. All remembering depends on the formation of a clear neural trace in the brain. Initial impressions are important because the mind clings just as tenaciously to incorrect impressions as it does to correct impressions. To get something right the first time, so that you don't have to unlearn and relearn, be attentive and cautious when you encounter anything new. Go very slowly at first. Place your emphasis on accuracy, not on speed.

Striving to Understand. Psychologists interested in cognitive processing say that you must make sure you understand new material before you try to remember it. A good way to ensure understanding is to recite or write the author's ideas in *your own words.* If you cannot do so, then you do not understand the author's ideas, and you will not be able to remember what you do not understand. You cannot fashion a clear, correct memory trace from a fuzzy, poorly understood concept. In the classroom, do not hesitate to ask the instructor to explain a point that is not clear to you.

The Basic Background

Your understanding of what you *hear,* what you *read,* what you *see,* what you *feel,* and what you *taste* depends entirely on what you already know—the knowledge and experience you have in your background. When listening to a speaker, you understand the successive points that he or she is making as long as you can interpret those points in terms of something you are already familiar with. But the moment the speaker refers to a concept like the *Zeigarnik effect* or to a word like *serendipity*—a concept or a word that is not in your background—then you are lost. The new concept or word stands alone as an isolated sound; you cannot attach an accurate meaning to it. At this point, you may need to stop the speaker and ask for an explanation or definition. Experienced speakers, however, usually know when they are putting forth concepts and words that are not popularly known, and they provide the audience with an example or analogy. (To satisfy your curiosity, the *Zeigarnik effect* is the tendency to remember uncompleted tasks better than completed tasks, and *serendipity* is the faculty of making fortunate discoveries by accident.)

Many students make the mistake of thinking that the basic courses they take in their freshman year are a waste of time. These courses create the background essential for all their later courses. Budding technicians or engineers should realize that when they start studying these basic courses, they have already begun their careers. Your professional life begins with your freshman courses.

Meaningful Organization

Writers strive for clarity by organizing their material in some way. Deep processing helps you discover organization. Deep processing for organization creates long-lasting memories. You process deeply when you strive hard to grasp the underlying significance of a fact or idea by seeking some kind of organizational principle that relates the fact or idea to other facts or ideas. If there is no obvious pattern, then try to rearrange the material to create one for yourself. Otherwise, you will have to rely on rote memorization, mechanically repeating words over and over until you have learned them.

It would take you a long time to memorize these numbers; but if you could discern a logical pattern to them, remembering them would be easy. Try to find the logical pattern before reading the explanation at the bottom of this page.[6]

281	319	243	035
414	652	576	368

Facts and ideas that are organized in a meaningful way are going to be easier for you to recall than those that are in a jumble. Here are some techniques for bringing order to a mass of data.

The Category and Cluster System. When you have a large list of items to remember, try to cluster similar items around a natural heading or category. Once clustered and categorized, the items will resist the decaying power of forgetting. Just as the stem holds together the individual grapes, so categories and clusters hold together individual facts and ideas.

This hanging-together is especially useful during an exam: Remembering one item in the cluster is usually the key to remembering all the items. For example, it would take a long time to memorize by rote the following words that you might encounter in a geology course:

Slate	Diamond	Sapphire
Bronze	Lead	Aluminum
Iron	Marble	Silver
Emerald	Steel	Brass
Gold	Limestone	Ruby
Granite	Platinum	Copper

[6]The numbers following the 2 in 281 are obtained by alternately adding 6, then 5, then 6, then 5, and so on. For example, if you add 6 to 2, you get 8. If you add 5 to 8, you get 13. If you add 6 to 13, you get 19, and so on.

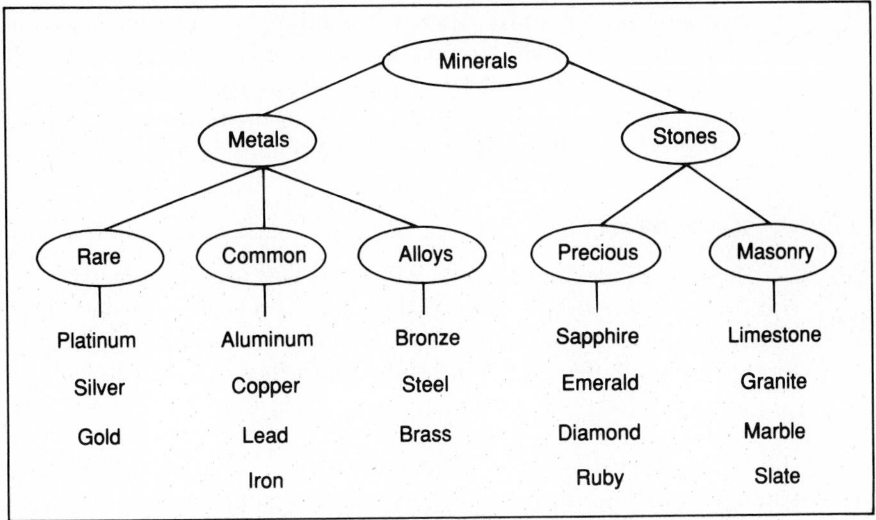

FIGURE 5.1 The Category and Cluster System of Organizing Items

However, when these words are organized into categories and are clustered as shown in Figure 5.1, memorization is relatively easy and remembering strong.[7]

The Magical Number Seven Theory. Experiments have revealed the exciting possibility of remembering vast quantities of material that is organized into categories or blocks. G. A. Miller of Harvard University found that the immediate memory span of an adult appears fixed at approximately seven separate chunks of information. Whether the seven chunks are big or small doesn't matter; only the number matters.

Organize your information into seven general categories; then add bits of information within these categories. Later, by remembering the names of the categories, you'll also remember, by association, the bits of information that each contains. The names of the seven chunks must always be in your own words so that the seven chunks together form a continuous story in your mind. You are sure to find words that tie together the seven chunks. As Miller says, "Our language is tremendously useful for repackaging material into a few chunks rich in information."[8]

---

[7]This example is from Jerome Kagan and Ernest Havemann, *Psychology: An Introduction*, Fourth Edition (New York: Harcourt Brace Jovanovich, 1980), p. 153. Reprinted by permission of the publisher.

[8]G. A. Miller, "The Magical Number Seven, Plus or Minus Two: Some Limits on Our Capacity for Processing Information," *Psychological Review* 63 (March 1956): 81–97.

First and Last on a List. Here is something to remember about organizing information: The items you place at the head of a list and those you place at the end of a list are recalled with greater accuracy than those in the middle of the list.[9] Therefore, when you are trying to memorize a list of items, give items in the middle of the list some extra attention.

Recitation

Recitation is saying aloud the ideas that you want to remember. No principle is more important than recitation for transferring material from the short-term memory to the long-term memory. Recitation creates a powerful force because it makes you think and thinking leaves a trace in your memory.

After you have gathered your information in note form and have categorized and clustered your items, recite them. Cover your notes with a blank sheet of paper; expose only the title or name of one category; and then recite aloud the material in that category. After reciting, expose your notes and check for accuracy. You should not attempt to recite the material word for word. Instead, use the words and manner that you would use if you were explaining the material to your roommate. When you can *say it,* then you *know it.*

Recitation may also be used with a textbook. After you read through a headed or subheaded section consisting of a page or two, stop reading and test yourself on what you have just read by reciting aloud the key ideas. Once you have recited and seen that you understand the ideas thus far in the chapter, you will read and recite later portions with greater understanding and efficiency.

How Recitation Works. While you are reading the words in a sentence or paragraph, your short-term memory holds them in mind long enough for you to gain the sense of the sentence or paragraph. However, short-term memory has a very limited capacity; and as you continue to read, you displace the words and ideas of the initial paragraphs with the words of subsequent paragraphs. This is one reason why you don't remember everything in the first part of a chapter by the time you reach the end of the chapter, when you read continually without pausing to recite.

When you *recite* or *contemplate* the idea conveyed by a sentence or paragraph, the idea has a chance (not guaranteed) of moving on into your long-term memory. Actually, only part of the rehearsed (recited) material goes into long-term memory. The rest of it, usually the part you are least interested in,

[9] B. B. Murdock, Jr., "The Retention of Individual Items," *Journal of Experimental Psychology* 62 (December 1961): 618–25.

remains in limbo and then returns to short-term memory, where it is forgotten. Whether new information is stored or dumped depends on whether you recite it out loud and whether you are interested in the information.

Why Recitation Works. Recitation is far more effective than merely reading and rereading. Because you know that you will be stopping to recite after reading each headed section within a chapter, you are motivated to understand. Recitation lets you know how you are doing. A correct recitation is an immediate reward that helps keep your motivation strong. An incorrect recitation is punishment that motivates you to study harder.

Recitation strengthens the original memory trace, because your mind must actively think about the new material. The physical activity of thinking, pronouncing, and even hearing your own words involves not only your mind but also your body in the process of learning. The more physical senses you use in learning, the stronger the neural trace in your brain will be. To promote recall, it is important to make outward, physical motion a part of the learning process. Students who silently read their assignments, no matter how diligently, often wonder why they remember so little after several days have passed. They do not realize that it is inefficient and ineffective to use the eyes alone as a means of absorbing information. Reciting aloud or writing the information, even sketchily, is better by far.

How Much Recitation? How much time should you spend reading and how much time reciting? The answer to this question was provided by a 1917 series of experiments that almost every textbook dealing with reciting turns to generation after generation. These landmark experiments, performed by Arthur I. Gates of Columbia University, show that regardless of the kind of material studied, more material is retained when a greater proportion of the study time is spent in reciting.[10] Reciting ensures both immediate recall and long-term recall.

Gates's experiments suggest that when you read a textbook chapter containing many facts, names, and principles, then 80 percent of your time should be spent in reciting and 20 percent in reading. This proportion pertains to subjects such as economics, psychology, sociology, and history. When you are memorizing reading material such as biographies, 60 percent of your time should be spent in reading and 40 percent in reciting. Gates also concluded that recitation should begin early in the learning process. In other words, you should not wait until you have read all the material before you begin to recite.

[10]Arthur I. Gates, "Recitation as a Factor in Memorizing," *Archives of Psychology* 7, no. 40 (1917).

Consolidation

Psychologists believe that neural traces need some time—from four or five seconds to about fifteen minutes—to jell or consolidate. Experiments with rats and hamsters offer concrete evidence of this phenomenon. In rats, the neural trace must persist in the brain for at least ninety seconds before a temporary memory can be converted or consolidated into a permanent one. In human beings, the neural trace must persist for only a few seconds, perhaps four or five.

The principle of consolidation may be at work when you recite or write the ideas and facts that you read. As you recite or write, you hold each idea in mind for the four or five seconds that are needed for the temporary memory to be converted into a permanent one. Another practical application of the principle of consolidation is in reviewing your notes immediately after class. If the reviewing is done by recitation, you are not only consolidating the new information but also strengthening its neural trace in your brain.

A. M. Sones's experiment demonstrating the value of review is illuminating.[11] One group of students had no review immediately after a class meeting; a second group had a five-minute review test. With only this five-minute advantage, the second group recalled one and a half times as much material as the group that had no immediate review, when both groups were tested six weeks later.

Distributed Practice

In *distributed practice* the student uses relatively short study periods broken up by rest intervals. In *massed practice* the student studies continuously until the task is completed. Many experiments show that, in general, there is an advantage to distributed practice. Several short sessions of intense concentration are more productive than one long, grinding-it-out session. The optimal length of the study period, of course, varies with different individuals as well as with the nature of the material being studied.

Distributed practice is more efficient than massed practice for these reasons:

1. Distributed practice prevents physical and emotional fatigue.
2. Motivation is stronger when you work within short blocks of time.
3. Distributed practice wards off boredom with subjects that are not very interesting.

[11] A. M. Sones, "A Study in Memory, with Special Reference to Temporal Distribution of Reviews," University of Iowa, *Studies, Aims and Progress in Research*, no. 72 (1943): 65–72.

4. Once energized, the neural learning processes seem to continue working during the rest period.

A practical application of the principle of distributed practice would be to make use of the small blocks of time (often only ten minutes) that occur between classes. After a lecture ends and while you are walking to your next class, try to recall the entire lecture—or as many of its ideas as possible.

Immediate and Long-term Gains. In an extensive experiment, Irving Lorge found that, with the introduction of distributed practice, students immediately improved their performance.[12] However, if distributed practice was stopped while the students were still working on the experiment, their performance decreased. There was an immediate reaction to both injection and withdrawal of distributed practice.

Bertram Epstein experimented to find out whether distributed practice has an effect on retention.[13] He tested his groups immediately after learning and then two weeks and ten weeks after the original practice. He found distributed practice to be superior to massed practice for both immediate and long-term retention.

Use of Massed Practice. In some cases, massed practice is superior to distributed practice. In work such as the writing of a paper, massed practice is often essential. For example, the exact locations of the little stacks of notes spread over the desk are held in mind with precision; the discrete bits of information are precariously suspended in mind to be fitted in like jigsaw-puzzle pieces at the appropriate time; and, the organizational pattern, though dimly perceived, is beginning to take shape. To stop at this point would be disastrous. The entire effort would collapse. So, in creative work, or work that needs to be overviewed at one sitting, it is far more efficient to overextend yourself—to complete that stage of the process—than to take a break or otherwise apply the principle of distributed practice.

Imagery: Mental Visualization

One half of the human brain thinks in words; the other half thinks in pictures. If you depend only on the words you read, you'll be using only half

[12]Irving Lorge, *Influence of Regularly Interpolated Time Intervals upon Subsequent Learning,* Contributions to Education, no. 438 (New York: Bureau of Publications, Teachers College, Columbia University, 1930).

[13]Bertram Epstein, *Immediate and Retention Effects of Interpolated Rest Periods on Learning Performance,* Contributions to Education, no. 949 (New York: Bureau of Publications, Teachers College, Columbia University, 1949).

of your brain; but if you convert the words into pictures, then, with both words and pictures in mind, you'll be using your whole brain. By drawing a picture, you'll actually be breaking the description in a textbook into its components, and you'll understand the material far more thoroughly than if you had only read the description.

Figure 5.2 is an example of how one student converted a few descriptive paragraphs about amoebas into a diagram. The student was interested not only in identifying the parts of the amoeba but also in spelling the words correctly. The student drew this diagram several times without the aid of notes and during the labeling step checked carefully to make sure that the spelling was correct.

Needless to say, when a question about amoebas appeared on a test, the student handled it easily, keeping in mind the picture of the amoeba.

Even when material doesn't lend itself to making a drawing, you can still devise a mental image. According to Dr. Joseph E. Shorr of the Institute for Psycho-Imagination Therapy in Beverly Hills, California, "The human memory would be worthless without the capacity to make mental pictures." If you need to remember that Abraham Lincoln was born in 1809, picture a log cabin with the date 1809 over the doorway. The image does not have to be a good one; it only has to be something that will jog your memory. (Chapter 10 is a detailed discussion of how to teach yourself to think visually.)

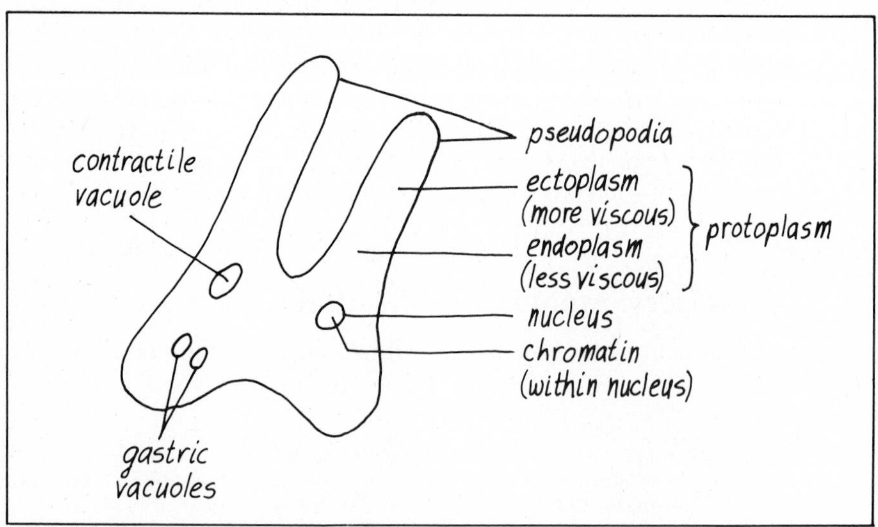

FIGURE 5.2 Structure of the Amoeba

Association

Suppose you have just been introduced to a heavyset man named Mr. Perkins. To remember his name, you immediately associate it with a heavy coffeepot *perking*. You even visualize the perking pot and smell the aroma of freshly brewed coffee.

What you have done is tie the *new* information (Mr. Perkins) to *old* information (perking coffeepot) that is already well established in your memory. When you meet Mr. Perkins at some future time, you will recall the perking coffee pot, which will prepare you to say, "Hello, Mr. Perkins. It is so nice to see you again."

Association is the basis of many memorization techniques. As William James said, "The more other facts a fact is associated with in the mind, the better possession of it our memory retains." How do you use the principle of association when you study? Simply by making a reasonable association when you come to a fact that you want to retain. Here's an example: "The boiling point of water varies with the air pressure and therefore with elevation. It is 212°F at sea level, and it decreases about 1°F for every 550 feet above sea level." If you ran across this information while studying a textbook, you might make a strong association by saying *aloud,* "This is what I'd reply if I were asked a question about air pressure or elevation and boiling points." Then you would repeat the information, again aloud, in your own words. If you later read such a question on an exam, chances are good that you'd recall the association and the information. There would be a linkage.

REMEMBERING WITH MNEMONICS

To combat forgetting, many students use *mnemonic devices*—easily remembered words, phrases, sentences, or rhymes that are associated with difficult-to-remember principles or facts. Almost all people use a mnemonic or two without realizing it. Probably the most widely used mnemonic device is the old jingle by which most of us learned the irregularities of our calendar:

Thirty days hath September,
April, June, and November.
All the rest have thirty-one,
Except February alone.

Rivaling this days-in-the-month mnemonic is one for spelling:

i before *e* except after *c*
or when sounding like *a*
as in neighbor and weigh.

Many people have private mnemonics, such as "surround the *r* with *a* for the word sep*ara*te."

The cardinal rule for dealing with masses of information is to *organize* the data in some way that makes sense. A mnemonic device is an organizational system, pure and simple. It is an ordinary means to an important end. Gerald R. Miller conducted a study to evaluate the effectiveness of mnemonic devices as aids to study.[14] He found that students who used mnemonic devices raised their test scores (by 77 percent in one case). Students who made up their own mnemonics attained higher test scores than when they used no mnemonics. Students who used mnemonics constructed by the instructor scored higher than when using mnemonics made up by themselves.

Miller recognizes that the use of too many mnemonics can overload the memory, thus reducing their effectiveness. Nevertheless, he argues that learning a large number of mnemonics well creates no greater hazard for the student than learning a large amount of material in the traditional way. If you use mnemonic devices, you must make certain to memorize the sentence, word, or jingle thoroughly, for the slightest error can throw you off completely.

Devising Mnemonics

It is best to acquire knowledge through understanding, rather than by parroting. Occasionally, however, you will be required to know facts that defy organization or that cannot be connected in a meaningful way. Then you will have to invent or adopt a mnemonic device to help you remember. When you do so, keep in mind that a mnemonic is an organizational device, and use your mnemonics only until you know the material so well that you no longer need them.

Associative Mnemonic. Sometimes you can associate a fact with something you know that has no real connection with the fact. For example, to remember that the Tropic of Capri*corn* is in the Southern Hemisphere, you can associate it with the *corns* on your feet—that is, with *your* south. As another example, use the *n*'s to remember that lines of lo*n*gitude run *n*orth and south; because the word *latitude* does not have an *n,* lines of latitude run west and east.

[14]Gerald R. Miller, *An Evaluation of the Effectiveness of Mnemonic Devices as Aids to Study,* Cooperative Research Project No. 5-8438, University of Texas at El Paso, 1967. Supported by Office of Education, U.S. Department of Health, Education, and Welfare.

Make-a-Word Mnemonic. The letters of a "made" word help you remember key words. Here's an example: The task is to make a mnemonic for these five ways to help prevent heart attack and stroke:

1. After age 40, get a medical checkup every year.
2. Do not smoke.
3. Keep your weight down.
4. Exercise moderately and wisely.
5. Get sufficient rest.

To devise a make-a-word mnemonic, proceed as follows:

1. Underline the key word in each item, as is done in the list above.
2. Write down the first letter of each key word. Here, we have A, S, W, E, and R.
3. Make a word or several words from the first letters of the key words. Change the order of the letters as necessary to do so. Here, we can make the word SWEAR, which will help us recall the five key words:

S moke
W eight
E xercise
A ge 40
R est

Your mnemonic may be a real word or a word that you just made up. When you use a made-up word, be sure you will be able to remember it.

Make-a-Sentence Mnemonic. This is a variation on the make-a-word mnemonic. It is devised as follows:

1. Underline the key word in each main point in your notes.
2. Write down the first letter of each key word.
3. Construct an easy-to-remember sentence using words whose first letters are the same as the first letters of the key words.

As an example, here are eight main points taken from a long article about what to do when you are in a building that is on fire. The key words are underlined.

1. In a burning building, feel the door with your hand. If it is hot, the room or hall on the other side is on fire.

2. If the door is cool, check the air coming under the door. If it is cool, there's probably no fire on the other side.
3. Still, don't take chances. Open the door just a crack while kneeling, with your face turned away. Listen and smell for fire and smoke.
4. When you leave, shut all doors and windows.
5. If your room is smoke-filled, crawl with your nose about one foot above the floor.
6. Never use an elevator; use a stairway.
7. If you are trapped, use wet cloths to protect your face, hands, and breathing passages.
8. Hang something out of a window to attract attention.

The first letters of the key words are D, A, C, S, C, S, W, and H. An easy-to-remember sentence using words beginning with the first letters of the key words is

Danger Always Causes Some Cats Some Where (to) Howl.

The letters need not appear in the same order as the key words. However, here the sequence of steps was considered to be important, so the order was presented.

In general, it is easier to make a sentence using the initial letters of the key words than to mold the initial letters into a word or two, especially if the order of the points is to be maintained. Of course, if the initial letters are mainly consonants, both can be difficult. To get around the problem of too many consonants, try to choose some key words that begin with a vowel.

Classic Mnemonic Devices

Here are some mnemonic devices that have been handed down and used by generations of students.

Astronomy. In astronomy, the favorite of students is the sentence that reminds them of the order of the planets (Mercury, Venus, Earth, Mars, Jupiter, Saturn, Uranus, Neptune, Pluto):

Men Very Easily Make Jugs Serve Useful and Numerous Purposes.

Biology. The first letters of the words in the following sentence stand for *kingdom, phylum, class, order, family, genus, species, variety:*

Kings Play Cards On Fairly Good Soft Velvet.

Geography. Remembering the names of the Great Lakes is easy with *homes* in mind, but remembering them in order is not so easy. Here's a mnemonic device that organizes them from west to east (Superior, Michigan, Huron, Erie, Ontario):

Super Machine Heaved Earth Out.

History. The royal houses of England (Norman, Plantagenet, Lancaster, York, Tudor, Stuart, Hanover, Windsor) are most difficult to remember without this mnemonic device:

No Plan Like Yours To Study History Wisely.

Mathematics. Students of mathematics use this rhyme to remember the value of pi, the ratio of the circumference of a circle to its diameter (3.1415926535895+). The key is the number of letters in each word:

3 1 4 1 5 9 2 6 5
How I wish I could determine of circle round

3 5 8 9 5
The exact relation Arkimedes found.

Medicine. Even doctors and pharmacists have jingles to keep certain chemicals straight. To distinguish between cyan*ates,* which are harmless, and cyan*ides,* which are extremely poisonous, they use this device:

-ate, I ate; -ide, I died.

Spelling. The greatest number of mnemonic devices are aids to spelling. Here's how to remember the correct way to spell two words that confuse many students:

A principal is a pal.
A principle is a rule.

COMMERCIAL MEMORY COURSES

Many students prefer to combat forgetting by taking memory courses given by commercial enterprises. The techniques used in such memory courses vary, but the majority require the memorization of a master list of words called *pegs.* Each word is numbered, and a strong association is made between the number and the word. For example, *one* is *bun, two* is *shoe, three* is *tree, four* is *door, five* is *hive,* and so forth. To remember a shopping list consisting of butter, sugar, sausage, bacon, and bread, you would form a bizarre image associating the first peg word with the first item on the list, the second peg word with the second item, and so on. For example, for butter you might visualize a pound of butter atop a *bun* left out in the sun with the butter melting all over it. For sugar, you could visualize a *shoe* filled with loose sugar.

In the supermarket, to recall the grocery items you would simply recall the well-memorized peg words in numerical sequence. Almost automatically, with each peg word would come to mind the item associated with it. However, if you went to the store the next day for milk and eggs, you would have to associate the milk with the bun, and yesterday's butter might interfere with today's milk.

In other words, because the same symbols are used for many different lists, the peg system is useful only for things that you want to remember for a short time. Obviously, this system is all right for grocery lists. However, it has two important limitations with regard to school work: First, it can be used with only one list of items for only one exam at any time. Second, no permanent knowledge is gained, for items so memorized are quickly forgotten. Peg words should be used only when you have to survive a battle (quiz or exam), so that you can stay on to win the war (pass the course).

MEMORY NEEDS TIME

No two people learn at exactly the same rate, yet the learning patterns for most people are quite similar. We all experience lulls in our learning. Progress is usually slow and steady at first, but then for a period of time there might be no perceptible progress even though genuine effort is being put forth. This "no progress" period is called a *plateau.* After days, weeks, or even a month of effort, suddenly a surprising spurt in learning occurs and continues until another plateau is reached.

A generally accepted explanation for the plateau is that the individual skills, the bits and pieces, must undergo consolidation. During the plateau period they are gradually combined into a more or less unified whole, and then the stage is set for another spurt in learning. Plateaus can occur at any time in the learning cycle, and they can have short or long durations.

When you reach a plateau, do not lose heart. You may not see any progress, but learning is going on nevertheless. Once everything is in place, you'll be rewarded for your effort.

SUMMARY

How quickly do I forget what I read?

After twenty-eight days, 81 percent of what you have read is gone. The bulk of that information is actually forgotten on the very first day.

How quickly do I forget what I hear?

In a study done on the members of the Cambridge Psychological Society, those who attended a seminar forgot over 90 percent of what they had heard in just two weeks. Remembering what you have heard is more difficult than remembering what you have read.

When forgetting is real, what causes it?

Several theories try to explain the causes of forgetting. Some theories attribute forgetting to fading and retrieval problems, others to problems of interference and motivation.

What is deep cognitive processing?

It's a term that psychologists and educators use to mean deep thinking. To ensure that information you want to remember stays firmly embedded in memory, you need to use deep cognitive processing. You need to *understand* the information thoroughly, *analyze* it from many angles, and *relate* it to information that you already know. Ten important principles of deep cognitive processing can help you hold on to information instead of surrendering it to forgetfulness.

What about the principle of selectivity?

If you try to remember everything, there's a good chance that you'll remember next to nothing. Hermann Ebbinghaus, a German psychologist, showed that if you needed one minute to memorize six items, you would need fifteen minutes to memorize twelve items. What that means in terms of study is that to facilitate remembering, you have to condense and summarize the information to be learned.

How does the poker-chip technique relate to the principle of selectivity?	In poker, the most valuable chips are blue, followed by the red chips and then the white chips. Accordingly, in players' stacks of chips, white chips predominate and blue chips are most scarce. When you study, if you can select the blue-chip (main) ideas from your notes, you will have selected the most important information. The red- and white-chip ideas that remain will be subideas and details, and you'll need to refer to them only when the blue-chip ideas require extra support.
How can I organize ideas in a meaningful way?	The category and cluster system involves grouping similar items around a natural heading or category. Once grouped together, these ideas will be easier to remember than they would be if left unorganized. The magical number seven theory reveals that you are capable of remembering as many as seven different categories and that the categories may be as large as you choose to make them. Finally, be aware that the items that occur first or last on a list are the easiest to remember.
What is the principle of recitation?	Recitation is saying aloud the ideas that you want to remember—not just reading them directly from your notes or textbook but rephrasing them in your own words. Recitation helps you feel confident that you truly know the material and haven't just memorized it.
Why does recitation work?	The act of reciting moves important information from your short-term memory to your long-term memory, where it is more likely to last.
Wouldn't rereading be just as good as or better than recitation?	No. Reciting is like taking a mini-quiz. You're motivated to learn because you have to supply the right answer. At the same time, reciting, unlike rereading, provides you with instant feedback. If you haven't

supplied the right answer, you know right away. Each time you recite, you strengthen the memory trace, and the fact that reciting involves not just thinking but speaking and hearing as well does still more to ensure that information is not easily dislodged by forgetting.

How much reciting should I do?

The more reciting you do, the greater is your chance of retaining the information you want to remember. Experiments have suggested that you should spend 20 percent of your time reading and 80 percent reciting.

What is the principle of consolidation?

According to the principle of consolidation, information has to be given time to sink in before it will be safely nestled in your long-term memory. If must be held in short-term memory for a period of anywhere from four seconds to fifteen minutes in order to stick. Recitation and review perform this task admirably.

What is the difference between distributed practice and massed practice?

Distributed practice is working in fits and starts, taking time out at regular intervals for rest. Massed practice, in contrast, is starting and continuing a task in a single, uninterrupted session.

Which method is better?

In most instances, the advantage goes to distributed practice. Fatigue and boredom are less likely to occur because of the rest periods. The breaks provide your memory with some consolidation time and increase your motivation as well. Massed practice is superior in just a few cases—primarily with research papers or creative assignments requiring that a certain mindset or train of thought be maintained.

What's behind the principle of imagery?

The principle of imagery suggests that you convert words into pictures whenever possible. When you do so, your information is in two forms rather than one, and thus you are more likely to remember it.

What is the principle of association?	Basically, association involves attaching new information to information that you already know.
What are mnemonics?	Mnemonics are easily remembered words, phrases, sentences, or rhymes that help you remember otherwise difficult-to-recall information. If you can easily rattle off the colors of the rainbow or the notes on a musical staff, you are probably using a mnemonic.
How effective are mnemonics?	Nothing beats learning the facts in earnest, but in situations where information appears to defy organization, mnemonics have been found to have a positive effect on test scores.
What are learning plateaus?	These are periods when you appear to be making no real progress even though you feel that you are making an effort. Experts say that these lulls in learning are not uncommon and that they are usually an indicator that what you have learned thus far is being consolidated. Therefore, try not to be discouraged when your returns don't seem to equal your investments. Once your memory has had time to consolidate, your dividends should be more than ample.

HAVE YOU MISSED SOMETHING?

1. *Sentence completion.* Complete the following sentences with one of the three words listed below each sentence.

a. The experiments of Ebbinghaus showed that remembering 12 syllables took fifteen times longer than remembering ________.

3 6 11

b. According to interactive interference theory, the fact that is most likely to be lost is the ________.

oldest newest middle

c. Reactive interference theory generally applies to information that is ______________________________.

complicated old-fashioned disliked

2. *Matching.* In each blank space in the left column, write the number preceding the phrase in the right column that matches the left item best.

_____ a. 7

_____ b. Interference theory

_____ c. 1

_____ d. Poker chip

_____ e. Retrieval theory

_____ f. 14

_____ g. Pseudo-forgetting

_____ h. Mnemonic

1. Theory that says that old facts cause us to forget new facts
2. Memory aid used for recalling difficult principles and facts
3. "Losing" a memory that you never had
4. Technique designed to aid selectivity
5. Number of days after which you will have forgotten 46 percent of a textbook chapter
6. Number of categories of information that the average adult can remember
7. Number of days after which you will have forgotten over 90 percent of a lecture
8. Theory that stresses the importance of organizing information

3. *True-false.* Write *T* beside the *true* statements and *F* beside the *false* statements.

_____ a. Recitation can be done either silently or out loud.

_____ b. Little worthwhile learning takes place without an intention to remember.

_____ c. The greatest amount of forgetting occurs on the very first day.

_____ d. Deep cognitive processing eliminates the need for forming a long-lasting memory trace.

_____ e. Remembering what you've read is more difficult than remembering what you've heard.

4. *Distributed practice.* Write "yes" next to the clear advantages of distributed practice.

_____ a. Prevents fatigue

_____ b. Increases motivation

_____ c. Replaces recitation

_____ d. Wards off boredom

_____ e. Aids consolidation

_____ f. Promotes creativity

5. *Multiple choice.* Choose the phrase that completes the following sentence most accurately, and circle the letter that precedes it.

In order to apply deep cognitive processing successfully, you must

a. analyze your information from all angles
b. understand the fact or idea in your own words
c. relate what you've learned to what you already know
d. all the above

PART

III

Your Notes

CHAPTER 6

Listening to Take Good Notes

Learn how to listen and you will prosper even from those who talk badly.

Plutarch (A.D. 46–120), Greek biographer and philosopher

A recent survey revealed how much time college students spend in four types of communication:

Listening	53%
Reading	17%
Speaking	16%
Writing	14%

Now hear this! You can't learn if you don't listen. With dozens of noises and thoughts vying for your attention, acquiring good listening skills takes hard work and practice; but the effort is worth making, and the rewards are long lasting. This chapter discusses

- Listening versus hearing
- Keys to effective listening
- Comprehensive listening

and finally

- The listening attitude

istening is the first step in note taking. In order to take good notes, you have to be a good listener—and that means an active listener. Merely hearing all the words is not enough; you must really listen to them.

LISTENING VERSUS HEARING

Hearing and listening are not synonymous. *Hearing* is the act of perceiving sound by the ear. If you are not hearing-impaired, then hearing for you is a spontaneous act that occurs independently of your will. *Listening,* by contrast, is something you consciously choose to do; listening is paying attention so that your brain absorbs the meaning of words and sentences. This process leads to the understanding of facts and ideas.

Listening, unlike hearing, does not occur automatically. The absorption of meaning leading to understanding requires two activities:

1. *Paying attention:* You stick to one task in spite of distractions.
2. *Concentration:* You focus your thoughts upon one problem.

Concentration does not mean thinking only one thought. Concentration means holding a central issue in mind while you accept or reject ideas that are related to that issue. In the words of F. Scott Fitzgerald (1896–1940), author of the novel *The Great Gatsby,* "The test of a first-rate intelligence is the ability to hold two opposed ideas in mind at the same time." If you pay attention and concentrate, you will become an active listener able to synthesize new information with facts and ideas already known.

A good way to begin concentrating is to anticipate the lecture. Before class, look over your notes from the last lecture, and take a minute to speculate about what your instructor is going to talk about today. If the lectures follow your textbook, peek ahead to see what's coming. Once the lecture starts, let your mind dart ahead (during pauses) to anticipate what's coming next. You'll be alert, engrossed in the material, and concentrating 100 percent. Another way to start the process of concentration is to look at the course syllabus.

You cannot attain concentration by concentrating on concentration. Your attention must focus on the lecture. Deep cognition, or deep thinking, is vital. When you hear a lecture, the words enter your short-term memory where they have to be swiftly processed into ideas. Active listening sets that process in motion. If your instructor's words are not processed through active listening that results from attention and concentration, they will be dumped from short-term memory and will be gone forever. If you process the words into ideas, in a flash the ideas will be stored in your long-term memory.

Research has shown that an average student remembers about 50 percent of a ten-minute lecture when tested immediately and 25 percent of the same lecture when tested forty-eight hours later. These poor results occur when students are unable to package the lecturer's ideas into easily remembered units.

Where do you stand as a listener? Figure 6.1 presents a short quiz that will let you know. If your score is less than 90, you need to improve your listening skills by breaking poor habits and adopting the habits of good listeners. Figure 6.2 lists ten skills that will make you a better listener. Each skill is discussed in detail in the next section of this chapter.

KEYS TO EFFECTIVE LISTENING

Don't compartmentalize. Use good listening skills both inside and outside the classroom.

Finding Areas of Interest

In the classroom, you're a captive audience for the duration of the lecture. This time will be totally wasted if you decide not to listen. Some students try to use a lecture period to read their textbooks, but doing so is a waste of time because the negative attitude permeating their thinking will interfere with concentration. Concentration will also be interfered with by the ongoing lecture.

It is best to listen intently, take notes vigorously, and show interest by your facial expression. These outward manifestations of interest will create genuine internal interest.

Outside the Classroom. In personal listening, you have a chance to redirect an uninteresting topic. Listen intently, sincerely, and politely, but at appropriate moments ask questions about aspects of the topic that interest you most.

Judging Content Not Delivery

Listeners are sometimes terribly rude or downright cruel when a lecturer's delivery fails to measure up to some preconceived standard. Try to approach each lecture with a humane attitude. Block out negative thoughts, and determine to concentrate totally on what's being said. Listen seriously and take notes (note taking is the subject of Chapter 7). If you do, you'll

How often do you find yourself engaging in these ten bad habits of listening? Check the appropriate columns.

	Frequency					
How often do you . . .	**Almost always**	**Usually**	**Sometimes**	**Seldom**	**Almost never**	**Score**
Decide that the topic is boring?						
Criticize the speaker?						
Overreact by disagreeing?						
Listen only for bare facts?						
Outline everything?						
Fake attention?						
Yield to distractions?						
Avoid listening to tough technical information?						
Let emotion-laden words arouse personal antagonism?						
Waste thought speed by daydreaming?						
Total score						

Tally your score as follows:

Almost always	2
Usually	4
Sometimes	6
Seldom	8
Almost never	10

Interpret your score as follows:

Below 70	Need training in listening
70 to 90	You listen well
Above 90	Extraordinarily good listener

FIGURE 6.1 Listening Habits

Adapted from Ralph G. Nichols and Thomas R. Lewis, Listening and Speaking, *p. 166. Originally published by Wm. C. Brown Group, 1954. Reprinted by permission of the authors.*

Keys to Effective Listening	The Poor Listener	The Good Listener
1. Find areas of interest	Tunes out dry topics.	Seizes opportunities: "What's in it for me?"
2. Judge content not delivery	Tunes out if delivery is poor.	Judges content, skips over delivery errors.
3. Hold your fire	Tends to enter into argument.	Doesn't judge until comprehension is complete.
4. Listen for ideas	Listens for facts.	Listens for central themes.
5. Be a flexible note taker	Is busy with form, misses content.	Adjusts to topic and organizational pattern.
6. Work at listening	Shows no energy output, fakes attention.	Works hard; exhibits alertness.
7. Resist distractions	Is distracted easily.	Fights or avoids distractions; tolerates bad habits in others; knows how to concentrate.
8. Exercise your mind	Resists difficult expository material; seeks light, recreational material.	Uses heavier material as exercise for the mind.
9. Keep your mind open	Reacts to emotional words.	Interprets emotional words; does not get hung up on them.
10. Thought is faster than speech; use it	Tends to daydream with slow speakers.	Challenges, anticipates, mentally summarizes, weighs the evidence, listens between the lines to tone and voice.

FIGURE 6.2 Ten Keys to Effective Listening
Source: Reprinted by permission of Unisys Corporation.

emerge from the lecture with a positive self-image. You will also learn something.

Outside the Classroom. In personal listening, your kind smile and relaxed attitude can help put the speaker at ease. Don't make the speaker uncomfortable by being aloof or impatient.

Holding Your Fire

In college you're bound to hear ideas that are different from or even contrary to those you hold. When this happens, your knee-jerk reaction may be to speak up immediately to defend your position. If you decide to attack, you will be too preoccupied to listen attentively to the rest of the lecture. You will be assessing the damage that is being done to your pet ideas, devising an embarrassing question to ask the lecturer, and fantasizing about the results once the lecturer has been "shown up." With such thoughts churning around in your mind, it's no wonder that the rest of the lecture gets tuned out.

You must learn not to get overly excited about a lecturer's point until you are certain you thoroughly understand it. Hold your fire! Do not automatically assume that you are right and someone else is wrong. What a self-centered view that is! Instead, listen intently to understand thoroughly the viewpoint expressed by the lecturer. Only after you have done so should you venture, not to attack, but to ask intelligent questions for clarification and explanation.

Outside the Classroom. When you are listening to your peers, interruption usually comes easily and quickly, and what could have been a profitable discussion often disintegrates into a shouting match. Remember: You learn much, much more by listening than by talking. When you talk, you're repeating what you already know. When you listen, you're open to ideas and facts that are probably new to you.

Listening for Ideas

As a college student, don't imitate the detective who says, "The facts, ma'am, just stick to the facts." When you take notes, you do need to take down the facts, but in doing so, try to see what the facts are leading to. Try to see what principle or what idea they are supporting. Try to see how the pieces of the puzzle fit into the building of the big picture. This approach will keep you concentrating at a 100 percent level.

Outside the Classroom. When your peers pour out facts, try to go one step further by thinking, "What is his motivation to tell me this?" Or, "What is she leading up to?" Your aim is not to psych out anyone; instead, it is to keep your mind fully occupied and agile.

Being a Flexible Note Taker

Flexibility in note taking depends on informed listening. Informed listening means that the listener is able to identify the organizational patterns used by the speaker. When you have detected a pattern, then you can anticipate the form of the message and adjust the way you record your notes. Here are some of the organizational patterns that you will encounter.

1. *Chronological pattern.* When events are described, notice whether the speaker describes them year by year, week by week, or even hour by hour.

2. *Process pattern.* You'll often encounter this pattern in the sciences, where the steps in a process are described in the order in which they must occur to put something together or to blend ingredients.

3. *Enumeration pattern.* When you hear the lecturer say, "Here are the ten most common poor listening habits," prepare to make a list of ten items.

4. *Problem-cause-solution pattern.* This is a convenient and effective way for a speaker to package a lecture. First the problem is identified; next the cause or causes are enumerated; then the solution is given. Once you hear the problem, you can generally start to anticipate the cause and the solution.

5. *Inductive pattern.* The speaker identifies a number of incidents and draws a conclusion from them. The speaker's main point will be something like this: "So, on the basis of all these facts, we come to this overriding principle, which is so-and-so."

6. *Deductive pattern.* This pattern is the reverse of the inductive pattern. Here, the principle or general statement is given first and then the events or proofs are enumerated.

Outside the Classroom. When you are listening to any talk or conversation, try to detect the organizational pattern that the speaker is using. If there is none, speculate on how the ideas or facts being poured forth could be better organized if one of the six patterns just described were used.

Working at Listening

A good listener is alert, outwardly calm but inwardly dynamic, and sits toward the front of the classroom. While taking notes, the listener may nod in agreement or look quizzical when the presentation becomes unclear. Such activity promotes comprehension and learning by the listener and provides encouragement to the speaker.

Outside the Classroom. Active listening results in better understanding for the listener and is appreciated by the speaker.

Resisting Distractions

There are distractions aplenty in the classroom: antics of other students, whisperings, the speaker's dress and mannerisms, outside noise, and outside views. The best way to resist distractions and maintain your concentration is to rivet your eyes on the speaker when you have a chance and focus on taking notes the rest of the time.

Outside the Classroom. Refrain from being so impolite as to watch some other person or activity while pretending to listen to the person speaking to you. Keep your eyes on the speaker just as you would want a listener to look at you while you are speaking.

Exercising Your Mind

More than just occasionally, sit in on lectures in fields that you know very little about. Try hard to follow the lecturer's chain of thoughts and ideas. Portions of the lecture will be like Greek to you, but you're bound to understand parts. Such listening is hard work; but like hard work in the gym to strengthen your muscles, the hard work of listening will strengthen your will to concentrate and your power to persist.

Outside the Classroom. When a discussion is going on among your friends who are majoring in subjects that are foreign to you, listen and ask questions. You'll be surprised how willing they'll be to answer you.

Keeping Your Mind Open

There are many touchy subjects of great importance in the news. You may have taken a strong position on some and a lukewarm position on others. When a lecturer uses inflammatory words to express a position contrary to yours, you are likely to harbor negative feelings toward the lecturer.

It is hard to believe that a word or phrase can cause an emotional eruption. Among poor listeners, that is frequently the case, however; and even among very good listeners fireworks occasionally go off. Words that are red flags for some listeners include *activist, liberal, conservative, evolution, creationism, communist, feminist, abortion,* and *pro-life.*

Dealing with highly charged language is similar to dealing with a fear or phobia. Often the emotional impact of the words can be decreased through a frank and open discussion. Genuinely listen to the other point of view. You might learn something that you didn't know before.

Outside the Classroom. Be kind and fair to your friends. Don't spring to the attack. Hold your tongue and listen.

Thought Is Faster Than Speech

When a lecturer speaks slowly, a listener has moments of free time to dart off on mental sidetrips and return to grasp the lecturer's next idea. To keep your mind from wandering, concentrate mightily on what the lecturer is saying. When you have time to think between ideas, first mentally enumerate the ideas that have been expressed and then, at the next opportunity, summarize them. Keep alternating in this fashion throughout the lecture.

Outside the Classroom. In a conversation with your peers, do the same throughout the talk: Listen, then enumerate; listen, then summarize.

COMPREHENSIVE LISTENING

The following quotation illustrates the inherent difficulty of oral communication:

> I know you believe that you understand
> What you think I said, but I am not sure
> That you realize that what you heard is not what I meant.

In order for communication to occur, both the speaker and the listener must act responsibly. The speaker's responsibility is to make points clearly. The listener's responsibility is to understand what the speaker says. Comprehensive listening occurs when the listener encourages the speaker to fully articulate his message, thus enabling the speaker to be more clear. If a speaker's message is not clear and the listener asks a clarifying question, both the speaker and the listener benefit. The speaker is encouraged and gratified to know that the audience is interested. The listener can concentrate on what the speaker has to say and can feel good about raising a question that was probably troubling less intrepid members of the audience.

A professor at the University of Virginia conducted a survey and found that 94 percent of her students had failed to understand something in at least one class lecture during the semester. Seventy percent of the students had not asked clarifying questions even though they knew they could. When asked why they had remained silent, they answered, "I was afraid I'd look stupid," "I didn't want to make myself conspicuous," "I was too proud to ask," "I was too confused to know what question to ask."

The way to dispel the fear of asking is to remember that the only dumb question is the one that was never asked. The way to dispel confusion is to acknowledge it by saying, "I'm confused about the last point you made," or "I'm confused about how the example pertains to your main point." In this situation, as in most, honesty is the best policy.

Sometimes the lecturer, to create a dialogue or to see whether the class is understanding the material, will ask you a question. When this happens, a good and fair response is to begin by paraphrasing or even repeating the question. Doing this keeps you on the right track, gives you a chance to warm up your thinking on the subject, and buys you some time to compose a reasonably good opening statement and to gather your thoughts.

THE LISTENING ATTITUDE

Although you can take many steps to improve your listening, the prerequisite to effective listening is a positive mental attitude. You must walk into the classroom convinced that the lecturer has something useful to say. If you have any doubts, take a moment to think about the kind of preparation that goes into a typical lecture. The lecturer had to do the searching, reading, selecting, discarding, and organizing of information from dozens of books—a task that can take hundreds of hours. You can reap the benefits of all that effort in a single lecture.

In listening, your most productive attitude is the sympathetic one. Show that you are *with* the speaker by having a pleasant expression on your face, by keeping your eyes on the speaker when you're not writing notes, and by nodding your head whenever you agree with what has been said. These actions do not automatically imply total acceptance of all the lecturer's points, but they do serve as expressions of interest.

By showing interest, you are treating the speaker as you would want to be treated. You draw an enthusiastic flow of words and ideas from the lecturer. Most important, you concentrate as you've never concentrated before.

With this head start on concentration, as well as a genuine desire to learn, you have begun the process of serious listening. To keep it going, show up in the classroom with sharp pencils and a good-sized notebook. Start taking notes the moment the speaker begins. To take intelligent notes, you will have to listen intently and jot down information quickly and efficiently. The next chapter gives you the lowdown on taking notes.

SUMMARY

Aren't listening and hearing basically the same?	No. Hearing is a spontaneous act. Listening, by contrast, is something you choose to do. Listening requires you not only to hear what has been said but to absorb the meaning as well.
How do I go about absorbing meaning?	Absorption of meaning requires three activities: (1) dynamic listening, (2) paying attention, and (3) concentration.
What's the best way to concentrate?	Start with anticipation. Look at your notes from the last lecture or peek ahead in your textbook. Either way, you'll be cultivating the mindset that is needed for 100 percent concentration during a lecture.
What is deep cognition?	Deep cognition, or deep thinking, is the process that moves information from the uncertainty of your short-term memory to the safety of your long-term memory.
What are the ten keys to effective listening?	The ten keys are (1) Finding areas of interest; (2) Judging content rather than delivery; (3) Holding your fire when you disagree with what's being said; (4) Listening for ideas, not just facts; (5) Being a flexible note taker; (6) Working at listening instead of faking attention; (7) Resisting outside distractions; (8) Exercising your mind with challenging material; (9) Keeping your mind open, even when you hear emotional words; (10) Putting new ideas to work during a lecture instead of just daydreaming.
What is comprehensive listening?	Comprehensive listening has to do with the feedback between speaker and listener. The speaker has an obligation to make her words understandable to the listener. The listener, in turn, must let the speaker know when he doesn't understand.
What's the best way to let the speaker know that I don't understand?	Ask questions. A surprising number of students are too embarrassed to ask questions. The only dumb questions, however, are the ones that go unasked.

What should I do if the lecturer asks *me* a question?	Simply start by paraphrasing or repeating the question. That will keep you on track, give you some time to warm up your thinking, and enable you to compose a well-focused opening statement.
What is most likely to help me become a good listener?	A positive mental attitude. If you have a positive attitude toward the lectures you attend, your chances of extracting the important information you need are excellent. Furthermore, enthusiasm is contagious. When the speaker sees that you are listening intently, the speaker's energy level is bound to rise and so will the overall interest level of the lecture.

HAVE YOU MISSED SOMETHING?

1. *Sentence completion.* Complete the following sentences with one of the three words listed below each sentence.

a. Through listening, the meanings of words and sentences are ______.

reflected increased absorbed

b. A good listener places great emphasis on the speaker's __________.

delivery appearance facts

c. In listening, the most productive attitude is ____________________.

combative sympathetic emotional

2. *Matching.* In each blank space in the left column, write the number preceding the phrase in the right column that matches the left item best.

_____ a. Attention	1. Percentage of students who are hesitant to ask a clarifying question
_____ b. Evolution	2. Sometimes faked by a poor listener
_____ c. Facts	3. Common pattern in science lectures
_____ d. 53 percent	4. Percentage of communication time devoted to listening
_____ e. Process	
_____ f. Questions	

_____ g. 70 percent

_____ h. 25 percent

5. May be a red flag for some listeners
6. Percentage of a lecture that is remembered after forty-eight hours
7. Can benefit both the speaker and the listener
8. Often the sole concern of a poor listener

3. *True-false.* Write *T* beside the *true* statements and *F* beside the *false* statements.

_____ a. Roughly 50 percent of a ten-minute speech is forgotten immediately.

_____ b. The good listener tunes out dry topics.

_____ c. Concentration means thinking only one thought at a time.

_____ d. The only dumb question is the one that is never asked.

_____ e. Words are processed into ideas through deep cognition.

4. *Good listener.* Write "yes" next to the characteristics of a good listener.

_____ a. Argues with the speaker, either silently or out loud

_____ b. Remains flexible to the speaker's organizational pattern

_____ c. Pays attention to form rather than content

_____ d. Sees difficult material as a challenge rather than as a threat

_____ e. Uses the speaker's pauses to ponder what has been said

_____ f. Tries to tune out any distractions

5. *Multiple choice.* Choose the phrase that completes the following sentence most accurately, and circle the letter that precedes it.

Listening is

a. strictly mechanical
b. the same as hearing
c. not automatic
d. all the above

CHAPTER 7

Note Taking

"The horror of that moment," the King went on, "I shall never, never forget!" "You will, though," the Queen said, "if you don't make a memorandum of it."

Lewis Carroll, pen name of Charles Lutwidge Dodgson (1832–98), author of *Alice's Adventures in Wonderland*

The bright-eyed cub reporter in the old movies really knew what he was doing. He scribbled down facts and ideas in a pocket pad. Although note-taking techniques have changed since then, the reason for taking notes is the same as it's always been: Note taking helps information stick in your memory. Whether you're capturing the words of a world leader or a classroom lecturer, you need to take notes quickly and efficiently. This chapter gives you the scoop on proper note taking. It reports on

- The importance of notes
- Tips and tactics
- The Cornell Note-taking System
- Types of notes
- Combining textbook and lecture notes

and finally

- Abbreviations and symbols

any students attribute their academic and professional success to what they learned from classroom lectures. This is not surprising because professors and instructors are at their best when they are teaching and inspiring through lecturing. If you expect to learn from lectures, you must take notes. You must, like the cub reporter of old, get the information down in black and white.

THE IMPORTANCE OF NOTES

Forgetting can be *instantaneous* and *complete.* Note taking is a vital skill in college because forgetting occurs so quickly and so thoroughly. Many experiments suggest that unless you mentally rehearse the information you receive, you are unlikely to retain it in your short-term memory for more than about twenty seconds.[1] Hermann Ebbinghaus, the German psychologist who investigated remembering and forgetting, found that almost half of what is learned is forgotten within an hour.[2] Recently, psychologists carrying out experiments similar to Ebbinghaus' confirmed his findings.

The following true story further confirms the rapidity and massiveness of forgetting. Three professors eating lunch in the faculty lounge had this conversation:

> CLYDE: Did you hear last night's lecture?
> WALTER: No, I was busy.
> CLYDE: Well, you missed one of the best lectures in recent years.
> LEON: I agree. The four points that he developed were gems.
> CLYDE: I never heard anyone make his points so clear.
> WALTER: I don't want you to repeat the lecture, but what were those four points?
> LEON: (Long silence) Clyde? (Passage of two or three minutes; seems like an hour.)
> LEON: Well, I'd better get back to the office.
> CLYDE: Me too!
> WALTER: Me too!

Neither Leon nor Clyde was able to recall even a fragment of any point made in the previous night's lecture. Each of them forgot the four points because neither of them had transferred the points from short-term memory to long-term memory by silently reciting them. Instead, they both had recited

---

[1]Douglas A. Bernstein, Edward J. Roy, Thomas K. Srull, and Christopher D. Wickens, *Psychology* (Boston: Houghton Mifflin, 1988), p. 293.

[2]Hermann Ebbinghaus, *Memory.* Translated by Henry A. Ruger and Clara E. Bussenius (New York: Dover Publications, 1964 [1913]), p. 76.

that the speaker was clear, forceful, and wise, and that he had made four points—and they remembered only what they had recited.

The only sure way to overcome forgetting is by taking notes, then taking your notes back to your room to study and recite.

TIPS AND TACTICS

If you turn these tips and tactics into habits, your notes will be the envy of your classmates. Use these tips and tactics until they are second nature to you.

Telegraphic Sentences

Sixty years ago, when telephones were not so numerous as they are today, important messages, both personal and business, were sent by telegraph. The sender paid by the word; so the fewer the words, the lower was the cost. A four-word message such as "Will arrive three pm" was a lot less expensive than an eleven-word message: "I will arrive home promptly at 3 o'clock in the afternoon."

When you take notes, use telegraphic sentences. Leave out unnecessary words. Use the key words only. Ignore rules of grammar. Write down a streamlined version of the lecturer's key points. Two examples of the telegraphic style are given in Figure 7.1.

Modified Printing Style

Terrible handwriting need not prevent you from taking legible notes. You can give up your old way of writing and adopt the modified printing style. Your writing will be surprisingly rapid and amazingly clear. Anyone can adopt this style and use it to write neatly and clearly.

Here is how the individual letters look in the modified printing style:

a b c d e f g h i j k l m n o p q r s t u v w x y z

If you have your own way of forming some of the letters, use it. What flows naturally from your pen or pencil will be swifter and easier than a forced change. Figure 7.2 shows the style used in a paragraph.

Lecturer's words in a marketing course

In selling, you can overcome a customer's objections to almost any product if you can come up with a good idea. Here are two examples: first, a lady who objected to a square flyswatter bought it when the sales manager said, "These are square, madam. They get them in the corners." Second, a lady who wanted round clothespins, bought the square ones when the clerk said, "They don't roll out of reach under a sink." So, don't sell the steak - sell the sizzle.

Student's telegraphic sentences

1. People buy ideas, not products.
   a. Ex. square flyswatter = "get in corners."
   b. Ex. square clothespins = "won't roll - sink."
   c. Don't sell steak -- sell sizzle.

Lecturer's words

The US Patent Office has granted numerous patents for perpetual motion machines based upon applications with complete detailed drawings. Some years ago, though, the patent office began requiring working models of such a machine before a patent would be granted. Result: no patents granted for perpetual motion machines since that time.

Student's telegraphic sentence

Perpetual motion machine (drawings) = many patents.
Required working model = no patents since.

FIGURE 7.1 Examples of Telegraphic Sentences

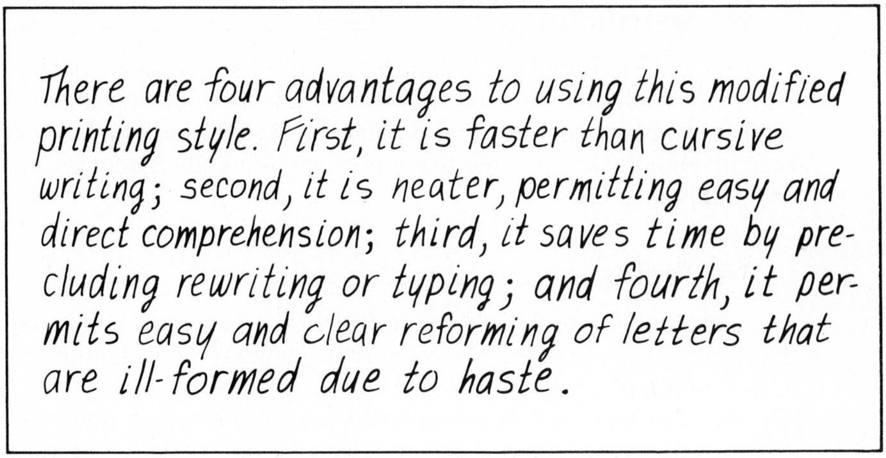

There are four advantages to using this modified printing style. First, it is faster than cursive writing; second, it is neater, permitting easy and direct comprehension; third, it saves time by precluding rewriting or typing; and fourth, it permits easy and clear reforming of letters that are ill-formed due to haste.

FIGURE 7.2 Modified Printing Style

The Two-Page System

When you need to scramble to keep up with a fast-talking lecturer, you may find this two-page system helpful. Here's the way it works: Lay your binder flat on the desk. On the left-hand page, record main ideas only. The left-hand page is your primary page. On the right-hand page, record as many details as you have time for. Place the details opposite the main ideas that they support. After the lecture, remain in your seat for a few minutes and fill in any gaps in your notes while the lecture is still relatively fresh in mind.

The Cassette and Tape Taboo

Do not use a tape or cassette recorder. If you do, you'll be wasting time and not learning very much. When a lecture is on tape, you cannot review it in five or ten minutes; you have to replay the entire lecture. Worst of all, you cannot use the technique of reciting, which is the most effective learning technique known to psychologists. Furthermore, you also lose the advantage of visual learning—that is, seeing the words and seeing the relationship between the written ideas.

Some students create written notes as they listen to the tape in the privacy of their rooms. Don't you see the waste of time? The notes could have been taken directly during the "live" lecture.

No Shorthand

Don't take lecture notes in shorthand. Shorthand notes cannot be studied effectively while they are still in symbol form. Besides, shorthand symbols still have to be transformed into regular words. If you need a fast method to keep up with the lecturer, use the abbreviations and the symbols listed at the end of this chapter.

No Typing

Scribbling is a bad habit. Write legibly the first time. Don't rationalize that you'll type your notes when you return to your room. Typing your notes is a waste of time, opportunity, and energy. You'll need almost a full hour to decipher and type one set of scribbled lecture notes. The hour you spend typing could have been extremely productive if you had spent it reciting notes taken during the lecture. Typing can exhaust you physically, mentally, and emotionally, leaving you unfit for the task of learning.

Contrary to what most people think, almost no learning takes place during the typing of scribbled notes. The act of deciphering and typing requires almost total concentration, leaving scant concentration for comprehending the facts and ideas being typed.

Signal Words and Phrases

Most college lecturers speak about 120 words per minute. In a fifty-minute lecture, you hear up to six thousand words expressing ideas, facts, and details. To impose some recognizable order on those ideas, facts, and details, lecturers use signal words and phrases.

Signal words and phrases themselves do not express ideas, facts, and details. They do, however, convey important information of a directional and relational sort. If you, as a note taker, know the importance and meaning of signal words and phrases, you'll be able to perceive the organization of the lecture, the direction of the lecture, and the relationship among the ideas, facts, and details. A list of signal words and phrases is given in Figure 7.3. Being able to recognize signal words and phrases will improve your reading, writing, speaking, and listening, as well as your note taking.

The Final Barrage

Pay close attention to the end of the lecture. Speakers who do not pace themselves well may have to cram half of the lecture into the last five or ten minutes. Record such packed finales as rapidly as you can. After class, stay in

Categories and Examples	When you hear these words, immediately think . . .
Example Words to illustrate for example for instance	"Here comes an example. The lecturer wants to make clear the point just made. I'd better write this down; otherwise I'll forget it."
Time Words before, after formerly subsequently prior meanwhile	"Hm-m! A time relationship is being established. Let's see, what came first and what came last, and what came in-between?"
Addition Words furthermore in addition moreover also	"After listing everything, they always seem to have one more thing to add. Well, I'd better get it and write it down."
Cause and Effect Words therefore as a result if . . . then accordingly thus, so	"There's that cause and effect word. I'd better quickly write down the word *effect* in my notes at this point. Later, I'll go back and write the word *cause* to label the preceding points."
Contrast Words on the other hand in contrast conversely pros and cons	"Now we're getting the other side of the picture, the other person's story, the research that contradicts what has already been said."
Enumeration Words the four steps . . . first, second, third next finally	"Ten steps is a lot! I'd better number them and list them in order."
Emphasis Words more importantly above all remember this	"Sounds like a hint that this idea is something important and something to remember."
Repeat Words in other words in the vernacular it simply means that is, briefly in essence	"Simplifying a complex idea or simplifying a long-winded explanation. I'd better note this simplified version."

FIGURE 7.3 Signal Words and Phrases

Categories and Examples	When you hear these words, immediately think . . .
Swivel Words	
however nevertheless yet, but still	"A warning that there's a little bit of doubt or 'give-back' on the point just made. I'd better note this qualifying remark."
Concession Words	
to be sure of course granted indeed though	"I see. These are similar to the swivel words. The lecturer is admitting that the opposition has a point or two."
Summary Words	
in a nutshell to sum up in conclusion	"Great! I'll try to get this summary word for word; then I can study it thoroughly when I get to my room."
Test Clues	
This is important. Remember this. You'll see this again. Here's a pitfall.	"Sounds like a potential test item. I'd better get this one word for word."

FIGURE 7.3 Signal Words and Phrases *(continued)*

your seat for a few extra minutes to write down as much as you can remember.

Instant Replay

As soon as you leave the lecture room, while walking to your next class, mentally recall the lecture from beginning to end. Visualize the classroom and the lecturer and any blackboard work. After mentally recalling the lecture, ask yourself some questions: What was the lecturer getting at? What really was the central point? What did I learn? How does what I learned fit in with what I already know? If you discover anything you don't quite understand, no matter how small, make a note of it and ask the instructor before the next class to explain it.

Avoiding Ice-Cold Notes

During your first free period after class, or that evening at the latest, read over your notes to fill in gaps and to give yourself an overview of the lecture.

Review your notes while the lecture is still fresh in your mind. Ice-cold notes are frustrating and are time wasters. Days after a lecture, you do not want to be gazing at your own writing and wondering, "What did I mean by that?"

Two Dozen Dos and One Dozen Don'ts

The twenty-four dos and twelve don'ts that follow are the warp and woof of note taking. Weave them into a magic carpet of your own design and glide over all the rough spots of note taking.

Dos

1. Look over previous notes before class. (Maintains continuity.)
2. Attend *all* lectures. (It's a continuing story.)
3. Be academically aggressive. (Sit up straight with "rolled-up sleeves.")
4. Take a front seat to see and hear better. (You won't dare snooze.)
5. Use a large, loose-leaf binder. (Gives ample room.)
6. Carry lined loose-leaf ($8\frac{1}{2} \times 11$) sheets to class. (Insert into binder on return.)
7. Write on only one side of sheet. (Spread out for review.)
8. On top sheet, record course, lecturer, and date. (In case of spill.)
9. Begin taking notes immediately. (Don't wait for inspiration.)
10. Write in short, telegraphic sentences. (Parsimoniously meaningful.)
11. Make notes complete for later understanding. (Don't sit there puzzling.)
12. Use modified printing style. (Clear letters, not scribbles.)
13. Use lecturer's words. (Lecturers like to see their words in exams.)
14. Strive to detect main headings. (As if you peeked at the lecturer's notes.)
15. Capture ideas as well as facts. (Get the drift too.)
16. Keep your note-organization simple. (Easy does it.)
17. Skip lines; leave space between main ideas. (Package the ideas.)
18. Discover the organizational pattern. (Like putting together a puzzle.)
19. If the lecture is too fast, capture fragments. (Jigsaw them together later.)
20. Leave blank spaces for words to fill in later. (Thus avoid voids.)
21. Develop your own abbreviations and symbols. (Not too many, but enough.)
22. Record lecturer's examples. (If you don't, you'll forget.)

23. Identify your own thought-notes. (What's mine? What's the lecturer's?)
24. Keep separate loose-leaf binders for each course. (Don't combine notes yet.)

Don'ts

1. Don't sit near friends. (Can be distracting.)
2. Don't wait for something "important." (Record everything.)
3. Don't convert lecturer's words. (Takes time and invites imprecision.)
4. Don't look for facts only. (See ideas too.)
5. Don't give up if the lecturer is too fast. (Some is better than none.)
6. Don't stop to ponder. (Do so later in your room.)
7. Don't over-indent. (You'll run out of right-side space.)
8. Don't doodle. (Breaks concentration and eye contact.)
9. Don't use spiral-bound notebooks. (Can't insert handouts.)
10. Don't consider any example too obvious. (Copy it!)
11. Avoid using Roman numerals. (You'll get tangled up.)
12. Avoid too many abbreviations. (Trouble deciphering later.)

THE CORNELL NOTE-TAKING SYSTEM

The notes you take in class are really a hand-written textbook. In many instances, your lecture notes are more practical, meaningful, and up-to-date than a textbook. If you keep them neat, complete, and well organized, they'll serve you splendidly.

To help students organize their notes, I developed the Cornell Note-taking System forty years ago at Cornell University. It is used in colleges not only in the United States but also in foreign countries, including China. The keystone of the system is a two-column note sheet.

Use 8½ by 11 paper to create the note sheet (see Figure 7.4). Down the left side, draw a vertical line 2½ inches from the edge of the paper. End this line 2 inches above the bottom of the paper. Draw a horizontal line across the bottom of the paper, 2 inches above the paper's edge. In the narrow (2½″) column on the left, you will write cue words or questions. In the wide (6″) column on the right, you will write lecture notes. In the space at the bottom of the sheet, you will summarize your notes. Note: You can use this system if you use lined notebook paper, too. You can disregard the red vertical rule and make your own rule 2½″ from the left edge of the paper. Or you can make

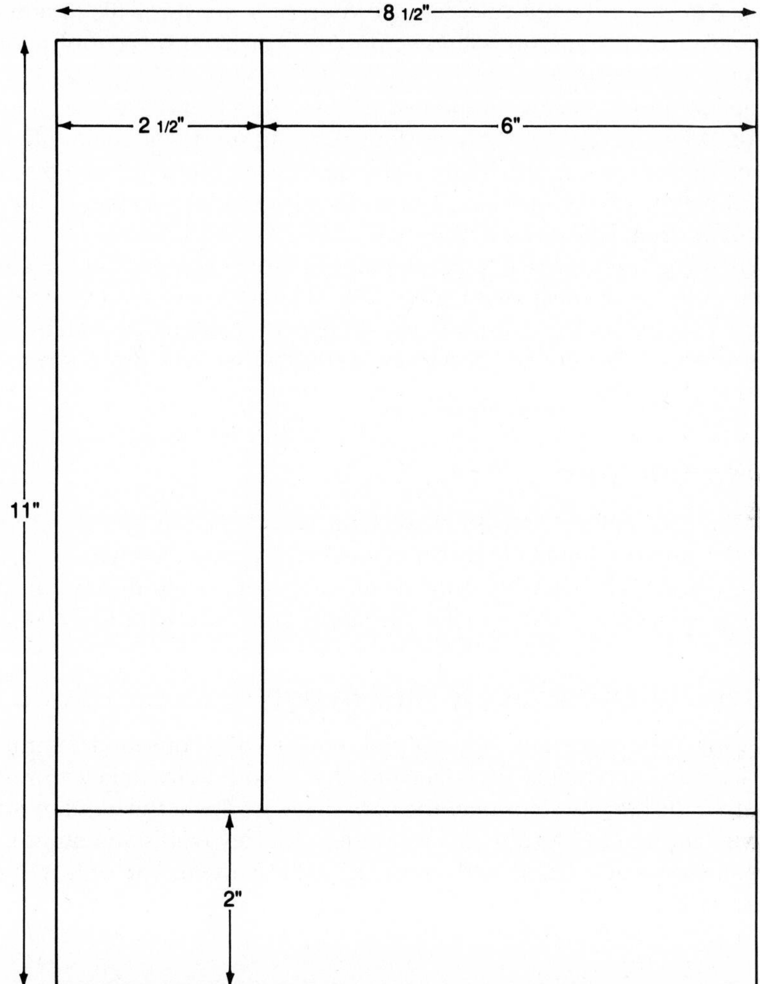

FIGURE 7.4 Note-Sheet Format for the Cornell Note-taking System
During a lecture class, the student writes notes in the wide (6″) column. To study from the notes, the student writes either cue words or questions in the narrow column and a summary in the space at the bottom of the note sheet.

the rule 2½″ from the red rule, leaving yourself 4″ for the wide note-taking column. In either case, you will have the 2½″ left-hand space for important cue words and questions.

There are two versions of the Cornell System: (1) the Six R version, (2) the One Q/Five R version. Both versions have six steps. The main difference between them is in step 2. The six steps are listed in Table 7.1 and discussed in detail below. Notice that step 2 in the Six R version is *reduce*; in the One Q/Five R version, step 2 is *question*.

When you use the Six R version, you will write cue words in the narrow column of the note sheet (see Figure 7.5). When you use the One Q/Five R version, you will write questions in the narrow column (see Figure 7.6). Which version is better? Give each one a try, and see which one works best for you.

Step 1: Record

In the wide column, record as many facts and ideas as you can. Use telegraphic sentences, but make sure that weeks after the lecture your notes will still make sense. Write legibly. Directly after class or at your first opportunity, fill in any blank spaces that you left and clarify your handwriting if necessary.

Step 2: Reduce (Six R version only)

During your first study opportunity, reread your notes and rethink the entire lecture. Then reduce each fact and idea in your notes to key words and phrases. In the narrow column of the note sheet, jot down the word or phrase that you have extracted from the fact or idea. The key words and phrases will act as memory cues. Later, when you see or hear them, you will recall the full fact or idea.

TABLE 7.1 Steps in the Cornell Note-taking System

Step	Six R Version	One Q/Five R Version
1[a]	Record	Record
2	Reduce	Question
3	Recite	Recite
4	Reflect	Reflect
5	Review	Review
6[a]	Recapitulate	Recapitulate

[a]Notes made in class (step 1) and the summary written during study time (step 6) are placed in the wide column of the note sheet.

	Psych. 102 – Prof. Goldsmith – Sept. 14th (Mon.)
	A. Build Self-Confidence – 15 steps
Weaknesses & strengths	1. Assess strengths & weaknesses a. Set goals accordingly
Life's goal	2. Decide what you'd like your life to be a. Rework your thinking to bring inner script up to date
Negatives	3. Bury all <u>negative</u> memories a. Forgive others & self b. Remember past successes – even minor ones
Guilt & shame	4. Wipe out any guilt & shame a. Don't allow these thoughts mental entrance
Personality defects	5. Don't attribute present behavior to personality defects a. Real causes might be economic, political, social, etc.
Points of view	6. Events may be seen differently by different people a. Rejections or put-downs might not be actual
Negative labels	7. Never label yourself negatively a. Such as: stupid, ugly, failure, incorrigible
Criticism	8. Accept criticism of a <u>specific</u> <u>action</u>, but not of <u>you</u> as a person a. Accept constructive criticism graciously
Failures blessing	9. Failures can be a blessing -- goals not right for you a. Avoids later let-down
Inadequacy	10. Don't tolerate people, jobs, situations that make you feel inadequate a. If can't change them or you -- walk out
Relax	11. Take time to relax & meditate -- hobbies a. Keep in touch w/ your inner self
Social	12. Be social -- enjoy other people a. See their needs and help them
Playing it too cool	13. Don't overprotect your ego -- it's resilient a. Better to try & fail, than to clam up; numbing!
Goals: long-range short-range	14. Develop long-ranged goals, also short-ranged ones a. Evaluate progress & whisper word of praise in your own ear
Not an object – active actor – <u>live</u> your life	15. You're not a passive object -- you can make things happen a. You're a product of millions of years of evolution & made in God's image b. Don't worry about <u>how</u> to live your life, lose yourself -- be absorbed in <u>living</u> it

Through deep thinking, decide what you want to be. What to do with your life. Write out long-term & short-term goals. Eliminate totally & permanently <u>all</u> <u>negative</u> feelings & occurrences past, present, & future. Do things. Try things. Ego can take set-backs. Don't withdraw to solitary "safety." Enter the stream of life. Be busy swimming in it.

FIGURE 7.5 The Six R Version
The narrow column contains key words and phrases.

Questions	Notes
	Psych. 105 - Prof. Martin - Sept. 14 (Mon.)
	MEMORY
	A. Memory tricky - Can recall instantly many trivial things of childhood; yet, forget things recently worked hard to learn & retain.
	B. Memory Trace
How do psychologists account for remembering?	1. Fact that we retain information means that some change was made in the brain.
	2. Change called "memory trace."
What's a "memory trace"?	3. "Trace" probably a molecular arrangement similar to molecular changes in a magnetic recording tape.
What are the three memory systems?	C. Three memory systems: sensory, short-term, long-term.
How long does sensory memory retain information?	1. Sensory (lasts one second)
How is information transferred to STM?	Ex. Words or numbers sent to brain by sight (visual image) start to disintegrate within a few tenths of a second & gone in one full second, unless quickly transferred to S-T memory by verbal repetition.
	2. Short-term memory [STM] (lasts 30 seconds)
What are the retention times of STM?	a. Experiments show: a syllable of 3 letters remembered 50% of the time after 3 seconds. Totally forgotten end of 30 seconds.
What's the capacity of the STM?	b. S-T memory - limited capacity = holds average of 7 items.
	c. More than 7 items -- jettisons some to make room.
How to hold information in STM?	d. To hold items in STM, must rehearse -- must hear sound of words internally or externally.
What are the retention times of LTM?	3. Long-Term memory [LTM] (lasts a lifetime or short time).
What are the six ways to transfer information from STM to LTM?	a. Transfer fact or idea by:
	(1) Associating w/information already in LTM
	(2) Organizing information into meaningful units
	(3) Understanding by comparing & making relationships.
	(4) Frameworking - fit pieces in like in a jigsaw puzzle.
	(5) Reorganizing - combing new & old into a new unit.
	(6) Rehearsing - aloud to keep memory trace strong

Three kinds of memory systems are sensory, which retains information for about one second; short-term, which retains for a maximum of thirty seconds; and long-term, which varies from a lifetime of retention to a relatively short time.

The six ways (activities) to transfer information to the long-term memory are: associating, organizing, understanding, frameworking, reorganizing and rehearsing.

FIGURE 7.6 The One Q/Five R Version

The narrow column contains questions.

Step 2: Question (One Q/Five R version only)

During your first opportunity, reread your notes and rethink the entire lecture. Then formulate questions based on your notes. In the narrow column of the note sheet, opposite the fact or idea in your notes, write a brief question that can be answered with the information in your notes. Writing questions helps to clarify meanings, reveal relationships, establish continuity, and strengthen memory. It also sets the stage for studying for exams.

Step 3: Recite

Reciting is saying each fact or idea in your notes out loud, in your own words, and from memory. Recitation is an extremely powerful aid to memory. Recitation makes you think, and thinking leaves a trace in your memory. Experiments show that students who recite retain 80 percent of the material; students who reread but do not recite retain only 20 percent when tested two weeks later. Without retention, there is no learning.

Cover up the wide column of your note sheet with a piece of blank paper, exposing only the cue words or questions in the narrow column. Read each cue word or question aloud; then recite *aloud* and in *your own words* the full facts and ideas brought to mind by the cue word or the answer to the question. After reciting, slide the blank sheet down to check your answer. If your answer is incomplete or incorrect, straighten out the information in your mind and then recite your answer aloud again. Recite until you get the answer right. Proceed through the entire lecture in this way.

Why recite aloud? The sound of your voice stimulates your thinking process. It is this thinking that leaves behind in your memory some neural trace to which you may return later, as to a filing cabinet, to retrieve a fact or idea. Reciting aloud is the most powerful single technique known to psychologists for implanting facts and ideas in your memory.

Why recite using your own words? Cognitive theorists have discovered that people do not remember verbatim what they hear or read. Rather, they remember the meaning that they gave to a fact or idea that they heard or read, and the meaning was expressed in words that they used when they were thinking about the fact or idea. In sum, you remember the meaning you gave to a fact or idea as you processed it in your mind through the use of your own words.

Step 4: Reflect

Professor Hans Bethe, nuclear physicist and Nobel Prize winner, said that "creativity comes only through reflection." Reflection is thinking about and applying the facts and ideas that you've learned. You reflect by asking yourself questions such as these: What is the significance of these facts? What principles are they based on? How can I apply them? How do they fit in with what I already know? What is beyond these facts and principles?

Reflection leads to advantageous learning—learning that is done voluntarily and with enthusiasm and curiosity, learning that is propelled by a burning desire to know something. What distinguishes advantageous learning from regular learning is your mental attitude. Knowledge gained through advantageous learning will still be with you long after you have taken your final examination.

Step 5: Review

In Chapter 5 you learned that yesterday's knowledge interferes with today's knowledge and today's knowledge interferes with yesterday's knowledge. The battle between remembering and forgetting goes on continuously. The best way to prepare for examinations is to keep reviewing and keep reciting the sets of notes that you'll be held responsible for.

Every evening, before you settle down to study, quickly review your notes. Pick up a designated set of notes and recite them. Short, fast, frequent reviews will produce far better understanding and far better remembering than long, all-day or all-night sessions can. After reciting, move immediately into your regular study routine.

Step 6: Recapitulate

Writing a recapitulation, or summary, is not easy, but the rewards are great. Recapitulating is a sure-fire way to gain a deep understanding of the facts and ideas in your notes, and reviewing summaries makes studying for exams a breeze. If you take the time to summarize your notes, your understanding deepens because you have the whole picture instead of an assortment of facts.

Write your summary in the space below the horizontal line at the bottom of the note sheet. Summarize according to one of these plans:

1. Summarize the content of each note sheet.
2. Summarize the content of the entire lecture on the last note sheet for that lecture.
3. Do both 1 and 2.

The third option yields the greatest reward. When you review your notes for exams, you'll be able to see the steps you took to arrive at your final, last-page summary.

TYPES OF NOTES

There are various types of notes that you can use: topic-explanation notes, sentence notes, topic-idea notes, paragraph notes. The nature of the subject, the lecturer's style, and your personal preference will determine which you choose. Be sure to use the Cornell System format with all four types.

Topic-Explanation Notes

Take a look at Figure 7.7. When the lecturer said, "There are two kinds of magic used in many primitive societies," the note taker was ready to list and enumerate them. Notice that the note taker fortified the two kinds of magic with good examples. Later, the note taker wrote key words and phrases in the narrow column.

Sentence Notes

In most instances, sentence notes written in a telegraphic style will be the most efficient way to record a lecture. Be flexible, though, because (as Figure 7.8 shows) you might have to switch from one type of notes to another.

	Oct. 10 (Mon.)-Soc.102-Prof. Oxford ①
	A. Two kinds of magic
Sympathetic= clay model	1. Sympathetic-make model or form of a person from clay, etc., then stick pins into object to hurt symbolized person.
Contagious= fingernail clippings	2. Contagious magic a. Need to possess an article belonging to another person. b. Ex. Fingernail clippings. By doing harm to these objects, feel that harm can be thus transmitted.

FIGURE 7.7 Topic-Explanation Notes

	Oct. 10 (Mon.) - Soc. 102 - Prof. Oxford ②
	A. Animism
Stick has power	1. Object has supernatural power
Power = mana	2. Power called mana (not limited to objects)
	a. Objects accumulate mana
	Ex. Good canoe - more mana than poor one.
	b. Objects can lose mana
Can gain or	c. People collect objects w/lots of mana
lose mana	d. Good person's objects collect mana
	e. People, animals, plants have mana, too.
Good people have	Ex. Expert canoe builder has mana -
lots of mana	imparts mana to canoe
	f. Chief has lots of mana - dangerous to
	get too close to chief - mana around head.

FIGURE 7.8 Sentence Notes

	Oct. 27 (WED.) - Economics 105 - Prof. Terry ①
	Some Basic Laws & Principles
What is the Law	1. Law of Diminishing Returns
of Diminishing	a. Refers to amount of extra output (pro-
Returns?	duction) we get when we add additional
	inputs; but, after a point, the extra inputs
	yield decreasing amounts of extra output.
What is	b. Malthus's views depended on this law =
Malthus's Law?	Just so much land, but population
	could increase more rapidly than food
	supplies.

FIGURE 7.9 Topic-Idea Notes

	Nov. 6 (MON) - World Lit. 106 - Prof Warnek ①
	Greek Race
What is the Greek concept of a well-rounded man?	1. Unity = well-rounded Early Greeks vigorous. Goal was to be well-rounded: unity of knowledge & activity. No separate specializations as law, literature, philosophy, etc. Believed one man should master all things equally well; not only knowledge, but be an athlete, soldier, & statesman, too.

FIGURE 7.10 Paragraph Notes

Topic-Idea Notes

The topic-idea format is often useful in history, economics, and philosophy courses. The lecturer mentions a topic and then expands on it. Notice that in Figure 7.9 the "paragraph" about the law of diminishing returns is broken up by two subtopic indicators to show separate ideas.

Paragraph Notes

If the lecturer is expounding on an idea in a straightforward fashion, don't try to impose some sort of topic and subtopic organization where there is none. Instead, write short, telegraphic sentences and end up with an almost solid paragraph, as shown in Figure 7.10.

COMBINING TEXTBOOK AND LECTURE NOTES

The format shown in Figure 7.11 is ideal for lectures that mainly explain and amplify the textbook. First, in the middle column, record your notes on a previously assigned textbook chapter. Then, when you take lecture notes in the right-hand column, you can avoid repeating material you already have,

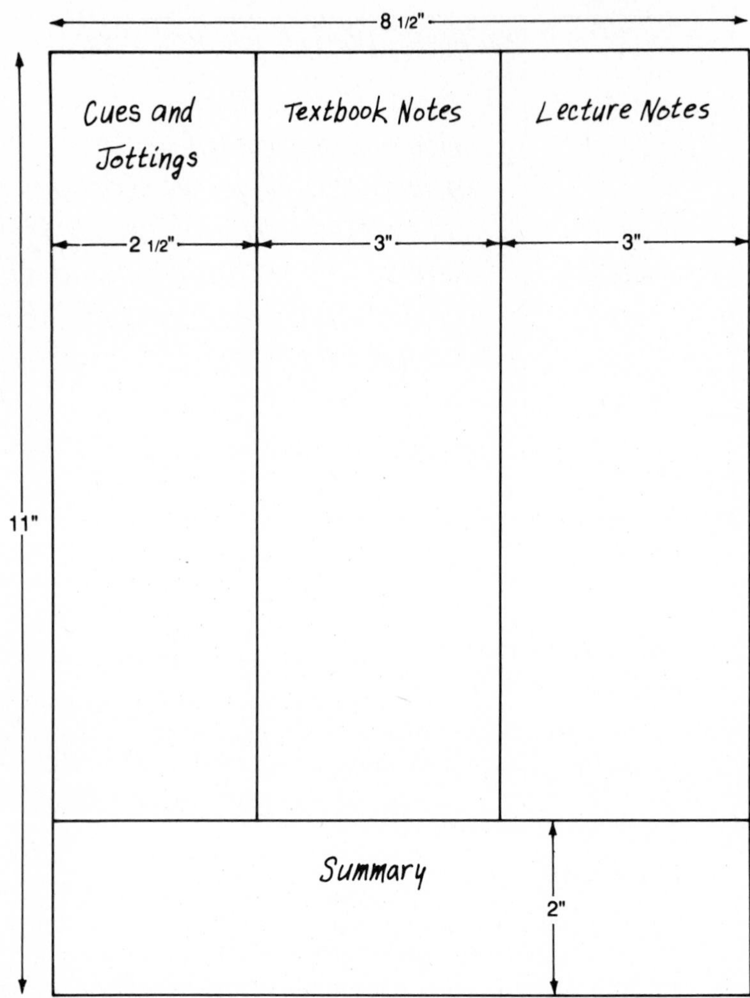

FIGURE 7.11 Cornell System Format for Combining Textbook and Lecture Notes

while you add the lecturer's explanations, examples, and supplementary comments. When you become accustomed to the lecturer's ways, you will be able to judge how much space to leave between items in the middle column in order to keep lecture notes and textbook notes directly opposite each other. The cue words or questions that you write in the left column should pull the two sets of notes together.

ABBREVIATIONS AND SYMBOLS

You should use only the abbreviations that fit your needs and that you will remember easily. A good idea is to introduce only a few abbreviations into your note taking at a time. Overuse may leave you with notes that are difficult to read. Here are some rules to keep in mind.

1. Symbols are especially helpful to students in engineering and mathematics. Lists of commonly used symbols are given in most textbooks and reference books.

$\neq$	does not equal
$\underline{f}$	frequency

2. Create a family of symbols.

○	organism
⊙	individual
Ⓢ	individuals

3. Leave out the periods in standard abbreviations.

cf	compare
eg	for example
dept	department
NYC	New York City

4. Use only the first syllable of a word.

pol	politics
dem	democracy
lib	liberal
cap	capitalism

5. Use the entire first syllable and only the first letter of a second syllable.

subj	subject
cons	conservative
tot	totalitarianism
ind	individual

6. Eliminate final letters. Use just enough of the beginning of a word to form an easily recognizable abbreviation.

assoc	associate, associated
ach	achievement
biol	biological
info	information
intro	introduction
chem	chemistry
conc	concentration
max	maximum
rep	repetition

7. Omit vowels from the middle of words, and retain only enough consonants to provide a recognizable skeleton of the word.

bkgd — background
ppd — prepared
prblm — problem
estmt — estimate
gvt — government

8. Use an apostrophe.

gov't — government
am't — amount
cont'd — continued
educat'l — educational

9. Form the plural of a symbol or abbreviated word by adding "s."

□s — areas
chaps — chapters
co-ops — cooperatives
$\underline{f}$s — frequencies
/s — ratios

10. Use "g" to represent *ing* endings.

decrg — decreasing
ckg — checking
estg — establishing
exptg — experimenting

11. Use a dot placed over a symbol or word to indicate the word *rate.*

$\dot{\updownarrow}$ — vibration rate
$\dot{\underline{f}}$ — frequency rate

12. Generally, spell out short words such as *in, at, to, but, for,* and *key.* Symbols, signs, or abbreviations for short words will make the notes too dense with "shorthand."

13. Leave out unimportant verbs.

14. Leave out the words *a* and *the.*

15. If a term, phrase, or name is initially written out in full during the lecture, substitute initials whenever the term, phrase, or name is used again.

Initial writing: Modern Massachusetts Party
Subsequently: MMP

16. Use symbols for commonly recurring connective or transitional words.

& — and
w/ — with
w/o — without
vs — against
∴ — therefore

SUMMARY

Why should I take notes?	The answer is simple: because forgetting is massive and instantaneous. Forgetting wipes out information like a tornado. Note taking provides disaster relief.
What do the research of Hermann Ebbinghaus and the Leon-Clyde anecdote demonstrate?	Ebbinghaus found that in just twenty minutes we lose nearly half of what we've learned. The Leon-Clyde episode showed how quickly two intelligent men can forget the key points of a lecture that both thought was brilliant. Both point to the necessity of taking notes to combat forgetting.
How do I begin taking notes?	A good way to start is with telegraphic sentences. Students who try to write down a lecture word for word are asking for trouble. The secret is to record only the key words. This streamlined version will save you time, yet provide you with the information you need.
What's the best way to take notes—with printing or with cursive?	Neither. Use the modified printing style. It provides the best of both worlds. It's fast and neat, and it saves you time that you might otherwise spend recopying.
Are there some time wasters in note taking?	Yes. There are at least three that you should avoid: (1) Never tape a lecture. (2) Don't use shorthand. (3) Don't recopy or type your notes.
How can I use the speaker's signals to my advantage?	Expressions such as "in contrast to" or "to sum up" act as signals and help you identify the pattern of organization the speaker is following. If you can follow the speaker's organizational pattern, you'll have little trouble fitting in the facts and ideas along the way.
What do you mean by instant replay?	As soon as you've left the classroom, take a moment to relive the lecture mentally from start to finish. After you've replayed the lecture in your mind, take a few moments to reflect on what the instructor has said and what it all means.

When should I review my notes?	Right away if possible. The longer you wait, the more you'll forget. Review your notes while the lecture is still fresh in your mind.
What is the Cornell Note-taking System?	The Cornell System is a time-honored technique for getting the most out of your notes. The keystone of the system is its format, a 6-inch area for your lecture notes and a 2½-inch left-hand margin for cue words or questions. There are two versions of the Cornell System: the Six R version and the One Q/Five R version. Both have six steps. The main difference between them is in step 2.
What is step 1?	Step 1, recording, simply involves taking notes. The notes go in the 6-inch column. Record as many of the lecturer's key ideas as you can. Use telegraphic sentences to get the information on paper quickly.
What is step 2?	Step 2 in the Six R version is reducing the key facts in your notes to cue words. Step 2 in the One Q/Five R version is formulating some cue questions.
What are cue words?	Cue words are key words or phrases written in the 2½-inch column that act as cues to help you to recall a full fact or idea.
How do I use cue questions?	Simply dream up a question that can be answered with the information from a full fact or idea.
What is involved in step 3, reciting?	When you recite, you say each key fact or idea in your notes out loud, in your own words, and from memory. If you are using the Six R version, your memory will be triggered by the key words in the 2½-inch margin. If you are using the One Q/Five R version, a thoughtful question will focus your response. In either case, the fact that you recite out loud will reveal immediately whether your answer is correct.
What is the reflection step?	Reflection involves thinking about and applying the concepts and ideas that you

learn. It triggers advantageous learning—learning that is done voluntarily and with enthusiasm. Advantageous learning has the best chance of lasting.

How often should I follow step 5, reviewing?

As often as possible. Reviewing is really the workhorse of both methods. How much you review will determine whether you will be able to remember important information days and weeks from now. If you make an effort to do a quick review of your notes every evening before you begin studying, you'll do a good job of maintaining your hard-earned knowledge.

What about the sixth and final step, recapitulation?

In short, it means summarizing. If you take the time to summarize your notes, your understanding will deepen because you'll have the whole picture.

Is there more than one way to summarize?

Yes. You have three choices: (1) Summarize the content of each note sheet. (2) Summarize the entire lecture at the bottom of the last note sheet for that lecture. (3) Do both 1 and 2. The third choice is worth the extra effort.

Can lecture and textbook notes be combined?

Yes. Combining lecture and textbook notes is especially important if the lecturer repeats what is in the textbook. Use a three-column format: one column for your lecture notes, another for the notes from your textbook, and the third for your cue words or questions.

Are abbreviations and symbols a help in note taking?

Used sparingly, abbreviations and symbols can be a help. A few key abbreviations can save you time and space. If you use too many abbreviations and symbols, your notes will be difficult to read.

HAVE YOU MISSED SOMETHING?

1. *Sentence completion.* Complete the following sentences with one of the three words listed below each sentence.

a. Much of the information that a person receives is no longer available after a few ________________.

minutes hours weeks

b. The Leon-Clyde anecdote illustrates the problem of ________.

note taking forgetting recapitulation

2. *Matching.* In each blank space in the left column, write the number preceding the phrase in the right column that matches the left item best.

_____ a. Two-page system	1. Can reveal where the lecture is heading
_____ b. Forgetting	2. Used cue words or questions
_____ c. Cornell System	3. Is both instant and massive
_____ d. 2½-inch column	4. Ideal format for coping with speedy lecturers
_____ e. 6-inch column	5. Is not recommended as a method of note taking
_____ f. Recapitulation	6. Used for classroom lecture notes
_____ g. Shorthand	7. Time-tested method for taking notes
_____ h. Signal words	8. Note-taking step that involves writing summaries

3. *True-false.* Write *T* beside the *true* statements and *F* beside the *false* statements.

_____ a. Notes written in the modified printing style must be retyped.

_____ b. Nearly 47 percent of material learned is forgotten in just twenty minutes.

_____ c. Taping the lecture is an efficient way to get all the information you need.

_____ d. Almost no learning takes place during the act of typing.

_____ e. A well-written stack of notes can function as a second textbook.

_____ f. The last five or ten minutes of a lecture often contain the greatest concentration of information.

4. *Note-taking dos.* Write "yes" next to the tips that are recommended for optimal note taking.

_____ a. Look over your previous notes before class.

_____ b. Use Roman numerals in outlining your notes.

_____ c. Capture the ideas as well as the facts.

_____ d. Differentiate your thoughts from the lecturer's thoughts.

_____ e. Write on both sides of your note sheets.

_____ f. Skip lines and leave space between main ideas.

_____ g. Begin taking notes immediately.

_____ h. Keep your notes in spiral-bound books.

5. *Multiple choice.* Choose the phrase that completes the following sentence most accurately, and circle the letter that precedes it.

Telegraphic sentences provide you with

a. verbatim notes
b. a secretary-style transcription
c. streamlined information
d. typed documentation

CHAPTER 8

Learning from Your Textbooks

There is a great difference between knowing a thing and understanding it.

Charles Kettering (1876–1958), American electrical engineer and inventor

Are you going hungry? Some students devour their textbook assignments, yet never learn a thing. That's because learning from a textbook involves more than just reading. It means digesting what you read. A textbook assignment needs to be read actively in order to provide food for thought. This chapter discusses

- Getting acquainted with your textbooks
- Mining prefaces and introductions
- Study systems for textbooks

specifically

- The SQ3R Method
- 3Rs for academic survival

and finally

- The Questions-in-the-Margin System

ecause you and your textbooks are going to spend a quarter or a semester together, you'd better become friends. How? By getting acquainted.

GETTING ACQUAINTED WITH YOUR TEXTBOOKS

Buy all your textbooks immediately after you register. This is a wise policy even if your school allows a period in which you can attend many courses before deciding on a final few. Get a head start by reading the tables of contents, prefaces, introductions, and any other up-front material in all your books. Underline important words and sentences, and make notes in the margins. (Of course, if you think you may not ultimately take a course whose books you've bought, don't make these marks! Save your receipts to return all unused books.) Then, while you still have the time, leaf through each of your books. Look at the pictures, tables, and diagrams; read the captions. Read chapter titles and headings and subheadings that interest you. This will give you a good idea of what the book is like and where you will be going during the semester. Later, you'll be glad you did, for you'll be able to see how the various parts of the course fit together.

Reading the Preface

The authors of most textbooks are dealing with serious subjects. Consequently, they write in a serious, scholarly vein. They may be warm and congenial people, but they can appear, in their writing, to be cold and faceless. The only place where most authors can drop their scholarly style and let their hair down is in the preface. There you have a chance to meet and get to know the authors as people. Once you do, you'll find that you can converse and even argue with them as you read the text. Now and then, you'll find yourself saying, "No, I don't agree with that statement" or "What do you mean by that?" You wouldn't make such a statement to a cold, unanswering textbook if you couldn't visualize a live hand behind the writing.

Every textbook would be much more meaningful if the authors could visit your classroom and give a short, informal talk. Thereafter, your textbooks would have far greater meaning. Since personal appearances are usually out of the question, the next best thing is to let the authors talk with you in the preface.

For instance, one student struck pay dirt on page 54 of a ninety-page preface to *A Treatise of Human Nature* by David Hume (1711–76), a Scottish philosopher. Hume wrote in his preface, "If I find the root of human nature, I'll be able to explain all human actions." The student accurately interpreted this sentence to mean that Hume would be using a psychological and not a traditional philosophical approach. Thus, with this proper mental set established, the student was able to read Hume's *Treatise* fairly rapidly and with clear understanding. Students who had not read the author's long preface read the book with a mental set directed at ascertaining Hume's philosophy. Most of those students never understood what David Hume was trying to explain.

In prefaces you can find valuable information such as (1) what the author's objective is, (2) what the author's objective is not, (3) the organizational plan of the book, (4) how and why the book is different from other books about the same subject, and (5) the author's qualifications for writing the book. As a practical exercise, you might find it interesting to read the preface of this book, if you have not already done so. See how much you can gain toward understanding not only the book but also the author.

What the Author's Perspective Is and Is Not

> This little book aims to give a certain perspective on the subject of language rather than to assemble facts about it. It has little to say of the ultimate psychological basis of speech and gives only enough of the actual descriptive or historical facts of particular languages to illustrate principles.[1]

It is a tremendous advantage to know the author's objective, for then you'll read and interpret the text from the correct point of view. Otherwise, reading could be quite a struggle, and the facts could seem to be completely unconnected. The author of the quotation just given is saying, "Keep your eye on the *perspective,* not on the facts." Being told what the author is *not* trying to do helps make the objective even clearer. Here, the author says, in effect, "No, this is not a list of facts, as many other books are." Being so warned, you'll refrain from drifting into the wrong pathway of thought while you are reading.

The Organizational Plan of the Book

> This book is organized, therefore, neither along chronological lines nor the less obvious logical line of proceeding from simple narration to varying emphases. The arrangement is, if anything, psychological.[2]

Having the organizational plan is like having a road map. You'll know not only what the authors are doing but also where they are going. In the

---

[1]Edward Sapir, *Language* (New York: Harcourt Brace Jovanovich, 1921), p. v.
[2]William M. Sale, Jr., James Hall, and Martin Steinmann, Jr., eds., *Short Stories: Tradition and Direction* (Norfolk, Conn.: New Directions, 1949), p. xii.

example above, you're told what patterns the editors of the anthology are following and not following, which makes the plan of the book especially clear.

> **How and Why the Book Is Different**
>
> Many histories of philosophy exist, and it has not been my purpose merely to add one to their number. My purpose is to exhibit philosophy as an integral part of social and political life; not as the isolated speculations of remarkable individuals.[3]

Knowing how and why the book is different is valuable information. It is easy to think that a new book on a subject is just "more of the same old stuff." When authors point out why their book is different and why their version or approach is necessary, you will read with greater awareness and greater comprehension.

> **The Author's Qualifications**
>
> It is obviously impossible to know as much about every philosopher as can be known about him by a man whose field is less wide; I have no doubt that every single philosopher whom I have mentioned, with the exception of Leibniz, is better known to many men than to me. If, however, this were considered a sufficient reason for respectful silence, it would follow that no man should undertake to treat of more than some narrow strip of history.[4]

Writers usually try, in some subtle way, to let the reader know that their book is written by a scholar, an expert on the subject. In the example above, the writer develops a very fine logical point in an interesting manner. He admits that he is an expert on the German philosopher Leibniz (1646–1716) but not on the broad field of philosophy. He maintains that his lack of knowledge will not prevent him from writing on the broad topic because if writers tackled only their pet subjects, no one would be able to give an overview on any subject.

Reading the Introduction

There are four good reasons to read the introduction to a book:

1. The introduction is usually well written, because the writer knows that it is the book's show window—especially for prospective customers looking the book over to decide whether to buy it.

---

[3]Bertrand Russell, *A History of Western Philosophy* (New York: Simon and Schuster, Inc., and London: George Allen Unwin, Ltd., 1945), p. x.
[4]Ibid.

2. Having only limited space, the writer packs the introduction with facts and ideas. As a reader, you will gain a lot from reading a relatively few pages.
3. Reading the introduction puts you on firm footing for the rest of the book, making future assignments easier, requiring less time, and helping you achieve a higher level of mastery than you otherwise would have achieved.
4. With your underlinings and notes in the margin, you can quickly review the introduction time after time, to give yourself a warm-up as well as a door into each assigned chapter.

Figure 8.1 is a densely packed introduction containing information of great and immediate value for the sharper reading of textbooks. It is from a book titled *Six-Way Paragraphs.*[5] The book's sole purpose is to teach students how to spot main ideas. One hundred paragraphs are provided for practice. To prepare students for such practice, the introduction strives to explain the ins and outs of the paragraphs found in textbooks. As you read it, be aware of not only *what* the writer says but also *how* he says it and his *purpose* for saying it.

STUDY SYSTEMS FOR TEXTBOOKS

The old saying "Practice makes perfect" holds true for most activities. Is it true for the reading of textbook chapters? Some say it is not. Others say it is if the reader uses a specially constructed system to read and study the textbook chapters.

In the remainder of this chapter, you will be reading about three specially constructed systems: (1) the SQ3R Method, an old standby; (2) the 3Rs System, which consists of just three essential steps; (3) the Questions-in-the-Margin Technique, which is brand new. If one of these systems fits your personality, style, and academic needs, then adopt it. If you can't find a perfect fit, then select, modify, and adjust the parts of these three systems. Tailor one so that it is right for you.

THE SQ3R METHOD

The SQ3R Method was devised during World War II by Francis P. Robinson, an Ohio State University psychologist. The aim of the system was to help military personnel enrolled in special programs at the university to read

[5]Walter Pauk, *Six-Way Paragraphs* (Providence, R.I.: Jamestown Publishers, 1974).

what: wants you to focus on the paragraph - unit
how: brings you and the writer together
purpose: wants you to look at the paragraph through the eyes of the writer

The paragraph! That's the working-unit of both writer and reader. The writer works hard to put meaning into the paragraph; the reader works hard to take meaning out of it. Though they work at opposite tasks, the work of each is closely related. Actually, to understand better the job of the reader, one must first understand better the job of the writer. So, let us look briefly at the writer's job.

what: each paragraph has but one main idea
how: shows you how a writer thinks
purpose: to convince you to look for only one idea per paragraph because writers follow this rule

To make his meaning clear, a writer knows that he must follow certain basic principles. First, he knows that he must develop only one main idea per paragraph. This principle is so important that he knows it backwards, too. He knows that he must not try to develop two main ideas in the same, single paragraph.

what: the topic of the main idea is in the topic sentence, which is usually the first one
how: the writer needs to state a topic sentence to keep his own writing clear and under control
purpose: to instill confidence in you that the topic sentence is an important tool in a writer's kit and convince you it is there, so, look for it!

The next important principle he knows is that the topic of each main idea must be stated in a topic sentence and that such a sentence best serves its function by coming at or near the beginning of its paragraph. He knows, too, that the more clearly he can state the topic of his paragraph in an opening sentence, the more effective he will be in developing a meaningful, well-organized paragraph.

what: developing main ideas through supporting material
how: "more to a writer's job," still keeps you in the writer's shoes
purpose: to announce and advance the new step of supporting materials

Now, there is more to a writer's job than just writing paragraphs consisting of only bare topic sentences and main ideas. The balance of his job deals with *developing* each main idea through the use of supporting material which amplifies and clarifies the main idea and many times makes it more vivid and memorable.

what: (a) main ideas are often supported by examples, (b) other supporting devices listed.
how: still through the writer's eyes

To support his main ideas, a writer may use a variety of forms. One of the most common forms to support a main idea is the *example.* Examples help to illustrate the main idea more vividly. Other supporting materials are anecdotes, incidents, jokes, allusions, comparisons, contrasts, analogies, definitions, exceptions, logic, and so forth.

To summarize, the reader should have learned from the writer that a textbook-type paragraph usually contains these three elements: a topic sentence, a main idea, and supporting material. Knowing this, the reader should use the topic sentence to lead him to the main idea. Once he grasps the main idea, then everything else is supporting material used to illustrate, amplify, and qualify the main idea. So, in the final analysis, the reader must be able to separate the main idea from the supporting material, yet see the relationship between them.

FIGURE 8.1 The Content of an Introduction
Source: Walter Pauk, Six-Way Paragraphs *(Providence, R.I.: Jamestown Publishers, 1974), pp. 7–8. Reprinted by permission of Jamestown Publishers.*

faster and to study better. The letters in the name of the system stand for *survey, question, read, recite,* and *review.* Robinson described the SQ3R Method and explained its benefits:

> These five steps of the SQ3R system—survey, question, read, recite, and review—should result in faster reading, and fixing of the important points in the memory. You will find one other worthwhile outcome: Quiz questions will seem familiar because the headings turned into questions are usually the points emphasized in quizzes. By predicting actual quiz questions and looking up the answers beforehand, you know that you are effectively studying what is considered important in the course.[6]

The five steps of the SQ3R Method are described and explained as follows[7]:

---

[6]Francis P. Robinson, *Effective Study,* 4th ed. (New York: Harper & Row, 1970), p. 32.
[7]"SQ3R Method" from *Effective Study* by Francis P. Robinson. Copyright 1941, 1946 by Harper & Row, Publishers, Inc. Copyright © 1961, 1970 by Francis P. Robinson. Reprinted by permission of the publisher.

S Survey

Glance through all the headings in the chapter, and read the final summary paragraph (if the chapter has one). This survey should not take more than a minute, and it will show you the three to six core ideas on which the discussion will be based. This orientation will help you organize the ideas as you read them later.

Q Question

Now begin to work. Turn the first heading into a question. This will arouse your curiosity and thereby increase comprehension. It will bring to mind information you already know, thus helping you understand that section more quickly. The question also will make important points stand out from explanatory details. You can turn a heading into a question as you read the heading, but it demands conscious effort on your part.

R_1 Read

Read so as to answer that question, but read only to the end of the first section. This should not be a passive plodding along each line, but an active search for the answer.

R_2 Recite

Having read the first section, look away from the book and try briefly to recite the answer to your question. Use your own words, and cite an example. If you can do this, you know what is in the book; if you cannot, glance over the section again. An excellent way to do this reciting from memory is to jot down brief cue phrases in outline form on a sheet of paper.

Now repeat the second to fourth steps for each successive section: That is, turn the next heading into a question, read to answer that question, and recite the answer by jotting down cue phrases in your outline. Read in this way until the entire lesson is completed.

R_3 Review

When you have read through in this way, look over your notes to get a bird's-eye view of the points and their relationships to each other. Check your memory by reciting the major subpoints under each heading. This can be done by covering up your notes and trying to recall the main points. Then expose each major point and try to recall the subpoints listed under it.

3Rs FOR ACADEMIC SURVIVAL

The 3Rs System is perfect for students who like to move quickly into a textbook chapter, or for those who face exams with little time for intensive study. The three Rs stand for *read, record,* and *recite*—the three essential steps for mastering textbook assignments. If you like its simplicity, you can also use the 3Rs System to implant facts and ideas in your long-term memory. Just emphasize the third step: Keep reciting the facts and ideas until overlearning occurs.

R_1 Read

Read several paragraphs; then go back to the first paragraph and ask yourself, "What do I need to know in this paragraph?" Read and reread until you find out.

R_2 Record

Once you have identified and can briefly say aloud what you need to know, underline only the key words, phrases, and sentences that identify this information. Later, when you review, your eyes will immediately focus on these, the essential parts of the paragraph. You won't have to reread the whole paragraph again when you review. Then do one more important thing: Jot in the margin an ever-so-brief question that asks for the information underlined. Question forming is very important in this system. Go through the entire chapter paragraph by paragraph.

R_3 Recite

Start at the first page of your assignment and cover up the printed page with a blank sheet of paper, leaving the questions in the margin exposed. Then, in your own words, recite aloud the answers. After reciting, check for accuracy. Recite until you've completed the chapter. Remember: If you don't know the answer now, you won't know it tomorrow in class or be able to write it on an exam. So, while you still have the chance, keep trying until you get the answer right.

THE QUESTIONS-IN-THE-MARGIN SYSTEM

The Questions-in-the-Margin System incorporates seven important steps needed to master any subject. Each step thoroughly done in sequence will

SURVEY	Read the title and speculate about what the chapter will be about. Read the headings to determine what ideas and facts will be presented. Read any summarizing section.
QUESTION	Turn each heading into a question by adding such words as "what," "how," or "who." Then read to answer the question.
READ	Read several paragraphs; then come back to the first paragraph and ask questions such as these: What is the main idea? How do the supporting materials support it? What do I need to know in this paragraph?
QUESTIONS IN MARGINS	Think deeply; then formulate and write a brief, telegraphic question in the margin. Next, underline very sparingly only the key words and phrases that make up the answer. The less underlining, the better.
RECITE	Counteract forgetting by reciting. Cover your textbook page, exposing only your questions in the margin. Then, in your own words, recite aloud the answers. After reciting, check for accuracy. Recite until you've completed the chapter.
REVIEW	Immediately after reciting, take a fresh look at each question; mentally glimpse and hold the answer for a few moments. In this way, work through the entire chapter. This overview of questions and answers will tend to snap the separate parts together like pieces of a jigsaw puzzle, enabling you to see the chapter as a whole. Intersperse reviews throughout the semester.
REFLECT	Manipulate the ideas and facts mentally. Turn them over, speculate on them, compare one with the other, notice where they agree and differ. Organize them under larger categories, or compress them into smaller units. Finally, free them from the chapter by weaving them into your existing knowledge.

FIGURE 8.2 The Questions-in-the-Margin System

help you see the author's facts and ideas more and more clearly. When you finish the seventh step, you will feel as though you had put the last piece of a jigsaw puzzle in place: You will see the full picture, which will image itself indelibly in your memory. Figure 8.2 is an overview of the system.

Step 1: Surveying a Textbook Chapter

Surveying has various uses, but its greatest use is in mastering textbook assignments. It is the grease that makes subsequent reading and studying more efficient. A good scholar would no more begin reading a chapter without first skimming it than an automotive engineer would run a car without first greasing it. The grease does not supply the power, but without it the gasoline would not be of much use.

If you skip this step, you will lose time, not save time. If you burrow directly into one paragraph after another, you'll be unearthing one compartmentalized fact after another, but you won't see how the facts relate to each other. Psychologists call this not-seeing-the-big-picture condition *tunnel vision*.

Here is how a student who had developed the technique of surveying to a fine art described this step:

> I first spend two or three minutes trying to get the full meaning out of the title of the chapter. I even wonder briefly why the author picked such a title. Then I shove off by saying to myself, "Let's see what he has to say about this subject."
>
> Next, I read the first couple of paragraphs in the regular way. If I don't do this, it's like coming into the middle of a conversation: I can't make head or tail of it.
>
> Then I let the printer guide me. My eyes dart to the big-type headings and subheadings. I read them because I know that they are like the small headlines for newspaper items. They are little summaries. I then read a sentence or two underneath these headings. My eyes float over the rest of the material looking for other islands of information. They might be marked by clues such as italicized words, underlined words, and changes in the type.
>
> When I first started to skim, I used to skip all the illustrations, charts, and diagrams. But after getting burned on exams, I found I could learn a lot very easily just by reading the captions and noticing what the lines on the diagrams and graphs meant. At least for me, illustrations stick in my mind better than words do; so during an exam, I take advantage of this. I close my eyes and see the illustration on the blackboard of my mind.
>
> I'm always careful to read the last paragraph or last section marked "summary." That's where the author gathers together all the main ideas of the chapter.
>
> Finally, I pause for a few minutes to bring all these pieces and fragments together before I begin reading and taking notes on the chapter. Sometimes to bring things together, I go back to the beginning of the chapter and leaf through the pages without reading, just looking at what I have already looked at.
>
> There are a few other things that skimming does for me. First, I no longer put off studying. Skimming is easy, so I don't mind getting started. Second, once I get into the chapter, I find that most of the chapters contain some interesting information, so I become interested. Third, because I am interested in the material, I concentrate better. And fourth, the topics that I find by skimming somehow make good topic headings for my notes.

When you skim, don't dawdle. Move along with good comprehension, but go slowly enough to get the facts, ideas, and principles accurately. Once assimilated, a mistake is hard to eradicate.

There are four practical reasons why surveying can make a real and immediate difference in your reading.

1. Surveying Creates a Background. When you don't have some prior knowledge about the subject matter of an assigned chapter, you read slowly and have difficulty understanding the material. When you come to something that you recognize, your reading speed quickens and your comprehension grows. The difference is your prior knowledge. Surveying prepares you for reading by giving you some background information about a chapter. Surveying counteracts tunnel vision. Once you have viewed the broad canvas, you will see how individual ideas fit into the complete picture.

When you skim a chapter, you spot and pick up topics by reading headings and subheadings. You pick up ideas by reading the first and last sentences of paragraphs. You become familiar with the names of people and places by skimming these names. You grasp the general objective of the chapter by reading the introductory paragraph, and you get an overview by reading the summarizing paragraph at the end of the chapter. You won't know any of these facts and ideas cold, of course. But when you meet them again during your careful reading, you will recognize them, and this familiarity will give you confidence and understanding.

2. Surveying Provides Advance Organizers. According to David P. Ausubel, a learning-theory psychologist, a preview of the general content of a chapter creates *advance organizers,* which help students learn and remember material they later study closely. The familiar landmarks act as topics or categories under which ideas, facts, and details may be clustered. John Livingston Lowes, a professor of literature at Princeton University, characterized such familiar landmarks as *magnetic centers* around which ideas, facts, and details cluster like iron filings around a magnet.

George Katona, a psychologist, tested the effectiveness of advance organizers with two groups of students. One group was asked to read a selection in which a general principle of economics was stated in the first sentence. The second group was given the same selection, but with the first sentence deleted. When the students in the first group were tested, they not only remembered the specific content of the paragraph better than the second group, but they were able to apply the general principle to all the examples in the selection. Without the first sentence, which was an advance organizer, students in the second group viewed the examples as separate, unrelated entities and were unable to see that the examples could be clustered under the one umbrella of a common principle in economics.

3. Surveying Limbers the Mind. For an athlete, a pregame warm-up limbers muscles, and it also limbers the psyche and brain. An athlete knows that success comes from the coordination of smoothly gliding muscles, a positive attitude, and a concentrating mind. The prestudy survey of a textbook achieves for the scholar what the pregame warm-up achieves for the athlete.

4. Surveying Overcomes Mental Inertia. How often have you said with impatience and exasperation, "Let's get started!" Getting started is hard. According to Newton's first law of motion, "A body in motion tends to remain in motion; a body at rest tends to remain at rest."

Many students find it difficult to open a textbook and begin to study. If you are one of them, use surveying to ease yourself into studying. Surveying does the job: It gets you started.

You need not always survey an entire chapter as the first step. You may begin by surveying the first part before you read it. Later, as you work your way through the chapter, you may want to skim farther ahead, page by page, as you read and study to understand.

Step 2: Turning Headings into Questions

The people who have *answers to give* when they are finished reading are usually those who had *questions to ask* before and during their reading. Asking questions works for one main reason: The questions force you to concentrate and to observe the words keenly, directly, and selectively as you read. When you don't have a question in mind, your eyes just glide over a paragraph, and you never realize that the printed words are alive with answers. In the words of John Lubbock (1834–1913), naturalist, banker, writer, neighbor of Charles Darwin, and coiner of the words *paleolithic* and *neolithic*, "What we see depends mainly on what we look for."

As you read, you should interrogate the writer, not simply stare at the words. You must approach each paragraph like an inquiring reporter, with definite and searching questions. The better your questions, the better will be your comprehension.

How do you formulate warm-up questions as you read and study a textbook? One technique is to turn each heading into a question. For example, the main heading "Basic Aspects of Memory" could be turned into the question "What are the basic aspects of memory?" The technique is simple, but it works. Here are some additional examples:

Subtopic Heading	*Question Formulated*
The Memory Trace	What is a memory trace?
Rate of Forgetting	How fast do we forget?
Organization of Recall	How is recall organized?
Decay Theory	What is the decay theory?

Once you have turned a heading into a question, you read the material under the heading to answer your question. If the question is answered early in the discussion, ask another, based on what you have read.

There are general questions that you can use in reading about almost any topic. Some readers prefer to ask these general questions to uncover specific facts and ideas. Other readers just enjoy conversing with the writer through the use of a general question-and-answer technique. In either case, an active, searching attitude is created. Here are some of the general questions:

- What does this paragraph tell me?
- What are the important supporting details?
- Does this example make the main point clear?
- What evidence does the writer give?
- What is the underlying principle?
- If this fact or idea is true, then what logically follows?
- If it is true, how does it affect my existing knowledge?
- How does this paragraph fit in with this chapter?
- What questions might I be asked about this paragraph?

Some practical readers ask not only "What is the author saying?" but also "How can I use this information?" If you ask such questions, make it a rule to try to answer them. Say something. Say anything that makes sense to you. Without effort, there's no gain.

A great deal is said these days about learning how to think: Books are written; lectures are given; and teachers exhort. The subject of thinking can be summarized in this one line: Thinking at its highest level is asking the right, relevant question.

Step 3: Reading Paragraph by Paragraph

After surveying the chapter, return to the first paragraph and read it thoroughly enough to answer only one question: What did the author say in this paragraph? If you are unable to answer this question at first, you must reread the paragraph until you can; otherwise you will not gain a functional understanding of the paragraph.

This is a crucial step. You must not move ahead to succeeding paragraphs if doing so means leaving the present paragraph unsettled. You may push on beyond a problem paragraph for the purpose of gaining context, but always with the intention of coming back to the problem paragraph. Remember that understanding a succession of paragraphs leads to comprehension of the chapter.

Guard against the habit of moving your eyes over the lines of print without grasping the writer's ideas. Read for the ideas and concepts behind the words. Pause at the end of each paragraph or at the end of a series of paragraphs, and in your own words describe the writer's main idea and the supporting details. Answer the question "What did I learn in this paragraph?" When you have described, you have understood.

The Topic Sentence. Use the topic sentence to help you break into the meaning of each paragraph. The topic sentence often contains the main idea or points to the main idea.

In Figure 8.3, the first sentence, the topic sentence, states the main idea. The rest of the paragraph is a long list of concrete examples supporting the main idea. The last sentence is not a continuation of the list; it rounds out or completes the paragraph. Incidentally (but importantly), notice how the writer sustains the mood of despondency from the opening sentence, through the examples, into the last clause of the last sentence.

Textbook Troubleshooting. As you read and study your textbook, your businesslike side should keep asking, "Am I getting it?" If the answer is, "It's getting pretty vague," you should take immediate action.

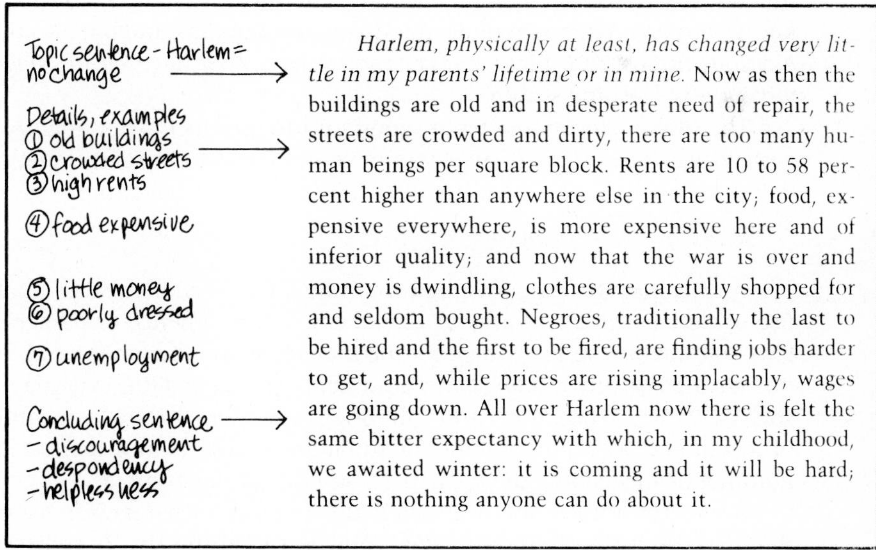

Harlem, physically at least, has changed very little in my parents' lifetime or in mine. Now as then the buildings are old and in desperate need of repair, the streets are crowded and dirty, there are too many human beings per square block. Rents are 10 to 58 percent higher than anywhere else in the city; food, expensive everywhere, is more expensive here and of inferior quality; and now that the war is over and money is dwindling, clothes are carefully shopped for and seldom bought. Negroes, traditionally the last to be hired and the first to be fired, are finding jobs harder to get, and, while prices are rising implacably, wages are going down. All over Harlem now there is felt the same bitter expectancy with which, in my childhood, we awaited winter: it is coming and it will be hard; there is nothing anyone can do about it.

FIGURE 8.3 The Topic Sentence
Source: James Baldwin, Notes of a Native Son *(Boston: Beacon Press, 1955), p. 57.*

1. Go back a couple of paragraphs to pick up the thread of the writer's ideas again.
2. Read ahead a couple of paragraphs to see where you're going.
3. Open your dictionary and look up any words that you are not sure of and that might be holding you back.
4. Reread the troublesome paragraph aloud, using exaggerated expression and emphasis to get at the meaning of what's being said. Such reading aloud, especially with expression, brings concentration back to a 100 percent level.

The Corson Technique. Dale Corson, former president of Cornell University and dean of the College of Engineering, observed that engineers and other students in science and mathematics must often crack the meaning of an idea or concept one sentence at a time. If comprehension does not occur even at this snail's pace, then you must ask your instructor for help. "But before you do," says Dr. Corson, "ask yourself this question: What is it that I don't understand?"

Under no circumstance should you go to the instructor, open the book, and with a broad sweep of your hand say, "I don't understand this." When you go for help, you should be able to say, "I understand and follow the writer's idea up to this point and even beyond this point, but for some reason this particular section has no meaning for me." That way, the instructor knows not only what you understand and don't understand but also that you did your utmost to achieve understanding. You now have set the stage for a meaningful learning session.

The Corson Technique has a wonderful by-product. After analyzing and verbalizing your problem, after you have viewed it from several angles, you will most likely have solved it yourself. You may not have to discuss it with anyone else.

Additional Reading Strategies. When you read sentences, make full use of signal words and organizational clues. If a sentence or paragraph begins "on the one hand," watch for the inevitable "on the other hand," which introduces the other side of the argument. Innocent little everyday words such as "since," "because," and "although" are as important in relating parts of a sentence as a plus, minus, or square-root sign is in a math equation. Ignoring or misreading them can get you into serious trouble.

If you get bogged down in a difficult sentence or paragraph, try reading the material without any modifying phrases. Find the simple subject of the sentence, the verb, and the simple object, to avoid getting lost in a maze of language. When the framework shows through clearly, so that you can grasp the main idea, then go back and read the material with all its "trimmings," to get its full sense.

After you finish a paragraph and summarize it, don't plunge immediately into the next paragraph. Pause for a minute or two, to think about the meaning of the paragraph you just read. Such a thinking pause provides time for the main idea to consolidate, to sink into your memory.

Whenever you encounter a difficult, unusual, or new word or term in your textbook, look it up in a glossary or dictionary. Put these words and terms, with their definitions, on 3×5 cards. You can learn these words and terms by carrying the cards and looking them over whenever you have a chance.

When you feel bored, do not reward your boredom by slamming your book shut and leaving empty-minded. Above all, don't reward yourself by going to a movie. If you get bored, give yourself the limited objective of extracting one nugget of knowledge, be it ever so small. Then, with that *accomplished,* you have *earned* the right to a break or a movie.

Step 4: Writing Questions in the Margins

The question-in-the-margin step is different in purpose from the question step of the SQ3R Method. In the SQ3R Method, the purpose of the question is to keep the reader alert, concentrating, and looking for an answer to the limited question that was asked. The question step of SQ3R directs the reader to turn headings and subheadings into questions. Obviously, putting "what" or "how" in front of a heading does not transform it automatically into a deep and searching question. A heading that is limited to begin with will remain limited after the addition of "what" or "how."

To be sure, this does not mean that the question step in SQ3R is not a good one. It serves a definite and valuable purpose when you are reading paragraphs or sections of the textbook for the first time. However, it is hard to imagine that you will be able to formulate a provocative question on textbook material before you have read, understood, and thought about the material. Merely asking a question before reading does not in any way guarantee that an answer will be forthcoming, regardless of how hard you read. Coming up with answers is not easy. Usually you have to dig hard for a comprehensive, accurate answer, and that is why the question-in-the-margin step comes into the system at this time—after you have read a paragraph thoroughly.

Once you have read a paragraph thoroughly and have been able to answer questions such as "What is the main idea here?" or "What are the important points made here?" you are ready to formulate and write a brief, telegraphic question in the margin of your textbook. After writing the question, you should then, for the first time, underline very sparingly only the key words and phrases that make up the answer. The less underlining you do, the better (see Chapter 9 for a detailed discussion of making notes in your textbook). Later, when you review for an exam, your eyes and mind will be directed to the words and phrases that deliver the meaning directly and efficiently. When you underline only the key words and phrases, you have to think, and thinking is what makes understanding and remembering possible.

Go through the entire chapter in this way: reading thoroughly to understand the passage; writing a brief, meaningful question; and underlining sparingly. Figure 8.4 shows the questions-in-the-margin technique applied to a textbook page.

Step 5: Reciting Based on the Questions in the Margin

After formulating questions on the entire chapter, go back to the beginning of the chapter and cover the printed text with a blank sheet of paper, exposing only the questions you've written in the margin. Read the first question aloud, and answer the question in your own words. Slide the blank sheet down to check your answer. If your answer is wrong or incomplete, recite it aloud again. Do this until you get the answer right. Go through the entire chapter in this way. Your aim is to establish in your memory an accurate, crystal-clear impression, because that's what you want to return to later

WRITING GOOD PAPERS IN COLLEGE

What 2 aspects lead to success?

The techniques of writing a good paper are easy to follow. You should remember two important aspects that lead to success. First, start work early on the paper. Second, if you have a choice, choose a subject that you are interested in, or that you can develop an interest in.

What 3 elements might make up a paper?

Much of your work in college involves absorbing knowledge; when it comes to writing papers, you have the opportunity to put down on paper what you've learned about a subject, and perhaps your opinions and conclusions on the subject.

What's the key in choosing a topic?

If not sure of a topic, do what?

Writing is an important form of communication. To communicate well you must have something you really want to say. So if you have a choice of topics, choose one that intrigues you. If it isn't one that everyone else is writing on, all the better. If you're not sure about your choice of topic, do a little preliminary research to see what's involved in several topics before you make a final decision. Remember the caution about allowing yourself enough time? Here's where it comes into play. Take enough time to choose a topic carefully (see Chapter 15 for specific pointers).

FIGURE 8.4 Writing Questions in the Margin

during an exam. If the impression in your memory is fuzzy at this time, it will be even fuzzier three or four weeks later.

Why Recite Aloud? Reciting aloud forces you to think, and it is this thinking that leaves behind in your memory a neural trace to come back to. You must believe, without an iota of doubt and without a moment of hesitation, that forgetting is and will continue to be your major academic problem. Forgetting erodes, corrodes, and thwarts learning. Forgetting never lets up. It works continuously to expel from memory what you worked so hard—often far into the night—to put there. Don't let forgetting get the upper hand. You can bring forgetting almost to a standstill by using the power of recitation.

Reciting promotes concentration, forms a sound basis for understanding the next paragraph or the next chapter, provides time for the memory trace to consolidate, ensures that facts and ideas are remembered accurately, and provides immediate feedback on how you're doing (and when you know that you're doing well, you will make progress). Moreover, experiments have shown that the greater the proportion of reciting time to reading time, the greater is the learning. Students who spent 20 percent of their time reading and 80 percent reciting did much better than students who spent less time reciting and more time reading.

When you recite aloud, don't mumble. Express the ideas in complete sentences, using the proper signal words. For example, when you are reciting a list of ideas or facts, enumerate them by saying "first," "second," and so on. Insert words such as "furthermore," "however," and "finally." When you do so in oral practice, you will do so most naturally in writing during an exam.

The New Way: Reciting and Visualizing. Visualizing is a powerful new technique for increasing your learning and your remembering. As you recite, instead of just mouthing the answer, picture yourself as a scholar-orator standing by your seat in the classroom reciting your answer to the instructor. Although you are actually sitting at your desk in your room and reciting in a lively manner, in your mind's eye you are standing in the classroom speaking, explaining, and gesturing.

Many successful athletes use visualization all the time. They burn such a positive image in their minds that it becomes part of the subconscious, and they expect the performance that they visualized to be carried out in actuality. Dwight Stones, a former U.S. Olympic high jumper, is very well known for the way in which he visualizes each jump before he actually makes it. There's nothing subtle about Stones. As he stands staring at the bar, his head bobs and you can almost visualize his jump yourself. His little routine might almost be comical except for one thing: Stones has won countless gold medals in international competition, and so instead of being laughed at for his peculiar routine, he is widely imitated by younger athletes who literally and figuratively are hoping to reach the heights that Stones has achieved.

Picture yourself in a classroom writing the answer to an essay question. Visualize the entire scene: the classroom, the other students, the instructor, the exam being handed out, your reading the questions. Now look at your textbook; read the question in the margin aloud; think for a few moments how you plan to organize and deliver your answer. Then, as if you were in an exam, recite softly to yourself and at the same time write your answer as you would if the exam were real. Try to *see* yourself in the classroom, thinking and writing forcefully and successfully. In this way you'll be creating in your brain cells a deep, well-defined pattern that will be easy to come back to and follow when the real exam is given. In Chapter 10, you will learn more about how to think visually.

Step 6: Reviewing Immediately and Later

Immediately after you have recited the whole chapter, you should finish the session with a general, relaxed overview, using the questions in the margins as cues. The purpose of the general overview is to put together all the separate questions and answers—to snap them together like the parts of a jigsaw puzzle and reveal the chapter as a whole.

This overview is made not by reciting the whole business over again—you've had enough of that for a while. Rather, look thoughtfully at each question in the margin, mentally glimpse the answer, and hold the answer in mind for a few seconds. Proceed through the entire chapter in this way. Don't make this process a chore. Actually, it could be a pleasant process, similar to taking a sweeping glance at a lawn you've finished mowing or a room you've straightened up. Take a last mental look at the questions and answers, and try to see the chapter as a whole.

The immediate review is important—very important—but it is not enough. You should review thoroughly and often. Later reviews should be conducted in the same way as the immediate review: using questions in the margins as cues, one page at a time, aloud, and in your own words. These later reviews will keep you in a state of preparedness for quizzes and exams. There will be no need to cram your head full of ideas and facts on the night before an exam. All you'll need is a refresher, in the same form—one more review.

As you review, look for ways to connect or categorize, to put like things together and to place opposite things opposite each other. Look for common characteristics, differences, or functions by which to categorize facts and ideas. This type of analysis puts you in control and gives you the chance to use your creativity—to bring the textbook to life and bring order to the mass of information you are required to learn. Categorizing also puts to practical use the Magical Number Seven Theory, described in Chapter 5—the finding that the immediate memory seems to be limited to seven categories, which can be as broad as you care to make them.

The best time for a fast review of your textbook is the half hour before going to bed. Things learned then have a way of lingering in the conscious mind during the time before sleep comes and in the subconscious mind after sleep comes.

Step 7: Reflecting on Facts and Ideas

After you learn facts and ideas through recitation and immediate review, let your mind reflect on them. Let it speculate or play with the knowledge you've acquired. To engage in reflection is to bring creativity to your learning. Ask yourself such questions as these: What is the significance of these facts and ideas? What principle or principles are they based on? What else could they be applied to? How do they fit in with what I already know? From these facts and ideas, what else can I learn? When you reflect, you weave new facts and ideas into your existing knowledge. They then become part of your regular stock of thinking tools.

There's a huge difference between proficiency and creativity. You can become proficient by studying your textbooks and lecture notes, but you will never be creative until you try to see beyond the facts, to leap mentally beyond the given. You must reflect on the facts and ideas, because creativity comes only through reflection, not from recitation and review.

To survive academically in college, you have to recite. To grow in creativity and in wisdom, you have to reflect.

The Reciter . . .	*The Reflector . . .*
• Follows strictly the ideas and facts in the textbook	• Pursues ideas and facts through additional reading in the library and goes to original works
• Is bound by the course outline	• Uses the course outline as a point of departure
• Is diligent and disciplined in memorizing but keeps ideas and facts at arm's length	• Is adventuresome and experimental and internalizes facts and ideas
• Is so busy reciting that the framework of the course is vaguely seen or missed	• Is likely to see the framework of the course and to talk to the instructor because of ideas occurring during reflection

• Understands the literal meaning but not the implications of assignments	• Applies learning to various situations
• Learns and accepts facts and ideas in the sequential order of the textbook	• Thinks, hypothesizes, speculates, and then tests ideas independently

Use reflection often. Reflection is a skill you can take with you wherever you go and use in spare moments. You can reflect while walking from one building to another, standing in line, waiting for a friend, or riding a bus. People who have made great discoveries have reported that some of their best insights came in unlikely places and at odd times. A classic example is that of Archimedes (287?–212 B.C.), the greatest mathematician of ancient times, who discovered the natural law of buoyancy while taking a bath. He became so excited that he ran naked through the streets shouting, "Eureka!"

Begin with the facts and ideas you have learned, and become curious about them. Look at them in different ways, combine them, separate them into the basics, try to find out what would happen if the opposite were true, and so on. This may be difficult at first, but it will become easier as your creativity grows. Continue your reflection until your ideas take definite shape. Don't leave them vague. If you need more information, an encyclopedia or a standard source book on the subject will often help you bring fuzzy ideas into focus.

The only type of learning that becomes a permanent part of you and increases your innate wisdom is *advantageous learning*—learning that occurs when you take a voluntary, extra step beyond the mere memorization of facts. That extra step is reflection. In the words of the philosopher Arthur Schopenhauer (1788–1860): "A man may have a great mass of knowledge, but if he has not worked it up by thinking it over for himself, it has much less value than a far smaller amount which he has thoroughly pondered."

SUMMARY

What's the best way to get the semester off to a good start?	Buy all your books just as soon as you've registered, so that you will have time to read the table of contents, preface, introduction, and other up-front material in each textbook.
What good is the preface?	The preface is the one place where most authors drop their scholarly style. As a result,

you may get a clear picture of the man or woman who has written your textbook. In addition, the preface provides information not available elsewhere: what the author's objective is and is not, how the book is organized, how and why the book is different from other books on the same subject, and the author's qualifications for writing the book.

With all that information in the preface, what's the point of the introduction?

Whereas the preface deals in matters broad and general, the author's introduction is often narrow and specific. From the introduction you'll learn the underlying principles of the book. Many students refer to the introduction before they tackle each new chapter, just to be sure that they're on the right track.

How does the SQ3R Method of study work?

In five steps—survey, question, read, recite, and review—the SQ3R Method helps you approach reading assignments systematically. First you survey the headings in a chapter and read the summary at the end. Then you turn these headings into questions. Read so as to answer that question, then look away from the book and briefly recite the answer you've found. Review your notes to get a bird's-eye view of all the points you've raised and their relationship to one another. SQ3R should result in faster reading and efficient learning.

How does the 3Rs System work?

The 3Rs System is for students who work well under the pressure of time and exams. The three steps—read, record, and recite—are simple and direct. First read several paragraphs, then return to the first paragraph and ask yourself what you need to know in the paragraph. Then underline key words, phrases, and sentences containing that information. Jot a brief question that asks for this underlined information. Cover the pages of your assignment and try to answer the questions you've posed in the margins. Recite in this way until you finish the chapter.

How does the Questions-in-the-Margin System work?

This technique combines the simplicity of the 3Rs System with the long-term effectiveness of SQ3R. It has seven clear and helpful steps.

What is the first step in the Questions-in-the-Margin System?

Before you begin to read a textbook assignment in earnest, survey, or skim, it first. The few minutes that you spend surveying a chapter can be invaluable.

Isn't surveying a waste of time?

No. Surveying a chapter can help you in at least four ways: (1) Surveying provides you with background information. (2) Surveying provides advance organizers—familiar landmarks that act as topics or categories around which you can cluster ideas, facts, and details. (3) Surveying readies your mind for the task of reading the textbook chapter. (4) Surveying overcomes mental inertia by easing you into a task (reading your textbook) that you might otherwise have put off.

What is the second step in the Questions-in-the-Margin System?

In the second step, you turn the chapter headings into questions, or you ask some general questions that can be applied to any topic. In either case, you suddenly have a purpose for reading. As a result, you don't simply stare at the words, you interact with them. Remember: Students who have *answers to give* when they finish reading are usually those who had *questions to ask* while they read.

What does the third step, reading paragraph by paragraph, entail?

When you begin to read a textbook chapter, it is crucial for you to understand one paragraph before you move on to the next. You should read and reread until you are able to answer the question "What did the author say in this paragraph?"

Is there a key to understanding the meaning of a paragraph?

Yes. The topic sentence of each paragraph generally contains the main idea or points to the main idea. It is often the first sentence in the paragraph.

What should I do if I can't make sense of a paragraph?

There are five techniques to get yourself out of a jam: (1) Go back a few paragraphs to pick up the thread of the author's ideas. (2) Read ahead a paragraph or two to see what's coming. (3) Grab a dictionary and look up any words that are acting as stumbling blocks. (4) Reread the troublesome paragraph out loud using exaggerated intonation to get at the meaning of the author's words. (5) If the first four techniques don't work, use the Corson Technique: Identify specifically what's causing you trouble. When you take pains to pinpoint a problem, you often wind up solving the problem. If you're still stumped, take your specific question to your instructor.

Are there any other ways to get a lot out of my reading?

Yes. Here are a few: (1) Be on the alert for signal words and organizational clues that tell you where the author is going. (2) To make sense of an especially complex sentence, simplify things by reading the material without any modifiers. (3) Pause after each paragraph so that your mind has a chance to absorb new information. (4) Transfer new and difficult words to 3 × 5 cards, where they can be studied and mastered so that you won't have to look them up again. (5) If you begin to lose interest in your reading, instead of closing the book and giving up, make an effort to extract at least one more piece of information before you move on to something else.

How does step 4, writing questions in the margins, differ from step 2?

In step 2 you were asked to formulate questions primarily to keep you alert and to keep you reading. When you have read a paragraph carefully and thoroughly, you should be able to ask deep and meaningful questions about it—the kind of questions that you are likely to find on an exam. Once you've written a question in the margin, go back to the text itself and underline the key words and terms that aid in answering your question.

Is there any point in going beyond step 4? Isn't writing questions in the margin the way to gain important information?

If you want to remember information, you must recite it. When you have formulated questions for the entire chapter, go back over the text and read your questions aloud one at a time, answering them correctly before you move on. Reciting out loud forces you to think while you recite and helps keep forgetting in check.

How do I apply step 6, reviewing?

Begin with an immediate review. As soon as you've finished reciting a chapter, take a moment to look over your notes in an effort to pull things together in your mind. Formulating the "big picture" improves the likelihood that the facts from the chapter will remain in your memory.

How do I go about reflecting?

Begin by questioning the things you learn. Wonder about their significance, the principles on which they are based, and other ideas they might be applied to. In short, try to see beyond the facts and ideas in the pages of your textbooks.

HAVE YOU MISSED SOMETHING?

1. *Sentence completion.* Complete the following sentences with one of the three words listed below each sentence.

a. Frequent and thorough reviews help to eliminate the need for ____.

recitation cramming reflection

b. When you use the Questions-in-the-Margin System, you should underline the textbook ____________.

sparingly frequently initially

c. Learning is most likely to occur when the proportion of reciting time to reading time is ______________.

high equal low

2. *Matching.* In each blank space in the left column, write the number preceding the phrase in the right column that matches the left item best.

_____ a. Reflection	1. Time-honored way to study textbooks
_____ b. 3Rs System	2. Pinpoints what you don't understand
_____ c. Recitation	3. Reveals author's objectives
_____ d. Review	4. Brings creativity to learning
_____ e. Preface	5. Step not found in the 3Rs System
_____ f. SQ3R Method	6. A three-step study method
_____ g. Corson Technique	7. A powerful weapon for combating forgetting
_____ h. Visualization	8. Adds a new dimension to the learning process

3. *True-false.* Write *T* beside the *true* statements and *F* beside the *false* statements.

_____ a. The first few pages of a textbook should usually be skipped.

_____ b. The Questions-in-the-Margin System has seven steps.

_____ c. Surveying a chapter provides advance organizers.

_____ d. Visualization will weaken the power of recitation.

_____ e. Answers to questions in the margin may be written as well as recited.

4. *The preface.* Write "yes" next to the common characteristics of a textbook preface.

_____ a. Tells what the author's objective is

_____ b. Deals with matters narrow and specific

_____ c. Explains why the book is different from other books on the same subject

_____ d. Serves as a guide for upcoming chapters

_____ e. Tells what the author's objective is not

_____ f. Presents the organizational plan of the book

5. *Multiple choice.* Choose the word that completes the following sentence most accurately, and circle the letter that precedes it.

The Questions-in-the-Margin System ultimately aids your mind's ability to

a. recall
b. recognize
c. reflect
d. rephrase

CHAPTER 9

Making Notes in and from Your Textbook

A book is a very good institution! To read a book, to think it over, and to write out notes is a useful exercise; a book which will not repay some hard thought is not worth publishing.

Maria Mitchell (1818–89), astronomer, the first woman admitted as a fellow to the American Academy of Arts and Sciences

Studying a textbook without a pen or pencil in your hand is like reading with your eyes closed. Whether the notes you take are written in your textbook or in a separate notebook, one thing is certain: In order to remember important ideas, you must make written notes. This chapter describes two systems of textbook marking and one of note taking done in a separate notebook, and it provides guidelines for

- The Standard System
- The Questions-in-the-Margin System
- The Separate Notes System
- Reading and taking notes on collateral material

and finally

- Using your notes

There's almost no limit to the amount of work you can put into studying your textbooks. It is hard work, but it can be pleasurably rewarding if it's done right. To do it right, you must mark up the pages of your textbooks or take notes in a separate notebook. Taking notes on textbook material forces you to concentrate and makes reviewing not only easier but also more profitable. In the absence of chapter notes, reviewing for an exam is like starting from scratch, from square one. The more careful your note taking, the more knowledge you'll gain from reviewing. You have three systems to choose from:

- Standard System: underlining and jotting notes in the margins
- Questions-in-the-Margin System: writing questions in the margins and selectively underlining
- Separate Notes System: summarizing each textbook paragraph in a separate notebook

THE STANDARD SYSTEM

Here are some guidelines for using the Standard System to mark up your textbooks.

1. *Finish reading before marking.* Never mark until you have finished reading a full paragraph or a headed section and have paused to think about what you've just read. This no-marking procedure prevents you from grabbing at everything that looks important at first glance. During your initial reading, it may be difficult to tell whether the author is stating a new idea or using new words to restate an idea previously discussed. You need to understand the full context of a paragraph or section before you decide what to mark.

2. *Be extremely selective.* Mark so that when you review later, only meaningful words, phrases, and sentences stand out. You'll appreciate your good original judgments, decisions, and discipline.

3. *Use your own words.* Jottings in the margins should be in your own words. Because your own words represent your own thinking, they are powerful cues to the ideas on the page.

4. *Work swiftly.* Be efficient. Don't dawdle. Read, go back for a mini-overview, make your markings and jottings. Then move on.

5. *Work neatly.* Neatness is scholarly. Neatness at first takes conscious effort but not extra time. When you review, your neat jottings and markings will etch sharper, clearer, more incisive images in your mind.

6. *Use cross-referencing.* If you find an idea on page 64 that has a direct bearing on an idea on page 28, draw a little arrow pointing upward and write "28" by it in the margin. Then turn back to page 28 and, alongside the idea there, draw an arrow pointing downward and write "64" by it. In this way you tie the two ideas together both in your mind and in your reviewing.

7. *Be systematic.* Figure 9.1 contains twelve suggestions for marking textbooks. Notice especially the use of single and double underlines; the use of asterisks, circling, and boxing for important items; and the use of the top and bottom margins for long notations or summaries. If some of these ideas appeal to you, work them into your marking system. Be sure to use them consistently so that you will remember instantly what they mean.

Textbook marking can be a useful aid to study and review, but marking must be done with thought and care. Otherwise it becomes busy-work. Drawing lines and boxes and inserting symbols and question marks can give you a false sense of accomplishment if you are not thinking deeply about what you read. Besides, if you overmark your book, you will defeat your purpose: quick identification of important points. When you review, you will find yourself trying to decipher a code instead of reviewing ideas. Figure 9.2 shows a page that is overmarked but still makes good use of some of the Standard System techniques.

Remember that the "you" who reviews the marked book will not be quite the same "you" who did the marking. As the term progresses, your knowledge grows. By the end of the term, many things that seemed so important to underscore, box, circle, star, question, comment on, or disagree with at the beginning of the term you will be accepting as commonplace. Your early marks may hamper your review. So use the help that marking can give you, but don't go overboard.

On the following pages are examples of appropriately marked textbook pages. Figure 9.3 shows how a brief marginal note can expand a title into a summary that will be invaluable for review. It gives the dates of the Crusades, since dates are important, and ties them to a date that is instantly meaningful—1492. The cryptic "13C" is an abbreviation for "thirteenth century." Notice also the summary notes in the margin and the circles representing concepts and geographical locations to be looked up. Underlining is used sparingly and effectively, so that review will be easy.

Figure 9.4 shows how material can be organized by numbering key concepts. If they are already numbered for you in the text, that's great. If they are not, then impose your own organization. Add your own numbers—and letters, too, if they are needed for subtopics. In any case, carry the numbers and letters over to your marginal notes, so that later you can recall the entire

EXPLANATION AND DESCRIPTION	*SYMBOLS, MARKINGS, AND NOTATIONS*
1. Use double lines under words or phrases to signify main ideas.	Radiation can produce mutations . . .
2. Use single lines under words or phrases to signify supporting material.	comes from cosmic rays . . .
3. Mark small circled numbers near the initial word of an underlined group of words to indicate a series of arguments, facts, ideas—either main or supporting.	Conditions change . . . ① rocks rise . . . ② some sink . . . ③ the sea dashes . . . ④ strong winds . . .
4. Rather than underlining a group of three or more important lines, use a vertical bracket in the margin.	had known . . . who gave . . . the time . . . of time . . .
5. Use one asterisk in the margin to indicate ideas of special importance, and two for ideas of unusual importance. Reserve three asterisks for principles and high-level generalizations.	* When a nuclear blast is . . . ** People quite close to the . . . *** The main cause of mutations . . .
6. Circle key words and terms.	The (genes) are the . . .
7. Box words of enumeration and transition.	[fourth,] the lack of supplies . . . [furthermore,] the shortage . . .
8. Place a question mark in the margin, opposite lines you do not understand, as a reminder to ask the instructor for clarification.	? The latest . . . cold period . . . about 1,000,000 . . . Even today . . .
9. If you disagree with a statement, indicate that in the margin.	Disagree Life became . . . on land only . . . 340 million years . . .
10. Use the top and bottom margins of a page to record ideas of your own that are prompted by what you read.	Why not use carbon dating? Check on reference of fossils found in Tennessee stone quarry.
11. On sheets of paper that are smaller than the pages of the book, write longer thoughts or summaries; then insert them between the pages.	Fossils Plants = 500,000,000 years old Insects = 260,000,000 " " Bees = 100,000,000 " " True fish = 330,000,000 " " Amphibians = 300,000,000 " " Reptiles = 300,000,000 " " Birds = 150,000,000 " "
12. Even though you have underlined the important ideas and supporting materials, still jot brief cues in the side margins.	Adapt – . . . . fossil – . . . . layer – . . . .

FIGURE 9.1 Using the Standard System to Mark Textbooks

Color Vision in Animals

Color vision is extremely puzzling to the physiologist; we have no satisfactory theory of color vision, nor can we explain how we see color. For example, we cannot explain why we see white light if we mix spectrally pure red (656 mμ) and blue-green (492 mμ), or why the sensation of spectral green can be perfectly matched by a mixture of yellow and blue. We do know, however, that all shades of color can be matched by appropriate mixtures of three so-called primary colors: red, yellow, and blue. A deviating color vision, known as color blindness, is associated with reduced acuity for shades of green or red (or both). It is quite common in man, occurring in about 8 per cent of all males and 0.6 per cent of females.

From our own experience, each of us knows that he sees colors and that these colors have names, and by inference we assume (although we have no proof) that when somebody says "red" he has the same experience we have. Such inference, however, is completely unjustified when it comes to animals of a different species, with whom we cannot talk; but even so, we can discover some facts about color vision in animals. We really want the answers to two questions: first, whether an animal can see light of a given color at all and, secondly, whether different colors are perceived differently so that they can be distinguished.

Some simple tests can often answer our first question. If a chicken is fed in a darkroom that has rice grains scattered on the floor and the grains are illuminated with spectral colors, the animals will pick up all the grains in red, yellow, and green light, but not the ones in blue light, although these are clearly visible to us. Evidently the chicken eye is not able to perceive blue as light. In a similar fashion we can show that honeybees are insensitive to red, and, by using red light, we can observe their life in the "darkness" inside the hive without disturbing them. On the other hand, bees are sensitive to ultraviolet, which we do not see.

Our second question—can animals distinguish colors? —has been answered by training experiments. If, for example, bees are trained to feed from a dish of sugar solution placed on a yellow disk, they will rapidly learn to seek food on a yellow background. If the full dish is now placed on a blue background and an empty dish on the yellow, the bees will continue seeking food on the yellow background. With a careful application of this and other training experiments, we are able to show that bees can distinguish colors (although we do not know *what* they see). In similar ways, it has been shown that at least some teleost fishes can discriminate colors, but elasmobranchs cannot. Turtles, lizards, and birds have color vision, but most mammals, except man and monkeys, are unable to discriminate color.

FIGURE 9.2 Too Much Marking
A well-meaning but overly conscientious student can defeat the purpose of marking. When you try to emphasize too much, you emphasize nothing. *Source: Text from* Animal Physiology *by Knut Schmidt-Nielsen, pp. 89–90. Copyright © 1960 by Prentice-Hall, Inc., Englewood Cliffs, N.J. Reprinted by permission of the publisher.*

The Crusades

1096 - to late 13C. - and 200 years before Columbus

From the time when they occurred to the present, the crusades have commanded public attention and called forth innumerable chronicles, histories long and short, and even poems. Their place in the historiographical tradition of Europe is thus assured, and the very word crusade has become familiar in our vocabulary. But if historians, mediaeval and modern, have agreed that the crusades were interesting and important, they have differed widely in explaining their origins and interpreting their significance. Indeed, it might be questioned whether they belong in a discussion of the mediaeval church. They were, however, launched originally by the papacy; and the church's role, though it diminished, was never negligible. In this brief account it will be possible only to summarize the more generally accepted conclusions.

Causes 1. Seljuks

Manzikert

First, it is clear that the eight large expeditions from 1096 to the later years of the thirteenth century, as well as the many less important ventures, were occasioned by the political and military successes of Islam. In particular, they were a response to a comparatively new menace presented in the second half of the eleventh century by the Seljuk Turks. The Seljuks had overrun the Bagdad caliphate and as a consequence of a resounding victory over a Byzantine army at Manzikert in 1071 opened the way to the conquest of Asia Minor. Byzantium had faced Islam across the straits before, but never had it lost the entire hinterland of Asia Minor.

2. 11C energy; Cluny; Expansion

Second, the crusades were made possible by the religious, political, and economic energy so characteristic of the eleventh century. The Cluny reform reached a climax in the second half of the century, and it was not difficult for an ecclesiastically militant church to direct its forces to the military defense of Christendom and the recovery of the Holy City, Jerusalem. Politically and economically, eleventh-century Europe was entering one of those periods of expansion which have characterized its civilization down to modern times.

FIGURE 9.3 Simple Marking of a Textbook Page

Source: Reprinted from Marshall W. Baldwin, The Mediaeval Church. *Copyright 1953 by Cornell University. Used by permission of Cornell University Press.*

Memory

> 1. Three stages of memory
> a) acquisition
> b) retention
> c) retrieval

To begin with, we must distinguish among three stages which are implied by any act of remembering. Consider a person working on a crossword puzzle who is trying to recall an eight-letter word meaning "African anteater." If she does, we can be sure that she succeeded in all three stages of the memorial process. The first is **acquisition.** To remember, one must first have learned; the subject must somewhere have encountered this particular item of biological exotica. During this acquisition stage, the relevant experiences presumably left some enduring record in the nervous system, the **memory trace.** Next comes **retention,** during which the information is filed away for later use (until the next crossword puzzle). The final stage is **retrieval,** the point at which one tries to remember, to dredge up this particular memory trace from among all others. Many failures to remember are failures of retrieval and not of storage. Our subject may be unable to come up with the correct answer at the time, but when she later sees the solution she realizes that she knew it all along. "Of course, Aardvark!"

> 2. Methods of retrieval
> a) recall
> b) recognition

A previously acquired item of information can be retrieved in two ways: **recall** and **recognition.** An individual who is asked to recall must produce an item or a set of items. "Where did you park your car?" or "What is the name of the boy who sat next to you in third grade?" are examples of recall questions. The experimental psychologist typically tests for the recall of materials that were learned in the laboratory; this assures that any failures in recall are not simply failures of original acquisition. Thus a subject might have to learn a dozen unrelated adjectives which he will later be asked to recite. Recall need not be verbal. An example is the retention of a motor skill such as playing golf; here memory is best assessed by observing how the subject hits a golf ball and not by how he talks about his swing. Another example is the memory of visual patterns. This is sometimes tested by the method of reproduction in which the subject tries to draw what he has seen. (Unfortunately, such reproduction failures may only prove that he cannot draw and not that he cannot remember.)

A memory trace can also be tapped with a recognition test. A person who is shown an item must indicate whether he has encountered it before, either in general ("Did you ever see this face before?") or in a particular context ("Is this one of the girls who played on your high school field hockey team?"). In the laboratory the subject is usually asked to pick out the previously learned item from among several false alternatives. Examples are multiple-choice or true-false tests which clearly put a greater premium on recognition than do essay or short-answer fill-in examinations, which emphasize recall.

FIGURE 9.4 Marking a Textbook: Numbers and Letters

Source: Reprinted from Psychology *by Henry Gleitman, by permission of W. W. Norton & Company, Inc. Copyright © 1981 by W. W. Norton & Company, Inc.*

the entire "package." In this instance, only the bare key words were placed in the margin, primarily for use as cues in reciting. Too much information in the margin will make reciting too easy.

THE QUESTIONS-IN-THE-MARGIN SYSTEM

The guidelines for using the Questions-in-the-Margin System to mark up your textbook are surprisingly few.

1. *Survey* an entire chapter.
2. *Return* to the first paragraph and read it thoroughly to answer this question: "What's important here?"
3. *Write* a brief, telegraphic question in the margin of your textbook that requires for an answer the important point or points that you perceive in the paragraph.
4. *Underline* only the key words, phrases, and sentences that make up the answer to the question you wrote in the margin.

These four steps provide you with the essential questions and the appropriate answers. With this strong, uncomplicated system, you need nothing else (see Chapter 8 for a detailed discussion of this system).

Figure 9.5 is an example of how to formulate the questions. Your questions may be specific or general—whichever best helps you master the facts and ideas in your textbook. To add interest and variety, make up some true-false questions as well as some fill-ins. The closer your questions are to actual test questions, the better will be your memory of the facts and ideas.

THE SEPARATE NOTES SYSTEM

Here are some guidelines for making separate notes on the material in your textbooks.

1. *Use the Cornell Note-taking System format.* Mark a 2½-inch margin on the left of your paper, leaving a 6-inch-wide area on the right in which to make notes (see Figure 7.4, page 000). Use the narrow margin for key words. This is the ideal format for recording, reciting, and reviewing. Figures 9.6 and 9.7 illustrate this format.

	Watch Out For Quicksand!
What happened to Jack Pickett? *How long did it take?*	While hiking in the swamplands of Florida, Fred Stahl watched Jack Pickett disappear before his eyes. Pickett had stepped onto what looked like an innocent patch of dry sand and then started to sink. Within fifteen minutes, Pickett had disappeared completely beneath the surface.
Is quicksand real?	Pickett was a victim of quicksand. If you think quicksand is something found only in adventure novels or films, you're making a big mistake. And that mistake could cost you your life.
What did a geologist say about Q.S.? *Where is Q.S. found?*	Geologist Gerald H. Matthes, who once escaped from quicksand himself, always gave this message to hikers: "Anyone who ever walks off the pavement should learn about quicksand." It can be found almost anywhere.
If Q.S. is firm, what to do? *If Q.S. is soft, what to do?* *Why not raise your arms?* *What kind of movements to make?* *What kind, not to make?* *Two ways to get out of Q.S.?* *Final advice?*	Here are some of Matthes' tips on how to prevent being helplessly sucked under by quicksand. First of all, if you step into quicksand that is firm enough, you may be able to run out. But you have to move fast. If, however, the sand pulls your legs in too quickly for you to escape this way, throw yourself flat on your back. That's right – you can actually float in quicksand. Don't make the common mistake of raising your arms. Resting on the surface, your arms can help you to float. Any movements you make should be slow and deliberate. Quick, jerky movements can cause you to be completely sucked in, just as Jack Pickett was. Try doing a slow breaststroke or slowly rolling yourself to firm ground. Above all, don't panic.

FIGURE 9.5 Questions-in-the-Margin System

Key Words	Notes on the Chapter
Contour Lines	General Rules for contour lines
1. Steep slope	1. Steep slope – lines close together.
2. gentle slope	2. Gentle slope – lines are spread.
3. Cross	3. Lines never cross
4. streams	4. Lines crossing streams – bend upstream.

FIGURE 9.6 The Cornell Format Used for Material Emphasizing Facts

Key Words	Notes on the Chapter
Song of Roland defeat french valor magic horn no love story knighthood	Song of Roland (medieval epic) One of the noblest poems in Europe. Celebrating a defeat, the french fought with such supreme valor that the defeat was vindicated. Roland had a magic horn which Charlemagne could hear. Poem is wonderfully concentrated on a single incident. Virtually no love story. A rugged, primitive poem. The finest ideals of knighthood have been crystalized in it.

FIGURE 9.7 Notes on Material Emphasizing Ideas and Relationships

2. *Finish reading before you take notes.* Never write a note until you have finished reading a full paragraph or a headed section. This prohibition will keep you from summarizing everything that looks important at first glance.

3. *Be extremely selective.* Pick out the essentials and write them concisely. This rule is probably the most difficult of all to follow, because to be selective you must read critically and think about what you have read. Then you'll be able to summarize each paragraph in *one sentence.* Don't try to master every idea, fact, and detail in the book; get the important ideas and the basic principles. Don't try to rewrite the textbook in longhand, for you won't be accomplishing a thing. Simply read the paragraph and reread it if necessary, decide *at that time* what is important, and write your one-sentence summary.

4. *Use your own words.* After finishing the paragraph or section, ask "What is the author's main point?" Recite it, and then quickly write it in the words you just spoke. Do not mechanically transfer words from the textbook to your notebook. You will be by-passing your mind and wasting time and energy.

5. *Write full sentences.* Do not make notes in outline form. Rather, write full sentences expressing full thoughts. This is what you will have to do during an exam. Also, when you review and restudy, you will be able to perceive each idea instantly. Neat writing will also be of help when you review.

6. *Be swift.* You don't have all day and night for note taking. Keep alert and press for efficiency. Read, go back for a mini-overview, recite the author's idea, and write it. Then attack the next portion of the chapter.

7. *Don't forget visual materials.* Important diagrams, like important facts and

	Chester G. Starr, Jr., The Emergence of Rome, Ch. I: "Geography and People of Ancient Italy" Geography is very influential factor. Italy, long-narrow peninsula in center of Med. Sea. Physical Aspect: Italy divided into 2 sections — peninsula — Med. land imp. in ancient times, other — north of Po R. impt. medieval and modern times. Plains in Italy very hilly — stone villages on hillsides so more room for farming. Climate: Winter - westerly winds with rainstorms. Spring — Sahara blast — drought in summer. Rome: two months without rain. Po Valley — water from Alps.

FIGURE 9.8 Telegraphic, Categorized Notes
The student will jot key words in the left margin during review. *Source: Adapted from Edward W. Fox,* Syllabus for History *(Ithaca, N.Y.: Cornell University Press, 1959). Reprinted by permission of the author.*

ideas, should be transferred to your notebook, recited, and reviewed. In biology, for example, a sure way of memorizing the structure of the amoeba is to sketch it, with all parts labeled. Take notes regarding the important aspects of maps, charts, and tables as well; they are vital parts of your text.

Figure 9.6 shows the kind of notes you might use for material that requires an orderly listing of facts, principles, or rules. Though at first glance the notes in this example may appear to be a formal outline, they are not. The facts in the wide column under "general rules for contour lines" form a simple list, and the sentences are almost complete.

Figure 9.7 shows notes on material that deals more with ideas and their relationships than with facts. Here you would be reading for concepts and theories that are likely to span many paragraphs. You would skim in your overview to get an idea of what the main concepts are and how extensively they are treated. Your task then would be to summarize and condense many paragraphs into one or two.

Slow readers often find that note taking forces them to concentrate better, and they go through each chapter faster than before. Rapid readers slow down a bit, but they learn to read with a new thoroughness.

Edward W. Fox, Cornell University's great teacher, lecturer, and historian, had this to say about note taking:

> Notes are a means to an end and not the end in themselves. Some system is desirable, but a very common failing among beginning students is to develop a method so complicated and formal that it wholly defeats its purpose.
>
> Notes taken in paragraph form on a page with a . . . left-hand margin are the most generally useful. Elaborate arrangements tend to confuse, and the traditional topical form, the use of Roman numerals, capital letters, Arabic numerals, and small letters, etc., with much indentation, has a fatal tendency to imply a logical analysis rather than elicit one.[1]

So you see, it is not only the study-skills experts who advocate note taking. Figure 9.8 is an example taken from Edward Fox's book *Syllabus for History.* In this example, the telegraphic style is combined with categorization, for more powerful notes. Notice, however, that the notes preserve the basic elements of regular sentence structure, even though they are telegraphic. The abbreviations "imp." and "impt." both mean "important."

READING AND TAKING NOTES ON COLLATERAL MATERIAL

In many undergraduate courses, assignments and lectures focus on a single textbook, but instructors often assign outside reading in other publications. Reasons for assigning the extra work include the following:

1. To amplify topics treated in the textbook or mentioned in class lectures
2. To go into greater detail—for example, by assigning original documents or primary sources
3. To expose students to another point of view or a different philosophy
4. To bring background material into discussions

Instructors generally do not expect you to master such collateral material as thoroughly as you master your textbook. Nevertheless, once the assignment has been made, you must cope with it, even though in addition to the collateral reading you have all your regular assignments to do. Clearly, you cannot spend an inordinate amount of time, but you must learn something from your collateral reading. Here are some suggestions for doing so.

[1]Edward W. Fox, *Syllabus for History* (Ithaca, N.Y.: Cornell University Press, 1959). Reprinted by permission of the author.

	I. <u>Introduction</u>
Experiment in living close to nature.	Thoreau voluntarily withdrew from a civilization which he felt was getting too complicated. He spent 2 yrs., 2 mos., and 2 days living at Walden Pond to regain the simplicity of life which comes when one lives close to the soil.
	II. <u>Thesis</u>
Each man should pause to decide just how he should spend his life. Is he paying too dearly for unessentials?	In a complex civilization, the fast flowing current of unessentials stemming from custom, tradition, advertising, etc., somehow sweeps a man away from the genuine goals in life. Only by temporarily cutting oneself off from civilization, could man realize that his life need not be so complex. By getting back to nature to rethink the basic issues of life, man could chart his course, and attempt to steer his life in accordance with these standards (not the expediencies set up by the pressures of complex civilization).
	III. <u>Body</u>
	Thoreau did not wish to hold up progress or civilization; rather, he wished that man would be more contemplative and selective in his actions.
Man should awaken and become aware of real life.	Thoreau chronicled his experiences at Walden Pond. He wanted to become familiar with nature. a. He built his own hut. b. Average cost of living a week was 27 cents. c. He observed nature: trees, birds, animals, etc.
Live simply & you will live more fully.	He believed that every man ought to measure up to the best he could do. What the best is, depends upon the individual. To have a standard to measure up does not mean that all must have the same, but every man should measure up to a standard in the best way he is able to.
	IV. <u>Summary</u>
Urged people to reject unessentials, and get back to fundamentals.	Thoreau wanted to demonstrate that many so-called necessities were not necessary at all. He wanted man to observe, appreciate, and evaluate what was important in life. Once man had set his sights upon the good life, he should follow it without compromising.

FIGURE 9.9 Notes in the Form of a Highly Condensed Summary

1. Try to figure out why the book was assigned. You might ask the instructor. If you find out, then you can skim the book looking for pertinent material, disregarding all the rest.

2. Read the preface. As you already know from Chapter 8, the preface provides inside information. It may tell you how this book is different from your textbook.

3. Study the table of contents. Notice especially the chapter titles to see whether they are like those in your textbook or different. If the chapters with similar titles contain the same information as the chapters in your textbook, then read the chapters that do not duplicate your textbook's coverage. (Do this with topics covered in your classroom lectures, too.)

4. If you have not yet found an "angle," read the summarizing paragraph at the end of each chapter. Make brief notes on each chapter from the information thus gained. With these notes spread out before you, try to see the overall pattern. From the overall pattern, come up with the author's central thesis, principle, problem, solution, or whatever.

5. Don't leave the book with only a vague notion of what it is about. You must come up with something so definite that you can talk about it the next day or write about it two weeks later. Do not waste time on details, but be ready to answer general questions: What was the author's central approach? How was it different from that of your textbook? How was it the same? Look for the central issues around which everything else is organized.

6. Have the courage to think big. If you lack courage, you'll waste time on minor details that you won't remember. Select the big issues and concentrate on them.

When a highly condensed summary of a book or long selection is required, you need a special approach. The introduction–thesis–body–conclusion sequence is useful in forcing you to understand the material and the way the author develops and supports it. (See Chapter 18 for a full explanation of this approach.) Furthermore, a summary that follows this sequence can be highly condensed; you may be able to capture the main ideas of a collateral book in only a page or two of notes. Figure 9.9 is an example.

USING YOUR NOTES

When you have read and comprehended an assignment and have made notes on the central points, you are ready to practice the active recall that will convert facts and concepts into knowledge you can retain and use. Read over your notes to be sure that they say what you mean and are clear enough to mean the same thing weeks and even months later.

If you have not already done so, now is the time to take the final step and summarize the notes you have made. If you have used the Cornell Method for taking separate notes, study the left-hand column key words and the right-hand notes to which they pertain. Write a brief, informative summary at the bottom of the page. If you have used either the Standard System or the Questions-in-the-Margin System, you can summarize your left-hand column notes at the end of the chapter or on a separate piece of paper.

Then study one section of your notes at a time. Cover a portion of the right-hand section with a piece of paper and, from the cues, try to recall the section, reciting aloud or even writing it out. Look again at your notes to see what errors you made or what you forgot. Repeat the process until you can accurately repeat the material in your own words. (This is the same procedure recommended for effective study of lecture notes in Chapter 7.)

There is no better way to prepare for an examination than by training yourself to reproduce your notes without looking at them.

SUMMARY

What's the purpose of marking my textbook?	Marking your textbook promotes concentration and thereby increases understanding. Marks both in the margin and on the text itself simplify reviewing.
What are my options for taking notes?	You have a choice of three systems: (1) the Standard System, (2) the Questions-in-the-Margin System, (3) the Separate Notes System.
What steps are involved in the Standard System?	There are seven steps: (1) Finish reading before marking. (2) Be extremely selective. (3) Use your own words. (4) Work swiftly. (5) Work neatly. (6) Use cross-referencing. (7) Be systematic.
Are there pitfalls to textbook marking?	The major pitfall is overmarking. Your purpose is to aid concentration and review, not to decorate your textbook with circles, underlines, and squiggles. Keep in mind that your learning increases as the semester goes on, so try not to mark too many things that will seem obvious to you in a few weeks. Overmarking will only slow down your review.

What are the guidelines for the Questions-in-the-Margin System?

Survey the entire chapter to get a feel for it. Then read one paragraph at a time. At the end of each paragraph, take a moment to decide what's important. Once you've done this, try to formulate a question that will draw out the paragraph's main point or points. Then underline the words, terms, or phrases that make up the answer to your question.

What are the guidelines for taking separate notes?

Use note paper that has been ruled for the Cornell Note-taking System format. Read a full paragraph before you begin taking notes. Write down only the essentials and, to ensure understanding, express them in your own words. Write complete sentences, swiftly and neatly. Don't ignore the visuals: Treat an important diagram like an important idea. Neither should be left out of your notes.

What are collateral readings?

Collateral readings, also known as outside readings, are books and articles that your instructor assigns to supplement your regular textbook in some way.

Should I approach these readings as I do assignments in my textbook?

No. Instructors generally want you to take a broad view of collateral readings. Start by deciding why your instructor assigned the book. The preface and table of contents usually provide clues, as do summarizing paragraphs at the end of each chapter. Your goal is to grasp the author's main thesis as well as the principles that are applied, the methodology that is used, and the problems and solutions that are mentioned. In short, concentrate on big issues rather than on details.

Should I stop once I've taken notes?

No. Capitalize on what you've learned in the note-taking process by summarizing your notes. If you've used the Cornell System, summarize in the 2″ section at the bottom of the page. If you've used the Standard System or the Questions-in-the-Margin

System, summarize either at the end of the textbook chapter or on a separate sheet of paper. Then cover the right-hand material and use the key words in the left-hand column to recite your notes.

HAVE YOU MISSED SOMETHING?

1. *Sentence completion.* Complete the following sentences with one of the three words listed below each sentence.

a. Try to summarize a textbook paragraph in a single ____________.
   word   phrase   sentence

b. Your questions in the margin should always be ______________.
   specific   general   telegraphic

c. Too much information in the margin will tend to make reciting too ______________________________________.
   easy   long-winded   difficult

2. *Matching.* In each blank space in the left column, write the number preceding the phrase in the right column that matches the left item best.

_____ a. Summarizing
_____ b. Reviewing
_____ c. Overmarking
_____ d. Outlines
_____ e. Amplification
_____ f. Preface
_____ g. Context
_____ h. Selectivity

1. Needed before you can mark efficiently
2. Can create a false sense of accomplishment
3. Can be used in understanding collateral materials
4. Lets only meaningful words, phrases, and sentences stand out
5. Primary activity in the Separate Notes System
6. Should not be used for separate note taking
7. One of the purposes of collateral readings
8. Becomes easier when textbooks are marked

3. *True-false.* Write *T* beside the *true* statements and *F* beside the *false* statements.

_____ a. The Questions-in-the-Margin System works best when used in conjunction with other note-taking methods.

_____ b. Marking your textbook forces you to concentrate.

_____ c. Marginal jottings should be expressed in your own words.

_____ d. True-false questions can be used with the Questions-in-the-Margin System.

_____ e. You can never really overmark your textbook.

_____ f. The "you" who marks your textbook is not the same as the "you" who reviews it.

4. *Separate notes.* Write "yes" next to the guidelines for taking separate notes.

_____ a. Write notes in full sentences.

_____ b. Note each main idea immediately.

_____ c. Use the Cornell note-taking format.

_____ d. Use the instructor's words whenever possible.

_____ e. Pay attention to visual materials.

_____ f. Be extremely selective in the ideas you master.

5. *Multiple choice.* Choose the word that completes the following sentence most accurately, and circle the letter that precedes it.

Rapid readers who take notes

a. read even more quickly
b. read with a new thoroughness
c. no longer need to concentrate
d. all the above

CHAPTER 10

Thinking Visually

A picture shows me at a glance what it takes dozens of pages of a book to expound.

Ivan Turgenev (1818–83), Russian aristocrat and author

No one likes to see things go to waste; yet every time you study your notes or review a textbook chapter, you are using only the left side of your brain. All students are experienced in writing and reading words. Few, however, deal as confidently with pictures as with words and make effective use of the brain's right side. To study effectively, you need to learn how to convert the words in a textbook into pictures or word maps of your own. You also need to be able to interpret and understand these and other visual displays when you see them in textbooks. This chapter is devoted to the encoding ("writing") and decoding ("reading") of pictures and other graphic materials. In it, you'll learn about

- Converting textbook words into pictures
- Using hierarchical concept maps
- Understanding visual materials
- Graphs
- Tables

and finally

- Diagrams

he human brain is divided into two hemispheres: left and right. Each hemisphere has specialized capabilities and processes different types of information. The left hemisphere operates in a rational, analytical manner. It processes verbal information. It is the seat of language and logical thinking. It organizes and categorizes information. The right hemisphere operates in an intuitive, holistic manner. It processes visual and spatial information. It is the seat of creativity and imagination. It combines separate elements to form coherent wholes.

Note taking, lecturing, reading, and analytical thought are left-brain skills. Recognizing patterns, configurations, shapes, and forms; intuitive thought; and visualization are right-brain skills. Students spend most of their time developing left-brain (verbal) skills: memorizing facts, analyzing bits of data, organizing and categorizing chunks of information. Students who also develop right-brain (nonverbal) skills—thinking pictorially, focusing on the whole instead of on separate parts, trusting intuition—are taking advantage of both of the ways in which the brain makes learning possible.

According to Allan Paivio of the University of Western Ontario, who has done a great deal of research on memory, if you commit facts and ideas to memory through words only, you are using only half of your brainpower.[1] When a fact or idea that you memorized through words (and stored in the left hemisphere of your brain) is also memorized through a picture or sketch (and is stored in the right hemisphere of your brain), you set up a powerful combination in your memory. You can draw on this combination later when you need to recall the fact or idea.

CONVERTING TEXTBOOK WORDS INTO PICTURES

For holistic learning to take place, the left side of your brain must cooperate and harmonize with the right side. This cooperation is easy to gain if you make it a habit to convert words into actual pictures or diagrams in your notes, or to convert words into mental pictures or images on the blackboard of your mind. Verbal descriptions often lend themselves quite easily to visual representation. Unfortunately, in many textbooks, pictures and diagrams are not as numerous as they should be. When a key concept lacks a picture, you can act as your textbook's illustrator by drawing what you read.

[1]Allan Paivio, *Imagery and Verbal Processes* (New York: Holt, Rinehart and Winston, 1971), pp. 522–23.

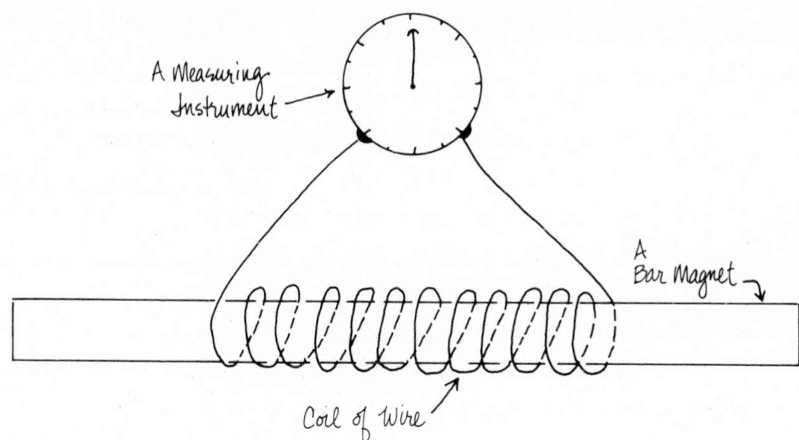

FIGURE 10.1 A Descriptive Paragraph Made Visual

Here is an example of how words can be converted into a picture. The following paragraph describes an experiment conducted by the English physicist and chemist Michael Faraday (1791–1867):

> In 1831, Michael Faraday, one of Britain's greatest scientists, did the experiments which completely demonstrated the close relationship between electricity and magnetism. One of his famous experiments was to take a coil of wire and connect the ends across an instrument capable of measuring tiny currents. By quickly pushing a bar magnet through the coil he was able to produce a small current in the coil and to measure that current. What he was really doing was to change the strength of the magnetic field in the coil by inserting and removing the magnet. The more rapidly he changed the field the more current he could generate.[2]

Figure 10.1 is an example of how one student converted this descriptive paragraph into a diagram, which helped the student not only to understand the described process but to visualize and remember it as well. If a question about Faraday's experiment appeared on a test, it is not hard to imagine how well a student with this picture in mind would do.

If an idea is particularly abstract, you may have to rely on a technique known as *mapping*.

---

[2]J. D. Jukes, *Man-Made Sun* (New York: Abelard-Schuman, 1959), p. 33.

USING HIERARCHICAL CONCEPT MAPS

Concept maps are word diagrams. They may be used to organize and to make visible, in a logical and connected manner, the information presented in your textbooks. Concept maps have a variety of purposes:

1. To reinforce textbook passages that contain important facts and ideas that you wish to understand thoroughly and remember permanently
2. To clarify textbook passages that are difficult to understand or to grasp fully because of their many parts
3. To organize and clarify textbook passages that are not well written
4. To pull together several main ideas that are separated by other ideas
5. To make a one-page summary of a textbook chapter or of an entire textbook
6. To review for exams
7. To make summaries of lecture notes
8. To organize ideas for writing papers or making speeches

A concept map shows not only the ideas, facts, and details but also their interrelationship. Ideas are arranged in a hierarchy: The most inclusive ideas precede less inclusive ideas and are connected to them with linking lines (see Figure 10.2).

Arranging ideas in hierarchical order is relatively easy when you encounter a well-written passage, because the main heading of the textbook introduces the major concept, and the first sentence, which is often the topic sentence, introduces the main idea. The sentences that follow are usually the supporting details.

Figure 10.2 is a concept map of a passage about the divisions of the nervous system, which appears in an undergraduate psychology textbook. Notice that the ideas are arranged in hierarchical order, from most inclusive ideas to least inclusive ideas. This concept map can be read from top to bottom or from bottom to top. The encircled ideas are linked by lines that are labeled with a word or phrase to show relationships.

Constructing Concept Maps

Concept maps are composed almost entirely of nouns that stand for key concepts and key terms. The connecting lines are labeled mostly with verbs and conjunctions like *and*. The main steps in constructing concept maps are as follows:

1. ***Read*** thoroughly the passage to be mapped, trying to comprehend as much of it as possible.

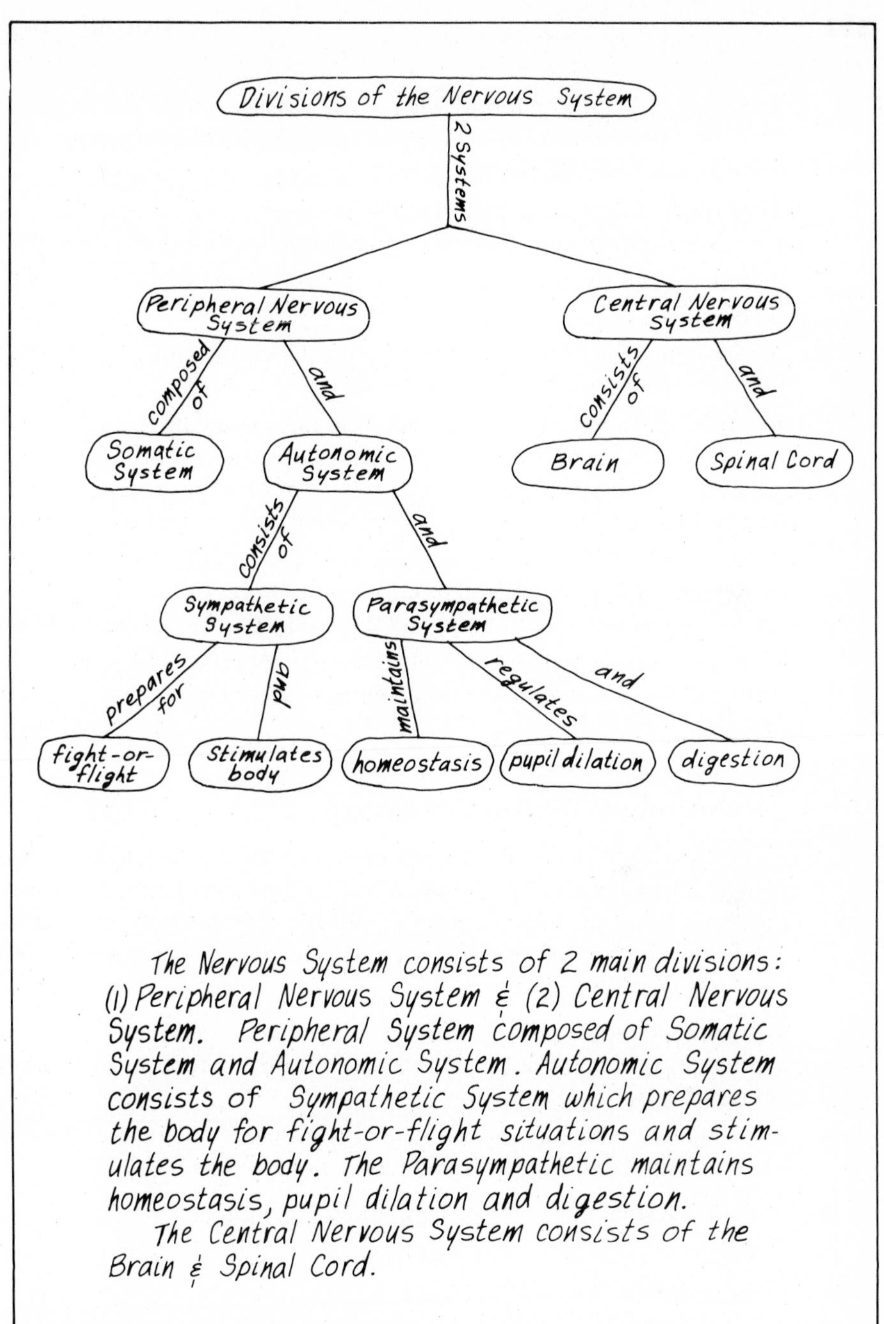

FIGURE 10.2 Hierarchical Concept Map of a Passage in a Psychology Textbook
Source: Kathy Wallace.

2. *Select* the most important idea in the passage—the idea to which all the other concepts can be related and subsumed. Write this important idea at the top and center of your paper.

3. *Reread* the passage and identify the words that stand for key concepts by circling them in your textbook or by listing them on a separate sheet.

4. *Rank* the concept words hierarchically, from most inclusive to least inclusive.

5. *Arrange* the concept words on your paper, not only according to hierarchy but also according to relationship.

6. *Link* the concept words by drawing lines showing the connections between and among them. Label the lines with a word or word phrase that explains the relationships. If an idea relates to other ideas represented in another portion of the map, show the relationship by drawing a broken line to indicate cross-linkage.

7. *Review* your concept map. Can you add any other information to the map? Can you think of another way that your map can be better developed?

8. *Write* one or more paragraphs summarizing the concept map. The better organized your map, the easier writing a meaningful paragraph will be.

Mapping a Textbook Passage

The facsimile textbook passage entitled "An Important Tool: The Language of Measurement" is used here to demonstrate the main steps in constructing a concept map. Figure 10.3 shows the passage, which is the raw material for the concept map shown in Figure 10.4. The student who mapped the passage took these steps:

1. After reading the passage carefully, the student identified "scientific measurement" as the most important idea and drew a circle around that expression (see Figure 10.3).

2. Using "scientific measurement" as a conceptual umbrella, the student selected and circled these words and phrases as key concepts:

metric system	Fahrenheit thermometer
Celsius	32
Fahrenheit	100
temperature scales	212
French scientists	converting Celsius readings to Fahrenheit
1799	

thermometers
mercury
Celsius thermometer
0 (zero)
converting Fahrenheit readings to Celsius
length
weight

3. The student ranked the list of key concepts hierarchically from most to least inclusive:

metric system
length
weight
French scientists
1799
temperature scales
Celsius
Fahrenheit
thermometers
Celsius thermometer
Fahrenheit thermometer
mercury
0 (zero)
100
32
212
converting Celsius readings to Fahrenheit
converting Fahrenheit readings to Celsius

4. The student next arranged these key concepts according to rank and linked them to show their interrelationship (see Figure 10.4).

5. After completing the concept map, the student reviewed it.

a. Information known from prior knowledge or gathered from any other portion of the textbook (such as from Table 21.1 in Figure 10.3) may be added to the map.
b. Relationships should be checked to make certain that they are logical.
c. The map should be rearranged or recopied if the student envisions a configuration that is better. Such rethinking increases the meaningfulness of the concept being mapped and takes the student well beyond the understanding gained through rote memorization.

6. The student wrote a paragraph about the concepts on the map. Following the labeled lines linking one idea to another makes writing a relatively easy process.

An Important Tool:
The Language of Measurement

Learn the language of scientific measurement. Most commonly used are the metric system and the Celsius and Fahrenheit temperature scales. Learn to think meaningfully in these quantities and measures, so that you will not be reading mere words and symbols.

For example, you should know that the word *metric* comes from *meter*, which is the principal unit of length in this system. The metric system was developed by French scientists in 1799 and is now used everywhere in the world for scientific work. Table 21.1 (page 370) compares some metric units with English units of measurement.

You will want to know about the Celsius and Fahrenheit temperature scales, too. The thermometers for both look alike and have the same size tubes; both are filled with mercury; and the mercury rises and falls to the same levels. They differ in the way the scale is graduated. On the Celsius thermometer the point at which water freezes is marked 0 (zero), while on the Fahrenheit thermometer it is marked 32. On the Celsius scale the boiling point is 100, while on the Fahrenheit it is 212.

On the Celsius thermometer, then, there are 100 equal spaces or degrees between the freezing and boiling points of water. On the Fahrenheit thermometer, there are 180 degrees between the freezing and boiling points. Thus,

> To change Celsius readings to Fahrenheit readings, multiply by 180/100, or 9/5, and then add 32.
>
> To change Fahrenheit readings to Celsius, subtract 32 and then multiply by 5/9.

Table 21.1 Comparison of Certain Metric and English Units of Measurement

Metric System		*English System*	
		Length	
Meter	=1.093 yards	Yard	=0.9144 meter
	=3.281 feet	Foot	=0.3048 meter
	=39.370 inches	Inch	=0.0254 meter
Kilometer	=0.621 mile	Mile	=1.609 kilometers
		Weight	
Gram	=15.432 grains	Grain	=0.0648 gram
	=0.032 troy ounce	Troy ounce	=31.1 grams
	=0.0352 avoirdupois ounce	Avoirdupois ounce	=28.35 grams
Kilogram	=2.2046 pounds avoirdupois		
Metric ton	=2204.62 poundsa avoirdupois	Pound	=453.6 gram
Carat	=3.08 grains avoirdupois	Short ton	=0.907 metric ton

FIGURE 10.3 Science Passage to Be Mapped

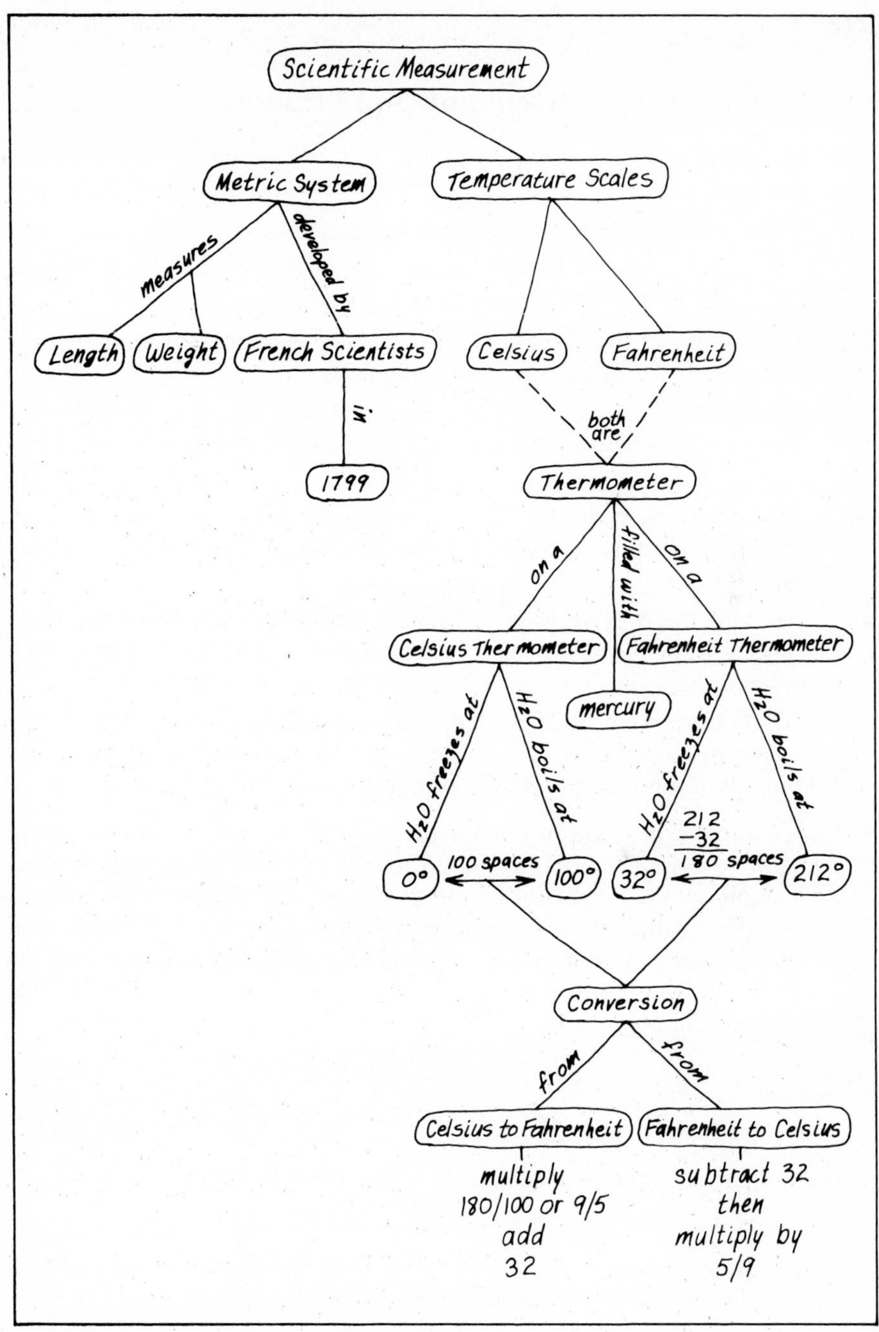

FIGURE 10.4 Concept Map of Science Passage
Source: Dr. Marino C. Alvarez.

Mapping Written and Oral Presentations

Mapping is an ideal way to organize your thoughts to prepare a paper or to make an oral presentation. Here are the steps you take:

1. Decide on a topic that you are interested in.

2. Make a random list of concepts that might be part of your paper or talk. The longer the list, the better it is.

3. Look over the list to locate four or five general, divisional concepts. Distinguish these concepts by *boxing* them in.

4. Look over the list a second time to choose concepts that pertain directly to your topic. Distinguish these concepts by *circling* them.

5. Start constructing the map. Center the topic at the top of the page. Put the divisional, boxed-in concepts across the page below the topic. Add the circled concepts, according to rank, under the appropriate divisional concepts.

6. Link the concept words with lines showing the connections between and among the concepts. Label these lines with a word or a phrase to explain relationships.

7. Review your concept map. Can you add any information to the map? Can you see a better way to organize the concepts? If a better idea strikes you, don't hesitate to remake your map.

A concept map can provide the skeletal structure for almost any paper or talk. To complete the project, go to a library to accumulate detailed information on 3 × 5 cards for all the divisional and subdivisional concepts.

For writing papers or preparing for talks, the concept map is a sure and convenient way to establish a logical organizational structure. The information on the 3 × 5 cards will provide the facts and details you need to elaborate on each concept.

Advantages of Mapping

The advantages of mapping include the following:

1. Notes are organized in a visual mode.
2. Notes that previously seemed separate and compartmentalized suddenly have a visible, connected structure.
3. Ideas, facts, and supporting material are placed at proper levels of rank, making the items meaningful.
4. Students who are visually oriented become better learners.

5. Both hemispheres of the brain are used: the left, which processes words; and the right, which processes pictures.
6. The visual images of concept maps are likely to stick in the memory longer and more accurately than words alone.
7. Mapping may be used as an alternate or supplementary method to unravel a difficult textbook passage.
8. Concept maps provide a bird's-eye view of an entire course when the main concepts are shown with linking lines establishing relationships.

Set your sights high, but don't be disappointed with less-than-perfect maps at first. Your maps will improve as you go along. Also, your map of a specific passage need not be exactly like someone else's. The structuring, organizing, and thinking that go into the making of concept maps will enable you to communicate your thoughts easily and meaningfully.

UNDERSTANDING VISUAL MATERIALS

Textbooks in the sciences, in sociology and psychology, and in business and economics contain an abundance of tables, graphs, diagrams, and pictures. Such visual materials can convey a great amount of information in a relatively small space. This information is as important as verbal information and may be more so; yet many students who feel pressed for time simply flip past a table or graph, thinking "Ah! Here's a page that I don't have to read."

When you flip past a page of visual material with no more than a passing glance, you are shortchanging yourself in two ways: You are missing important information, and you are skipping a first-rate opportunity to do some pure thinking. Here's why: Because the page contains *visual* information, you must transform it into *verbal* information. You have to stop and do all the thinking, but once it is done you will have thought through the information and stored it as both verbal and visual data. You will understand it and remember it with great clarity for a long time.

The best way to master nonverbal material is through intensive study of every table, graph, diagram, and picture that you encounter in your assigned reading. This may sound like the hardest way to learn, but actually you will be accomplishing several things. You'll be learning a skill that will be useful today, tomorrow, and in future assignments. As you use this skill, you'll become increasingly proficient. Furthermore, you'll be learning important material directly and efficiently—material that you need to learn anyway. Finally, there is the motivating reward of a job well done and done well in advance of exam time.

It is not at all difficult to read graphic materials. These materials are devised by specialists, who build four important qualities into each graphic item:

1. *Directness:* Visual materials are designed to draw the attention of readers immediately to the information that is to be seen.
2. *Simplicity:* The information is organized tightly, and needless details are avoided.
3. *Clarity:* Both visual format and meaning are set forth clearly.
4. *Accuracy:* Data are carefully checked, and only graphic forms that do not distort the data are used.

With these built-in qualities, visual materials should be neither complex nor confusing to you, but you still have to know how to read them. Once you do, you'll find that reading graphics is both a pleasure and a welcome break from the constant bombardment of printed words.

How to Read Graphs, Tables, and Diagrams

Here are some suggestions for reading graphs, tables, and diagrams:

1. *Survey the graphic.* Look it over to get a general impression.
2. *Read the title.* Read carefully, for the title often tells you *what* the data represent, *where* they were collected, and *when.* The title also gives you the subject matter.
3. *Determine the units of measurement.* There is a big difference, for example, between percentages of the whole and actual measurements. Also notice whether graphs begin at zero or at some other measurement.
4. *Check headings or labels.* Read the headings over columns (vertical) and alongside rows (horizontal) in tables, to be sure you know what they represent. Read the labels alongside the axes in graphs.
5. *Read the footnotes and headnotes.* Footnotes or headnotes provide further information and often a key to symbols.

How to Read Pictures

Most readers give pictures no more than a passing glance. Pictures, however, should be analyzed systematically:

1. Read the title of the picture and the place it depicts. Also read all notations and explanations.
2. Make a general survey, looking for the "message."
3. Look closely at the different parts of the picture. Like Sherlock Holmes, take in detail after detail.

4. Try to find the connection between the picture and the text. Ask yourself, "Why did they include it?"
5. Try to make generalizations and draw inferences from the information you have gleaned.

Things to Watch Out For

Factual data—especially statistics—can be placed in graphic formats that distort the data. Unscrupulous people may use this device to strengthen arguments or make data appear favorable to their cause. The book *How to Lie with Statistics*[3] exposes some of the devious tricks that are used and is also fun to read. For example, you should be wary of the word *average,* and you should try to find the highest and lowest figures that went into each average. Two companies may have an average salary of $29,000. But if the range of salaries in one company is from $6,000 to $90,000, whereas in the other company the range is from $20,000 to $35,000, then the salary policies of the two companies are quite different.

Don't be overly impressed by the steepness of the lines in graphs. Look at the side of every graph to find the scale—the value of each increment. Units of $100 will make a line much steeper than units of $1,000. Always convert what you see into words; otherwise you'll remember the steepness or flatness but not the real information that is being presented.

Remember that visual relationships can be tricky. The frame around a diagram can actually change the way you see the diagram. For example, this is a diamond-shaped figure:

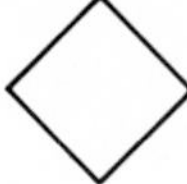

But notice that when the same figure is placed in a frame,

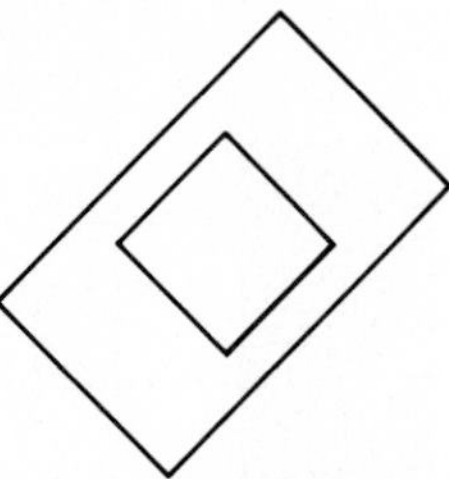

it becomes a square. The size and shape of a chart or graph can also affect what you see. Data that may be quite neutral or ordinary can be made to

[3]Darrell Huff, *How to Lie with Statistics* (New York: Norton, 1954).

appear startling by the form and scale of the graphic. If you read graphics carefully, you'll see them in the proper way, rather than as someone else may expect you to see them.

GRAPHS

In your reading, you'll come across dozens of graphs that seem to differ in a variety of ways. On closer inspection, however, you'll find that they are all modifications of four basic types: bar graphs, circle graphs, line graphs, and combination graphs.

Bar Graphs

Bar graphs have two scales. The horizontal scale usually measures time, and the vertical scale measures some quantity or amount. Figure 10.5 is a graph that you can read easily and directly. Bar graphs effectively show simple trends, such as the steady increase in the size of PAC contributions to Senate and House candidates. Since the values are in millions, you must add six zeros to the numbers shown on the vertical scale.

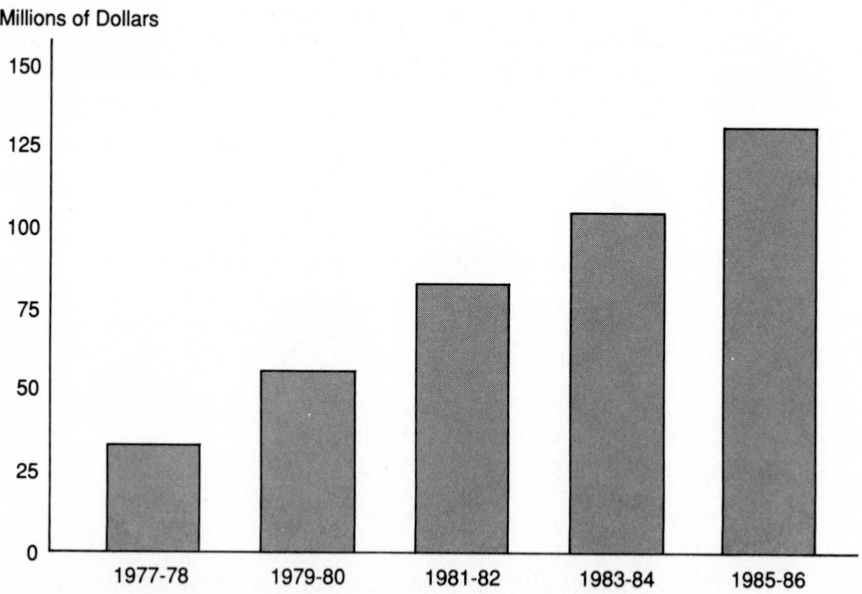

FIGURE 10.5 PAC Contributions to Senate and House Candidates, 1985–86
Source: World Eagle, *November 1987, vol. XI, no. 3, p. 28.*

In Figure 10.6, the horizontal scale measures time and the vertical scale measures population figures. The light and the dark regions compare population increases over time. The graph also contrasts increases in the developing and developed regions of the world.

Figure 10.7 is a bar graph that shows the relation between two quantities as well as their magnitudes. The relation is shown directly, clearly, and forcefully by placing bars side by side. The grid lines help you assess values quickly and easily. The key distinguishes the columns for "net earnings" and for "cash dividends paid."

Circle Graphs

No graph can do a better job than the circle graph (also known as the pie chart) when it comes to showing the *proportional parts* of the whole (see Figure 10.8). It is probably the easiest of all graphs to read, because there are no vertical or horizontal lines to follow or any amounts to interpret. The chart clearly shows the proportions, and the amounts are given directly. Notice that in Figure 10.8, the "all others" category is represented as if it were a single exporter; in fact, it is comprised of several (we don't know how many) nations. The source from which this circle graph is taken cites the following

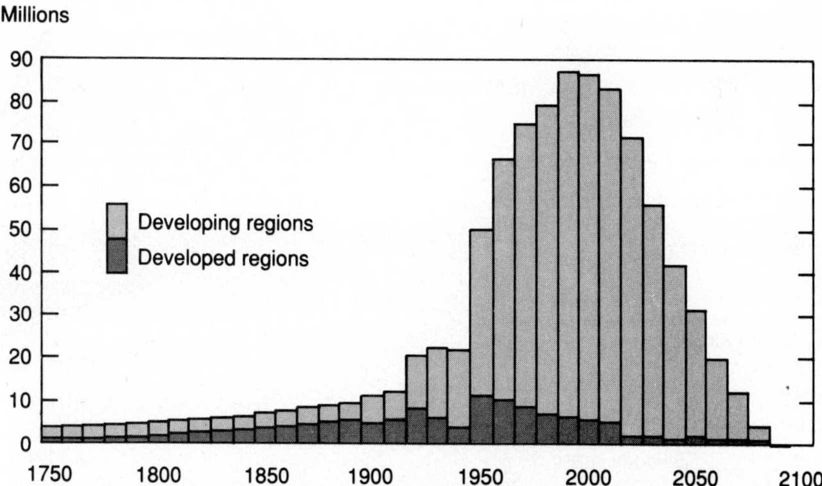

FIGURE 10.6 Population Growth in Developing and Developed Regions of the World, 1750–2100.
Average annual increase in numbers per decade. *Source: Thomas W. Merrick, with PRB staff, "World Population in Transition,"* Population Bulletin, *Vol. 41, No. 2 (Washington, D.C.: Population Reference Bureau, Inc., reprinted January 1988), p. 4.*

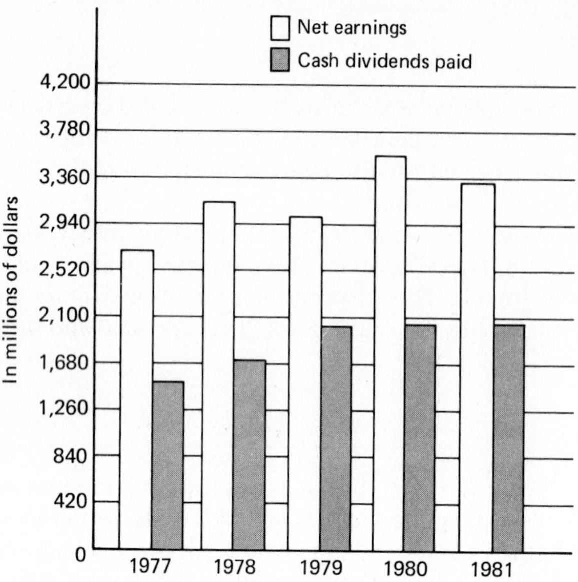

FIGURE 10.7 Net Earnings and Cash Dividends Paid
Source: International Business Machines Corp. *Annual Report 1981, p. 25.*

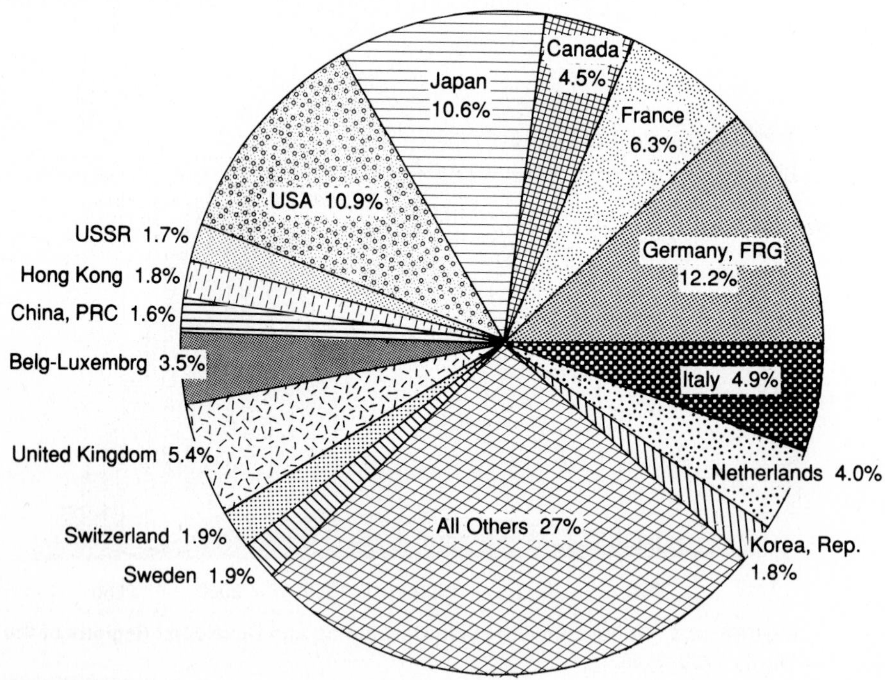

FIGURE 10.8 The Top 15 Exporting Nations in 1986
Source: World Eagle, *February 1988, vol. XI, no. 6, p. 10.*

figures: In 1986, the value (in U.S. dollars) of exports from the top 15 exporting nations was $1.4512 trillion, and total exports for the world that year were estimated at $1.9916 trillion.

Line Graphs

Line graphs are widely used because they can be adapted to all kinds of quantitative data. Like the bar graph, the line graph has two scales at right angles, one vertical and the other horizontal. If time is one of the variables, it is usually shown on the horizontal scale.

In Figure 10.9, the sentence below the line graph immediately orients you to the graph's full meaning. Notice, on the horizontal scale, that each year is divided into months. By placing a ruler on the graph, you can get a fairly good idea of the hourly wage for any of the months shown. Why didn't

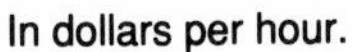

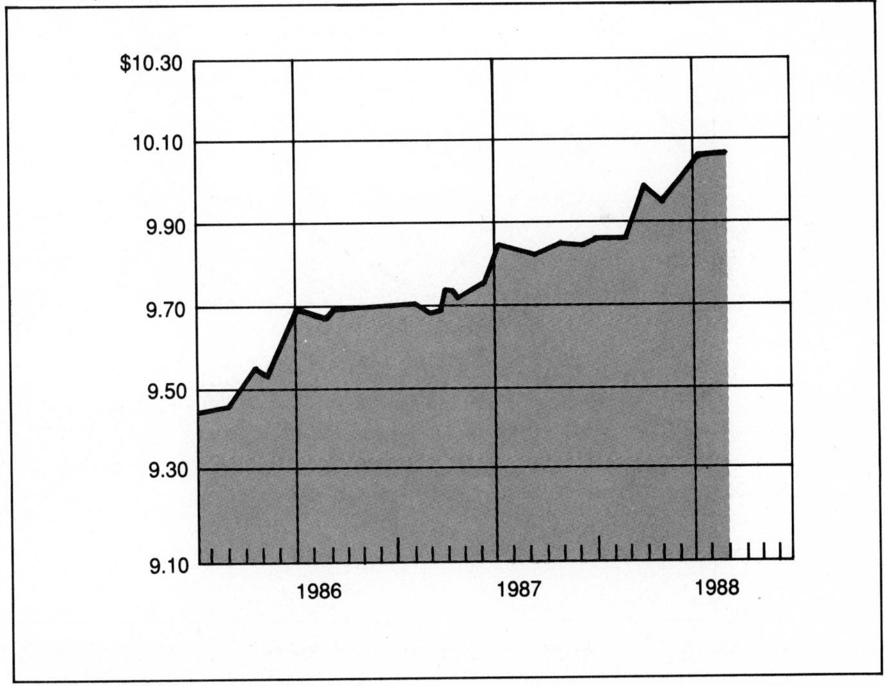

AVERAGE HOURLY PAY of factory workers in February remained unchanged at $10.07 from the preceding month, the Labor Department reports.

FIGURE 10.9 Hourly Earnings

Source: The Wall Street Journal, *March 9, 1988, p. 1. Reprinted by permission of* The Wall Street Journal, *© Dow Jones & Company, Inc. 1988. All rights reserved.*

the artist use a bar graph to show the wages month by month? A bar graph would have been too crowded if thirty-seven columns, one for each month, had been jammed into the space allotted to the figure. A single line makes a clean, inviting graph.

Figure 10.10 is a more complex line graph. The ages of women in the labor force between 1950 and 1985 are shown horizontally; the percentages they occupy in the labor force are shown vertically. There are five lines, one for each of the years in which a group was studied. Notice the peaks in certain age groups. This graph wants you to see that certain groups have higher

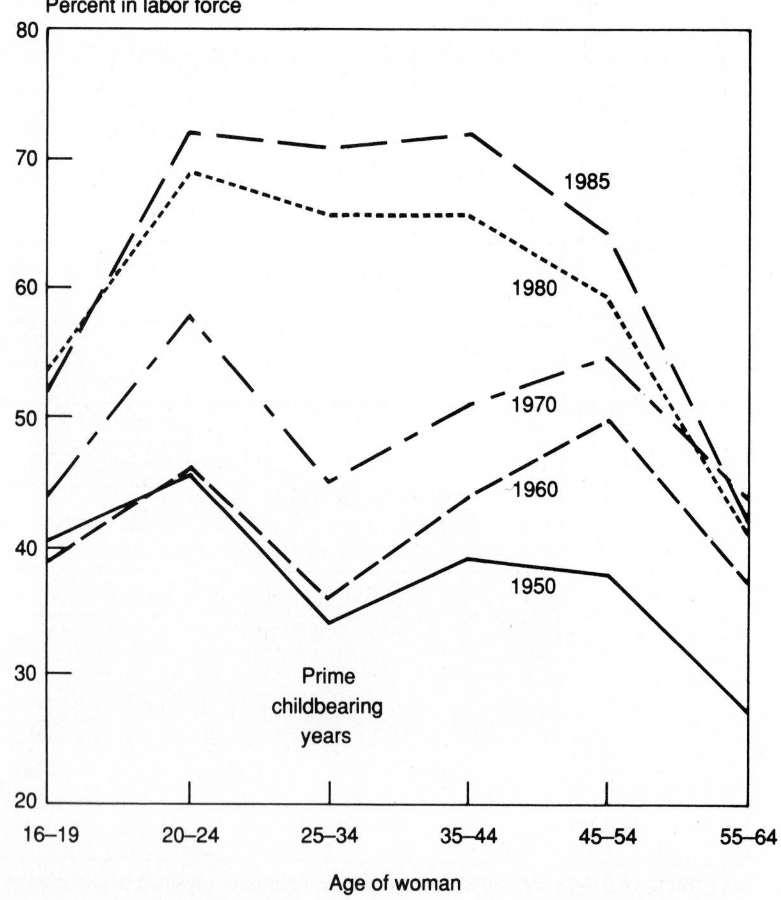

FIGURE 10.10 Labor-Force Participation for U.S. Women by Age, 1950–85
Source: Population Today, *vol. 15, no. 2 (February 1987), p. 2; data are from the U.S. Bureau of Labor Statistics. Originally in Martin O'Connell and David E. Bloom,* Juggling Jobs and Babies: *America's Child Care Challenge, Population Trends and Public Policy Report No. 12 (Washington, D.C.: Population Reference Bureau, Inc., February 1987), p. 5.*

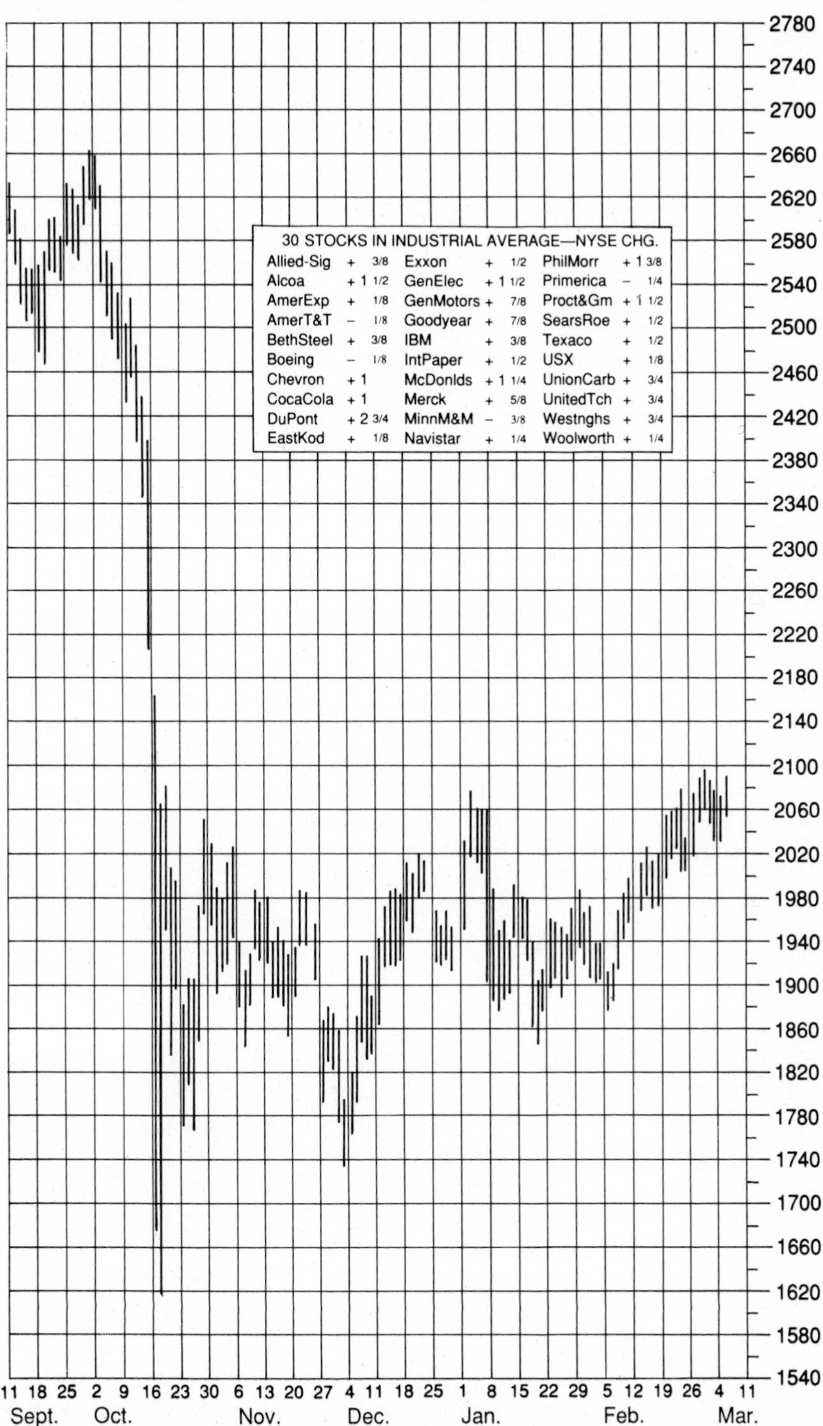

30 STOCKS IN INDUSTRIAL AVERAGE—NYSE CHG.

Allied-Sig	+ 3/8	Exxon	+ 1/2	PhilMorr	+ 1 3/8
Alcoa	+ 1 1/2	GenElec	+ 1 1/2	Primerica	– 1/4
AmerExp	+ 1/8	GenMotors	+ 7/8	Proct&Gm	+ 1 1/2
AmerT&T	– 1/8	Goodyear	+ 7/8	SearsRoe	+ 1/2
BethSteel	+ 3/8	IBM	+ 3/8	Texaco	+ 1/2
Boeing	– 1/8	IntPaper	+ 1/2	USX	+ 1/8
Chevron	+ 1	McDonlds	+ 1 1/4	UnionCarb	+ 3/4
CocaCola	+ 1	Merck	+ 5/8	UnitedTch	+ 3/4
DuPont	+ 2 3/4	MinnM&M	– 3/8	Westnghs	+ 3/4
EastKod	+ 1/8	Navistar	+ 1/4	Woolworth	+ 1/4

FIGURE 10.11 The Dow Jones Industrial Averages from September 11, 1987, to March 8, 1988

Source: The Wall Street Journal, *March 9, 1988, p. 54. Reprinted by permission of* The Wall Street Journal, *© Dow Jones & Company, Inc. 1988. All rights reserved.*

labor-force participation rates than others and that the total percentages for certain groups have changed with time.

Combination Graphs

Some graphs are neither bar graphs nor line graphs but have characteristics of each. The makers of combination graphs often use great imagination and creativity to display complex information in an easy-to-understand format. The graph used to show the monthly Dow Jones Industrial Average (of the prices of thirty industrial stocks on the New York Stock Exchange) is an example of this type of ingenuity. The dramatic graph in Figure 10.11 horizontally displays the weeks between September 11, 1987, and March 8, 1988. The symbol used to show the monthly average is a short line. The top of the line indicates the highest average reached during the month. The bottom of the line indicates the lowest average reached during the month. Notice the severe drop in stock value in October 1987.

TABLES

Tables are used to present a large amount of factual information (usually statistics) in a compact, orderly arrangement that makes complex relationships immediately clear. For example, Table 10.1 shows how life expectancy varies with age, race, and sex. The table is easy to read and presents a tremendous amount of information within a relatively small amount of space.

DIAGRAMS

Some textbooks—in science and engineering, for example—contain diagrams on almost every page. A labeled diagram helps you understand the interrelationship of a system's components. If you study diagrams so thoroughly that you can reproduce them from memory, you will know the subject cold, not only for the next exam but also for the long pull.

Figure 10.12 shows how hot water is used to produce electricity in a nuclear reactor. After leaving the reactor, water goes to a steam generator. The water in the reactor's cooling loop is kept at a very high pressure—more than 2,000 pounds per square inch (this is equivalent to the pressure at a depth of one mile in the ocean). Because of this great pressure, the water can be heated to 600 degrees Fahrenheit without boiling. The pressure in the steam line, however, is less, so that the water in it boils and passes through the turbine as steam. In a nuclear reactor, the reactor core and the steam generator replace the conventional fuel furnace. The reactor shown in Figure

TABLE 10.1 Expectation of Life at Birth, 1920–78

	Total			White			Black and Other		
Year	Total	Male	Female	Total	Male	Female	Total	Male	Female
1920	54.1	53.6	54.6	54.9	54.4	55.6	45.3	45.5	45.2
1930	59.7	58.1	61.6	61.4	59.7	63.5	48.1	47.3	49.2
1940	62.9	60.8	65.2	64.2	62.1	66.6	53.1	51.5	54.9
1950	68.2	65.6	71.1	69.1	66.5	72.2	60.8	59.1	62.9
1955	69.6	66.7	72.8	70.5	67.4	73.7	63.7	61.4	66.1
1960	69.7	66.6	73.1	70.6	67.4	74.1	63.6	61.1	66.3
1965	70.2	66.8	73.7	71.0	67.6	74.7	64.1	61.1	67.4
1970	70.9	67.1	74.8	71.7	68.0	75.6	65.3	61.3	69.4
1971	71.1	67.4	75.0	72.0	68.3	75.8	65.6	61.6	69.7
1972	71.1	67.4	75.1	72.0	68.3	75.9	65.6	61.5	69.9
1973	71.3	67.6	75.3	72.2	68.4	76.1	65.9	61.9	70.1
1974	71.9	68.1	75.8	72.7	68.9	76.6	67.0	62.9	71.3
1975	72.5	68.7	76.5	73.2	69.4	77.2	67.9	63.6	72.3
1976	72.8	69.0	76.7	73.5	69.7	77.3	68.3	64.1	72.6
1977	73.2	69.3	77.1	73.8	70.0	77.7	68.8	64.6	73.1
1978	73.3	69.5	77.2	74.0	70.2	77.8	69.2	65.0	73.6

Source: U.S. Department of Commerce, Bureau of the Census, *Statistical Abstract of the United States, 1980* (Washington, D.C., 1980), p. 72.

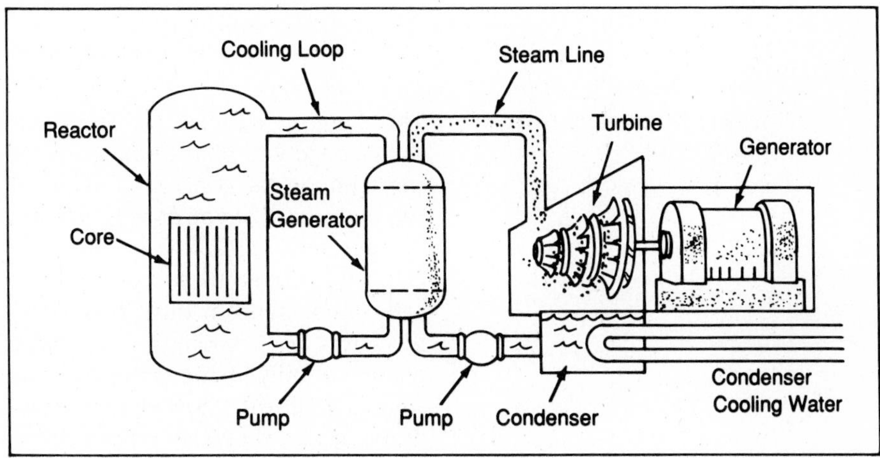

FIGURE 10.12 A Pressurized-Water Nuclear Reactor
Source: From Physics For People Who Think They Don't Like Physics, by Jerry S. Faughn and Karl F. Kuhn, © 1976 by Saunders College Publishing, a division of Holt, Rinehart and Winston, Inc., reprinted by permission of the publisher.

10.12 is a pressurized-water reactor. Roughly half of the power reactors built in the United States are of this type.

SUMMARY

How can I convert words into pictures?

Verbal descriptions are often easily transformed into visual representations. When a key concept lacks a picture, act as your textbook's illustrator and draw what you read. If the idea is particularly abstract, you may have to devise concept maps.

What are concept maps, and what are they used for?

Concept maps are word diagrams. They are a visual approach to the information that you read. Textbook passages that are important or hard to understand can be converted into concept maps to make them easier to understand and remember. You can often summarize anything from a chapter to a whole book in a one-page concept map. In addition, concept maps can be used to review for exams, to summarize lecture notes, and to plan speeches or papers.

How can I make my own concept maps?

There are eight steps: (1) Thoroughly read the passage you plan to map. (2) Select the most important concept, and put it at the top and center of your paper. (3) Reread the passage, and circle or list other key concepts. (4) Rank these concepts hierarchically—that is, from most inclusive to least inclusive. (5) Arrange the concepts on your paper, not only by hierarchy but by relationship as well. (6) Show the relationships by drawing a line between related concepts and labeling these lines with a word or phrase that explains the relationship. (7) Review your concept map, not only to make sure you understand it but to be certain that it is complete and arranged in the best way possible. (8) Write a brief summary explaining your concept map.

How can concept maps help out in written and oral presentations?

As soon as you've selected a topic, you can put concept mapping to work for you. List concepts that you might include. From this list, identify four or five divisional concepts. Draw a box around each. Go back and identify the concepts that are more specific. Circle them. On a sheet of paper, write your topic at the top. Place your divisional concepts on the second row. Then add all the circled concepts, ordered by rank and placed under the appropriate divisional concepts. Draw lines between related concepts, and describe their relationships in a word or two along the linking lines. Take a moment to review your map to see whether you have arranged things in the best way possible. If you have not, don't hesitate to rearrange your map.

How should I approach graphs, tables, and diagrams?

Try to arrive at a general impression, and then zero in on details such as the title, the units of measurement, the headings or labels, and footnotes or headnotes.

Do graphic materials present any pitfalls?

Yes. Graphic materials are just as susceptible to distortion as words are. You should pay attention to the scale of the graph, its overall size, and the material to which it is being related. Altering any of these variables can sometimes have a drastic effect on the graph's interpretation.

What are the basic types of graphs?

There are four basic types: (1) bar graphs, (2) circle graphs, (3) line graphs, and (4) combination graphs.

How does a bar graph work?

These graphs make use of two scales. The horizontal scale usually measures time; the vertical scale usually measures some quantity or amount. Bar graphs are excellent at illustrating trends.

When is a circle graph normally used?

The circle graph is often used to relate parts proportionally to the whole. In this type of graph, the relative sizes of the pieces that make up the pie are what is important.

How do you read a line graph?	Like the bar graph, the line graph is often used to illustrate trends. Bar graphs are most effective with a limited amount of information. Line graphs can be used to illustrate a great deal of information clearly and simply.
What are combination graphs?	Combination graphs are usually a mixture of bar and line graphs. They are an effort by designers to integrate the precision of the bar graph with the clarity of the line graph.
What advantage does a table have over a graph?	All graphs, even line graphs, are somewhat limited in the amount of information that they can present clearly. Tables can present a great deal of information in a relatively small amount of space. Their only drawback is that they sacrifice the visual quality that most graphs possess.
When are diagrams most commonly used?	Diagrams are frequently found in science and engineering textbooks. Their purpose is to illustrate the interrelationship of a system's components. Because diagrams appeal to the right side of the brain, they can do a great deal to aid in the remembering of complex information.

HAVE YOU MISSED SOMETHING?

1. *Sentence completion.* Complete the following sentences with one of the three words listed below each sentence.

a. If you commit facts and ideas to memory through words only, you are using only half of your ____________________.

wordpower brainpower intuition

b. The left side of the brain tends to be ____________________.

ethical creative logical

c. Mapping can benefit students who are visually ____________________.

impaired oriented deficient

2. *Matching.* In each blank space in the left column, write the number preceding the phrase in the right column that matches the left item best.

_____ a. Right hemisphere

_____ b. Divisional concept

_____ c. Hierarchical ranking

_____ d. Bar graph

_____ e. Concept map

_____ f. Diagram

_____ g. Line graph

_____ h. Circle graph

1. Is a hierarchically arranged word diagram
2. Processes visual and spatial information
3. Is generally boxed not circled
4. Goes from most inclusive to least inclusive
5. Effectively shows simple trends
6. Emphasizes the relationship of parts to the whole
7. Can be adapted to all types of quantitative data
8. Helps clarify the interrelationship of a system's components

3. *True-false.* Write *T* beside the *true* statements and *F* beside the *false* statements.

_____ a. Words can rarely be converted into pictures.

_____ b. A concept map should be accompanied by a written summary.

_____ c. Visual images tend to stay in memory longer than words alone.

_____ d. Statistics are straightforward and difficult to distort.

_____ e. Science textbooks frequently contain illustrative diagrams.

_____ f. Mapping can give compartmentalized ideas a connected structure.

4. *Graphics.* Write "yes" next to the characteristics of good graphics.

_____ a. Splashy

_____ b. Direct

_____ c. Simple

_____ d. Small

_____ e. Clear

_____ f. Accurate

5. *Multiple choice.* Choose the word that completes the following sentence most accurately, and circle the letter that precedes it.

   Combination graphs possess the characteristics of

   a. bar and circle graphs
   b. circle and line graphs
   c. diagrams and concept maps
   d. bar and line graphs

PART

IV

Tests and Examinations

CHAPTER 11

Preparing for Exams

Dig a well before you are thirsty.

Chinese Proverb

Are you overcome by test anxiety? Do your palms sweat? Do your hands shake? Do your thoughts become a blur? Or do you stay cool as a cucumber and still get grades that aren't so hot? Whether you're nervous but knowledgeable or fearless but failing, the solution is the same. This chapter shows how preparation can give your test scores a boost. It discusses

- Test anxiety
- Organizing your time
- Organizing your notes
- Helping yourself
- Cramming

and finally

- Making the most of exam time and its aftermath

he grade on your exam is to you what the financial bottom line is to a corporation. Both are a measure of success. Although some students learn far more than their grades indicate, in general if solid learning took place, the grade will be respectable perhaps 9.5 times out of 10.

TEST ANXIETY

Doing poorly on a quiz or an exam is frequently blamed on test anxiety, a phenomenon that one student summed up in the following way: "I get so uptight when the test sheet is handed out that I totally blank out and can't come up with answers that I *know* that I know." A frightening situation, to be sure. But why are test-anxious students so convinced that they actually knew the right answers?

The Cause

Immediately after an exam, many students take a look at their textbooks and lecture notes and find the right answers highlighted or underlined. These were the ideas that they studied, the facts and principles that they read and reread. Yet when the time came to write them on the test sheet . . . nothing! What was the problem?

For many students the root cause of test anxiety lies in confusing recall with recognition. There is an important distinction between them. Recall occurs when you retrieve a piece of information from your memory without any hints or cues. Recognition is aided by cues. Recognition occurs when you identify a piece of information because of the context in which it is presented.

If someone were to ask you to name the capital of Massachusetts and you came up with the answer—Boston—you'd be demonstrating pure recall. If someone were to ask you to name the man who discovered Florida in 1513, you might be stumped. "I know the answer," you might say, "but I just can't can't come up with it." But if you were given a list of explorers to choose from

Sir Francis Drake

Jacques Cartier

Ponce de Leon

Vasco da Gama

you probably would have no trouble identifying Ponce de Leon as the discoverer of Florida. You *recognized* his name. You did not recall it even though it may have been buried in your memory. You needed a hint to trigger the answer.

The method of study used by many students brings learning to the recognition stage but not to the point of recall: They read and reread, underline and circle, highlight and symbol-mark. This sort of studying can be costly. If you were asked in an exam to name the man who discovered Florida, you would have gotten a zero on that question. Undoubtedly, when you went back to your notes, you would have found "Ponce de Leon" clearly circled, and you would have concluded that test anxiety had prevented you from coming up with the answer. The real cause of your problem, though, was failure to study your notes to the point of recall.

If the question had been a multiple-choice question, you would have been in luck. As you progress through college, however, multiple-choice questions will become less and less common. *Most questions on tests require recall, not mere recognition.* Thus, counseling, a more relaxed attitude, or greater will power will not wipe out test anxiety. The only thing that will both reduce anxiety and increase success is studying to the point of recall.

Does that mean that test anxiety doesn't exist? Anyone who has had the symptoms knows that test anxiety definitely exists. But test anxiety is not the cause of test failure; test failure is the cause of test anxiety. The only way to break out of this vicious circle is to succeed on tests. The way to succeed is to apply a systematic study method that enables you to recall all or almost all that you study.

Your efforts should begin even before the semester does and intensify at the semester's end as you apply the system before, during, and even after the final exam. The earlier you begin, the better you'll do, but you can put the system into practice even in mid-semester.

The Cure

The cure for test anxiety is a simple one: preparation. Advance preparation is like a fire drill: It teaches you what to do and how to proceed, even in a high-stress situation, because you've been through the procedure so many times that you know it by heart. In order to be prepared, it is important to be well-acquainted with your textbooks, to faithfully take notes on both lectures and readings, to use a note-taking format that promotes real learning, and to spend as much time as possible reciting your notes. Then, when the time comes to begin studying specifically for a quiz or an exam, you will have a strong foundation of learning on which to build.

Buy Textbooks Early. Buy your textbooks early; then, before classes start, read carefully the preface of each book to get acquainted with the

	SOME NONSENSE ABOUT LECTURES
Why is it bad to take notes?	You will be sure to hear that you can get more out of a lecture if you don't take notes. This could be true if you took an examination right after the lecture. But you don't: you take one weeks or months later, and you can forget a lot by then. You can't review the lecture without good notes.
Why is it bad to write main ideas after hearing the whole idea?	You may hear that you should take notes only on the main points of a lecture. This just doesn't work. Noting a point after you have decided that it is important interferes with your listening to the next point. On the other hand, don't think you must record every word the lecturer says: rather, be alert to take down the facts and ideas which form the step-by-step development of the topic.
Why is it bad to reflect on ideas during a lecture?	You may hear that you should reflect upon the lecturer's ideas as they are being presented. This is highly impractical. When you emerge from your reflections on point one, you are apt to hear the lecturer say, "and point number four is. . . ." This does not mean that you should take notes unthinkingly, like a tape recorder. But extended reflection should come later, assisted by complete notes taken during the lecture.
Why is it bad to convert lecturer's words into your own?	You may hear that you should convert the lecturer's words into your own. This also is seldom possible in a fast-moving lecture. Formulating concepts in your own words should come later in your study time.
	You may hear that you should take notes in formal outline — I.A, 1.a, etc. The outline form does have some advantages in organizing the material, but it has disadvantages too. By the time you decide whether a point is

FIGURE 11.1 Textbook Notes Using the Questions-in-the-Margin System

author. In the preface, the author may tell you why he or she wrote the book, how it is different from other books on the same subject, and so forth. Once you have a sense of the author as a real, live person, you'll be able to carry on a conversation with the author when you study the textbook. For example, when an author of an economics book writes, "There's a direct connection between money growth and inflation," you can ask, "Oh, yes? What's your proof?" Such a dialogue can convert the silent words of print into an audible and more easily remembered conversation, yielding fuller comprehension and making the facts and ideas all the more memorable.

Use the Questions-in-the-Margin System for Textbook Notes. When the first assignment is given, read a page or two to get into the subject matter and then go back to the first paragraph and ask, "What's the main idea here?" Once you have decided on the main idea, write a brief question in the margin of the page. Then, opposite each question, underline very sparingly and selectively the key words and phrases that make up the answer (Figure 11.1). Go through the entire chapter in this way.

Use the Cornell Note-taking System for Classroom Lectures. Take complete notes of every classroom lecture. Your objective is to capture on

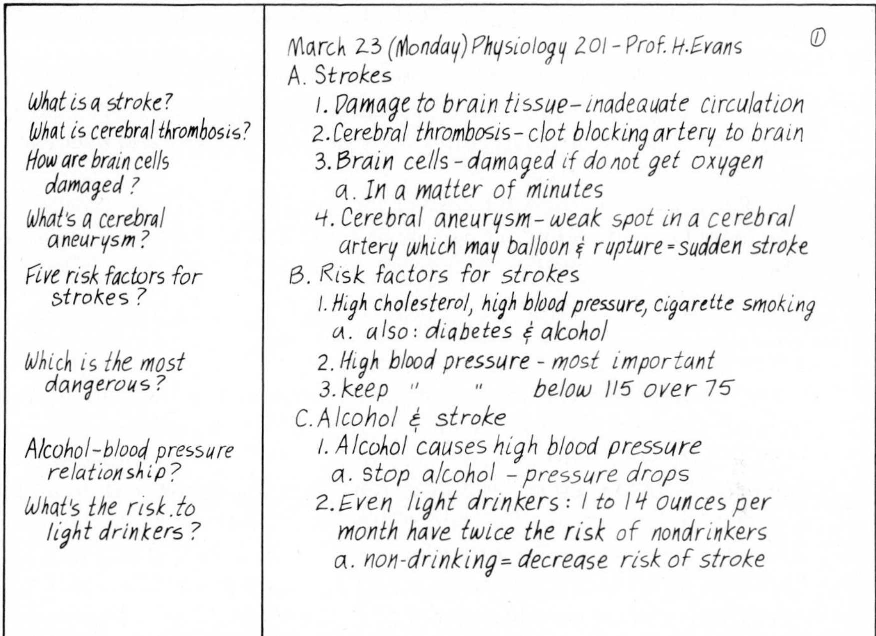

FIGURE 11.2 Lecture Notes in the Cornell Format

paper the lecturer's facts and ideas so that you can study them thoroughly. In class, write swiftly, but neatly. Use the Cornell Note-taking System. The format for the note sheets is shown in Figure 7.4, on page 145. Remember that the wide (6") column on the right is where you write the notes of the lecture. Don't crowd them. Leave plenty of white space. When you get back to your room, read your notes from beginning to end, recreating in your mind the original lecture. As you think about each fact and idea, make sure you have understood it clearly; then, in the narrow (2½") column on the left write a brief, meaningful question. Figure 11.2 shows lecture notes with questions written in the narrow column.

Recite Your Lecture Notes and Textbook Chapters. Recitation is the most powerful method known to psychologists for embedding facts and ideas in your memory. Before putting your lecture notes away, cover the notes in the wide column, leaving exposed the questions in the narrow column. Read the first question aloud, and recite the answer. Recite aloud, using your own words. After reciting, look at your notes in the wide column to see whether your recitation was on target. Proceed in this way until you have answered all the questions in the narrow column.

Use the same recitation technique for your textbook chapters. Cover the textbook page, exposing only the questions written in the margin of each page. Recite the answers in your own words. Recite over and over again until you get the answer right.

Remember: If you can't answer the questions now, you haven't learned the material, and you won't be able to recall it later during the exam. During the exam, you won't have forgotten anything because you failed to learn anything in the first place.

Keep Up-to-Date in Your Coursework. Your preparation for exams must begin on the very first day of classes and continue throughout the entire semester. To study effectively for an exam, the decks must be clear—that is, your coursework must be up-to-date. Your mind and your time should focus steadily on the upcoming test. If you must spend any time getting caught up—completing assignments that you should have done earlier in the semester—you seriously endanger your performance on the exam. If you stay on top of your assignments throughout the semester, they won't come back to haunt you when it's time to study for finals.

BEFORE THE EXAM

If you are taking five courses, each consisting of about forty classroom lectures and twenty textbook chapters, you are responsible for two hundred lectures and one hundred textbook chapters. How do you organize your notes and your time to study all this material?

Organizing Your Time

Schedule the time available to you in the week before finals. Use the format shown in Figure 11.3. Fill in the time blocks that will be taken up by meals, meetings, job (if you have one), and recreation. Next fill in your classes. Under no circumstances should you miss any of these. You'll be responsible for the lectures themselves, and you will want to hear the instructor's answers to students' questions about the exam. Fill in the time you will need to complete term papers and other assignments. Make sure you get them done *before* exam week. You don't want unfinished business to interfere with your study or to distract your thinking during exams.

You should find that some extra time is available toward the end of this

	M	Tu	W	Th	F	S	S
7:00							
8:00							
9:00							
10:00							
11:00							
12:00							
1:00							
2:00							
3:00							
4:00							
5:00							
6:00							
7:00							
8:00							
9:00							
10:00							

FIGURE 11.3 Sample Weekly Schedule Form

week. Use it to study for your exams. Fill in the exact study times and subjects. Instead of simply writing "Study" in the time blocks, write exactly what you will study: "Study economics, chaps 1 to 10" or "Summarize sociology notes." Make a schedule that you'll be able to follow, and then follow it.

Toward the end of the week before finals, make up another schedule—this one for exam week. Fill in the times for your exams and for your meals and recreation. Remember that you must be in tip-top shape mentally, emotionally, and physically if you are to do your best on the exams. Don't skip meals, recreation, or sleep to get in more study.

By finals week, the bulk of your preparation should be completed, and most of your summaries should be in order. Leave a block of time immediately before each exam to review the summary sheets for that exam. The less time you allow between this last review and the exam, the less forgetting will take place. Review calmly and thoughtfully, and carry this calm, thoughtful behavior right into the exam room.

Organizing Your Notes

The best way to study for an exam is to consolidate your lecture and textbook notes into sets of summary sheets and then recite them. As you make up the summary sheets, you are accomplishing three things. First, you are reviewing the notes you took throughout the semester, adding to the information you have retained. Second, you are categorizing information under specific headings, which will help you retrieve it from your memory during the exam. Third, you are preparing a condensed set of notes that you can use as a refresher immediately before the exam.

Prepare one set of summary sheets for your lecture notes and one for your textbook notes, for each course. By categorizing notes into blocks of information, you should be able to reduce each set of notes to about ten pages. Details and background information will be in your mind, rather than on the summary sheets. The summary sheets will contain all the cues; therefore, they are ready for recitation.

Cornell System Summary Sheets. Figure 11.4 shows a Cornell System summary sheet that represents more than ten pages of notes taken during two lectures. Notice how the various points are categorized by century and are placed side by side for ease of comparison. The key words are brief as they should be; they hint at, but do not supply, each comparison.

Figure 11.5 shows a Cornell System summary sheet derived from textbook markings. The subcategories "Advantages" and "Disadvantages" were supplied by the student who took the notes. The material in each of these subcategories was originally scattered throughout the chapter.

To use one of these summary sheets for recitation, place a blank piece of paper over the right-hand column, look at the key words on the left, and recite. When you have recited the entire sheet, remove the blank paper to see whether you covered all the points.

Modified Outline and Paragraph Forms. Figure 11.6 shows a summary sheet in which the cue-word column is omitted. The key words themselves *are not omitted,* however. They are used as the headings and subheadings in this modified outline format.

To use this kind of summary sheet for recitation, place a blank sheet of paper over it. Then move the blank sheet down to expose the first heading

	Sociology 103 – Dr. Lind 19th CENTURY	20th CENTURY
Head of family	1. Patriarchal. Father head of family.	1. Now, individualistic & democratic
Stable- non extended fam.-	2. Family stable.	2. Family less stable.
	3. Many children and relatives under one roof = extended family	3. Smaller in size. Only two generations (parents & children)
non-mobile -	4. Non-mobile. Rarely moved "Old family homestead"	4. Mobility increased & residence changes often
women & work	5. Women: housework and children	5. Women: work outside & care for children after hours
sex-	6. Puritanical on sex matters.	6. Increasingly liberal
family types–	7. Family types in community alike	7. Greater variability in family type
family functions	8. Family had many functions: political, religious, economic	8. Now: function- procreation and socialization

FIGURE 11.4 Summary Sheet for Classroom Lecture Notes: Cornell System

(*A. Speech*), and recite. After reciting, expose the notes under the heading to check your accuracy. Then move the blank sheet down to expose the next heading, recite, and so on, until you reach the bottom of the sheet. Once you have reached the bottom of the page, take a few minutes to cast your eyes over the page to see the relationships and continuity among the various categories. This will give you a mental view of the whole.

The type of summary sheet shown in Figure 11.7 can be reviewed in the same way. The only difference between this sheet and the one shown in Figure 11.6 is that this sheet is in paragraph form. The main topics are still easy to identify and use as key words. The format you use should depend on the material and on your personal preference.

Helping Yourself

There are some more things you can do before your final exams, to ensure that you do your best.

1. Find out as much as you can about each exam. Ask your instructor about the types of questions (objective, essay, or both) that will be used. Find out

	Economics 102 - Professor Maxwell
I. Single Adv: 1. freehand 2. profits-his Disadv: 1. liable 2. "venture capital"	I. Single proprietorship ADVANTAGES 1. Can do what desires 2. All profit goes to owner DISADVANTAGES 1. All losses hurt owner (unlimited liability) 2. Commercial banks ordinarily will not provide "venture capital"
II. Partner – Adv: 1. Common pool 2. "vertical integration" 3. "horizontal " " Disadv: 1. death & change 2. liable	II. Partnership ADVANTAGES 1. Pool wealth, profits, losses 2. "Vertical integration" = gain control of resources, become own wholesaler 3. "Horizontal integration" = buy out competitors; add products; improve products DISADVANTAGES 1. Each time a member dies or leaves, a new partnership needs to be formed 2. Unlimited liability, even if own a small share
III. Corporation Adv: 1. legally formed 2. stock - capital 3. limited liability 4. perpetual – board Adv. to society: 1. production - eff. 2. continuation 3. creates capital 4. pays taxes	III. Corporation ADVANTAGES 1. Easy to form (legal permission needed) 2. Issue stock to raise capital; banker underwrites stock issue and sells to public. 3. Limited liability – Corp., distinct from its owners, can sue and be sued. 4. "Perpetual succession", or existence. Board of directors. ADVANTAGES TO SOCIETY 1. Technical efficiency - production of goods & services 2. Pool business risks - Continuation of production 3. Creates further capital for expansion or finance new 4. It is taxed

FIGURE 11.5 Summary Sheet for Textbook Chapter: Cornell System

The Hopi

A. Speech
  1. Uto-Aztecan family (Ute, Paiute, Shoshone)
B. Subsistence-Economic Life
  1. Skillful farmers-growing maize (mainstay), beans, squash.
  2. Main fields not irrigated-small gardens irrigated. Cotton.
  3. Domestic animals not important
    a. turkeys-for feathers
    b. sheep - for wool
  4. Wild flora-onions, potatoes, tobacco - yucca for soap.
  5. Hunting
    a. rabbit
C. Settlement & Houses
  1. Proximity of water
  2. Desire for security - mesa residence.
  3. Clay, sandstone, mud - terraced effect - hole in top, reached by ladder.
  4. Only women own houses.
    a. matrilocal residence-brings together matrilineal kin.
    b. kinship groups are strong.
D. Crafts
  1. Basketry (not too good).
  2. Loom work - wool has become the principal textile material.
  3. Pottery (coiled) painted.
E. Division of Labor
  1. Men
    a. most of farming
    b. spin, weave, tan skins, make clothing for selves & wives
    c. housebuilding: both sexes work
  2. Women
    a. make pottery
    b. tend gardens
F. Trade
  1. Other Pueblo
  2. Paiute, Apache, Navaho
G. Society - Lineage & Clan
  1. Typical matrilocal residence - Underlie the clan system.
  2. Houses owned by women — " " " "
  3. All-important ceremonials associated with maternal lineage.
  4. Clans are exogamous.
  5. Clans have totemic names, but do not believe descended from totem.
H. Family & Clan
  1. Boy accompanies father to cornfields; learns from him.
I. Government
  1. Chief - head of Flute ceremony.
  2. Power vested in hierarchical council of headmen.
  3. Town chief must learn long ceremonial chants.

FIGURE 11.6 Summary Sheet in Modified Outline Form
The separate column of key words has been omitted because the key words are in the outline.

Greek Race

Unity, well-rounded

The early Greeks were a vigorous people who constantly strove to achieve a well-rounded life — a unity of human knowledge. The Greeks did not have a departmental view. They believed that one man should know all things in one lifetime. The well-rounded Greek, in addition to being well versed in the arts, had to be an athlete, soldier, and statesman.

Competition

The Greeks loved competition. For example, they got together for athletic games each year. The athletic competitions best known to us were the games held at Mount Olympus and at Delphi.

Human-Image

A strong religious force permeated their lives. The early Greek religion was an interpretation of nature — polytheism. The Greek invested the gods with a human image in order to define these forces as tangible beings. These gods had greater power than humans, but they possessed human frailties. There was a close connection between government and religion. Every city was supposed to have been established by some god. For example, Athena was supposed to have founded Athens and the people were descended from her.

FIGURE 11.7 Summary Sheet in Paragraph Form

whether your instructor will allow partial credit, how long the exam will take, and whether textbooks, notes, calculators, or other equipment will be allowed in the exam room. See whether you can get a copy of last semester's exam, to see what kinds of questions were asked and to make sure you know the meanings of the words used in the directions. (For example, *interpret* doesn't mean the same as *evaluate* in an essay question.) Use all this information to direct your study effort and to make sure you have the equipment you need to take the exam.

2. As you recite from your summary sheets, pause between key words and ask yourself, "What kind of question would I ask on this material if I were the instructor?" Then write out your questions on a separate sheet of paper. You may end up with twenty or even thirty questions for each course. Use part of your study time for each course to sit down and answer these questions, as if they were the exam. Write out your answers just as you would for the exam itself. Then check your answers to see that they are complete and accurate. Don't worry about how close your questions might be to the actual questions. They will be close enough. The more questions you make up and answer, the greater is the chance that you'll encounter similar questions on the exam.

3. Study in the same way for both objective and essay exams. Some students believe that objective-type exams are easier, and they tend to study less for them than for essay tests. Others believe they should study details for objective exams and relationships for essay exams. Actually, you need to master the material just as thoroughly for one type as for the other.

4. Don't study by rereading the textbook. Rereading is neither an efficient nor an effective study method. Use your notes, underlinings, and marginal key words to study through summarization and recitation—they are hard to beat because they get you actively involved in your studying.

5. On 3 × 5 cards, make condensed notes to carry around with you. Using these cards during spare minutes is a splendid way to study throughout the day instead of bunching your study time into long, unbroken sessions.

6. Make concept maps as described in Chapter 10. On one or several sheets, write out the main concepts of the course; bolster these main concepts with supporting material; draw connecting lines to show relationships; and end up with a map of the course that shows you the full picture.

7. Take advantage of group study, if you are well prepared. If you have studied the material for the course thoroughly, group study is good because during a discussion you will be able to understand another's interpretation and see relationships. If, however, you are unprepared, you'll be wasting your time.

8. Think positively. Your attitude will influence how you do on an exam. A positive attitude begins with your feeling of preparedness; but even if you feel you haven't studied as successfully as you should have, don't think negatively. Remind yourself that you do know a good portion of the material and that your healthy physical, mental, and emotional state will help you think through the rest.

9. Don't expect to be helped in any way by going to a so-called relaxing movie on the night before an exam. Any such activity can only interfere with remembering. Instead, take a "grand tour" of the summary sheets for tomorrow's exam. Spread out the summary sheets and try to see the overall picture; try to get a panoramic view of the course. Then go to bed and get a good night's sleep. In the morning, have a leisurely and nourishing breakfast, take a last tour through your notes, and do well on the exam.

CRAMMING

Should students cram? Yes, if they don't know their material. But cramming, sometimes an unfortunate necessity, must be done according to a system if it is to be of any use.

Suppose that you have taken notes on almost every lecture but have not recited or reviewed your notes since you took them. Also, you have skimmed through each assigned textbook chapter, have underlined the chapters indiscriminately, but have not taken any separate notes. With the passage of time and with no reviews of the material, your retention is probably at the 10 percent level. Two days before the examination, you will be starting almost from scratch.

With all five of your courses in this state of nonpreparation, you have an almost impossible task before you. If you try to study day and night to learn every idea, fact, and detail for each course, you will learn almost nothing. The mind simply is not built to take in such chunks of undigested material in such a short time.

The Selectivity System

If your only chance to pass a course is to cram, then the one word to remember is *selectivity.* You must avoid falling into the trap of trying to learn too much. It will be extremely difficult to resist picking up important-looking bits of information along the way, but that is what you must do. Concentrate on essential facts, and use as much of your time as possible for *remembering* them.

Each textbook chapter has to be skimmed and searched, and the main ideas and pertinent supporting materials must be ferreted out and written, in your own words, on a separate summary sheet ruled in the Cornell format. The same must be done with your lecture notes.

When all the highlights have thus been noted, push aside the books and notebooks. Leave in front of you only the ten or so sheets of notes you took on the textbook and the ten sheets of notes taken from your classroom notes.

Now recite, recite, and recite. The notes you have selected will do you no good unless you embed them in your mind so that you can mentally carry them into the examination room. To make these notes your own, glance at the key words in the left margin, and recite the ideas, principles, and supporting details over and over again until you know them cold.

It is true that you have taken a chance by selecting only certain ideas, principles, facts, and supporting materials. But if you try to remember too much, you will end up with almost nothing; you cannot possibly memorize so much in such a short time. By judiciously selecting the very top ideas and memorizing them, you give yourself a good chance of passing the examination. You may not remember much after the exam, but the objective is to survive the battle so that you can come back next semester to continue the war.

Cramming Doesn't Replace Regular Study

Experiments have shown that people do not learn well or react logically in a crisis. These results apply directly to the student who tries to learn under the pressure of cramming. During the crisis of the examination, on questions that require thinking beyond the facts or with different facts, the student will be prone to panic and will answer a question with wrong material, make false, frantic starts, or just freeze. Studying under intense pressure seems to stifle flexibility in thinking and acting.

Through organized note taking, regular recitation, and systematic review, you can be ready to study for your final examinations. Then a few days spent with your summary sheets will organize vast amounts of material in your mind—far more than you could ever learn by cramming. Moreover, you will be rested, confident, and ready for the exams.

DURING THE EXAM

Getting Ready

Arrive at the examination room early, to get a good seat. Sit where the light is good for you; where the proctor will not disturb you as he or she paces up and down; where you can see the blackboard; and where there will be a minimum of distractions.

Do not sit near a friend. Friends are distractions. Any conversation before the exam is likely to interfere with the mindset you have developed for the exam. And, during the exam, you are likely to break concentration if your eyes meet those of your friend. If your friend leaves the room early, you may be tempted to leave early too, so you can discuss the exam. Finally, there is the danger of being accused of cheating because of a friendly but harmless word or smile.

Until the exam is passed out, silently rehearse some of the facts, formulas, and ideas that you've studied. This kind of thinking keeps distracting thoughts away. It also warms up your thinking apparatus, so that you will be able to give your full attention to the exam.

If you feel tense before or during the exam, use the Doctors' Method (discussed in Chapter 2) to get rid of your anxiety. Breathe in until your lungs feel completely full. Take a sudden, quick, extra breath through your open mouth. Let your breath out slowly. Repeat the three steps five, six, or seven times, depending on what feels right for you. They are hardly noticeable to others.

Listen carefully for additional instructions, before—and even after—you receive your copy of the exam. The instructions that are written on the examination itself are not always complete, or they may require clarification. If you have already received your copy, you may be tempted to read the exam, giving only half an ear to the spoken instructions. It pays to stop reading and listen, because the proctor's oral instructions may change or even negate some written instructions. You would, for example, be in hot water if you missed the proctor's instruction to "Do only three out of the five essay questions."

If the directions are not clear, and the exam hasn't started yet, immediately ask about them. Don't start any test with such a doubt in your mind. If the exam has already started, and you have a question—especially about procedure—raise your hand high. When the proctor comes to you, whisper your question.

Answering the Questions

Before you answer any questions, *read the directions carefully.* Then skim the entire exam, just enough to become slightly familiar with the types of questions asked and to see how much weight is assigned to each question. Next, quickly decide how much time you should spend on each question. Finally, begin answering the questions, but *do the easy questions first.* You will save time because you'll be able to get to work immediately; you'll feel better about the exam once you put a question or two behind you; and, with your thinking processes limbered and oiled, you'll be in a good position to attack the harder questions.

Check the time occasionally to see that you are keeping up with your question-answering schedule, but don't get worried if you're a bit behind. Use any time you gain to go back and check your answers and to make sure that your answers are numbered to correspond with the question numbers.

Don't get upset when you run into a question that you can't answer, and don't sit and ponder the question forever. Both of these responses are time wasters, and your time should be used for earning exam points. When you come to a tough question, read it again carefully. If you can, quickly outline some kind of logical or reasonable response and carry the response as far as possible, hoping to get some credit for the effort. Then put the question and answer out of your mind, and go on to the next question. If you can't write anything at all, either because your memory is "blocked" or because you just don't know, go on to the next question immediately. Return to the skipped question later.

Always take the full time allowed for the exam. If you finish early, go back to the questions you skipped and try to answer them. When there is no penalty for guessing wrong in a multiple-choice exam, leave no question unanswered. When there is a penalty, use this system: If five possible choices are given and you can eliminate two as being incorrect, then guess. If four choices are given and you can eliminate one, then guess. But if you cannot eliminate any choices, skip the question.

You can also use extra time to reread the questions, to make sure you understood the real intent of each one. You may want to change some of your answers. Research shows that students improve their scores by changing answers on objective tests *after giving the questions more thought.* (In one study, using a true-false test, the changing of *true* to *false* was more often correct than the changing of *false* to *true.*) So, after calm thought, if you think you should change an answer, do so. But don't change an answer simply because you are nervous about your original response.

Taking Standardized Tests

Standardized tests are preprinted tests, usually prepared by firms that specialize in testing. They are generally answered on machine-readable answer sheets. For example, the SAT and PSAT tests are standardized tests. Standard procedures are used to administer, score, and evaluate them, so that the test scores of all students all across the country can be compared without bias.

Here are five tips for taking these tests:

1. To record your answer, make a dark mark in the space provided, with *one firm stroke* of the pencil from top to bottom.
2. Because stray marks on the answer sheet may be picked up by the machine as incorrect answers, erase such marks cleanly.
3. If you change an answer, erase your previous mark thoroughly.
4. Occasionally check to see that you are recording your answers in the spaces that correspond to the proper questions in the test booklet.
5. Keep your test booklet very near the answer sheet to make the marking faster and more accurate.

AFTER THE EXAM

Directly after the exam, while your memories are still fresh, talk over the exam with several of your friends. The bigger the group the better, for then you'll be getting more information about how the others interpreted the questions and how they answered them. You'll benefit from knowing the techniques and thinking and reasoning processes they used. You'll see where and why you made mistakes, and where you succeeded. In addition, you'll be reviewing the subject matter of each question. Like other, more formal, reviews, this one too will help you remember the important facts and ideas.

Most final-exam papers are not returned to students, but tests and quizzes usually are returned. When you get back a test or exam paper, don't simply note the grade and file it "for future reference." It's yours and you "paid" for it, so use it to learn even more.

1. Go first to the questions you missed. Read and analyze them carefully to find out specifically what was wrong with your answers. Were they incomplete? Did you make careless mistakes? Did you really know the material?
2. Learn from your mistakes by taking the time to outline (or even write) better answers. You might reap an unexpected bonus by doing this, because instructors often repeat, on the next test, a question that many students missed.
3. Learn from your correct answers by analyzing why they were correct. You'll be pleasantly surprised at how much you can learn with this seldom-used technique.
4. Check to see which types of questions you did or did not do well with: definitions, interpretations, discussions, mostly facts, mostly ideas, and so forth. Check also to see where the questions came from: lectures, textbooks, outside readings, or discussions. Use this information to study more effectively for the next test.
5. Determine which of your study and test-taking techniques worked and which did not work. Modify your study and test-taking strategies accordingly.

If you feel the need to discuss your exam with the instructor, by all means do so. Before your meeting, write out the questions you want to ask; then ask them in a constructive manner. Find out what the instructor was trying to test with the questions, what ideas or facts he or she thought were important. This will help you to "read" future exam questions with greater accuracy. Above all, don't be negative. Don't argue with the instructor or complain about the wording of the questions. Don't explain that you knew the answer, but time ran out. Such negative arguments cannot possibly help you.

The most impressive thing you can do in any course is show steady progress. Few instructors give a term grade based only on cumulative average; the last examination in a course is usually far more important than the first. Suppose student A starts with an 85, dips to 75, rises slightly to 80, and on the final exam staggers through with a 72. Student B fails the first test with a 60, pulls up to 75, then to 80, and is a class leader with a 90 on the final. Student A actually has the higher average. But wouldn't you give the higher semester grade to student B if you were the instructor?

SUMMARY

What is recognition?

Recognition occurs when you're able to arrive at a correct answer after you have been given a number of answers to choose from. A multiple-choice question requires you to recognize the correct answer.

What is recall?

Recall involves remembering information without any choices or cues—that is, without the aid of recognition. Essay questions and even short-answer questions put an emphasis on this skill.

Where does test anxiety come in?

Test anxiety often occurs when you have studied only for recognition and not to the point of recall. When a question asks you to recall information, you panic and think you've forgotten. Of course, in reality you never really *knew* the information at all; you could only *recognize* it.

How can I overcome test anxiety?

Overcoming test anxiety involves changing your study habits by putting the emphasis on recalling information. After all, most test questions do the same.

How does the Questions-in-the-Margin System help me prepare for exams?

This technique forces you to pick out the key ideas from every paragraph and bolsters your ability to recall what you've read. Furthermore, because your marginal notes are written in question form, you immediately begin your preparation for test questions.

Can the Questions-in-the-Margin System be used for lectures as well?

Yes. Take your lecture notes on paper ruled according to the Cornell Note-taking System—that is, with a 6-inch column on the right and a 2½-inch column on the left. After the lecture is over, write thoughtful questions in the left-hand column just as you did in the margin of your textbook.

Where does reciting come in?

After you've taken notes and written questions, test your mastery of your lecture notes and of your textbook chapters. Cover the wide column of your notes with a blank sheet of paper and then ask yourself the questions that you've written. Recite your answers out loud and in your own words. Use the same technique with your textbook chapters. Because your answers will be covered, you'll be forced to recall what you know instead of just recognizing it.

How can I better organize my time in preparation for exams?

A week before exams, draw up a special time schedule, so that you can be sure that each block of time is well used. Before exam week begins, complete any back assignments and papers. You should still have time at the end of the week to focus on your upcoming exams. Designate time blocks for exactly what you want to study. Come up with specific goals that you can accomplish. But don't miss any meals, classes, recreation, or sleep in the process—they are all important to your exam performance.

Won't I need a schedule for exam week as well?

Yes. Make up one toward the end of the week before finals. With classes out of the way and back assignments completed, the bulk of your time should be devoted to reciting your summary sheets.

How do I consolidate my notes?

You can make summary sheets, condensed versions of a semester's worth of work. Look over all your notes and create two new sets of notes: one set for your textbook and one set for lectures. This time, record only the highlights from your original notes, making an effort to arrange them into smaller, more manageable categories. Use the Cornell System format for these sheets, or arrange your notes into paragraphs using headings and subheadings as your cues.

What other preparations can I make in order to be ready for exams?

Here are a few: (1) Ask your instructor about the exam. Will the questions be multiple choice or essay? Will notes, textbooks, or calculators be permitted? (2) As you study, try to anticipate the kind of questions the instructor is likely to ask. (3) Study the same way for objective and essay exams. (4) Rely on reciting and summarizing for your studying; rereading is both inefficient and ineffective. (5) Put condensed notes on file cards and carry them around to study in spare moments. (6) Use concept maps. (7) Take advantage of group study, but only if you are well prepared. (8) Study and prepare with a positive attitude; negative thoughts can undermine your success or make a bad situation worse. (9) Don't take the night off before an exam. Instead, spend the evening going over your summary sheets in order to get the big picture. Then go to bed and get a good night's sleep. In the morning, have a nourishing breakfast, and walk into the exam room feeling relaxed and confident.

Is there a right way and wrong way to cram?

Yes. If you must cram, be certain to do so as efficiently as possible. Be selective. Resist the temptation to learn everything; focus on learning only the essential facts. Do this in the following way. Skim each textbook chapter and write out only the main ideas on Cornell System summary sheets. Use a separate set of summary sheets for the main ideas from your lecture notes. Next, add cue words or questions in the narrow column. Finally, clear your desk of everything but your summary sheets, and then spend the rest of your time reciting until you know these notes by heart.

What can I do to prepare on exam day?

Get to the exam early so you can pick a good seat, one that's well lighted, in view of the blackboard, and away from distractions (including friends). While waiting for the exam to be passed out, silently rehearse any key facts and formulas. This encourages alertness and discourages distractions. If you feel tense, try one of the relaxation methods discussed in Chapter 2. Finally, read the test directions and listen for oral instructions, but don't try to do both at the same time. If you have questions about either, ask immediately: Don't begin the exam with any doubt in your mind.

What should my strategy be for answering questions?

Begin by figuring out how much time you can spend on each question. Then take care of the easy questions first. These early successes should bolster your morale and provide you with extra time. If you draw a blank on a tough question, reread it and do the best you can. If nothing comes, move on and return to the troublesome question only if you have time. Leave only when your time is up. Otherwise, use the extra time to go over skipped questions. If the questions are multiple choice and you are able to narrow the choices down, guess. You may also want to reread the other questions to be certain that you didn't misinterpret any of them.

Any hints for standardized tests?

Because standardized tests are usually graded by computers, not by human beings, you have to be certain that you aren't misinterpreted. Be sure to fill in your answer with a dark mark so the computer can read it. Make certain that any stray marks or old answers are erased completely. Check periodically to see whether the question you are answering corresponds to the spot on the answer sheet where you are marking.

What can I do after the exam?

Talk the exam over with a group of friends. You may learn where you went right and where you went wrong. If and when your test paper is returned, look it over to find out why your wrong answers were wrong and why your right answers were right. You might want to outline better answers for the questions you missed. Also, take note of the types of questions that you missed so that you can give them extra attention next time. Finally, figure out which study methods worked and which ones didn't, and adjust your routine accordingly.

Should I discuss the exam with the instructor?

If you're in search of constructive criticism or helpful advice, then by all means seek it out. You may learn something that will help you on a subsequent exam. But if you're just out to argue, forget it. It is far better to be seen as an enthusiastic student who is truly interested in learning and wants to improve. A show of steady progress often pushes a borderline grade up a notch.

HAVE YOU MISSED SOMETHING?

1. *Sentence completion.* Complete the following sentences with one of the three words listed below each sentence.

a. Test grades, like the financial bottom line, are an indication of ______ ______________________________.

interest   success   anxiety

b. Experiments have shown that people do not react logically in a ______ ______________________________.

test   library   crisis

c. It is a good idea to answer the easiest test questions ______________.

first   last   carefully

2. *Matching.* In each blank space in the left column, write the number preceding the phrase in the right column that matches the left item best.

____ a. Recall	1. Powerful method for embedding facts and ideas in memory
____ b. Recognition	2. Facilitates dialogue between reader and author
____ c. Anxiety	3. Extracting an idea from memory without any hints
____ d. Recitation	4. Must be done systematically, just like any other study technique
____ e. Background	5. Stored in your mind rather than on your summary sheets
____ f. Cramming	6. Should be read thoroughly before you ask any questions
____ g. Directions	7. The result, not the cause, of test failure
____ h. Preface	8. Remembering information with the help of cues

3. *True-false.* Write *T* beside the *true* statements and *F* beside the *false* statements.

____ a. Most test questions require recall rather than recognition.

____ b. It's all right to miss class during the week before exams.

____ c. The same basic recitation system can be used for both lecture and textbook notes.

____ d. You should study for essay and objective exams in the same way.

____ e. The instructions on your test paper may not always be complete.

____ f. After you've finished, it's a bad idea to discuss your exam with friends.

4. *Summary sheets.* Write "yes" next to the advantages of writing summary sheets.

____ a. Eliminate the need for recitation

____ b. Provide an immediate review

_____ c. Help to categorize your information

_____ d. Emphasize supporting details

_____ e. Provide a handy set of condensed notes

_____ f. Add information to what you already know

5. *Multiple choice.* Choose the phrase that completes the following sentence most accurately, and circle the letter that precedes it.

Extra time during an exam can be used to

a. return to questions you skipped
b. reread the questions you answered
c. change some of your answers
d. all the above

CHAPTER

12

Answering True-False, Multiple-Choice, and Matching Questions

To be able to discern what is true is true and what is false is false; this is the mark and character of intelligence.

Emanuel Swedenborg (1688–1772), Swedish scientist, inventor, and theologian

Do you know right from wrong? Can you recognize a correct answer when you see one? This chapter will help you do both—on tests and exams. It tells you

- What to look for in true-false questions
- How to analyze multiple-choice questions
- How to work through matching questions

rue-false questions, multiple-choice questions, and matching questions provide a very efficient way to test a student's knowledge of facts. With these types of questions, a fifty-minute test can cover a great deal of ground. Such questions are easy to grade, and the results depend only on knowledge; the student's writing ability doesn't get in the way of his or her answers.

The three types of questions are similar in one respect: The correct answer is provided; the student must identify it. In spite of this similarity, different techniques are used to analyze and answer true-false, multiple-choice, and matching questions.

WHAT TO LOOK FOR IN TRUE-FALSE QUESTIONS

In its simplest form, a true-false question is a statement that attributes a property or quality to one or more persons or things:

T F Birds can fly.

T F Students are creative.

T F Snakes are poisonous.

In the first statement, the ability to fly is attributed to (or connected with) birds. In the second, the quality of creativeness is connected with students. In the third, the property of being poisonous is attributed to snakes. On an exam you would circle *T* in all three cases, because all three statements are true. There are birds that can fly; there are students who are creative; and there are snakes that are poisonous. You should have no trouble with such simple, straightforward statements. The problem is that very few (if any) true-false statements are written so simply. Most contain qualifiers, negatives, or strings of qualities that make them more difficult to handle.

Watch Out for Qualifiers

Here's what happens when we add *qualifiers* to our basic true-false questions:

T F *All* birds can fly.

T F *Some* students are creative.

T F *Most* snakes are poisonous.

In each case, one small word—the qualifier—makes a big difference in the basic statement.

The first statement, "All birds can fly," is false, because birds such as the ostrich and the penguin cannot fly. The qualifier *all* overstates the connection between birds and flying. The second statement is true because *some* students are indeed creative. The qualifier *some* does not overstate or understate the situation. The third statement, "Most snakes are poisonous," is false; of the three thousand different kinds of land snakes, only about 250 are poisonous. Here again the qualifier leads to overstatement.

Qualifiers may be grouped into sets. The six most-used sets are

All—Most—Some—None (No)

Always—Usually—Sometimes—Never

Great—Much—Little—No

More—Equal—Less

Good—Bad

Is—Is Not

Within each set, the qualifiers may overstate a true-false statement, understate it, or make it just right. Memorize the six sets. They will help you answer many true-false questions.

Whenever one qualifier from a set is used in a true-false statement, substitute each of the others for it, in turn. In this way, determine which of the qualifiers in the set fits best (makes the statement just right). If that is the given qualifier, the answer is *true;* otherwise, the answer is *false.*

For example, suppose you are given the question

T F All birds can fly.

Substituting the other qualifiers in the "all" set gives you these four statements:

All birds can fly.

Most birds can fly.

Some birds can fly.

No birds can fly.

The statement beginning with the word *most* is just right, but that is not the statement you were given. Therefore, the answer is *false.*

Some qualifiers are "100 percent words." They imply that the statements they appear in are true 100 percent of the time. These words are

No	Every	Only
Never	Always	Entirely
None	All	Invariably
		Best

Such qualifiers are almost always connected with a false statement, because there are very few things in this world that are 100 percent one way or the other. Here are two examples:

All chickens make clucking sounds.

No true chicken can swim.

Always watch out for these qualifying words, but don't automatically consider a statement wrong simply because it contains one of them. To keep you honest and alert, some instructors will occasionally use them in true statements:

All stars are surrounded by space.

All human beings need food to survive.

No human being can live without air.

Qualifying words that fall between the extremes are generally used in true statements. Here are some in-between qualifiers:

Seldom	Most	Usually
Sometimes	Many	Generally
Often	Few	Ordinarily
Frequently	Some	

Here are two items in which these words are used:

T F *Many* birds fly south for the winter.

T F A balanced diet *usually* leads to better health.

To test your ability to recognize and work with qualifiers, do the exercise in Figure 12.1.

Check Each Part of the Statement

If any part of a true-false statement is false, then the whole statement is false. Be suspicious of a statement that contains a string of items, but don't conclude that it is false only because it contains the string. Here are two examples of statements with strings:

A long-term sales chart shows the dollar sales and sales trend by weeks, months, and years.

A warm-climate product, cocoa is grown in the Gold Coast of Africa, Nigeria, Brazil, Colombia, Venezuela, and in southern Norway.

The first statement is true because a long-term sales chart does show both dollar sales and the sales trend, which is indicated by the up-and-down

The following quiz, specifically designed both for students who have had a course in psychology and for those who have not, illustrates the importance of key words in objective questions. Take the quiz, picking out the key words and writing them in the space provided. In most cases, there is only one key word, but in a few instances, there are two or three. Also indicate in the right-hand column whether you think the statement is true or false. When you are finished, look below for the correct answers.

1. Geniuses are usually queerer than people of average intelligence. ____________ ___
2. Only human beings, not animals, have the capacity to think. ____________ ___
3. Much of human behavior is instinctive. ____________ ___
4. Slow learners remember what they learn better than fast learners. ____________ ___
5. Intelligent people form most of their opinions by logical reasoning. ____________ ___
6. A psychologist is a person who is trained to psychoanalyze people. ____________ ___
7. You can size up a person very well in an interview. ____________ ___
8. When one is working for several hours, it is better to take a few long rests than several short ones. ____________ ___
9. The study of mathematics exercises the mind so that a person can think more logically in other subjects. ____________ ___
10. Grades in college have little to do with success in business careers. ____________ ___
11. Alcohol, taken in small amounts, is a stimulant. ____________ ___
12. There is a clear distinction between the normal person and one who is mentally ill. ____________ ___
13. Prejudices are mainly due to lack of information. ____________ ___
14. Competition among people is characteristic of most human societies. ____________ ___
15. The feature of a job that is most important to employees is the pay they get for their work. ____________ ___
16. It is possible to classify people very well into introverts and extroverts. ____________ ___
17. Punishment is usually the best way of eliminating undesirable behavior in children. ____________ ___
18. By watching closely a person's expression, you can tell quite well the emotion he is experiencing. ____________ ___
19. The higher one sets his goals in life, the more he is sure to accomplish and the happier he will be. ____________ ___
20. If a person is honest with you, he usually can tell you what his motives are. ____________ ___

ANSWERS FOR EXERCISE IN KEY WORDS

The key words for each question were as follows: (1) usually, (2) only, not, (3) much, (4) better, (5) most, (6) psychoanalyze, (7) very well, (8) better, (9) in other subjects, (10) little, (11) stimulant, (12) clear, (13) mainly, (14) most, (15) most important, (16) very well, (17) usually, best, (18) quite well, (19) sure, happier, (20) usually. All the statements are false. The reasons for their being false can be found in the book from which they were taken or, very likely, in any general course in psychology.

FIGURE 12.1 An Exercise in Key Words (Qualifiers)

Source: Quiz reproduced by permission of McGraw-Hill Co., New York, from Clifford T. Morgan, Introduction to Psychology *(New York: McGraw-Hill, 1961), p. 2.*

movement of the graph. In addition, the time scale on the chart is marked in weeks and months as well as years.

The first nineteen words of the second statement are true. The last two words, "southern Norway," are false because cocoa grows only in warm climates—and Norway, both northern and southern, is freezing cold in winter. This one false item makes the entire statement false.

Some tricky (and usually false) statements are made up of two "substatements," both of which may be true. The two substatements are connected by a conjunction such as *therefore, thus, because, consequently,* or *so,* or a phrase such as *as a result.* What generally makes the statement false is that the second substatement doesn't logically follow from the first. In other words, the two parts are not directly related, although the statement is presented as if they are. For example, consider this statement:

> Thomas Edison invented the ticker-tape machine for recording stock prices and, *as a result,* he became famous.

It is true that Edison invented the ticker-tape machine and that he became famous in his lifetime. However, his fame was due not directly to his ticker-tape machine but to other inventions, including the electric light bulb, the phonograph, and the storage battery. For this reason, the statement is false.

Beware of the Negative

True-false statements that contain negative words and prefixes are difficult to sort out and answer. The negatives can upset or complicate your thinking. Negative words include *not* and *cannot,* and the negative prefixes are *dis-, il-, im-, in-, ir-, non-,* and *un-,* as in *inconsequential* or *illogical.*

Notice, in the following three statements, how the addition of negatives increases the difficulty of understanding what the statements mean—let alone deciding whether they are true or false.

> Thomas Edison's fame was due to his many practical inventions.
>
> It is illogical to assume that Thomas Edison's fame was due to his many practical inventions.
>
> It is illogical to assume that Thomas Edison's fame was not due to his many practical inventions.

When you are confronted with such a statement, begin by circling the negative words and negative prefixes. Then try to get the meaning of the statement without the negatives. Finally, reread the sentence to find out whether it is true or false in its entirety. Here, the first statement is true, the second is false, and the third is true.

Think "True"—and Guess When You Must

Most true-false tests contain more true statements than false statements, simply because they are made up by teachers. Since teachers would rather leave true information in your mind, they tend to stack the test with true statements. Of course, some teachers will fool you, but after the first test you'll know for sure.

On a true-false test, it is a good idea to guess at answers that you don't know, even if credit is subtracted for wrong answers. According to the laws of probability, you should get 50 percent right when you guess, even if you know nothing about the subject matter. If you can make intelligent guesses—knowing that there are more true than false statements—you should be able to do much better than that.

HOW TO ANALYZE MULTIPLE-CHOICE QUESTIONS

Most multiple-choice questions[1] are of the incomplete-statement type. A partial statement (called the *stem*) leads grammatically into four or five sentence endings, or options, listed directly under it. One of the options is the correct answer. The other (incorrect) options are called *distractors* or *decoys*.

Here is an example of a well-constructed multiple-choice question:

1. The almost perfect walls of granite boulders surrounding some lakes in Iowa were formed by

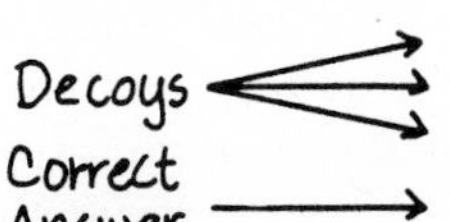

a. American Indians
b. prehistoric men
c. huge meteors
d. thick ice

This incomplete-statement question exhibits good construction in the following ways:

1. All options are grammatically consistent.
2. The stem is long, and the options are short.
3. Extraneous material is excluded from the stem.

[1]Some of the ideas in this section were inspired by James F. Shepherd, *The Houghton Mifflin Study Skills Handbook* (Boston: Houghton Mifflin, 1982), pp. 230–70.

4. The stem contains one central problem.
5. Double negatives are not used.
6. All options are plausible.
7. The correct option is no longer or shorter than the others.
8. Only one option is the correct or best answer.[2]

When the use of an incomplete statement would lead to an awkward stem or options, the question form is used, and the options are listed below the question.

Answering Multiple-Choice Questions

Before you even look at a question on a multiple-choice test, you must *read the directions carefully.* Some say, "Mark the one best answer," whereas others may require that you "Mark all correct answers." You will lose credit if you mark more than one answer in the first case, or if you miss a correct option in the second case. If the directions are not clear, then *ask.*

Begin each question by reading the stem all the way through. Then read the options all the way through. Don't be in a rush to mark the first option that sounds good. In some questions, *all* the options may be correct, and you have to choose the best one; you won't find it unless you read them all.

You should read all the options even when the question seems unfamiliar. One of them might provide you with a hint as to what the question is about. Furthermore, there's information in the options themselves—information that might help you remember what you need to know.

After you read the stem and the options, spend no more than a few seconds puzzling over the question. If it resists answering, cross out any options you have eliminated, mark the question so you will be able to find it easily later, and move on to the next question. But don't leave any question so fast that you do not give it the calm consideration it deserves. If you merely go through the motions, you're wasting time. The idea is to convert the easy questions into quick point-getters and leave enough time to go back to the questions you skipped.

When you have worked your way through the test, go back to the questions that you marked for reconsideration. This time, however, concentrate on eliminating options. The more distractors you can eliminate, the better your chance of finding the correct answer.

[2]William D. Hedges, "How to Construct a Good Multiple-Choice Test," *The Clearing House* 39 (September 1964): 9–11.

If you can somehow eliminate all the distractors, then you will have isolated the correct answer. If you can eliminate only one or two of the options, then you should guess at the correct answer. In the long run you will come out ahead by doing so, even if some credit is subtracted for each incorrect answer.

Here are some additional hints that may be of help to you in eliminating distractors and choosing the correct answer.

Try to Apply the True-False Technique

To use the true-false technique, you make a complete statement from the stem and each option, in turn. An option that results in a false statement is eliminated as a distractor. One that results in a true statement is probably the correct answer. As an example, consider this multiple-choice question:

2. Because of its lack of lumber, Syria has many "beehive" homes built of
 a. metal
 b. concrete
 c. marble
 d. mud brick

To judge the correctness of the first option, you would complete the stem as follows: Because of its lack of lumber, Syria has many "beehive" homes built of metal. Because Syria is a hot, dry, and rather poor country, you would probably decide that this statement is false. Metal (and concrete and marble as well) are too expensive and not readily available to the vast majority of people. The last option, *mud brick,* undoubtedly produced locally, would be inexpensive and available and would hold up in a country where rainfall is meager. (The correct answer is *d.*)

When you use this technique, don't be too quick to eliminate options; do so only after sufficient consideration. If you have eliminated three options but don't like the remaining option, you must go back and reconsider them all.

Stick to the Subject Matter of the Course

When a multiple-choice question includes options that you don't recognize or that seem out of place, don't get panicked into choosing one of them. The chances are great that the strange options are distractors. Here's an example:

3. Which of the following does not have satellites (moons)?
   a. Venus
   b. Cassiopeia
   c. Mars
   d. Perseus

You might reason as follows: "We've been studying planets and their rotation around the sun. I've heard of Cassiopeia, but we haven't studied it. I've never heard of Perseus. I bet both are decoys—I'll cross them off. We did study Venus and Mars. They are planets, but I don't remember which one has satellites and which one doesn't. Well, at least I've boiled things down to a fifty-fifty chance. I'll mark this question and come back to it later."

Later, when you return to the question, you might remember that Mars has a ring of satellites or moons around it. That would eliminate Mars, leaving Venus. You still might not remember whether Venus has satellites, but since that's the only option left, you would choose it. (*Venus* is the correct answer.)

Watch Out for Negatives and Extreme Words

We discussed negatives and extreme words in relation to true-false questions, and our discussion applies here as well. Whenever you find negative words such as *not* or *except* in the stem or in the options, circle them so they'll stand out. Then make sure you take them into consideration when you choose your answer. Here's an example:

4. Which materials are (not) used in making saddles?
   a. linen, canvas, serge
   b. wood and leather
   c. rubber and cork
   d. iron and steel

(The correct answer is *d.* The materials in *a, b,* and *c* are all used in saddles.)

Always circle 100 percent words such as *never, no, none, best, worst, always, all,* and *every;* and be suspicious of the options in which you find them. In fact, if you have to guess, first eliminate all the options that contain absolute words. Then choose your answer from the remaining options. As an example, see whether you can answer this question:

5. The author suggests that the desert
   a. climate is unpredictable
   b. heat is always unbearable

c. is totally devoid of rain
d. earthquakes pose a constant danger

You should have circled *always* in *b, totally* in *c,* and *constant* in *d,* to obtain *a* as the correct answer. You didn't even have to know what the question is about.

Foolish Options Are Usually Incorrect

Test writers occasionally include a silly statement as an option. Most likely, they become tired and simply dash off foolish statements to fill space. You should almost always view such statements as distractors worthy of being immediately crossed out. Here's an example:

6. The most important reason why the travel agents tested the Camel Caravan was to
a. judge the safety aspects of the trip
b. improve relations with the Arabs
c. get a free vacation
d. test the appeal of the Caravan for tourists

The foolish option is *c.* The correct option is *d.* Notice that options *a* and *b* make true statements, but the word *most* in the stem calls for option *d.*

The Option "All the Above" Is Usually Correct

When all the reasonable candidates for options will make the statement true, test writers frequently use "all the above" as an option. Doing so greatly simplifies the writing of such a question. Here's an example:

7. Until the first half of the second millennium B.C., an army laying siege to a city made use of
a. scaling ladders
b. siege towers
c. archery fire
d. all the above

(The correct option is *d.*)

One way to confirm the choice "all the above" is to find two correct answers in the options. For example, suppose you were sure that ladders and towers were used, but you weren't sure about archery fire. Then, if only one answer were permitted, that answer would have to be *d,* because *d* is the only option that includes *a* and *b.*

Numbers in the Middle Range Are Usually Correct

When all the options in a multiple-choice question are numbers, the answer is easy if you have memorized the correct number. Otherwise, you'll probably have to do some guessing. If you have no other information to go on, your chances of guessing correctly are increased if you eliminate the highest and lowest numbers. For some reason, test writers usually include at least one number lower than the correct answer and at least one number higher than the correct answer. This "rule" allows you to eliminate half of the options in the following example:

8. The "Great Pyramid" originally stood how many feet high?
   a. 281
   b. 381
   c. 481
   d. 981

You would eliminate 281 as the lowest number and 981 as the highest, leaving two middle-range numbers, 381 and 481. At this point you have a fifty-fifty chance of choosing correctly. Can you improve the odds?

You could compare the two remaining options to something you know, such as a football field. Then, 381 feet is slightly greater than a football field, perhaps not so high for a pyramid. But 481 feet is over 1½ times as high as a football field is long. That would really make a "Great Pyramid." (If you stuck with 481 feet, you would be correct.)

Check for Look-Alike Options

Test makers occasionally include, in one question, two options that are alike except for one word. Such a pair seems to indicate where the test maker's interest was focused, so it is logical to assume that one of the pair is the correct answer. The other options should, of course, be read carefully; they should be eliminated in favor of the look-alikes only in a guessing situation. For example, consider the question:

9. The author considers himself an authority on
   a. touring the Middle East
   b. Middle East rug dealers
   c. Middle East rug bargains
   d. behavior patterns of tourists

Even if you had no inkling of the correct answer, you would be wise to eliminate *a* and *d* and choose from the similar pair *b* and *c*. (The correct option is *b*.)

The test writer can keep you from using this technique by inserting two pairs of similar options. Then you would have to deal with four options:

10. The author considers himself an authority on
   a. behavior patterns of merchants
   b. Middle East rug dealers
   c. Middle East rug bargains
   d. behavior patterns of tourists

Check for Longer or More Inclusive Options

In multiple-choice questions, the correct option is often longer or more inclusive of qualities or ideas than the distractors. The length or inclusiveness results when the test writer must qualify or amplify a simple statement. So, be alert for a tightly packed or overly long option, as in this question:

11. The author says that rug buying in the Middle East is like courtship in that
   a. both parties fool each other
   b. both parties must trust each other
   c. both parties desire the same thing but begin with expressions of disinterest
   d. in rug buying, as in courtship, one dresses in one's best

(Here option *c* is correct.)

HOW TO WORK THROUGH MATCHING QUESTIONS

Matching questions provide a most efficient way to test knowledge in courses such as history (in which events, dates, names, and places are important) and psychology (for which numerous experiments, experimenters, results, and special terms and definitions have to be remembered). In a matching question, two vertical lists of items are placed next to each other. Each list contains a half dozen or more words or phrases, in random order. The task is to match the items in one list with those in the other list, according to a relation that is given in the directions for answering the question.

Figure 12.2 contains a matching question that will test your knowledge of inventors and their inventions. You may want to try it now, before you read the next section.

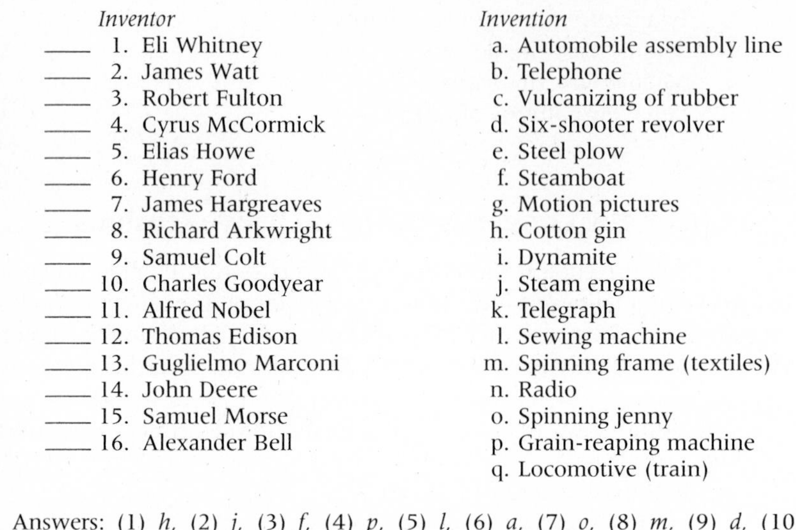

Match the inventions in the right-hand column with the inventors in the left-hand column by writing the proper letter in the space provided alongside each inventor's name. Use each item in the right-hand column only once.

Inventor	*Invention*
____ 1. Eli Whitney	a. Automobile assembly line
____ 2. James Watt	b. Telephone
____ 3. Robert Fulton	c. Vulcanizing of rubber
____ 4. Cyrus McCormick	d. Six-shooter revolver
____ 5. Elias Howe	e. Steel plow
____ 6. Henry Ford	f. Steamboat
____ 7. James Hargreaves	g. Motion pictures
____ 8. Richard Arkwright	h. Cotton gin
____ 9. Samuel Colt	i. Dynamite
____ 10. Charles Goodyear	j. Steam engine
____ 11. Alfred Nobel	k. Telegraph
____ 12. Thomas Edison	l. Sewing machine
____ 13. Guglielmo Marconi	m. Spinning frame (textiles)
____ 14. John Deere	n. Radio
____ 15. Samuel Morse	o. Spinning jenny
____ 16. Alexander Bell	p. Grain-reaping machine
	q. Locomotive (train)

Answers: (1) *h,* (2) *j,* (3) *f,* (4) *p,* (5) *l,* (6) *a,* (7) *o,* (8) *m,* (9) *d,* (10) *c,* (11) *i,* (12) *g,* (13) *n,* (14) *e,* (15) *k,* (16) *b.*

FIGURE 12.2 Matching: Inventors and Inventions

How to Answer a Matching Question

The following sequence of steps will help you work through any matching questions systematically and efficiently.

1. Read the directions. Then run your eyes down both columns to get a brief overview of the specific items you will be working with.
2. Read the top item in the left-hand column. Then look carefully and thoughtfully down the right-hand column until you find a match for it. Don't stop at the first likely match; instead, continue through to the end of the right-hand column, to make sure there is not a better match. (If the right-hand column has the longer entries, you can save reading time by looking for the matches in the left-hand column.)
3. When you are certain that you have found a match, fill in the proper letter or number. (If you match the wrong items, you'll not only lose credit on that match, but you will run into more trouble later.) If you're not sure, skip the item and come back to it.

Match the activities in the right-hand column with the names in the left-hand column by writing the proper letter in the space provided alongside each name. Use each item in the right-hand column only once.

	Names	*Activity*
____	1. Jesse Owens	a. Tennis
____	2. Pete Rose	b. Swimming
____	3. Joe Montana	c. Hockey
____	4. Kareem Abdul-Jabbar	d. Aviation
____	5. Wayne Gretzky	e. Basketball
____	6. Althea Gibson	f. Movies
____	7. Gertrude Ederle	g. Football
____	8. Amelia Earhart	h. Opera
____	9. Meryl Streep	i. Baseball
____	10. Beverly Sills	j. Boxing
____	11. Joe Louis	k. Track
		l. Soccer

Answers: (1) *k,* (2) *i,* (3) *g,* (4) *e,* (5) *c,* (6) *a,* (7) *b,* (8) *d,* (9) *f,* (10) *h,* (11) *j.*

FIGURE 12.3 Matching: Personalities

4. This is the secret: Continue down the left column, filling in all the matches *that you're sure of.* This will drastically and immediately reduce the number of items that are left when you have to make the more difficult matches. And the fewer the items, the better are your chances of being correct.
5. As you use each item in the right column, circle its letter or number to show that it has been used. (You may also want to add the number or letter of the item with which it has been matched. This keying of your matches will help you check your answers later.)

Don't do any guessing until you are almost absolutely sure you're completely stumped. If you make an incorrect match too soon, you'll remove a "live" item from later consideration; then a second match, which would have made use of that item, will also be wrong. So first do your very best; then, using common sense and hunches, go ahead and guess at the remaining matches.

In case you're not an expert on inventions, Figure 12.3 contains a matching question that features famous personalities of the past and present. If you didn't use the matching-question sequence for Figure 12.2, try it here.

How to Study for Matching Questions

If you know that your instructor includes a long matching question in almost every exam, here's the best way to prepare for it. As you read and mark your textbook, be alert for facts and ideas that are associated with people's names. On a separate sheet, list the names and facts opposite each other, so that you end up with two distinct vertical columns, as in the following example:

Names	Facts or Ideas	(Subject)
Susan B. Anthony	Women's movement	(Sociology)
Jack London	*Call of the Wild*	(Literature)
George Washington Carver	Agricultural chemist	(Science)
Lewis & Clark	American explorers	(History)
George A. Miller	Magic number seven	(Psychology)
William James	Pragmatism	(Philosophy)
Mozart	*Marriage of Figaro*	(Music)

To master your list, cover the fact column with a sheet of paper. Look at each item in the name column, and recite and write the corresponding fact or idea. Then, to make sure that you learn the material both ways, block out the name column and use the facts as your cues. The example given here includes items from various subject areas. The same steps can be taken in any single subject area.

SUMMARY

What makes some true-false questions so hard to answer?

The difficulty often occurs when the test maker uses qualifying words such as *all, most, some,* and *none.* You must know not only the main fact, but also whether the qualifying word overstates or understates the fact, making the statement false. Be especially watchful for words that allow no exceptions—that is, words such as *never, all, always, none,* and *every.* These words can change an otherwise true statement into a false one.

What if half of the statement is true and half is false?	Then the statement is false. Always judge the entire statement. Be especially careful when a statement contains a long list of items.
What else should I watch out for?	Watch out for negative and extreme words within the statement. To make sure you take them into consideration, begin your analysis of the question by drawing a circle around every negative word and prefix.
Should I guess on true-false tests?	Yes. You have a fifty-fifty chance of being right, and knowing something about the subject matter should give you the winning edge.
How should I answer multiple-choice questions?	Begin by reading the directions carefully. Then read each question carefully—both stem and options. Eliminate options (distractors) where you can. Try to use the options as clues, and try the true-false technique.
Should I answer each question before moving on?	No. Don't waste time on a question that you can't answer in a reasonable amount of time. Instead, cross out the options you have eliminated, mark the question so you can come back to it later, and go on to the next question.
What should I do when I return to a multiple-choice question?	Concentrate on eliminating distractors. Make full use of probability techniques by looking for foolish options, "all the above," and look-alike and long options. Guess when you are able to eliminate at least one option in a four-option question or two options in a five-option question.
What's the best way to work a matching question?	First read the instructions and all the listed items. Then mark only the matches you are sure of, one by one. Next, go back to the items that you have skipped, and try to match them. Guess only when you're completely stumped.

Why can I study for matching questions but not for the others?

You *can* study for all types of questions, but you can do some special studying for matching questions by making a list of likely matches and then learning your list.

HAVE YOU MISSED SOMETHING?

1. *Sentence completion.* Complete the following sentences with one of the three words listed below each sentence.

a. Negative and absolute words should be ______________.

avoided circled defined

b. In matching questions, the fewer the remaining choices, the better are your chances of being ______________.

incorrect correct alert

2. *Matching.* In each blank space in the left column, write the number preceding the phrase in the right column that matches the left item best.

_____ a. Stem
_____ b. Qualifier
_____ c. Guessing
_____ d. Distractor
_____ e. Overstatement
_____ f. Understatement

1. Incorrect multiple-choice option
2. Risk of the word *none*
3. Correct option makes it a true statement
4. Risk of the word *all*
5. A word like *usually* or *some*
6. A last resort for matching questions

3. *True-false.* Write *T* beside the *true* statements and *F* beside the *false* statements.

_____ a. Qualifiers make true-false statements easy to answer.

_____ b. Complicated true-false statements are usually false.

_____ c. Guessing is advised when you don't know the answer to a multiple-choice question.

_____ d. In a well-constructed multiple-choice question, the correct option is always the shortest.

_____ e. In a matching question, answers you've used should be circled or marked in some fashion.

_____ f. In a matching question, you should immediately guess at matches you are unsure about.

4. *Multiple choice.* Choose the phrase that completes the following sentence most accurately, and circle the letter that precedes it.

In a multiple-choice question, an option is usually correct if it is

a. longer and more inclusive than the other options
b. one of two look-alike options
c. the only nonabsolute option
d. all the above

CHAPTER 13

Answering Sentence-Completion and Short-Answer Questions

Whatever is almost true is quite false, and among the most dangerous of errors, because being so near truth, it is more likely to lead astray.

Henry Ward Beecher (1813–87), American preacher and writer

It takes a certain knack to answer questions briefly but accurately. This chapter tells you

- How to analyze sentence-completion questions
- How to write short answers

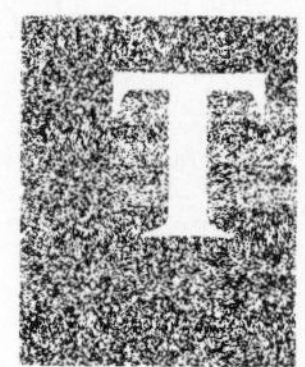

The types of questions discussed in Chapter 12 require only that you *recognize* the answer (or recognize whether a statement is true or false). The answer is already on the test paper, waiting for you to pick it out. To respond to sentence-completion and short-answer questions, which are discussed in this chapter, you must first find the correct information in your memory and then write it concisely. For sentence-completion questions, you are given a statement containing one or more blanks, and you must fill the blanks with words or phrases that make the statement correct. For short-answer questions, you are given a key word or phrase and must define, describe, or explain it in a few sentences.

Some students believe that having to supply the answers makes these types of questions more difficult than true-false, multiple-choice, and matching questions. However, the truth is that *guessing* is more difficult on completion and short-answer tests. You have to know the information to do well on *any kind of test.*

HOW TO ANALYZE SENTENCE-COMPLETION QUESTIONS

You have to supply very little information to answer a sentence-completion question—one or two words or perhaps a phrase. On the other hand, the test writer has to pack enough information into the incomplete statement so that you will know exactly what is wanted. All this information should be full of clues that will draw the correct answer up out of your memory. Sometimes even the physical make-up of the question can help you find the correct answer.

Finding the Clues and Filling the Blanks

One-Blank Statements. Most sentence-completion statements contain only a single blank, so you need to supply only one word. The easiest to complete are those in which the missing word comes at the very end of a sentence; then you have the uninterrupted context of the sentence to help you find the answer. Here's a long one-blank statement:

> In China there are about 80 million people named Chang; in France, the most common last name is Martin; in Germany it's Schultz; in Spain it's Garcia; in Russia it's Ivanov; and in the United States there are 2,400,000 ______________________________.

This statement provides a number of clues. There should be no doubt in your mind that what's wanted is the most common name in the United States, which is Smith. (Here, *Smiths* is the required answer.)

Two-Blank Statements. Two blanks with only a space between them indicate that a two-word answer is required. Often the two words are the first and last names of a person, as in the following example:

> The first person to suggest the use of daylight saving time was ______________ ______________.

Notice that both lines denoting implied words are of the same length. A careful test writer will make sure that all missing-word lines are of the same length, regardless of the actual lengths of the missing words. This is done to ensure that the lines don't serve as clues to the answers. (Here, the answer is *Benjamin Franklin.*)

When two blanks in a sentence-completion question are widely separated, you must treat them as if they occurred in separate sentences. There may or may not be a direct relationship between the missing words, so make sure that each filled-in word makes sense in its own part of the statement. Here is an example:

> Corn is the second most widely grown crop on earth today, after ____, and in the United States corn is the largest crop; however, no one in Europe knew about corn until ____ returned from the New World.

In the first portion of the sentence, the word *corn* tells you you're dealing with a grain. If you had read your textbook carefully (or if you hadn't, but used your common sense), you'd know the answer is *wheat.* The second blank demands a person's name; in this case, it is *Columbus.*

A Long Blank. A long blank indicates that a long answer is desired—a phrase, a clause, or even the equivalent of a sentence. Here is an example:

> Wedding rings have been worn on the third finger of the left hand since the days of ancient Greece, because the Greeks believed ________ ____.

To fill in this long blank, you would have had to read your assignments, because guessing wouldn't be practical or rewarding. However, you won't often find long blanks in completion questions, for two reasons: (1) They are difficult to grade because correct answers can vary so much. (2) Instructors don't want to get into arguments with students who claim that their answers are just as plausible as the so-called correct answer. (The answer is: *that a vein in this finger runs directly to the heart.*)

Grammatical Clues. Occasionally, a word in the incomplete statement will give you a clue to the missing word. For example, notice the form of the verb that follows the blank in this question:

> About 75 million meteors enter our atmosphere each day, but usually no more than _____ ever reaches the ground.

Because *reaches* is a singular form, the answer must be *one.*

Sometimes, a completion question will provide you with the *a*-or-*an* clue. This can help you reduce the number of possible answers. Here's an example:

> In addition to being one of this country's greatest statesmen, Benjamin Franklin also made lasting contributions to modern life as an ________.

After you finish reading this question, you should begin to run through Franklin's various interests. He was a diplomat, a philosopher, a printer, an author, an autobiographer, and an inventor. Right away you can see that the first three possibilities won't work. The word *an* in the question requires an answer that begins with a vowel. That leaves author, autobiographer, and inventor. Now you have to do a little thinking, based on the more important clue, "lasting contributions." As an author, Franklin wrote *Poor Richard's Almanack,* whose proverbs are still quoted occasionally. ("A penny saved is a penny earned" is probably the most famous of these.) His autobiography is no longer very popular. What about inventions? Among other things, Franklin discovered electricity, invented the lightning rod, and developed bifocals. Modern life would be quite different without these items, so *inventor* seems to be the best choice. (The correct answer is, indeed, *inventor.*)

The Question-asking Strategy

Whenever you are genuinely unsure about what specifically is wanted in a sentence-completion question, don't be afraid to ask. Before you raise your hand, however, have your question formulated in such a way that you can get the desired answer and, with it, the clue you need. As an example, here's a relatively simple completion question.

> Today, most of the olives we eat come from ____________________ or ____________________.

Although the sentence is well constructed, it is nevertheless unclear. The problem is that you know that olives are grown in Spain, Italy, Portugal,

Morocco, Libya, Algeria, and all along the northern African coast, but you wonder whether you should write in the two continents of Europe and Africa or the names of the two major olive-producing countries.

At this crucial point you should *not* call the instructor over and say, "I don't understand what you want!" If you do, you won't get much help. The instructor will simply tell you to do the best you can. Instead, you should say something like, "I have answers for this one, but I'm not sure whether you want me to list the continents or specific countries." In this case, the instructor would tell you to list specific countries. Then you would fill in the blanks with the two largest exporters of olives. (The correct answers are *Spain* and *Italy.*)

When Should You Guess?

You should begin every test by moving quickly through it once, to answer the questions you are reasonably sure of. Take the time to read each question carefully, and mark those you skip so you will be able to find them later. Then go through the test a second time, give each unanswered question some thought, and write as reasonable an answer as you can. You have nothing to lose, because there is usually no penalty for guessing on a sentence-completion question. A blank space is worth zero; but a good guess, based on common sense, can earn you some points. Here's an example:

> By using a system of rivers, bays, and canals called the ______________ ______________, it is possible to travel by ship from New England to Florida without once entering the usually rough open seas.

This sentence is long enough and descriptive enough to help you come up with a good guess, in the event you don't know the official name for the system. You might call it the "Inland Waterway." That's not the exact name, but it is very close, and you probably would get almost full credit for it. (The answer is *Intracoastal Waterway.*)

HOW TO WRITE SHORT ANSWERS

Figure 13.1 shows part of a typical short-answer test. Notice that only a limited space is provided for each answer. To save time and space, and to make sure that you don't have to do any massive erasing, *think* before you write. Give direct answers; concentrate on presenting information; and write in telegraphic sentences, unless the instructor specifically asks for complete

NAME, AND BRIEFLY DISCUSS OR DESCRIBE, THE FOLLOWING ANIMALS.	
Fastest animal:	The cheetah. for short distances, can top 70 miles per hour.
Fastest bird:	The swift, which can top 106 miles per hour; the fastest of all living creatures.
Non-flying birds:	The ostrich of Africa, the penguin of the Antarctic, the emu and the cassowary of Australia, the rhea of South America, and the kiwi of New Zealand.
Most poisonous snake:	The Australian tiger snake is the most poisonous snake in the world. There's enough venom in its glands to kill 300 sheep.
Most common domesticated animal:	The chicken, formerly a jungle fowl from Asia, domesticated about 1500 B.C. Now, about four billion chickens on earth. About 400 million in U.S. and about 560 million in Russia.

FIGURE 13.1 Short-Answer Questions with Answers

sentences. Even when you do write full sentences, make them simple; concentrate more on packing information into your answers than on achieving a graceful literary style.

As usual, you should work through a short-answer test twice—the first time to answer the questions you are sure of, the second time to work on those you skipped. When you go back to a question, think about it, and then write down any fragments of information that you may recall. Try to put the fragments in some logical order, to show that you know what you are doing. Take a stab at questions you are not sure about, but do so quickly; guesses usually don't earn many points on these almost-essay questions.

The best way to study for short-answer tests (and other types as well) is to make and recite summary sheets as discussed in Chapter 11.

SUMMARY

What's the trick to answering sentence-completion questions?	There are very few tricks or gimmicks to help you. Your best bet is to know your facts and ideas cold.
What's the best clue to use in answering sentence-completion questions?	The best clue is context—the incomplete sentence itself. Read the sentence thoughtfully, trying to get as much meaning out of it as possible. Even individual words can spark the recall of the correct answer.
Should I guess on completion questions?	When you are sure there is no penalty for guessing, fill in reasonable and serious answers to questions that stump you. But never give a "cute" or "wise" answer. It will almost always affect the test marker negatively.
What's the prime advantage of short-answer questions?	Short-answer questions enable the instructor to cover more ground on an exam, in less time, than does one essay question. So a short-answer test more completely covers the course material.
What's the secret to writing short answers?	Think before you write; then write telegraphic sentences, packed with information. If you're going to guess, do so quickly and then move on to the next question.

HAVE YOU MISSED SOMETHING?

1. *Sentence completion.* Complete the following sentences with one of the three words listed below each sentence.

a. In a completion question, the most important clues come from the ______________________________.

context lines instructor

b. Unless the instructor specifies otherwise, your short answers should be ______________________________.

literary telegraphic humorous

2. *Matching.* In each blank space in the left column, write the number preceding the phrase in the right column that matches the left item best.

_____ a. Information	1. Limited in a short-answer test
_____ b. Space	2. Study method for all kinds of tests
_____ c. Question	3. Normally awarded to a blank that is left blank
_____ d. Zero	4. More important than style in short answers
_____ e. Guessing	5. Used intelligently, it can clarify a confusing answer
_____ f. Recitation	6. Of limited value in a short-answer test

3. *True-false.* Write *T* beside the *true* statements and *F* beside the *false* statements.

_____ a. Two-blank statements often require a person's first and last name.

_____ b. You can depend on line lengths for clues in completion questions.

_____ c. Blanks that are widely separated are best treated as if they appear in separate incomplete statements.

_____ d. There's an element of the essay question in a short-answer question.

_____ e. If you do guess on a short-answer question, you should spend plenty of time pondering your answer.

_____ f. In a short-answer test, you should strive for direct answers.

4. *Multiple choice.* Choose the word that completes the following sentence most accurately, and circle the letter that precedes it.

Unlike a multiple-choice question, a short-answer question involves

a. recognition
b. recall
c. revision
d. reflection

CHAPTER 14

Answering Essay Questions

People like definite decisions
Tidy answers, all the little ravellings
Snipped off, the lint removed.

Gwendolyn Brooks (b. 1917), Pulitzer Prize–winning poet

Writing in your own words—that is perhaps the scariest part of answering an essay question. There are no blanks to fill in or answers to choose from. Everything must come from you and what you've learned. This chapter discusses

- How essay exams are graded
- Planning before you answer
- How to answer an essay question
- The content of an essay answer

and finally

- Important odds and ends

To answer an essay question, you must write from one or two paragraphs to several pages about a given topic. You are required not only to *recall* ideas and facts, but also to *organize* them into thoughtful, forceful sentences and paragraphs.

HOW ESSAY EXAMS ARE GRADED

Here is how over two hundred examination booklets in a popular introductory history course are graded at one college. The day of the exam, each grader in the history department has time to scan, but not to grade, the answer booklets. At a meeting the next day, each grader reads aloud what he or she thinks is the one best answer for each question. A model answer for each question is then agreed upon by the staff. The essential points in the model answers are noted by all the graders, for use as common criteria in grading the responses.

During the reading of the answers, one grader remarked, "Yes, this student mentioned points five and six . . . but I think he didn't realize what he was doing. He just happened to use the right words as he was explaining point four." These comments reinforce the importance of enumerating major points by numbering them, bold and dark—1, 2, and so on—and using transitional words to show how you got from one point to the next, so that no one thinks you just stumbled onto the answer.

Graders don't simply count facts, ideas, and dates. Most essay questions require *reasoning,* and graders look for it in your answers. In one survey, 114 college teachers were asked what they look for most when grading answers to essay questions. Here's how they responded:

Specific Quality	*Number of Responses*
Reasoning ability	103
Factual accuracy	84
Relevance to question	73
Good organization	71
Complete answers	71
Clarity	64

Notice that four of these point-getters are related to *how* students answer, and only two are related to *what* they answer. Of course, you must know the facts cold, because you can't reason and organize well or be clear and relevant if you don't know what you're writing about. But you must also present the facts in such a way that your answer exhibits the other important qualities. The remainder of this chapter tells you how to do so.

PLANNING BEFORE YOU ANSWER

You can do a number of things to help yourself once the essay exam has begun but before you have started to answer the questions. These actions will get you ready for the questions, get you into the first question, and help you work your way through the test.

1. *Make Notes on the Back of the Exam Sheet.* Even before you read the exam questions, unburden your mind by quickly jotting on the back of the exam sheet the ideas, facts, and details that you have memorized but think you might forget. This is almost like putting down a summary of your summary sheets. Furthermore, it is a positive action that will involve you in the exam immediately. Do not, however, spend more than a minute or so making these notations.

2. *Read the Examination Directions Carefully.* Notice especially whether you must answer all the questions and whether there are any time limits. Frequently, you may be given a choice of questions.

3. *Read All the Questions.* Before you write anything, read all the questions. If you have a choice among questions, select those for which you are best prepared. As you read the instructions for each question, underline or circle the key words, which tell you the form in which the answer is wanted. Then check the key words before you begin to answer the question. A list of key words and their meanings is given in Figure 14.1.

4. *Jot Cues Alongside Each Question.* While reading each question, quickly note a few words or phrases that immediately come to your mind. Later, when you begin writing, use these jottings and those on the back of the exam sheet to organize your answer.

5. *Plan Your Time.* It takes less time to follow these suggestions than to read them—especially in relation to the time you will gain through efficient handling of answers. Find out how much time is left after following these steps; then decide how much time to give to each question, and *stick to your plan.*

6. *Start with the Easiest Question.* Nothing inspires confidence and clear thinking more than getting off to a flying start with one question well answered. Don't sit and stare at the first exam question! Seize on an easy one, number the answer correctly, and start writing.

KEY WORD	*EXPLANATION*
Apply a principle	Show how a principle works, through an example.
Comment	Discuss briefly.
Compare	Emphasize similarities, but also present differences.
Contrast	Give differences only.
Criticize	Give your judgment of good points and limitations, with evidence.
Define	Give meanings, but no details.
Demonstrate	Show or prove an opinion, evaluation, or judgment.
Describe	State the particulars in detail.
Diagram	Show a drawing with labels.
Differentiate	Show how two things are different.
Discuss	Give reasons pro and con, with details.
Distinguish	Show main differences between two things.
Enumerate	List the points.
Evaluate	Discuss advantages and disadvantages, with your opinion.
Explain	Give reasons for happenings or situations.
Give cause and effect	Describe the steps that lead to an event or situation.
Give an example	Give a concrete example from your book or experience.
Identify	List and describe.
Illustrate	Give an example.
Interpret	State the meaning in simpler terms, using your judgment.
Justify	Prove or give reasons.
List	List without details.
Outline	Make a short summary with headings and subheadings.
Prove	Give evidence and reasons.
Purpose	How something fulfills an overall design.
Relate	Show how things interconnect.
Relationship	Connection between events, the linkage.
Review	Show main points or events in summary form.
Show	List your evidence in order of time, importance, logic.
Solve	Come up with a solution based on given facts or your knowledge.
State	List main points briefly without details.
Summarize	Organize and bring together the main points only.
Support	Back up a statement with facts and proof.
Trace	Give main points from beginning to end of an event.

FIGURE 14.1 Key Words in Essay Questions
This alphabetical list contains key words encountered in the directions for essay questions, along with brief explanations.

HOW TO ANSWER AN ESSAY QUESTION

Hugo Hartig suggests the following ten rules for answering essay questions.[1] The rules are not meant to tell you *what* to write, but rather *how* to compose and word your answers.

1. ***Understand the Question with Precision.*** It is important to read the question very carefully, so that you are clear about the *exact* idea that the professor is trying to get at. A good essay question is never vague or ambiguous, and if there is anything unclear about the question, do not hesitate to ask for a clarification from the instructor. You are going to be graded very largely on the *clearness* and *precision* of your answer, so obviously the question must also be clearly and precisely understood.

2. ***Strive for a Complete Answer.*** State your ideas explicitly. Do not leave anything to be inferred or concluded by the reader. Also define your terms as you go, to show that you know the full meaning of all the words that you are using. Explain all significant statements, to show that you know why they are significant. Show the complete process of your thinking. If your instructor has to "read between the lines" in order to get your point, he will mark you down. Make sure that every sentence actually has a definite point and definite purpose.

3. ***Use Facts and Logic, Not Vague Impressions or Feelings.*** Your personal likes or dislikes, emotions, attitudes or "feelings" are of no interest to anyone except yourself. Also, they are private: no instructor has the right to demand that you reveal your feelings in any way. Students sometimes believe that the purpose of a course is to teach them to "like" the subject, but this is absolutely not the case. Even in a course such as "Music Appreciation" the purpose is not to teach students to *like* music, but rather merely to *understand* it. In an essay exam, then, it is important to remember that liking or disliking is irrelevant; understanding is all important. The reason for this is the simple fact that teachers are not preachers, and, therefore, they are not in the business of persuading you to like anything or believe in anything.

4. ***Avoid Unsupported Opinions.*** An opinion that is not supported by some kind of logical or factual evidence is not worth anything at all, even if it is absolutely correct. For example, if you make the statement: "*Huckleberry Finn* is a masterpiece of American literature," and do not give any good reason to show that the statement is true, you get a zero on the statement. It is important to make significant statements, but it is equally important to show that they are either true, or untrue, on the basis of some convincing evidence or argument.

[1]This section is quoted, with permission, from Hugo Hartig, *The Idea of Composition* (Oshkosh, Wis.: Academia, 1974), pp. 29–32.

5. *Be Concise.* The most impressive answer is invariably the one that manages to get at the exact "heart of the matter" in the most direct and straightforward manner. It is important to make complete answers, and to explain and support everything you say; but it is even more important to say exactly the right thing, and not hide this gem of thought in a rambling discussion. If you must write out your ideas, to get them organized in your mind, do so on a sheet of scratch paper, and then write out your concise answer when you really have discovered the single most significant idea.

6. *Write Carefully So as to Avoid Errors.* Teachers almost without exception are very prone to make snap judgments about your general intelligence on the basis of your writing style. If you misspell common words, and make clumsy errors in sentence structure, or even if you write paragraphs that lack unity and coherence, many of your instructors are going to take it as a sure sign that you are sadly lacking in basic academic ability. Once a teacher thinks this about you, you will not get much credit for your ideas, even if they are brilliant. English teachers tend to be especially prejudiced in this regard.

7. *Be Natural and Sincere.* Avoid the use of high-sounding jargon, super-elegant language, phony fancy style, or so-called "fine writing." This does not impress anybody in regard to either your literary ability or your intelligence. On the contrary, many teachers will be insulted by it, because they will believe that you are trying to give them a "snow job." Any teacher who has read hundreds or thousands of papers becomes very sensitive to phoniness in student writing, because he sees so much of it.

8. *Organize Your Answer Intelligently.* Focus on either one central idea, or on several main points. In either case, follow the principle of "one idea—one paragraph." Write *deductive* paragraphs, in which you first state your important idea clearly and precisely, with adequate explanation. Then follow this statement immediately with factual or logical evidence that will support it adequately and convincingly. Sometimes it is helpful to underline your key statements in order to show that you are thinking systematically; but do not overdo it, or it will be less effective. In some cases, it may be helpful to use a brief introductory paragraph that states clearly in your own words exactly what the problem is that you are going to try to solve. A concluding paragraph that answers the "So What" question may also be effective.

9. *Keep It Simple.* Do not get involved in deep philosophical profundities. Especially avoid vague and fuzzy speculations that cannot be squared with ordinary common sense. Quite difficult and subtle ideas can be expressed in straightforward and simple language. If you can do this, your writing will be most impressive.

10. *Understand the Instructor's Pet Ideas.* In general, every instructor uses only a few basic approaches to his subject, and he probably keeps repeating these over and over again in his discussion of various aspects. An alert student can easily identify these "pet ideas" and work them out carefully in his own words. The student who does this is prepared not only to see through the instructor's questions quite readily, but he also knows exactly how to answer them, using the teacher's own methods of problem solving! Perhaps this is the very essence of grade getting in any course that depends heavily on essay exams.

THE CONTENT OF AN ESSAY ANSWER

Your answer must demonstrate that you (1) understand the question with precision, (2) know the necessary facts and supporting materials, and (3) can apply reasoning to these materials. Your only way to demonstrate that you know your stuff is through an organized answer. The following suggestions will help you get organized.

1. ***Do Not Write an Introduction.*** Don't start your essay with an introductory paragraph or even with a high-sounding sentence such as "This is, indeed, a crucial question that demands a swift solution; therefore. . . ." Such a general approach forces you to scatter your ideas, whereas the instructor is looking for a sharp focus. The instructor wants to know *how you answer the question.* It follows, too, that without a sharp focus, you will do serious damage to the unity of your answer. The result could be an answer that contains all the necessary details, but so mixed up that they do not convince the instructor that you know what you are talking about.

2. ***Answer the Question Directly and Forcefully in the First Sentence.*** Develop your essay from a strong opening sentence. The key to a direct answer is in a partial repeat of the question itself. By using the question as the stem of your answer, you cannot help but write a direct answer.

The example in Figure 14.2 shows how this principle works. The question asks for the student's opinion; therefore, it is quite correct to start the

Question: What do you think is the purpose of studying sociology?

Answer: I believe that the purpose of studying sociology is to make us aware and conscious that the people of the world are not one conglomerated mass; instead, people fall into various groups, societies, and economic systems.

FIGURE 14.2 A Direct Answer

sentence with "I believe." Notice that the first line in the answer includes some of the words that are used in the question. Such an approach keeps you honest; there can be no partial or off-focus answers. You have committed yourself to a direct answer.

3. *Expand on the First Sentence.* Now all you need to do is put down ideas, facts, and details to support your first sentence. Notice how easy and natural this approach is. When everything you write pertains to the first sentence, you cannot help but achieve unity; everything is not only pertinent but also hangs together.

In Figure 14.3, the question is directly answered in the first sentence. The answer revolves around the "characteristic shapes" of dunes. All the other sentences in this short essay are on the right track as they amplify the main point: the shape. Notice that this question has two parts. One part asks for a yes-no answer; the other asks the student to "describe." Simple diagrams would have been appropriate to help describe the different shapes of the dunes.

The essay in Figure 14.3 is a one-paragraph essay. For an extended essay (fifteen to thirty minutes), it is even more important that your direct answer come first, but in the form of a full paragraph rather than in a sentence. Then each of your subsequent paragraphs should expand on one of the sentences in the first paragraph. Again, the organization of the essay will develop easily and naturally.

In the opening sentence of Figure 14.4, the student places the answer in context, then immediately states his thesis sentence: "To help my students

Question: Are dunes recognizable after they have been covered with vegetation? Describe.

Answer: Yes, dunes can be recognized in the field after they have been covered by vegetation because dunes have characteristic shapes that cannot be entirely obscured or obliterated by vegetation. Dunes have a definite crest or summit, usually having a long windward slope and a much steeper leeward slope. They would be especially easy to recognize if they were barchans (crescent-shaped dunes). By studying the shape of the dunes, it is often possible to determine the direction of the prevailing winds over a region; thus a person can ascertain the present direction of the prevailing winds to see whether the windward slope and the winds coincide. Shape therefore indicates much more than whether a desert feature is or is not a dune.

FIGURE 14.3 A Paragraph-Length Essay

Question: Name and briefly describe several specific methods that a classroom teacher may employ to aid students in improving their reading skills. Consider this question in the context of the subject area in which you plan to teach.

Answer: I plan to teach high school English. To help my students improve their reading skills, I would teach them word analysis, how to read between the lines and interpret what they are reading, how to read with a purpose—and how to better understand the structure of what they are reading. I shall discuss each of these methods briefly:

(A) Reading ability is greatly improved when the student has a grasp of most of the words with which he is dealing. To increase my students' working vocabulary I would teach them how to analyze words in context. We would learn prefixes, suffixes, and roots and would learn how to analyze these and put them together. Word analysis would also involve figuring out words from their contexts. By practicing these skills, the students should be better able to handle new words in their future reading.

(B) Interpretative reading or reading between the lines is another means of improving reading. To help students interpret what they read, I would have them read practice passages—especially of poetry—and have them answer such questions as "What was the author's attitude toward Silas Marner, as reflected in her description of him?" or "What did the poet think of the girl about whom he wrote, 'Your face is like a rose'"?

(C) Reading with a purpose is basic to comprehension in any field. To get students used to reading with a purpose I would ask specific questions about the material, specifically about setting, character, etc. To get them used to reading for various purposes, I'd introduce various material—magazines, novels, poems, etc.

(D) I would try to improve students' reading skills by teaching them the structure of writings—the kinds of paragraphs, location of topic sentences, etc. Practice in writing would be beneficial.

To sum up, I would help my students improve their reading skills through word analysis, interpretative reading, reading with purpose, and analysis of the structure of writing.

FIGURE 14.4 A Longer Essay Answer

improve their reading skills. . . ." He next outlines the points he plans to cover and connects them with the rest of his answer by using a transitional sentence: "I shall discuss each of these methods briefly." Notice how the student makes his points stand out by lettering them, and notice his use of examples. These examples are supporting material; they convey to the instructor the student's full grasp of the topic under discussion.

4. *Use Transitions.* Transitions are often called directional words; they point to the turn in the road that the reader should take. When transitions lead from one idea to the next, the instructor finds the paper clear, logical, and refreshing. A number of transitional words are listed in Figure 14.5; try to use them when you have the chance.

5. *Don't Save the Best for Last.* Avoid the mistake of saving your best idea for a big finish. If it is not included in your direct answer in the first few lines, your point may never become clear to the instructor. Also, your point may never be worked into the organizational pattern of your answer, and the precious concept you were saving for last might end up unused.

The experienced writer knows that transitional words provide directional clues for the reader, that they show the relationship between sentences in a paragraph. For example, the word *furthermore* says, "Wait! I have still more to say on the subject." So the reader holds the previously read sentences in mind while reading the next few sentences. The following list suggests other words and expressions that you might find valuable.

Transitional Words and Expressions	*Intention or Relationship*
For example, in other words, that is	Amplification
Accordingly, because, consequently, for this reason, hence, since, thus, therefore, if . . . then	Cause and effect
Accepting the data, granted that, of course	Concession
In another sense, but, conversely, despite, however, nevertheless, on the contrary, on the other hand, still, though, yet	Contrast or change
Similarly, moreover, also, too, in addition, likewise, next in importance	No change
Add to this, besides, in addition to this, even more, to repeat, above all, indeed, more important	Emphasis
At the same time, likewise, similarly	Equal value
Also, besides, furthermore, in addition, moreover, too	Increasing quantity
First, finally, last, next, second, then	Order
For these reasons, in brief, in conclusion, to sum up	Summary
Then, since then, after this, thereafter, at last, at length, from now on, afterwards, before, formerly, later, meanwhile, now, presently, previously, subsequently, ultimately	Time

FIGURE 14.5 Transitional Words and Expressions

6. ***End with a Summarizing Sentence or Two.*** The final sentence or two in your answer should summarize (as in Figure 14.3) or repeat (as in Figure 14.4) the points made in your opening sentence or paragraph. Notice the transitional phrase "to sum up" in the last sentence of Figure 14.4; it clearly labels that sentence as a concluding statement.

IMPORTANT ODDS AND ENDS

1. ***Be Neat.*** A neat and legible paper or answer booklet does influence the grade. In a carefully controlled experiment, a group of teachers was instructed to grade a stack of examination papers on the basis of content and to disregard poor handwriting. Placed randomly within the stacks were word-for-word duplicate papers: one paper in good handwriting and the other in poor handwriting. In spite of their instructions, on the average the teachers gave the neater papers the higher grades—by a full letter grade.

2. ***Use Ink.*** Pencil is not appropriate for a written exam.

3. ***Write on Only One Side of Each Sheet.*** When both sides are used, the writing usually shows through, giving the paper a messy look. In addition, in an exam booklet, if you need to change or add something, you can write it on the blank page and draw a neat arrow to the spot where you want it inserted on the facing page.

4. ***Leave a Generous Margin, Especially on the Left Side.*** You will have a neater paper and provide space for the instructor's comments.

5. ***Leave Space Between Answers.*** This will allow you to add an idea or fact that may occur to you later. Such an idea may be blended into the answer by using an appropriate transitional phrase, such as "An additional idea that pertains to this question is. . . ."

6. ***Watch the Time.*** If you think you may run out of time, just outline your remaining points to show the instructor that you did, in fact, have the necessary material in mind. You will gain credit. If you have time left over, use it to go back over your answers to correct points of grammar or to insert clarifying words or phrases.

SUMMARY

What's the most important step in writing an essay answer?

Starting your first sentence with a full or partial repeat of the question is the most important step you can take to keep your answer on target. It forces a natural organizational pattern on your writing. Your opening sentence is a topic sentence, and all you do is expand it by explaining it, giving examples, and supporting it in general. Don't forget that last, strong, concluding sentence, which tells the grader that you're in control right to the finish line.

How can I show the grader that I'm thinking?

You must put down your facts accurately. You must also show that you can reason on the basis of those facts by organizing your essay well, keeping your comments relevant to the question, and writing clearly and neatly (without an abundance of erasures and cross-outs). When you reason beyond the facts, make sure you identify the reasoning or opinions as your own.

How can I be sure that I have read the essay question correctly?

There are two steps to take: (1) Make sure you underline key words such as *list, evaluate,* and *compare* in the instructions; then fix in your mind exactly how you will comply with these specific directions. (2) Quietly ask the instructor about anything you do not understand, including whether you have interpreted the question correctly. If you are fuzzy about the question, your answer is almost sure to be equally fuzzy.

HAVE YOU MISSED SOMETHING?

1. *Sentence completion.* Complete the following sentences with one of the three words listed below each sentence.

a. In essay questions, you are graded on your ____________________.

reasoning   handwriting   decisions

b. Your answer to an essay question must demonstrate that you understand the ____.

facts   dates   directions

2. *Matching.* In each blank space in the left column, write the number preceding the phrase in the right column that matches the left item best.

_____ a. Neatness	1. Explain in simpler terms
_____ b. Key words	2. Requires opinion plus evidence
_____ c. Evaluate	3. Has been known to affect essay grades
_____ d. Transition	4. Calls for arguments plus details
_____ e. Interpret	5. Says "Come along to this next sentence"
_____ f. Discuss	6. Should be underlined or circled in essay instructions

3. *True-false.* Write *T* beside the *true* statements and *F* beside the *false* statements.

_____ a. Vague impressions or feelings are helpful in an essay answer.

_____ b. Comparisons can include differences as well as similarities.

_____ c. It helps to be aware of the instructor's pet ideas.

_____ d. Graders sometimes use model answers to essay questions.

_____ e. It's best to tackle the toughest question first in an essay exam.

4. *Multiple choice.* Choose the phrase that completes the following sentence most accurately, and circle the letter that precedes it.

In taking an essay exam, you should

a. begin writing as soon as the exam begins
b. avoid unsupported opinions
c. write quickly and correct your errors later
d. add philosophical asides to spice up your answers

PART

V

Your Vocabulary and Reading Ability

CHAPTER 15

Improving Your Vocabulary

The difference between the right word and the almost right word is the difference between lightning and the lightning bug.

Mark Twain (1835–1910), pen name of Samuel Clemens, author of *Huckleberry Finn*

Numerous research studies in both the academic and the business worlds show a close relationship between a good vocabulary and success. A vocabulary that is large and precise can lead you to a wealth of knowledge. This chapter explains why building a vocabulary can be a worthwhile investment. It discusses the importance of

- Using a dictionary
- Recognizing word roots and prefixes
- Becoming interested in the origin of words
- Mastering difficult words
- Using the Frontier Vocabulary System

and finally

- Testing your vocabulary

hroughout your college years, new words will be flooding into your consciousness. Many of them are the keys to ideas and information that will be new to you. When students have trouble in a course, the trouble can often be traced back to their imperfect comprehension of terms that are essential to an understanding of subject matter. A first-year science or social science course may introduce you to almost as many new words as a first course in a foreign language—for example:

Chemistry	*Geology*	*Psychology*	*Sociology*
kinetic	syncline	decenter	ethnocentrism
colloid	moraine	synapse	sociometry
adsorption	diastrophic	receptor	superorganic
isomer	Pleistocene	mesomorph	mana

Then there are also words like *base* in chemistry and *accommodation* in psychology, which may not literally be new to you, but which have specific meanings within the context of a specific course and therefore must be learned as if they were new words.

For a college student, a large, wide-ranging vocabulary is not just something "nice" to have. It is a necessary tool for grasping fundamental ideas and facts. Words are the tools of communication, learning, and thinking. Like a mechanic with an inadequate tool kit, a student with an inadequate vocabulary cannot function effectively and efficiently. Because you cannot go to a hardware store and buy new words to complete your kit of communication tools, as you listen and read you must be on the lookout for words to add to your vocabulary. When you find such words, gather them in immediately. Write them down, in the sentence in which you found them, so you'll have their context. Then, as soon as you can, look them up in a good dictionary.

USING A DICTIONARY

The best way to learn new words is to keep a good dictionary close to your elbow and use it. Gliding over a word that you don't quite know can be costly. Consider this sentence: "The mayor gave *fulsome* praise to the budget committee." What does *fulsome* mean? If you think it means "full of praise," you're mistaken. Look it up in your dictionary.

Sometimes, you can get some idea of the meaning of a new word from its context—how it is used in your reading material. Use context when you can, but be aware that it has its limitations. Lee C. Deighton of Columbia

University points out three: (1) Context provides only the meaning that fits that particular situation. (2) You often end up with a synonym, which is not quite the same as a definition. (3) When you have to infer the meaning of a word, you can be slightly (or greatly) in error.[1] Your safest bet is to avoid all the guesswork and go straight to your dictionary.

As you study, consult your dictionary whenever you come to a word that you don't know precisely. Find the exact meaning you need; then go back to your textbook and reread the paragraph, with the *meaning* substituted for the word. If you become interested in a particular word, write it on a 3 × 5 card. Later, go back to the dictionary and investigate it. Write its meanings on the card, and keep the card and other like cards to look through and study occasionally. But don't break into your studying for a long session with the dictionary; save that for later.

Many scholars and businesspeople rely on a pocket dictionary as a handy source of definitions. Eddie Rickenbacker (1890–1973), auto racer, ace fighter pilot in World War I, and businessman, who left school when he was only 12 years old, made it a habit to carry a small dictionary in his pocket. In his autobiography, he recalled:

> Though much of my association was with mechanics and other drivers, I also had the opportunity to converse with men in higher positions, automotive engineers, and company officials. . . . I listened carefully and marked well the way such men constructed and phrased their thoughts. I carried a dictionary with me always and used it. I have never slackened in the pursuit of learning and self-improvement.[2]

Follow the example of thousands of successful people. Get yourself a pocket dictionary such as *New Webster's Best Pocket Dictionary* or *Webster's New World Vest Pocket Dictionary,* and always carry it with you. Instead of reading the print on cereal boxes, or looking at advertising placards on buses and subways, or staring into space, take out your dictionary and *read* it. Its definitions will be terse, consisting mainly of synonyms, but its value lies in its ability to spark a lifelong interest in words as well as increase your vocabulary. Of course, a pocket dictionary is no substitute for a larger, desk-size dictionary; but as a portable learning tool, the pocket dictionary is worth at least its weight in gold.

For your study periods, buy and use the best abridged dictionary that you can afford, but be aware that no word is ever fully defined even by a good abridged dictionary. The dictionary meaning is only an operational meaning that will solve your immediate problem. Words have multiple shades of

---

[1]Lee C. Deighton, *Vocabulary Development in the Classroom* (New York: Teachers College Press, 1959), pp. 2–3.

[2]Edward V. Rickenbacker, *Rickenbacker* (Englewood Cliffs, N.J.: Prentice-Hall, 1967), pp. 65–66.

meaning that add richness to our language. These various shades will become apparent to you as you keep reading, listening, and trying to use words in a variety of contexts.

Good abridged desk dictionaries include the following:

The American Heritage Dictionary (Houghton Mifflin Company)

The American College Dictionary (Random House)

Webster's New Collegiate Dictionary (G. & C. Merriam Company)

Webster's New World Dictionary of the American Language (World Publishing Company)

For intensive word study, however, there is no substitute for an unabridged dictionary. Locate the unabridged dictionaries in your library—usually they are in the reference room—and use them to supplement your own abridged desk dictionary. An unabridged dictionary gives more definitions, more about the derivations of words, and more on usage. Good one-volume unabridged words include *Webster's New International Dictionary of the English Language,* the *New Standard Dictionary of the English Language,* and the *Random House Dictionary of the English Language. The Oxford English Dictionary,* in twelve volumes plus supplements, is indispensable for the historical study of words but is more detailed than you will need for most purposes.

The reference librarian can help you find specialized dictionaries on various subjects. They list technical terms not always found even in unabridged dictionaries. However, your textbooks are usually the best sources of the definitions for such terms.

RECOGNIZING WORD ROOTS AND PREFIXES

Using the dictionary is an excellent way to increase your vocabulary one word at a time. However, if you would like to learn whole clusters of words in one stroke, you should get to know the most common roots and prefixes in English. A word *root* is the core of a word, the part that holds the basic meaning. A *prefix* is a word beginning that modifies the root. Table 15.1 lists some common word roots, and Table 15.2 lists some common prefixes.

It has been estimated that 60 percent of the English words in common use are made up partly or entirely of prefixes or roots derived from Latin and Greek. The value of learning prefixes and roots is that they illustrate the way much of our language is constructed. Once learned, they can help you recognize and understand many words without resorting to a dictionary. With

TABLE 15.1 Common Word Roots

Root	Meaning	Example	Definition
agri	field	agronomy	*Field*-crop production and soil management
anthropo	man	anthropology	The study of *man*
astro	star	astronaut	One who travels in interplanetary space *(stars)*
bio	life	biology	The study of *life*
cardio	heart	cardiac	Pertaining to the *heart*
chromo	color	chromatology	The science of *colors*
demos	people	democracy	Government by the *people*
derma	skin	epidermis	The outer layer of *skin*
dyna	power	dynamic	Characterized by *power* and energy
geo	earth	geology	The study of the *earth*
helio	sun	heliotrope	Any plant that turns toward the *sun*
hydro	water	hydroponics	Growing of plants in *water* reinforced with nutrients
hypno	sleep	hypnosis	A state of *sleep* induced by suggestion
magni	great, big	magnify	To enlarge, to make *bigger*
man(u)	hand	manuscript	Written by *hand*
mono	one	monoplane	Airplane with *one* wing
ortho	straight	orthodox	Right, true, *straight* opinion
pod	foot	pseudopod	False *foot*
psycho	mind	psychology	Study of the *mind* in any of its aspects
pyro	fire	pyrometer	An instrument for measuring temperatures
terra	earth	terrace	A raised platform of *earth*
thermo	heat	thermometer	Instrument for measuring *heat*
zoo	animal	zoology	The study of *animals*

one well-understood root word as the center, an entire "constellation" of words can be built up. Figure 15.1 shows such a constellation, based on the root "duct," from the Latin *ducere* ("to lead"). Notice that it makes use of twenty common prefixes and of other prefixes and combining words as well as various word endings. It does not exhaust all the possibilities, either; you should be able to think of several other words growing out of "duct."

Although knowing the meanings of prefixes and roots can unlock the meanings of unfamiliar words, this knowledge should supplement, not replace, your dictionary use. Over the centuries, many prefixes have changed in both meaning and spelling. According to Lee Deighton, "of the 68 prominent and commonly used prefixes there are only 11 which have a single and

TABLE 15.2 Common Prefixes

Prefix	Meaning	Example	Definition
ante-	before	antebellum	*Before* the war; especially in the U.S., before the Civil War
anti-	against	antifreeze	Liquid used to guard *against* freezing
auto-	self	automatic	*Self*-acting or self-regulating
bene-	good	benefit	An act of *kindness;* a gift
circum-	around	circumscribe	To draw a line *around;* to encircle
contra-	against	contradict	To speak *against*
de-	reverse, remove	defoliate	*Remove* the leaves from a tree
ecto-	outside	ectoparasite	Parasite living on the *exterior* of animals
endo-	within	endogamy	Marriage *within* the tribe
hyper-	over	hypertension	*High* blood pressure
hypo-	under	hypotension	*Low* blood pressure
inter-	between	intervene	Come *between*
intra-	within	intramural	*Within* bounds of a school
intro-	in, into	introspect	To look *within,* as one's own mind
macro-	large	macroscopic	*Large* enough to be observed by the naked eye
mal-	bad	maladjusted	*Badly* adjusted
micro-	small	microscopic	So *small* that one needs a microscope to observe
multi-	many	multimillionaire	One having *two* or *more* million dollars
neo-	new	neolithic	*New* stone age
non-	not	nonconformist	One who does *not* conform
pan-	all	pantheon	A temple dedicated to *all* gods
poly-	many	polygonal	Having *many* sides
post-	after	postgraduate	*After* graduating
pre-	before	precede	To go *before*
proto-	first	prototype	*First* or original model
pseudo-	false	pseudonym	*False* name; esp., an author's pen-name
retro-	backward	retrospect	A looking *back* on things
semi-	half	semicircle	*Half* a circle
sub-	under	submerge	To put *under* water
super-	above	superfine	*Extra* fine
tele-	far	telescope	Seeing or viewing *afar*
trans-	across	transalpine	*Across* the Alps

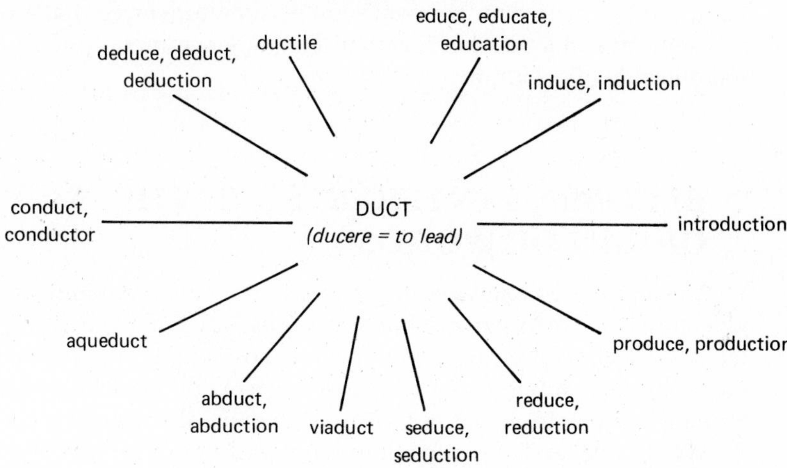

FIGURE 15.1 A Constellation of Words from One Root

fairly invariant meaning."[3] The other 57 prefixes have more than one meaning each.

For example, the prefix *de-* means "of" or "from"; yet the dictionary lists four different meanings for it:

1. It means "down" as in *descend,* which means to pass from a higher to a lower place.
2. It indicates separation as in *dehumidify,* which means to separate moisture from air, or in *decapitate,* which means to behead—that is, to separate the head from the rest of the body.
3. It indicates reversal as in *decode,* which means to convert from code into ordinary language, or in *depreciate,* which means to lessen in value.
4. It may be used to intensify as in *demonstrate,* which means to show or prove publicly, or in *declare,* which means to announce.

So learn as many of the common prefixes and roots as you can, but learn them for better and more precise understanding of words you already know and words that you have yet to look up in the dictionary. When you go to the dictionary, make sure that you spend some time on the prefixes and roots

[3]Deighton, *Vocabulary Development in the Classroom,* p. 26.

that make up each word. You will soon become convinced that a word is not an assemblage of letters put together like an anagram, but the true and natural outcome of evolution.

BECOMING INTERESTED IN THE ORIGIN OF WORDS

The four ingredients necessary to make vocabulary building a productive adventure are a keen sense of interest, a sense of excitement, a sense of wonder, and a feeling of pleasure when you choose words and the words choose you.[4] One sure way to pick up interest, excitement, wonder, and pleasure in your adventure with words is to learn the origin of words.

Words, like facts, are difficult to remember out of context. Remembering is greatly facilitated when you have a body of information with which to associate either a word or a fact. For words, interesting origins or histories will help provide a context. For example, a *hippopotamus* is a "river horse," from the Greek *hippos,* meaning "horse," and *potamos,* meaning "river."

Indiana is called the *Hoosier state,* and its people *Hoosiers.* Why? In the early days, the pioneers were gruff in manner; when someone knocked at the front door, a pioneer's voice would often boom, "Who's yere?"

You may have wondered why runners on a cross-country track team are called *harriers,* especially by sports writers. Actually, a harrier is a swift-running dog, useful in hunting rabbits.

If you were offered a *Hobson's choice,* would you know what was meant? Thomas Hobson owned a livery stable in seventeenth-century England. He loved his horses, and to prevent any one horse from being overworked, he hired them out in turn, beginning with stall number one. Customers had to take the horses they were given. Thus *Hobson's choice* means no choice at all.

Words that are illustrated with pictures are especially memorable. Figure 15.2, for example, is from a book entitled *Picturesque Word Origins.* Whenever you read or use the word *bribe,* its history will instantly rise to the top of your memory, and the picture will project itself onto the movie screen of your mind. What a powerful and enjoyable way to learn words!

Here are two lists of books that are sure to arouse your interest in words and, at the same time, increase your stock of words. The out-of-print books are worth looking for in libraries; those still in print can be obtained from their publishers.

---

[4]Ibid., p. 59.

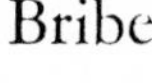

Bribe: once only a scrap of bread

The word *bribe* has degenerated morally while acquiring greater importance financially. It was once an honest scrap of bread. That was in the Late Latin form *briba.* The French borrowed it (*bribe*) in the sense "a lump of bread," "leavings of meals," something that might be given to beggars. When *bribe* first came into English it meant "a gift begged," then "a present." In modern use the "present" is frequently a large amount of money, and its purpose is to corrupt a person in a position of trust.

FIGURE 15.2 The Origin of the Word "Bribe"
Source: From Picturesque Word Origins. *© 1933 by Merriam-Webster, Inc., publishers of the Merriam-Webster® Dictionaries.*

Books Still in Print

Ciardi, John, *A Browser's Dictionary and Native's Guide to the Unknown American Language.* Published in 1980. Hard cover. The author discusses about a thousand words, including *baker's dozen* and *swindle.* Information and copies: Harper & Row Publishers, Inc., Keystone Industrial Park, Scranton, PA 18512.

Funk, Charles E., *A Hog on Ice, and Other Curious Expressions.* Published in 1948. Hard cover. The author discusses about 750 phrases, such as *kick the bucket* and *kangaroo court.* Some illustrations or drawings. Information and copies: Harper & Row Publishers, Inc., Keystone Industrial Park, Scranton, PA 18512.

Holt, Alfred H., *Phrase and Word Origins.* Published in 1961. Paperback. The author discusses over one thousand words and phrases from *armed to the teeth* to *wet your whistle.* Information and copies: Dover Publications, Inc., 180 Varick Street, New York, NY 10014.

Hook, J. N., *The Grand Panjandrum.* Published in 1980. The book's entries *haply* run the *gamut* from *frippery* and *furbelow* to *quaggy* and *sward.* Chapter themes include people, psychology, the five senses, medicine, measurements, the landscape, and plants. Includes an index and pronunciation guide and end-of-chapter word mastery tests. Information and copies: Macmillan Publishing Co., Inc., 866 Third Avenue, New York, NY 10022.

Maleska, Eugene T., *A Pleasure in Words.* Published in 1981. The author, a famous educator and creator of crossword puzzles, describes thousands of words through many humorous anecdotes. The book includes a section on how to construct your own crossword puzzle, in-chapter spelling, vocabulary, and etymology quizzes. Information and copies: Simon and Schuster, 1230 Avenue of the Americas, New York, NY 10020.

Mathews, Mitford M., *American Words.* Published in 1959 and again in 1976. Hard cover. The author discusses about two hundred words such as *podunk* and *hickory,* and many are illustrated by drawings. Information and copies: Philomel Books, 200 Madison Avenue, Suite 1405, New York, NY 10016.

Word Mysteries & Histories. Published in 1986 by the editors of the American Heritage Dictionaries. As the editors note in their preface, this book "[delves] into the stories behind the *bromides* and *bluestockings,* the *Amazons* and *eunuchs,* the *ignoramuses* and *shysters,* . . . the *prunes* and *pundits,* and the *wizards* and *zombies.*" Information and copies: Houghton Mifflin Co., One Beacon Street, Boston, MA 02108.

Out-of-Print Books

Ernst, Margaret S., *In a Word.* Published in 1939 by Alfred A. Knopf, New York. The author discusses (and James Thurber illustrates) about 250 words, such as *abundance* and *whiskey.*

Picturesque Word Origins. Published in 1933 by G. & C Merriam Company, Springfield, Mass. One hundred fifty-eight words are fully discussed, and forty-eight more are interestingly but briefly discussed under the categories of flowers, birds, animals, cloth, and gems. Forty-five of the words are graphically and meaningfully illustrated. (See Figure 15.2 on page 315.)

MASTERING DIFFICULT WORDS

There is no quick and easy way to a powerful vocabulary. Don't fall for any advertising that claims otherwise. The only sure way is overlearning by means of recitation. All you need is a dictionary and a stack of 3 × 5 cards. On the cards write the difficult words that you find in your textbooks and hear in the classroom. These are words you need to know to understand your coursework.

When you select a word, write it on one side of a 3 × 5 card. To provide a meaningful context, write the sentence or phrase in which the word occurs and underline the word. Next, look the word up in a dictionary and write the word out in syllables, including accent and diacritical marks so that you can pronounce it correctly. On the reverse side of the card, write the definition that is most appropriate for the context. For a technical term, write the definition given in your textbook. Special terms are usually defined when first introduced or else in a glossary. If you want to pursue your study of a word in more detail, record also, on the reverse side of the card, any information you find about its derivation; for this information you may need to consult an unabridged dictionary. Figure 15.3 shows three formats for your cards.

To study your cards, pronounce the word aloud correctly. Try to recall the definition without looking at it; then turn the card over to check your recall. If you fail, place a dot in the upper right-hand corner, on the front of the card. The next time you go through your cards, the dot will remind you that you missed on a previous try. When a card has three or more dots, it is time to give that word some special attention.

The advantage of 3 × 5 cards is that they are convenient to carry about for study at odd moments. At all times, have with you a few blank cards on which to record interesting words. Learning words that intrigue you will be immeasurably more valuable than memorizing a list made up for you by someone else.

USING THE FRONTIER VOCABULARY SYSTEM

Consulting the dictionary or probing the histories of words can help to increase your vocabulary word by word. One highly effective way to increase

(FRONT)

(REVERSE)

(a)

symbiosis

sym'bī-ō-sis

the intimate living together of two species with mutual benefit

(FRONT)

(REVERSE)

(b)

eyes like chrysoprase

chrys'-o-prase

an apple green variety of chalcedony

chalcedony (kăl-sĕd́-o-nĭ) = a translucent variety of quartz with waxlike luster

(FRONT)

(REVERSE)

(c)

"And I stand ready to oppose to the uttermost any group that seeks to limit or pervert the curricula of schools and colleges in order to impose upon them their own narrow and dogmatic preconceptions concerning matters that are properly the subject of free inquiry."

pre'con-cep'tion

pre = before; denoting before in time.
con = with, together, in conjunction.
cept = from capere = to take
A preconceived idea; hence, a prejudice; a prepossession.
preconceive = to conceive, or form opinion of, beforehand.

FIGURE 15.3 Vocabulary Cards in Varying Degrees of Detail
(a) A key term defined from the textbook. (b) A word in a meaningful phrase with a secondary definition given. (c) A word in full-sentence context, with information on parts and derivation and with a secondary definition.

your vocabulary is to use the Frontier Vocabulary System developed by Johnson O'Connor. The Frontier Vocabulary System is based on natural learning processes.[5] We know that a baby must crawl before it can walk and walk before it can run. We know, too, that a child can pronounce the sound *p* at about age 3½ but usually does not master the sound *r* until age 7½. Many other skills develop along with physical growth and general maturation. All learning processes have four characteristics:

1. Skills progress from the simple to the complex.
2. Each skill is developed in an orderly sequence of steps.
3. Each step is at a different level of difficulty.
4. No significant step may be skipped. Each step seems to develop the muscle or brain pattern that makes the next step possible.

From his analytical research, O'Connor concluded that learning new words is much like learning any other skill. We progress from simple words to more difficult ones in an orderly sequence. The difficulty or ease of learning a word does not depend on the length of the word, its frequency of use, its geographic origin, or its pronunciation, or on teachers, books, or parents. Instead, difficulty in learning a word depends on the complexity of the *idea* that the word stands for. Defining words with simple synonyms does not provide the learner with a background sufficient to think with the words. Because words stand for ideas, the ideas behind them must also be learned.

S. I. Hayakawa, the noted semanticist, agrees with this view. He questions the old-fashioned notion that the way to study words is to concentrate one's attention exclusively on words. Hayakawa suggests that words should be understood in relationship to other words—not only other words on the same level, but also words at a higher (more abstract) level and words at a lower (more concrete) level.

Principles Governing the Learning of Words

The following findings by O'Connor form the basis for the Frontier Vocabulary System:

1. The easiest words are learned first; then the harder ones are learned.
2. At the forward edge of the mass of all the words that have been mastered is the individual's *frontier.* Only a very few words *beyond the frontier* have already been mastered.

[5]Much of this discussion is based on an article by Dean Trembly, "Intellectual Abilities as Motivating Factors," *Japanese Psychological Research* 10, no. 2 (July 1968): 104–08.

ZONE OF KNOWN WORDS These are the words already mastered. They are used in reading, writing, listening, and thinking. The Edge of the Frontier
FRONTIER AREA The words in this zone are the frontier words. They are somewhat familiar.
ZONE OF TOTALLY UNKNOWN WORDS An occasional word, like an island in an unknown sea, might have been discovered and made one's own because of necessity.

FIGURE 15.4 The Concept of Frontier Words

3. The greatest learning takes place in the frontier area, which lies between the zone of known words and the zone of totally unknown words (see Figure 15.4).
4. The most significant characteristic of the words in the frontier area is that they are, to some extent, familiar. The maximum advancement in a person's mastery of words takes place in the frontier area, where hundreds of almost-known words need only a slight straightening out to make them familiar.
5. Learning becomes extremely inefficient and may actually break down whenever a person skips the frontier area and tries to learn totally unknown words.

Familiarity with a word in the frontier area means that you already know something about the word or its definition. You may, for example, know how to pronounce the word and know its general meaning. Or you may know one of its several meanings. The important point is this: By singling out such a frontier word and learning its specific meaning, or its several definitions, you can master the word with minimal time and effort.

By working continually in the frontier area, you can make rapid progress in mastering words. At the same time, you will continually be discovering new frontier words to conquer. As the process continues, the frontier area will push into the zone of totally unknown words.

Recognizing Frontier Words

To find your own frontier words, first become aware of your daily speech, and make a list of the unusual words you use. Next, be on the lookout for words that you recognize in reading but do not use in speaking and writing. From this source choose *only* the words that appeal to you. Listen attentively while other people speak. The chances are great that you will recognize and know the general meaning of all the words you hear. Choose from this stream of speech the words that appeal to you—words that you would like to incorporate into your own speech.

Later, after writing out the definition for each of your frontier words, look for its opposite. If it interests you, learn that word too. Learning pairs of contrasting words creates the strong force of spontaneous suggestion—either word suggests the other.

Making the Frontier System Work

Write each frontier word on a separate 3 × 5 card, underlined and in proper context. Once you have a small stack of cards, look up the words in an unabridged dictionary. Below your excerpted sentence, print the word with its syllables and diacritical markings.

On the back of the card, write the prefix and root that make up your word. Write the definition or definitions for your word and put an asterisk beside the definition that best fits the meaning of your word in its specific context.

Carry about a dozen of these completed cards in a pocket or purse so you can review them whenever you have a spare moment. Figure 15.5 shows the Frontier System format.

To master the words on the cards, do the following:

1. Always look at the front side of the card. Pronounce the word correctly; read the sentence completely; and then define the word, not necessarily in dictionary language but meaningfully in your own words. All this should be done before you look at the definition on the back.

(a)

FRONT

His silence implied that he, at least, did not disagree with my statement.

im-ply′ (ĭm-plī′)
im-plied′ (ĭm-plīd′)

REVERSE

[im = in] [plicare = fold]
[implicare = to fold in; to involve]

1. To express indirectly; to suggest; to hint or hint at.
*2. To involve when not expressly stated in words or by signs.

syn: involve.

(b)

FRONT

From his silence and manner, I inferred that he agreed with my statement.

in-fer′ (ĭn-fûr′)
in-ferred′ (ĭn-fûrd′)
in-fer′ring (ĭn-fûr′ring)

REVERSE

[in = in] [ferre = to bring (out)]

1. To derive by reasoning; to conclude from facts or premises.
*2. To surmise; to guess.

syn: deduce, conclude

FIGURE 15.5 Frontier System Cards
These two cards (*implied* and *inferred*) show a pair of words that are opposite or complementary. Such words, studied together, are bound to take on more precise meaning. Notice that the front of each card shows the new word underlined in a complete sentence. It also shows how to pronounce the word. The reverse of each card defines prefixes and roots and gives important dictionary definitions of the word. An asterisk is placed beside the definition that most nearly matches the use of the word on the front of the card. Synonyms are also given.

2. After you have defined the word to the best of your ability, turn the card over to check on the accuracy of your definition.
3. If you are not satisfied with your definition, place a dot on the front of the card, in the upper right-hand corner. The next time you go through your cards, the dot will remind you that you missed on a previous try. When a card has three dots, it is time to give that word some special attention.
4. After the small stack of cards has been mastered, place them in a file and pick up additional ones for mastering.
5. From time to time, review the words that you have mastered.

As you master the precise meaning of each frontier word, there will be a corresponding advance in your reading, writing, speaking, and thinking.

For each question in this section, choose the best answer and blacken the corresponding oval on the answer sheet.

Each question below consists of a word in boldface, followed by five lettered words or phrases. Choose the word or phrase that is most nearly opposite in meaning to the word in boldface. Since some of the questions require you to distinguish fine shades of meaning, consider all the choices before deciding which is best.

Example:

good: (A) sour (B) bad (C) red (D) hot (E) ugly

1. **ordinary:** (A) numerical (B) rational (C) impolite (D) staunch (E) abnormal
2. **ban:** (A) borrow (B) regret (C) permit (D) conquer (E) exaggerate
3. **compression:** (A) equality (B) expansion (C) exposure (D) endurance (E) excitement
4. **flicker:** (A) rise slowly (B) burn steadily (C) warm completely (D) fume (E) collide
5. **atheist:** (A) believer (B) scholar (C) recluse (D) expatriate (E) pauper
6. **fraudulent:** (A) dynamic (B) masterly (C) possible (D) genuine (E) abundant
7. **parasite:** (A) expert (B) imposter (C) instigator (D) self-assured snob (E) self-sufficient individual
8. **sparse:** (A) thick (B) tidy (C) wealthy (D) round (E) sticky
9. **denounce:** (A) overstate (B) acclaim (C) destroy (D) refuse (E) hasten
10. **serrated:** (A) undervalued (B) aggressive (C) smooth and even (D) loose and flexible (E) supremely confident
11. **fly-by-night:** (A) unbalanced (B) moderate (C) permanent (D) incredible (E) modern
12. **sterile:** (A) venal (B) productive (C) generous (D) variegated (E) unalloyed
13. **rejoice:** (A) defend against (B) shrug off (C) criticize (D) bemoan (E) discriminate
14. **cosmopolitan:** (A) indecisive (B) ineffectual (C) antagonistic (D) parochial (E) deferential
15. **fanaticism:** (A) optimism (B) hedonism (C) penitence (D) didacticism (E) apathy
16. **vestigial:** (A) fully developed (B) publicly announced (C) offensive (D) provincial (E) miraculous
17. **hypocritical:** (A) guileless (B) eccentric (C) perspicacious (D) untrustworthy (E) sagacious
18. **ebullient:** (A) staid (B) anxious (C) feminine (D) unique (E) respectful
19. **accolade:** (A) appetizer (B) censure (C) recoil (D) seizure (E) referendum
20. **propound:** (A) remove from consideration (B) defend without evidence (C) avoid without reason (D) view with humility (E) rescue from imprisonment
21. **divert:** (A) bore (B) rescue (C) espouse (D) judge fairly (E) question relentlessly
22. **exculpate:** (A) require (B) yield (C) reinstate (D) vivify (E) convict
23. **hackneyed:** (A) integrated (B) appealing (C) inventive (D) acceptable (E) improper
24. **alacrity:** (A) indolence (B) bravery (C) wisdom (D) pungency (E) retention
25. **burgeon:** (A) fail to prove (B) shrivel and die (C) pursue and capture (D) disobey regulations (E) speak incoherently

FIGURE 15.6 PSAT Vocabulary Test

Source: PSAT test questions are from the PSAT/NMSQT Student Bulletin, *College Entrance Examination Board, 1981. Reprinted by permission of the Educational Testing Service, copyright owner of the sample questions. Permission to reprint the sample PSAT material does not constitute review or endorsement by Educational Testing Service or the College Board of this publication as a whole or of any other sample question or testing information it may contain.*

For each question in this section, choose the best answer and blacken the corresponding oval on the answer sheet.

Each question below consists of a word in boldface, followed by five lettered words or phrases. Choose the word or phrase that is most nearly opposite in meaning to the word in boldface. Since some of the questions require you to distinguish fine shades of meaning, consider all the choices before deciding which is best.

Example:

good: (A) sour (B) bad (C) red (D) hot (E) ugly

Ⓐ ● Ⓒ Ⓓ Ⓔ

1. **promptness**: (A) excessive modesty (B) extreme rigidity (C) reluctance or apathy (D) hesitation or delay (E) embarrassment or shame
2. **indulge**: (A) adhere (B) abstain (C) divulge (D) exonerate (E) expiate
3. **commonplace**: (A) genuine (B) illogical (C) enormous (D) intermediate (E) extraordinary
4. **deaden**: (A) join (B) justify (C) stimulate (D) guard carefully (E) alter significantly
5. **rove**: (A) whisper (B) nourish (C) close up (D) squeeze dry (E) settle down
6. **relinquish**: (A) retain (B) conform (C) persuade (D) send forward (E) move together
7. **shrewd**: (A) glum (B) witless (C) sinister (D) penniless (E) mischievous
8. **outclass**: (A) initiate (B) oppress (C) keep secret (D) be inferior (E) arrange in order
9. **monochromatic**: (A) polygamous (B) multicolored (C) multitudinous (D) syndicated (E) bilateral
10. **foreshadowed**: (A) unwanted (B) unrecognizable (C) unobserved (D) unintentional (E) unanticipated
11. **dwindling**: (A) enterprising (B) advantageous (C) instructive (D) impulsive (E) growing
12. **desecration**: (A) isolation (B) decision (C) consecration (D) declaration (E) modification
13. **overt**: (A) hidden (B) ordinary (C) prone (D) barren (E) accidental
14. **flaccid**: (A) mountainous (B) fertile (C) thin (D) firm (E) young
15. **stoic**: (A) patriarch (B) mediator (C) progenitor (D) confederate (E) sensualist
16. **pique**: (A) prefer (B) show (C) carry (D) placate (E) startle
17. **cogent**: (A) unconvincing (B) uniform (C) argumentative (D) unthinkable (E) meditative
18. **castigation**: (A) belief (B) adroitness (C) propagation (D) adulation (E) indoctrination
19. **dichotomy**: (A) monotony (B) union (C) infinity (D) termination (E) abnormality
20. **ancillary**: (A) principal (B) irregular (C) subjective (D) contemporary (E) consonant

FIGURE 15.7 SAT Vocabulary Test

Source: SAT test questions are from Taking the SAT, *College Entrance Examination Board, 1981. Reprinted by permission of Educational Testing Service, copyright owner of the sample questions. Permission to reprint the sample SAT material does not constitute review or endorsement by Educational Testing Service or the College Board of this publication as a whole or of any other sample question or testing information it may contain.*

TESTING YOUR VOCABULARY

The tests in this section will give you a chance to test your vocabulary in private. These tests are much more difficult than traditional ones in which you are given a test word and are required to choose a second word that most nearly matches it in meaning. Here, you must choose the word or phrase that is most nearly *opposite* in meaning to the test word. Thus, you will be working with antonyms. You'll have to hold the meaning of the test word in your mind while searching the options for its opposite.

In the quiet of your room, without the pressure and exposure of a classroom, observe how you handle each test question. Notice whether the test word is familiar, vaguely familiar, or totally unfamiliar. If it is familiar, can you pick out its opposite with confidence? Do you know the meanings of some of the words in a vague, general sense, but not specifically? Are you able to pronounce each word accurately and with confidence?

Determine what your weaknesses are, and then do something about them by implementing the Frontier Vocabulary System. Remember, vocabulary is not a fixed trait like the color of your eyes or hair. A vocabulary is something that you can design and build in accordance with your personal specifications.

For now, take the tests in Figures 15.6 and 15.7. The correct answers are given in Appendix B, along with the percentages of students who answered each question correctly.

Students taking this kind of test are usually given separate answer sheets on which they indicate their answers by blackening an oval with a pencil. Readers of this book, lacking answer sheets, can simply circle the correct answers on the test.

SUMMARY

Is there really a connection between a good vocabulary and success?

Yes. Information is power, and the only way to send and receive information effectively is with the help of a large, wide-ranging vocabulary.

What is the best way to build up my vocabulary?

The best way to improve your vocabulary is to get into the habit of using your dictionary. When you don't know a word, look it up.

Can't I simply figure out a word's meaning from context?

Context can give you a rough idea of a word's meaning, but it has three limitations: (1) Context provides the meaning of a word in a very specific instance. (2) It gives you a synonym rather than a bona fide definition. (3) It requires guesswork, which may or may not be correct, by you.

What kind of dictionary should I use?

Few students can afford to buy an unabridged dictionary; however, most libraries keep several unabridged dictionaries on hand for reference. You should buy a good abridged dictionary to use when you are studying at your desk. You might also want to buy a pocket dictionary to carry around with you.

Is there any point in studying prefixes and word roots?

Yes. Sixty percent of the words commonly used in English have Latin or Greek prefixes and roots. The ability to recognize and understand the meaning of these prefixes and roots can give you a real edge.

What can be done in order to make vocabulary building a productive adventure?

You need a sense of interest, a sense of excitement, a sense of wonder, and a feeling of pleasure in order to make vocabulary building productive. One way to gain all four is by becoming interested in the origin of words.

How can I learn difficult words that turn up in my textbooks or in lectures?

Mastering words takes constant practice. The most effective way to get this sort of practice is by putting difficult words encountered in your textbooks and class lectures on 3 × 5 cards.

What's the advantage of 3 × 5 cards?

Such cards are portable. You can easily carry a stack of cards in a pocket or purse so they'll be available whenever you have a little free time.

What should I write on the cards?

Put each word on a separate card. Write the word and the sentence or phrase in which it occurs on the front of the card. Look up the word in a dictionary, and write its phonetic spelling on this side as well. On the back of the card, put the word's definitions as well as its derivation.

How do I study from the cards?

To master the word, pronounce it; read it in context; and then define it without looking at the back of the card. Then check the back to see whether you were correct. Go through a handful of vocabulary cards until you feel secure that you have mastered them.

What is the Frontier Vocabulary System?

The Frontier Vocabulary System is a vocabulary-building method that focuses on words that are slightly familiar to you rather than totally unknown. If you try to learn a word that is totally unknown to you, the chances are great that you will never remember it. But if you learn a word that lies in the frontier area of your vocabulary, you are likely to hold on to its meaning. What's more, with each new word you learn you'll be pushing into the zone of unknown words.

Should I find my own frontier words, or should I use an expert's list?

Make up your own list. Use words that *you* are slightly familiar with, rather than words that an expert has chosen for you.

How do I find my own frontier words?

There are four ways to start accumulating a list of frontier words: (1) Pay attention to the words that you use routinely in conversation. Are you sure that you are clear about their meanings? (2) Look for words that you recognize in reading but never use when you speak. There's a good chance that they are frontier words. (3) Listen to the conversations of others and see whether they use words that you would like to master. (4) Learn the antonyms of the frontier words that you find. Learning words in pairs does a great deal to cement them in your memory.

How do I master these frontier words?

Write each frontier word on a 3 × 5 card. Treat and study these words just as you treat the difficult words encountered in your textbooks and in lectures. Master the words by reading the front of the card out loud and reciting the word's definition from memory. Then check your progress by flipping over the card.

HAVE YOU MISSED SOMETHING?

1. *Sentence completion.* Complete the following sentences with one of the three words listed below each sentence.

   a. There is a close relationship between a good vocabulary and ____.

   prefixes synonyms success

   b. New vocabulary words should always be written in ________.

   pairs context cursive

   c. Definitions in most pocket dictionaries consist mainly of ______.

   synonyms derivations antonyms

2. *Matching.* In each blank space in the left column, write the number preceding the phrase in the right column that matches the left item best.

   ____ a. Accommodation
   ____ b. 60
   ____ c. Constellation
   ____ d. 57
   ____ e. Context
   ____ f. Prefix
   ____ g. Known words
   ____ h. Frontier area

   1. May reveal the meaning of a new word
   2. Takes on a specific meaning when used in psychology
   3. Percentage of English words derived from Latin or Greek
   4. Word beginning
   5. Zone of vocabulary used in reading, writing, speaking, and thinking
   6. Number of common prefixes that have multiple meanings
   7. A group of words with a common root
   8. Greatest learning takes place here

3. *True-false.* Write *T* beside the *true* statements and *F* beside the *false* statements.

   ____ a. A powerful vocabulary can be acquired very quickly.

   ____ b. No word is ever fully defined.

   ____ c. Key words and terms from your courses should be mastered like frontier words.

   ____ d. A knowledge of prefixes and roots will eliminate any need for the dictionary.

_____ e. Antonyms of words you already know can make excellent frontier words.

_____ f. The word *bribe* once referred to a scrap of bread.

4. *Frontier words.* Write "yes" next to the characteristics of frontier words.

_____ a. Are inexhaustible in their supply

_____ b. Are derived from the lists of experts

_____ c. Are located in the zone of unknown words

_____ d. Are the easiest words to master

_____ e. May be heard in conversation or read in a book

_____ f. Are familiar in one way or another

5. *Multiple choice.* Choose the phrase that completes the following sentence most accurately, and circle the letter that precedes it.

Three dots on a vocabulary card indicate that the word

a. has three different definitions
b. may require extra attention
c. has been properly mastered
d. consists of a common prefix and root

CHAPTER 16

Improving Your Reading Speed

When we read too fast or too slowly, we understand nothing.

Blaise Pascal (1623–62), French philosopher, mathematician, and scientist

Almost anyone who reads can read faster. The way to do so, however, is to strengthen your natural way of reading and thinking—not to use some artificial method. This chapter includes information and expert research on

- Eye movements during reading
- How much the mind can see
- Vocalization while reading

and finally

- A natural way to read faster

he simple question "How can I improve my reading?" does not have a simple answer. There are many different purposes in reading, many different reading techniques that can be used, and many ways in which reading can be "improved." However, when this question is asked by a student, it usually means, "How can I *speed up* my reading so I can finish my homework in half the time with high comprehension and almost complete retention?" There is no easy way to do so, despite the numerous brochures, newspaper and magazine articles, and television programs that extol the marvels of "speed reading." Many students, as well as the general public, are convinced that speed reading is a technique that is easy to learn and that can be used with any page of print. Unfortunately, speed reading is virtually useless to anyone who desires to learn from the printed page.

If you desire high comprehension and almost complete retention, you must use systematic study techniques. There is no other way to master your courses. This entire book is devoted to making learning a reality through the use of efficient study skills. This chapter and Chapter 17 focus on specific skills you can use in reading. Before examining them, however, we must discuss two aspects of reading: eye movements and vocalization. In doing so, we emphasize some negative aspects of speed reading, for two reasons. First, academic improvement through speed reading is just not in the cards, so don't spend your time, money, and energy on this dead end. Second, by clearing the decks of so-called easy ways to read and study, we set the stage for reading and studying systems that work.

EYE MOVEMENTS DURING READING

Facts About Eye Movements and Speed Reading

Newspapers have carried sensational stories about high school students who read at astronomical speeds. One student was clocked at the rate of 40,000 words per minute. Another student was timed at 50,000 words per minute! A peculiar characteristic of all such stories is that they include the statement, "with nearly 100 percent comprehension."

How fast is 40,000 words per minute? There are about 300 words on an average paperback book page. By dividing 300 into 40,000, we find that to read 40,000 words per minute, a person would have to read 133 pages per minute! The reader (or, more accurately, the page turner) would have less than half a second to spend on each page. Some students find it difficult to *turn* 133 pages in a minute, let alone see any words on those pages. Readers who are fast page turners might be able to see a word or two on each page as it flutters by, but this would hardly lead to "nearly 100 percent comprehension." Such readers could not possibly reconstruct the ideas contained in the 133 pages.

The basic premise of speed-reading advocates is this: The eye is able to see a vast number of words in one fixation. (A *fixation* is a focusing of the eyes on an object. The eyes must pause—they must be still—to fix on the object.) Some advocates say the eye can see phrases at a glance; others say entire lines; still others say paragraphs at a time; and a few say the eye can see an entire page at a glance. Let's look at the facts.

Eye-movement photography shows that the average college student makes about four eye fixations per second. Eye-movement photography also shows that the eye sees an average of only 1.1 words during each fixation. Seldom does any person, trained or untrained, have a usable span of recognition of more than 2.5 words.[1] Recent research using computers shows that good readers take in an average of about ten usable *letters* per fixation: four letters to the left of the center of fixation and five or six letters to the right of the center of fixation.[2] Thus, a reader may take in less than one long word, such as *informational*; or one complete word, such as *basketball*; or more than one word, such as *high grade*.

These facts indicate that only a most unusual person can see 10 words per second (2.5 words per fixation × 4 fixations per second). So, in sixty seconds it is arithmetically possible for the eye to take in 600 words. This calculation does not include the time needed to return the eyes to the beginning of each line and to turn pages.

There is no evidence that anyone's eyes can see a whole line of type "at a glance." So any advice to run your eyes down the middle of a page or column, to speed-read the page, is nonsense. All you'll get is a word or two from each line—a handful of scrambled words.

Richard Feinberg[3] reported that when a reader focuses on a word, "only four to five letters immediately around the fixation point are seen with 100 percent acuity" (sharpness). The letters of words half an inch from the point of fixation are seen with only 40 percent acuity, and those one inch from the point of fixation are seen with only 26 percent acuity. If the reader has less than normal vision, the fall-off in acuity is even more pronounced.

---

[1]Stanford E. Taylor, "Eye Movement in Reading: Facts and Fallacies," *American Educational Research Journal* 2, no. 4 (November 1965): 187–202.

[2]Keith Rayner, "The Perceptual Span and Peripheral Cues in Reading," *Cognitive Psychology* 7 (January 1975): 65–81.

[3]Richard Feinberg, "A Study of Some Aspects of Peripheral Visual Acuity," *American Journal of Optometry and Archives of American Academy of Optometry* 26 (February–March 1949): 1–23.

A knowledge of words, what they are and how they function, is the first and last essential of all liberal education. As Carlyle says, "If we but think of it, all that a University or final highest school can do for us is still but what the first school began doing—teach us to *read.*" When a student has been trained to make the words of any page of general writing yield their full meaning, he has in his possession the primary instrument of all higher education.

●

In these days when the nation is asking that its schools produce good citizens first and specialists second, there is a marked need for a rich and wide "universal" training of the mind. This book on reading is designed to forward the process by which the whole mind, intellectual and emotional, becomes a more accurate instrument for the reception and transmission of thoughts and sensations. If our system of education does not so train the minds of its students, if it does not teach them to recognize differences, to distinguish shades of meaning, to feel as by intuition not only the hypocrisy of the demagogue and the flattery of the bootlicker but also the depth of a statesman like Lincoln and the insight of a poet like Shakespeare, it fails of its purpose.

FIGURE 16.1 The Peep-Sight Experiment
See the text discussion for instructions. *Source: From E. A. Tenney and R. C. Wardle,* Intelligent Reading *(New York: Crofts, 1943), preface.*

An Experiment with Eye Movements

Here's how to find out how your eyes move during reading. Use any page of print, such as the text shown in Figure 16.1, mimeographed on a half sheet of paper. Punch a hole near the center of the page, as at the dot in Figure 16.1. Hold the page close to your own eye, with the printed side facing toward another person (the reader). As the reader silently reads the printed matter, watch his or her eyes through the peephole. You will immediately notice that the reader's eyes do not flow over the lines of print in a smooth, gliding motion. Instead, the eyes seem to jerk their way across the page, alternating fast, forward movements with momentary pauses, much like a typewriter carriage. The pauses are absolutely necessary, for they allow the eyes to focus on the type, to get a clear image of it. When the eyes are in motion, they record nothing but a blur on the retinas.

Instructions to the Reader. When you read the material, actually slow down your rate so that your partner will be able to count, as well as carefully observe, your eye movements. Don't try to manipulate your eyes in some unnatural way, such as by trying to focus on an entire line in one fixation; it won't work.

Calculations. You can make a rough calculation of the number of words perceived by the eyes by dividing the number of eye pauses into the total number of words on a line. For example, if the first line contains twelve words and the reader pauses eight times, the reader is taking in roughly one and one-half words per fixation.

HOW MUCH THE MIND CAN SEE

Our emphasis has been on the question "How many words can the eyes see in one fixation?" A more basic question is "How does the mind process the words that are imprinted on the retina of the eyes?" Suppose the eyes take in two words at a single fixation. Does the mind impose a meaning on both words instantly and simultaneously, or must it consider each word in sequence, one at a time, to get at the meaning of each word? If the mind can handle only one word at a time, however swiftly, wouldn't it be easier for the eyes to deliver to the mind one word at a time in the first place?

The Limitation of the Mind

Research done at the Massachusetts Institute of Technology, using M.I.T. undergraduates, gives scientific evidence that the mind can attend to only one word at a time. In one part of the study, as it was reported in *Scientific American,* "The letters of two different six-letter words were presented simultaneously in pairs for brief intervals of time. If the words were *canvas* and *dollar,* for example, *c* and *d* would appear in the first frame, *a* and *o* in the second frame and so on to the end of the words."[4] You can see how this test was presented by imagining that you yourself were shown the following frames one at a time:

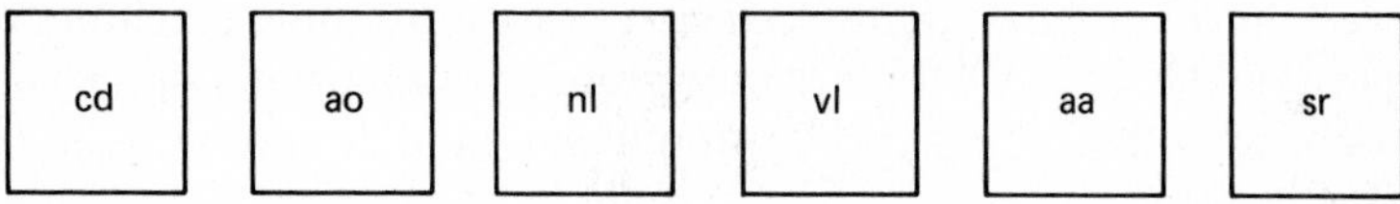

When the subjects were asked to identify either one of the two words, they scored correctly on 57 percent of the trials; but when they were asked to identify both words, the score was only 0.2 percent (one correct report in

[4]Paul A. Kolers, "Experiments in Reading," *Scientific American* 227, no. 1 (July 1972): 84–91.

420 trials). The researchers concluded that "even the skilled reader has considerable difficulty forming a perception of more than one word at a time."[5]

You often have the impression that you are seeing more than one word at a fixation because your eyes are moving rapidly from left to right, taking in words in rapid sequence. This process is almost like watching a movie. Although each film frame is a still picture, you "see" motion and action when the film is projected at a rate of twenty-four frames per second. Similarly, words projected on the brain at the rate of seven or eight words per second give the impression of living, moving ideas. Nevertheless, the brain is "viewing" only one word at a time.

Speed Reading and Remembering

A final objection to speed reading is that it does not give the mind time to consolidate new information.[6] Even if your eyes were able to take in several thousand words a minute (impossible) and your brain were able to comprehend the meaning of them all (impossible), your mind would not have time to consolidate the meaning before it was assaulted by the next batch of several thousand words. As you saw in Chapter 5, the brain requires a certain period of time in which to convert a temporary idea to a permanent one.

VOCALIZATION WHILE READING

For many years it has been thought that vocalizing while reading is a bad habit that should be eliminated. There are four types of vocalizers: the person who whispers each word aloud; the one who pronounces each word with lip movements; the one who moves only the vocal cords; and the one who thinks the sound of each word. Those who want to eliminate vocalization claim that vocalizing slows reading speed. This claim is probably true. However, the assumption that vocalization can and should be eliminated is highly questionable because there is no research to support it. On the contrary, there is strong evidence that vocalization of one kind or another is an essential part of all reading.

A Practical Experiment

Perhaps you don't believe that subvocalization (silent pronunciation) takes place in all readers to some extent or are not sure what subvocalization

[5]Ibid.
[6]R. S. Woodworth and H. Schlosberg, *Experimental Psychology* (New York: Holt, 1954), p. 773.

is. Silent pronunciation is not necessarily the syllable-by-syllable pronunciation of oral reading. Rather, when subvocalization takes place, the sound of the word is heard by the "inner ear" instantly and whole.

Here are two two-line bits of poetry. See whether you can read them by sight alone:

Beside the lake, beneath the trees,
Fluttering and dancing in the breeze.

'Twas too much heart to hide behind a cough
All heard the icy snap of the wintered bough.

Did both examples rhyme for you? The first two lines are a voice rhyme from "The Daffodils," a poem by William Wordsworth (1770–1850). They rhyme only if the words are vocalized, because *trees* and *breeze* do not rhyme for the eye. The second bit of poetry does not rhyme if the words are vocalized, because the mind recognizes the different sounds of *cough* and *bough*. The second two lines are an example of an eye rhyme; they rhyme only to the eye, and only because the rhyming words have the same ending.

If the first two lines rhymed for you but the second two lines did not, then you subvocalized as you were reading. We all subvocalize as we read; we must, in order to comprehend.

What Does Research Say?

Robert A. Hall, Jr., an internationally known linguist, has this to say about vocalization, or inner speech:

> It is commonly thought that we can read and write in complete silence, without any speech taking place. True, many people learn to suppress the movements of their organs of speech when they read, so that no sound comes forth; but nevertheless, inside the brain, the impulses for speech are still being sent forth through the nerves, and only the actualization of these impulses is being inhibited on the muscular level, as has been shown by numerous experiments. No act of reading takes place without a certain amount of subvocalization, as this kind of "silent speech" is called, and we normally subvocalize, when we write, also. Many slow readers retain the habit of reading out loud, or at least partially moving their lips as they read; fast readers learn to skip from one key point to another, and to guess at what must lie in between. The good rapid reader knows the subject-matter well enough to guess intelligently; the poor reader does not know how to choose the high spots or guess what lies between them. As the rate of reading increases, the actual muscular movements of pronunciation are reduced; but, just as soon as the going gets difficult, the rate of reading slows down and the muscular movements of pronunciation increase again, even with skilled rapid readers.
>
> From these considerations, it is evident that the activities of speaking and reading cannot be separated. Curiously enough, literary scholars are especially

> under the delusion that it is possibly to study "written language" in isolation, without regard to the language as it is spoken; this is because they do not realize the extent to which, as we have just pointed out, all reading and writing necessarily involve an act of speech on the part of both writer and reader.[7]

Åke Edfeldt, of the University of Stockholm Institute of Reading Research, has studied vocalization with a team of medical doctors who used electrodes to detect movement in the lips, tongues, and vocal cords of volunteer readers. After exhaustive medical tests, Edfeldt concluded:

> On the basis of the present experimental results, earlier theories concerning silent speech in reading may be judged. These theories often appear to have been constructed afterwards, in order to justify some already adopted form of remedial reading. In opposition to most of these theories, we wish to claim that silent speech occurs in the reading of all persons.
>
> In any case, it seems quite clear that all kinds of training aimed at removing silent speech should be discarded.[8]

Decades ago, E. L. Thorndike (1874–1949), American psychologist and lexicographer, said that "reading is thinking." Psychologists agree that thinking is silent speech. So if reading is thinking, and thinking is silent speech, then reading must also be silent speech. It seems that if we spend our time and energy trying to knock out vocalization, we are in fact trying to knock out comprehension. Vocalization cannot and should not be eliminated, because it is part of the reading process.

A NATURAL WAY TO READ FASTER

Speed-reading methods cannot be effective if they interfere with natural processes, or if they require that we read in a way that isn't natural to us. For example, vocalization is a natural and necessary function; methods that attempt to eliminate vocalization so as to increase reading speed cannot succeed. Methods that impose an artificial eye-fixation scheme must likewise fail.

The only effective way to increase your reading speed is to do so naturally—to do exactly what you have been doing but do more of it or do it faster. The method described in this section will help you read faster naturally. However, you must realize that it is *not* meant for textbook reading, where you must read (and often reread) slowly, to get the full meaning of each

[7]Robert A. Hall, Jr., *New Ways to Learn a Foreign Language* (New York: Bantam Books, Inc., 1966), pp. 28–29.
[8]Åke W. Edfeldt, *Silent Speech and Silent Reading* (Chicago: University of Chicago Press, 1960), p. 154.

sentence and paragraph. Use the method to increase the speed at which you read novels, magazines, journals, and newspapers. To read these materials at the slow textbook rate is a waste of your time; in such cases, the mind is eager to sprint, but the textbook reading habit limits it to a plodding pace.

Setting the Stage for Faster Reading

Here are five things to do or to keep in mind as you practice faster reading. They are fairly general in nature, but they are important to the method. Farther on, you will see, step by step, how to practice faster reading to increase your reading speed.

Establish a Base. Before you begin to read a new book, take a few minutes to think about its title and to look through the table of contents. Extract as much meaning as possible from both. For example, if your book were *The Adventures of Sherlock Holmes,* you would know that you had a handful of absorbing detective stories to read. Knowing the nature of the book will create a mindset highly favorable to reading; it will be derived from the two powerful forces of anticipation and concentration.

As you looked through the table of contents, your eyes might stop at "The Five Orange Pips." You would wonder to yourself, "Pips? I guess that's the British word for seeds. What else could it mean relative to oranges? Not the skin, of course. It must be the seeds." With pips and seeds on your mind, you would already be concentrating without having read a single word of the story. You would be working up a natural and powerful head of steam—a solid base from which to begin your reading.

Be Flexible. Match your reading speed to the material you are reading. If the book begins with introductory, "warm-up" material, move through it fast. But slow down a bit when you come to the first solid paragraph. You need to grab and hold in mind items such as names, places, and circumstances, for these are the magnetic centers around which ideas and details will cluster as you sprint through the pages. When the going gets easier, speed up again. As you read, be continually alert to slow down at paragraphs that are full of ideas and to speed up when you can. There is no reason to expect—or try—to read at a constant rate.

Follow Ideas, Not Words. Don't try to remember words. Simply use the words to visualize the ideas, facts, and actions that the author is presenting. Once you have done so, let the words drop out of your mind. Retain only the development of the story or the important ideas and facts.

Ignore Your Eye Fixations. Don't think about what your eyes are doing, for that will break both your reading rhythm and your concentration. The eye fixations will take care of themselves easily and naturally as you read along at your own pace. You don't need to think about eye fixations any more than you need to think about moving your feet while you walk. The feet take care of themselves, and so do the eyes.

Enjoy the Concluding Paragraph. Slow down for the last paragraph, and savor it. You will enjoy seeing how the author connects the various facts or events in an article or the various parts of a short story or novel.

This whole process—establishing a base, being flexible in reading speed, following ideas, ignoring eye movements, and enjoying the conclusion—leads not only to faster reading, but to intelligent reading as well.

How to Practice Faster Reading

For your first book, choose a novel that you've wanted to read but never had time for. The novel you use to practice reading faster should be on the light side; it is difficult enough to increase your reading speed without struggling at the same time with a tough book.

When you first begin practicing, don't push yourself. Otherwise, you'll find that your mind is unable to follow the story and tends to wander; this can create the bad habit of not concentrating. Read faster than you usually do, but slow enough so you can follow and *enjoy* the story. Remember, you want to build a good habit that has a future.

Do not, at any time, attempt to calculate your words-per-minute reading speed. If you do, speed for speed's sake will become your goal, rather than speed for efficient comprehension. You must avoid this misplaced emphasis.

The First Book. Push yourself to read the first book much faster than you've read before (but, again, at a pace at which you can follow the development of the story). Read at this fast pace for ten full minutes. Then read for ten minutes at a slightly slower pace—just to catch your breath, so to speak. Finally, read for another ten minutes at your fast pace.

This program will give you thirty minutes of practice, and that's enough for one day. Put the book aside, to be used only to practice faster reading. Practice every other day in this way, until you have finished the book.

The Second Through Fifth Books. As with your first book, practice faster reading every other day with your second through fifth books. Begin with a fast-reading session; follow that with a moderate-reading session; and

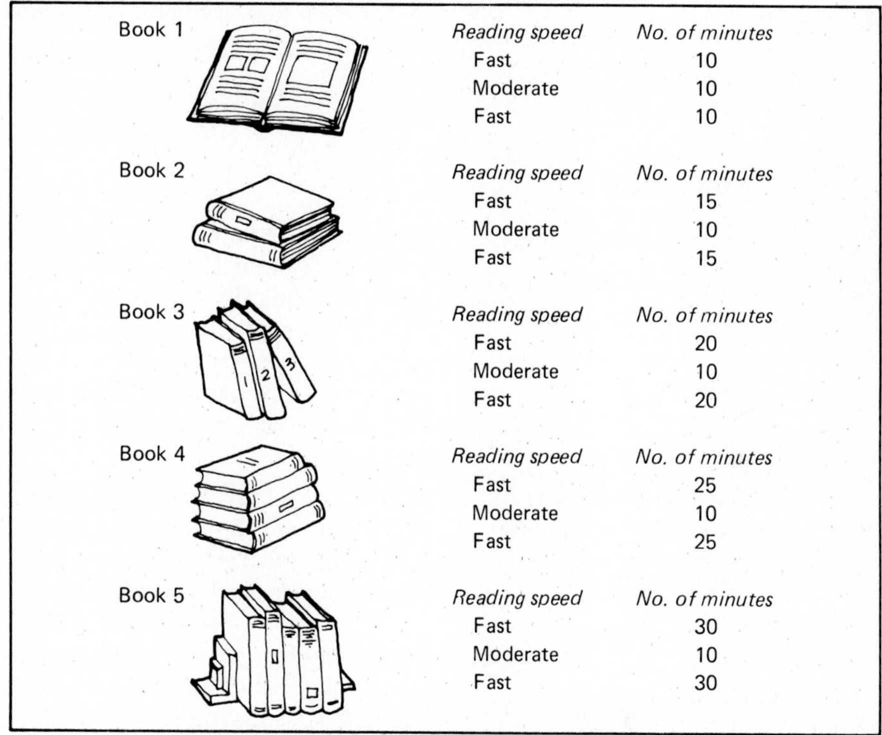

FIGURE 16.2 Durations of Reading Sessions for Practice Books One Through Five

end the practice with another fast-reading session. Figure 16.2 shows how long each of these sessions should be, for each book. In the fast-reading sessions, remember to read as fast as you can without losing your grasp of the story.

The Sixth Book and Beyond. After your fifth practice book, you've served your apprenticeship. Henceforth, read as fast as you can with comprehension, remembering to be flexible in these ways: First, when you begin to lose track of the development of a story, slow down until you pick up the track; then continue at high speed. Second, if you get tired but want to continue reading, slow down slightly for a while; later, if you feel like speeding up, do so gradually.

You must never continue to push for speed when you feel even a bit tired; if you do, you will begin to destroy the skill that you have developed through patient practice. If you start losing interest in a book, don't feel obliged to read it to the end. Put it aside, and pick up another book that seems more interesting.

SUMMARY

How does purpose affect reading?	Purpose determines how much time you'll spend in reading almost anything. For example, looking over a textbook chapter to gain familiarity before listening to a classroom lecture might take no more than half an hour, but reading the same chapter in preparation for a quiz might take three or four hours.
If 600 words per minute is the fastest possible reading rate, how have claims for rates of thousands of words per minute persisted?	Claims is all they are. No so-called speed reader has yet submitted to an impartial test. Any claim of over 600 words per minute would necessitate the skipping of many words. You, too, could make about four or five fixations on a page, turn it, and repeat this on page after page. After a minute of glancing and turning, you'd end up with a count of thousands of words per minute, but you would have understood nothing.
Are eye pauses and subvocalization really necessary during reading?	According to all the research, eye pauses and subvocalization are absolutely necessary. The pauses allow your eyes to focus on the words; subvocalization is required for comprehension.
Should I use the faster reading method on textbooks?	No. Textbooks are packed too full of ideas and facts for fast reading with complete comprehension. It would be a waste of time, for you would understand little and remember almost nothing. Use the method on the easier novels that you read for pleasure, as well as for magazines, newspapers, and journals.
What is a "natural way" to read faster?	You should practice reading faster using the same techniques that you use naturally, but push yourself to higher and higher speeds.

This method includes none of the artificial techniques advocated for so-called speed-reading systems, for such techniques only interfere with your natural development.

HAVE YOU MISSED SOMETHING?

1. *Sentence completion.* Complete the following sentences with one of the three words listed below each sentence.

a. Most students believe that improved reading means improved ________________.

comprehension vision speed

b. The best way to read faster is by reading ________________.

technically naturally artificially

2. *Matching.* In each blank space in the left column, write the number preceding the phrase in the right column that matches the left item best.

_____ a. Eye movement	1. Processes words one at a time
_____ b. Fixation	2. Blurs words on a page
_____ c. Subvocalization	3. Always accompanies reading
_____ d. The mind	4. Should not be applied to textbooks
_____ e. Faster reading	5. Allows the eyes to focus

3. *True-false.* Write *T* beside the *true* statements and *F* beside the *false* statements.

_____ a. Moving your lips when you read indicates a lack of intelligence.

_____ b. You need not read for comprehension when you practice faster reading.

_____ c. Your eyes can see only about ten printed letters at one time.

_____ d. Your eyes can see clearly only when they are not moving.

_____ e. You should practice faster reading every day.

_____ f. You should slow your reading down when you get tired.

4. *Multiple choice.* Choose the word that completes the following sentence most accurately, and circle the letter that precedes it.

   Reading for understanding does not require

   a. speed
   b. fixations
   c. thinking
   d. subvocalization

CHAPTER 17

Ten Techniques for Improving Your Reading Comprehension

To sit alone in the lamplight with a book spread out before you, and hold intimate converse with men of unseen generations—such is a pleasure beyond compare.

Yoshida Kenko (1283–1350), Japanese poet and Buddhist monk

Just as there is more than one way to skin a cat, there's more than one way to improve your understanding of what you read. This chapter features

- The intonation way
- The vocabulary way
- The background way
- Edward Gibbon's way
- The paragraph way
- The organizational-pattern way
- The page-at-a-time way
- Daniel Webster's way
- The pivotal-words way

and finally

- The skimming way

Reading comprehension cannot be improved through mechanical techniques like turning pages faster or moving the eyes in some artificial pattern. There is no magic in such actions. The magic comes only when you work at your reading skills.

Most methods for improvement suggested in this chapter require hard work, but the rewards are great. A few of them require only the willingness to try a new way of using old knowledge, and here, too, the rewards can be great.

THE INTONATION WAY

As you saw in Chapter 16, vocalization is part of the process of reading and comprehending. You can use it to read faster with a high degree of understanding. The most efficient use of vocalization is through *intonation,* which is the rise and fall of the voice in speaking. Reading with intonation means reading with expression. Intonation provides a natural means for combining individual words into meaningful mental "bites."

To use this system, let your eyes move rapidly across the page as usual. You need not make any sound, but let your mind swing along each line with an intonational rhythm that can be heard by your "inner ear." Read with expression. In doing so, you will be replacing the important *rhythm, stress, emphasis,* and *pauses* that were taken out when the words were put into written form.

The passage in Figure 17.1 has been divided into thought units. The clusters of words are separated by slash marks. (Of course, different readers would group these words into different clusters, depending on their individual intonation.) Read the passage silently, letting your eyes move rapidly over the lines and permitting your "inner voice" to cluster the words through intonation. You will probably notice how rapidly your eyes move and how easy it is to comprehend the meaning when you read with intonation.

To make silent intonation a regular habit, start by reading aloud in the privacy of your room. Spend ten or fifteen minutes on one chapter from a novel. Read it with exaggerated expression, as if you were reading a part in a dramatic play. This will establish your own speech patterns in your mind, so that you will "hear" them more readily when you read silently.

THE VOCABULARY WAY

There is probably no surer or sounder way to improve your reading permanently than by building a strong, precise vocabulary. In a precise vocabulary, every word is learned as a concept. You know its ancestry, its principal

> Athens and Sparta / were both Greek cities / and their people / spoke a common language. / In every other respect / they were different. / Athens rose high from the plain. / It was a city / exposed to the fresh breezes / from the sea, / willing to look / at the world / with the eyes / of a happy child. / Sparta, / on the other hand, / was built / at the bottom / of a deep valley, / and used the surrounding mountains / as a barrier / against foreign thought. / Athens / was a city of busy trade. / Sparta / was an armed camp. /

FIGURE 17.1 Reading by Word Clusters: The Intonation Way
Source: Reprinted from The Story of Mankind *by Henry B. van Loon and Gerard W. van Loon, by permission of Liveright Publishing Corporation. Copyright © 1972 by Henry B. van Loon and Gerard W. van Loon.*

definition as well as several secondary definitions, its synonyms and the subtle differences among them, and its antonyms. Then, when you encounter it in your reading, this vast store of knowledge flashes before you, illuminating the sentence, the paragraph, and the idea the author is trying to convey. (If you have not yet read Chapter 15 on building a precise vocabulary, this is a good time to do so.)

THE BACKGROUND WAY

You can improve your reading tremendously by reading good books. The first reason for this is that you'll be getting a lot of practice. Even more important, you'll be storing up a stock of concepts, ideas, events, and names that will lend meaning to your later reading. This kind of information is used surprisingly often.

Psychologist David Ausubel says that the most crucial prerequisite for learning is your already established background of knowledge. Ausubel means that if you are to understand what you read, then you must interpret it in the light of knowledge (background) you already have. A background is not something you are born with. You accumulate one through both direct and vicarious experiences. The vicarious experiences, of course, are those you acquire by listening, seeing films, and reading books.

Authors often make allusions to famous books, famous people, or well-known events. In many cases, you can miss these references and still understand the story. In some instances, however, an allusion will be crucial, and you will have to search for its meaning if it is not in your background. Consider this short passage by Robert Louis Stevenson (1850–94), Scottish novelist and poet:

> And not long ago I was able to lay by my lantern in content, for I found the honest man.

This sentence is composed of twenty simple words, many consisting of only two and three letters. It contains one word that is crucial to the understanding of the sentence. Go back and see whether you can pick it out before you read on.

The two words most often chosen are *honest* and *content.* Neither is the crucial word. That word is *lantern.* It is, however, no ordinary lantern to which Stevenson refers, but one that is associated with a real person in history. Whose lantern? The lantern of Diogenes. Diogenes was a fourth century B.C. Greek cynic and critic who walked the streets of Athens during the daytime, holding a lighted lantern, peering into the faces of passers-by, and saying that he was looking for an honest man. He was dramatizing the idea that it is difficult to find an honest man, even with a lighted lantern during the day.

Obviously, without knowing the story of Diogenes you cannot fully understand Stevenson's line, and that is only one example from millions. You cannot make every fact, myth, story, and poem part of your background. But you can, through your reading, enlarge your background and thus increase the effectiveness of your reading. In other words, you can improve your reading by reading.

Read the *great* books, for it is in these books that the wisdom of the ages is passed on to posterity. These books give you the chance to "talk" with princes, kings, philosophers, travelers, playwrights, scientists, artists, and novelists. Begin with the books and subjects that interest you, and don't worry about having only narrow interests. Once you begin reading, your interests will widen naturally.

Here are some books that will guide you in selecting books to read. They not only tell you about books but also suggest titles, lists, and plans.

Dickinson, Asa D. *The World's Best Books.* Bronx, N.Y.: Wilson, 1953.

Downs, Robert B. *Books That Changed America.* New York: Macmillan, 1970. A paperback edition is published by New American Library.

Downs, Robert B. *Books That Changed the World.* New York: New American Library, 1971. Paperback.

Downs, Robert B. *Famous American Books.* New York: McGraw-Hill, 1971. Paperback.

Downs, Robert B. *Famous Books: Great Writings in the History of Civilization.* Totowa, N.J.: Littlefield, Adams, 1975.

Downs, Robert B. *Books That Changed the South.* Totowa, N.J.: Littlefield, Adams, 1977. Paperback.

Fadiman, Clifton. *Reading I've Liked.* New York: Simon and Schuster, 1958. Paperback.

Fadiman, Clifton. *The Lifetime Reading Plan.* New York: Crowell, 1978. Distributed by Harper & Row.

Pauk, Walter. *Reading for Success in College: A Student's Guide to Recommended Books for College Background Reading and a Practical Handbook for Developing College Study Skills.* Clearwater, Fla.: Reston-Stuart Publishers, P.O. Box 4067, 1968. Paperback.

Weber, J. Sherwood. *Good Reading: A Guide for Serious Readers.* New York: New American Library, 1980. Paperback. A guide to the world's best books, prepared by the Committee on College Reading.

EDWARD GIBBON'S WAY

The great English historian Edward Gibbon (1737–94), author of *Decline and Fall of the Roman Empire,* made constant use of the great recall technique. This is simply an organized and rather intense use of one's general background. Before starting to read a new book, or before starting to write on any subject, Gibbon would spend hours alone in his study, or he would take a long walk alone to recall everything that he knew about the subject. As he pondered some major idea, he was continually surprised by how many other ideas and fragments of ideas he would dredge up.

Gibbon's system was highly successful. His old ideas were brought to the forefront of his mind, ready for use, and they could act as magnetic centers for new ideas and new information. Great recall promotes concentration.

THE PARAGRAPH WAY

You can improve your comprehension by stopping at the end of each textbook paragraph to summarize and condense it to a single sentence. To summarize and condense, you must understand the functions of three main types of sentences: the topic or controlling-idea sentence, the supporting sentence, and the concluding sentence. Figure 17.2 shows these three types of sentences in an actual paragraph.

The *topic* sentence announces the topic (or the portion of the topic) to be dealt with in the paragraph. Although the topic sentence may appear anywhere in the paragraph, it is usually first—and for a very good reason. This sentence provides the focus for the writer while writing and for the reader while reading. When you find the topic sentence, be sure to underline it so that it will stand out not only now, but also later when you review.

The bulk of an expository paragraph is made up of *supporting* sentences, which help to explain or prove the main topic. These sentences present facts,

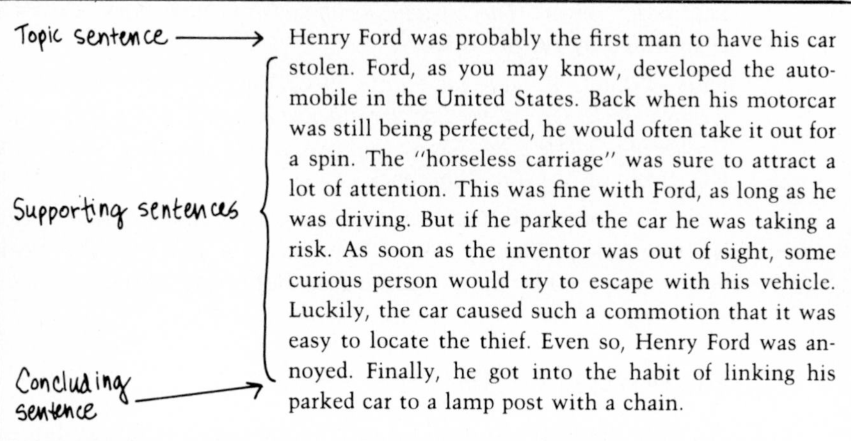

FIGURE 17.2 The Three Elements of an Expository Paragraph

reasons, examples, definitions, comparisons, contrasts, and other pertinent details. They are most important, because they sell the ideas.

The last sentence of a textbook paragraph is likely to be a *concluding* sentence. It is used to sum up a discussion, to emphasize a point, or to restate all or part of the topic sentence so as to bring the paragraph to a close.

Of course, the paragraphs you'll be reading will be part of some longer piece of writing—a textbook chapter, a section of a chapter, or a newspaper or magazine article. Besides expository paragraphs, in which new information is presented and discussed, these longer writings contain three types of paragraphs: introductory, transitional, and summarizing.

Introductory paragraphs tell you, in advance, such things as (1) the main idea of the chapter or section; (2) the extent or limits of the coverage; (3) how the topic is developed; and (4) the writer's attitude toward the topic. *Transitional* paragraphs are usually short; their sole function is to tie together what you have read so far and what is to come—to set the stage for succeeding paragraphs. *Summarizing* paragraphs are used to restate briefly the main ideas of the chapter or section. The writer may also draw some conclusion from these ideas, based on the evidence in the chapter, or speculate on the basis of that evidence.

All three types should *alert* you: the introductory paragraph of things to come; the transitional paragraph of a new topic; and the summarizing paragraph of main ideas that you should have gotten.

THE ORGANIZATIONAL-PATTERN WAY

The secret of good reading comprehension is thinking. You must think the words you see and give thought to the ideas they generate. This sounds simple, but it isn't. The problem is that your thoughts tend to wander as you read. When you are thinking about something else, you cannot think about what you are reading.

One way to keep your mind on your reading is to recognize and keep yourself aware of the organizational pattern that the author is using. Then you will think with the author as you read. For example, suppose you recognize that a paragraph is organized according to a chronological pattern. Then you would say to yourself, "Yes, I see what she's doing. She's describing the major events of the Great Depression as they happened, year by year." As you focused on the pattern, your mind would stay on your reading and you would be thinking about it.

Here are brief descriptions of the most commonly used organizational patterns. You should have no trouble recognizing them when you encounter them in your reading.

Time or Chronological Pattern. Events are presented in the chronological order in which they happened. This pattern can be recognized quickly from the author's use of dates and of phrases such as *in previous years, the next day,* and *two years later,* which denote the passage of time.

Process Pattern. Steps or events are presented in an orderly sequence that leads to a desired situation or product. A recipe and the instructions for assembling a bicycle provide examples of process patterns. They often include words such as, *first, after this, then, next,* and *finally.*

Place or Spatial Pattern. Items are presented or discussed on the basis of their locations or their arrangement relative to each other. For example, an author might use this pattern to describe the geographical features of the United States from the West Coast to the East Coast. In such a case, this pattern is often called the *geographical pattern.* It is also called the *topical pattern* when it is used to describe the organization of a corporation along the lines of purchasing, manufacturing, sales, and so forth. The progression from item to item is usually orderly and easy to follow: from left to right, from high to low, from north to south, or whatever.

Increasing-Importance Pattern. In this pattern, the most important or most dramatic item in a series is placed at the end. Each succeeding item is more important than the previous one, so a crescendo effect is created. Thus, this pattern is often called the *climactic-order pattern.*

Decreasing-Importance Pattern. In this pattern, the most important or most dramatic item in a series is placed at the very beginning. Such an organization grabs the reader's interest immediately, so there is a good chance the reader will stay with the writing all the way through.

Cause-Effect Pattern. This exceedingly important general pattern has such variations as the *problem-cause-solution pattern* and the *problem-effect-solution pattern.* Whatever the combination, you should be able to identify the various parts of the pattern—the problem, cause, effects, and solution—and think along with the author as you move from one part to the next.

Compare or Contrast Pattern. Writers *compare* things, events, or people when they emphasize similarities, and *contrast* them when they emphasize differences. Individual characteristics may be compared or contrasted one at a time, or lists of characteristics may be discussed as a group. In either case, the pattern can be recognized from the various similarities or differences and from the use of words such as *similarly, likewise, conversely,* and *on the other hand.*

THE PAGE-AT-A-TIME WAY

Thomas Babington Macaulay (1800–59) was an English statesman, historian, essayist, and poet. His greatest work, *The History of England,* at the time it was published outsold all other books except the Bible. Macaulay began reading adult books at the age of 3; but after consuming shelf after shelf of books, he suddenly realized that he wasn't gaining much knowledge for all his effort. He understood every word of what he read and seemed to comprehend what the writer was saying, but later he could not summarize the ideas presented or even describe, in general terms, what the writer had written. He described his solution to this problem as follows:

> At the foot of every page I read I stopped and obliged myself to give an account of what I had read on that page. At first I had to read it three or four times before I got my mind firmly fixed. But I compelled myself to comply with the plan, until now, after I have read a book through once, I can almost recite it from the beginning to the end.

There's something very basic, honest, and refreshing in the Macaulay way. There are no complicated formulas to follow. You simply stop at the bottom of a page and ask yourself, "In brief, what did the writer say on this page?" This technique will do for you what it did for Lord Macaulay. It will make you concentrate. It will also teach you to think continually while you read. Every time you pause for a brief recall, your memory will be getting stronger.

DANIEL WEBSTER'S WAY

Daniel Webster (1782–1852), American statesman and orator, had his own special technique for building concentration. Before reading a book, he would look at the table of contents, read the preface, and turn some of the pages. Then he would make lists of (1) questions that he expected to be answered in the book, (2) the knowledge he expected to gain from his reading, and (3) where the knowledge would take him. The three lists guided him through the book; his attention and concentration were intense.

THE PIVOTAL-WORDS WAY

No words are so helpful while you read as the prepositional phrases and conjunctions that guide your mind to and through the author's ideas. A word like *furthermore* says, "Keep going!" *However* says, "Easy! Hold up!" If you master the words and phrases listed below, you will almost immediately become a better reader.

Additive Words. These say, "Here's more of the same coming up. It's just as important as what we have already said."

also	further	moreover
and	furthermore	too
besides	in addition	

Equivalent Words. These say, "Both what I have just said and this too."

as well as	equally important	similarly
at the same time	likewise	

Amplification Words. With these, the author is saying, "I want to be sure that you understand my idea; so here's a specific instance."

as	in fact	such as
for example (e.g.)	like	that is
for instance	specifically	to illustrate

Alternative Words. These point out, "Sometimes there is a choice; at other times there isn't."

either/or	other than	otherwise
neither/nor		

Repetitive Words. These say, "I said it once, but I'm going to say it again in case you missed it the first time."

again	in other words	that is (i.e.)
to repeat		

Contrast and Change Words. These say, "So far I've given you only one side of the story; now let's take a look at the other side."

but	instead of	regardless
conversely	on the contrary	still
despite	on the other hand	though
even though	nevertheless	whereas
however	notwithstanding	yet
in spite of	rather than	

Cause-and-Effect Words. These say, "All this has happened; now I'll tell you why."

accordingly	for this reason	then
as a result	hence	therefore
because	since	thus
consequently	so	

Qualifying Words. These say, "Here is what we can expect; these are the conditions we are working under."

although	providing	whenever
if	unless	

Concession Words. These say, "Okay! We agree on this much."

accepting the data	granted that	of course
even though		

Emphasizing Words. These say, "Wake up and take notice!"

above all	indeed	more important

Order Words. With these, the author is saying, "You keep your mind on reading; I'll keep the numbers straight."

finally	last	second
first	next	then

Time Words. "Let's keep the record straight on who said what and especially when."

afterwards	meanwhile	subsequently
at the same time	next	then
before	now	ultimately
formerly	presently	until
later	previously	while

Summarizing Words. These say, "We've said many things so far. Let's stop here and pull them together."

briefly	in brief	to summarize
for these reasons	in conclusion	to sum up

THE SKIMMING WAY

Both students and business executives report that the workhorse of reading is skimming. Covering many speeds and uses, skimming can range from just fast reading to searching, which could hardly be classified as reading. Whether to use rapid reading or searching—or anything in between—depends on your purpose. Tailor skimming to your purpose; otherwise you'll waste time.

Here are five purposes for skimming and the techniques for each.

Searching for a Needle in a Haystack

If you want to find specific information (name, date, word, or phrase) in a textbook or article, searching may be used because it is recognition, not comprehension, that will give you the answer. To ensure that your eyes do not overlook the word or fact you seek, concentrate on it, keeping it in mind as your eyes run over the pages. Concentration will trigger your mind to pick it out of the sea of words. Once you have located the specific word or fact, pause and read at a normal rate the sentence or paragraph surrounding it to make sure, through context, that you have found what you were looking for.

When using the searching technique, if your time is short, resist the temptation to read the whole article. What you may really be doing, subconsciously, is putting off studying. But, if you do have time, follow your curiosity and finish the article. It may not help you on the next exam, but the knowledge gained will give you an edge and contribute to your general wisdom.

Looking for Clues

When you are seeking specific information but do not know in what words the information may appear, you must use a slower searching method. In this case, you won't be able to anticipate the exact words, so you must be alert for clues, which can appear in various forms.

In this kind of searching, you must infer the answer. For example, after reading an article about Paul Bunyan, a legendary giant lumberjack and folk hero, a student was asked a question about Paul Bunyan's birthplace. The answer was Canada, yet nowhere in the article did the word *Canada* appear. The answer had to be inferred from a sentence that stated that Paul Bunyan was born at the headwaters of the St. Lawrence River. Because the student discovered on a map that the headwaters are in Canada, she could answer the question.

When you are looking for clues, try to guess the form in which the information might appear. When you believe you have found the information you want, go back and read the paragraph to make sure, from context, that it is exactly what you seek.

Getting the Gist

Sometimes skimming may be used to get the gist of a book or article. You can use this technique to find out whether a book pertains to the topic you are working on. To get the gist, read both introduction and summary rapidly, as well as paragraphs that have topic sentences indicating that the paragraph contains important data.

This skimming method can help when you have a term paper to write. After you have looked through the card catalogue and have made a list of books that seem related to your topic, get the books and look through them to eliminate those that are not pertinent and to keep those that are. Obviously, you would waste time and energy if you attempted to read all the books on your list. To get the main idea of each book, look at the table of contents, or select a chapter with a title related to your topic and skim it for its outstanding ideas.

Overviewing a Textbook Chapter

An important use of skimming is discussed in Chapter 8: surveying or getting an overview of a textbook chapter before you read it thoroughly. Overviewing may be done to attain various degrees of comprehension. In most cases, this type of skimming calls for understanding captions, headings, subheadings, and portions of paragraphs well enough to locate key concepts in the chapter. Such skimming lets you see the relative importance of each part to the whole.

Skimming to Review

Skimming also can be used to review for an examination or for a recitation. After skimming chapters that you have previously read, studied, and noted, for effective study you should pause from time to time and try to recite the main concepts in each chapter or summarize the chapter. After finishing a textbook chapter, always review to understand the chapter as a whole, like a finished jigsaw puzzle.

SUMMARY

How can I use intonation silently?

Intonation in reading means saying the words silently—but saying them with expression or rhythm, not in a monotone. Just a little practice reading aloud will show you how it works. Reading with intonation requires close attention that will get you to concentrate. The end result will be high comprehension plus speed.

Why is a background of information important in reading?

Many words have meanings beyond their definitions, meanings that are derived from their use in various writings. Unless you are aware of these meanings, you will fail to understand them when you encounter such words. Moreover, even dictionary meanings are expanded and extended through use. The larger your background of information, the more of these meanings you will understand as you read.

Won't pausing to summarize each paragraph slow me down?	Yes. But what's the sense in moving through a whole chapter without learning or remembering anything? Reading a textbook chapter straight through will yield almost no long-term remembering, so you'll have to go back and read it again anyway. Overall, you'll save time by pausing to summarize—to make sure you understand each paragraph.
How does recognizing the organizational pattern help comprehension?	Once you recognize a familiar pattern, you know what's going on. You become part of the process. You therefore concentrate better, comprehending and absorbing facts and ideas because you know exactly how they are related and why the author has presented them in a particular sequence.
How does the paragraph way differ from the page-at-a-time way?	The idea in both systems is to pause, think, and summarize what you have read. Do so paragraph by paragraph when the writing is packed with facts, page by page when the material is written in a more leisurely narrative style.
How does knowing pivotal words help reading?	Pivotal words direct your reading and your thinking. They also point to ideas, modify or connect ideas, and even reverse ideas in midsentence. If you truly know the meanings of pivotal words, you will understand almost anything you read.
Why are there various methods of skimming?	The various methods and speeds in skimming let you tailor the method to fit the job.
What is the one rule for using skimming?	Use skimming as a tool. Determine what the main purpose of your assignment is, and then judge whether skimming can help you achieve your purpose.

HAVE YOU MISSED SOMETHING?

1. *Sentence completion.* Complete the following sentences with one of the three words listed below each sentence.

a. Edward Gibbon learned new ideas by letting his old ones act as ______________________.

magnets examples summaries

b. A summary paragraph or sentence usually restates ____________.

references information transitions

2. *Matching.* In each blank space in the left column, write the number preceding the phrase in the right column that matches the left item best.

_____ a. Intonation way	1. Advocate of a "list before you read" technique
_____ b. Paragraph way	2. Most crucial prerequisite for learning
_____ c. Macaulay	3. Involves efficient use of vocalization
_____ d. Pivotal words	4. Advocate of the "page-at-a-time" way
_____ e. Webster	5. Involves pauses for summarization
_____ f. Background	6. Helps you to understand the chapter as a whole
_____ g. Overviewing	7. Direct your thinking as you read

3. *True-false.* Write *T* beside the *true* statements and *F* beside the *false* statements.

_____ a. You should do all your reading out loud in the intonation method.

_____ b. A good vocabulary is one of the best tools for effective reading.

_____ c. Transitional paragraphs help you to follow the writer's train of thought.

_____ d. Supporting sentences are usually placed in the middle of a paragraph.

_____ e. You will read more effectively if you read great books.

_____ f. You should skim a chapter after you read it.

4. *Multiple choice.* Choose the phrase that completes the following sentence most accurately, and circle the letter that precedes it.

A description of the events leading up to World War I would probably be organized in the

a. process pattern
b. compare pattern
c. increasing-importance pattern
d. chronological pattern

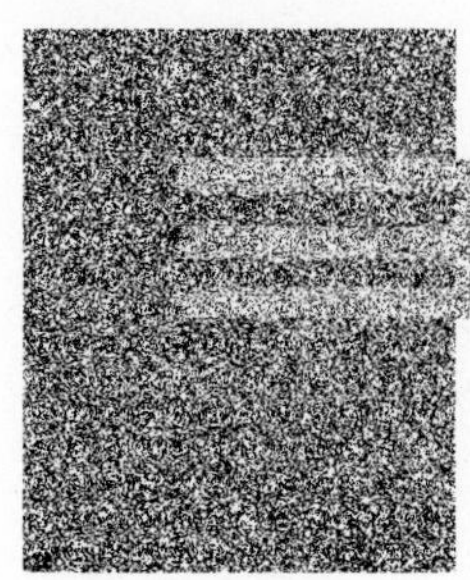

PART

VI

Special Skills

CHAPTER 18

Researching and Writing Papers

If your writing falls apart, it probably has no primary idea to hold it together.

Sheridan Baker (b. 1918), professor of English, author of *The Practical Stylist*

At worst, writing a paper can be a tedious ordeal. At best, it may be an adventure in learning. The difference lies in knowing how to approach your writing assignment—whether you have been asked to write a report, a theme, or a research paper. This chapter discusses

- Writing good papers
- Choosing a topic
- Doing research
- Recording information
- Organizing the paper
- Writing the research paper
- Editing your work
- Adding the missing elements

and finally

- Making the final copy

riting even a short paper can seem to be a tremendous undertaking. From the time the paper is assigned until the day it is due (or overdue), it can occupy your mind like no other type of assignment. But the truth is that writing a paper isn't much more difficult than reading about a subject in detail, taking notes on your reading, organizing your notes, and reciting them. You should already be doing these things when you study. The only added step is putting your recitation down on paper, to communicate it to others. If you take it one step at a time, you may even find—as many other students have found—that writing papers can be a most absorbing way to learn about a subject.

WRITING GOOD PAPERS

You may be asked to write any of several kinds of papers, depending on the subject and the instructor's approach:

Theme. Usually fairly short and based on your own conclusions, your experience, or your reading.

Report. A factual discussion (usually in one of the sciences) of the results of a piece of research. The format is usually supplied to you by the instructor.

Critical essay. Your opinion on a book or other piece of writing, usually assigned in an English or other language course.

Research paper. Of any specific length, but usually at least four double-spaced typed pages. Based on extensive research of published material on a subject. The topic may be left up to you, within fairly broad guidelines, or you may be given a specific assignment.

The most extensive type is the research paper. The others require less library work and may be handled a little differently. However, the techniques for writing a research paper, as discussed below, are applicable to any paper you write.

Most papers are assigned well in advance of the date they're due. If the assignment is given at the beginning of the term, set up a schedule on your calendar that allows plenty of time for your research, time to write at least three drafts or versions, and time to make the final copy before the paper is due. *Don't* start the night before.

The length of the paper is given in number of words or number of double-spaced pages required. The assigned length of the paper is chosen by the instructor to indicate how deeply you should get into the subject. A 500-word paper must focus on one specific aspect of a topic; 2,000 words or ten pages gives you room to cover the topic more broadly. For example, you might use 500 words to discuss one presidential candidate's stand on the issue of defense spending but ten or more pages to discuss his whole platform and its implications. Try to stay within the given limits, but don't think of them as exact length requirements.

Assignments may be clearly stated, so that you know precisely what you're expected to write on, or they may be phrased very generally. If you have any doubt about what your instructor expects you to cover in the paper, make an appointment to discuss it with him or her. Feel free to ask for suggestions as to approach and sources of information.

CHOOSING A TOPIC

Finding a topic is often the biggest stumbling block in writing a paper. It's essential that you know how to choose one easily and efficiently. There are three steps in the process of selecting a topic for a research paper. Some or all of them may also apply to other types of papers, depending on the particular assignment:

1. Choose a subject that interests you.
2. Narrow your subject.
3. Find a focus.

Choose Your Subject

If you are writing a research paper, you will most likely be able to choose a topic from a broad subject area. In that case, choose a subject that you are interested in, or that you can develop an interest in. If it isn't a subject that everyone else is writing on, all the better. If you're not sure about your choice of a subject, do a little preliminary research—in the library—to see what's involved in several subjects before you make your decision.

Suppose that you are very interested in the medical profession and have decided to write about that. But "medical profession" includes the training of doctors, their career patterns, their patient relations, the best way to build up a practice, foreign-born doctors, the shortage of doctors, and scores of other topics. How can you do justice to them all? Obviously you cannot. You will have to narrow your subject.

Narrow Your Subject

The most common criticism of research papers is that the topic is too broad. The problem lies in knowing when you have narrowed your topic enough. A Cornell professor of English suggests this method: Put your subject through three or four significant narrowings, moving from a given category to a class within that category each time. As an example, here is a sample narrowing for a paper of from ten to fifteen pages:

General Topic:	*The Civil War*
1st narrowing:	The Crucial Battles of the Civil War
2nd narrowing:	The Crucial Battle of Chancellorsville
3rd narrowing:	Lee's Tactics at Chancellorsville
4th narrowing:	"Stonewall" Jackson's Attack at Chancellorsville

Or suppose that after considering many different aspects of the medical profession, you feel that you are most interested in the shortage of doctors. The subject seems to be a natural one, because you immediately begin to speculate about it: Why don't the medical schools accept more medical students? But more students would mean more professors and enlarged facilities. Then why not shorten the number of years of training? All these ideas springing into your mind show that you have a natural interest in the topic; in fact, any of these ideas could be the focus for your paper.

Let us pause at this point to sum up the topics you have considered and the amount of narrowing that has been done. Here is what the summing up looks like:

General Topic:	*The Medical Profession*
1st narrowing:	The Shortage of Doctors in the U.S.
2nd narrowing:	Overcoming the Doctor Shortage
3rd narrowing (alternative):	Overcoming the Doctor Shortage by Accepting More Medical Students
3rd narrowing (alternative):	Overcoming the Doctor Shortage by Shortening the Term of Training
3rd narrowing (alternative):	Overcoming the Doctor Shortage by Government Subsidies

Because the shortage of medical doctors has been a subject of concern, many articles have been written about it in newspapers, magazines, and journals. Now it is time to go to the library and dig for more ideas in the *Readers' Guide to Periodical Literature.* You look in the *Readers' Guide* under the heading "Physicians," and you find a long list of titles of articles. But there is not even one article on any of the topics of the third narrowing. After looking through several more volumes of the *Readers' Guide* and finding only one or two titles on each topic, you decide to abandon the three topics because of the lack of material.

Going back to the current volume of the *Readers' Guide,* you begin looking for another topic with an emphasis on the shortage of doctors. The list of titles on the page looks somewhat like this:

Physicians

1. Family doctor: Medicine's newest specialty
2. Dilemma in Dyersville: doctors needed
3. Let's give foreign doctors a fair shake
4. Curing the doctor shortage: apprenticeships
5. Never marry a doctor
6. Medical assistant; the health team approach
7. Who is the doctor's doc?
8. Medical shortages abroad, too

Your eyes stop at title 4, "Curing the doctor shortage: apprenticeships." You sense that this topic could lead to an exciting paper. You imagine this article might take the approach that the doctor shortage could be cured by having select students learn how to become doctors by working under the supervision of practicing physicians. Your thesis could be on the side of apprenticeship. You need to find other articles that would support your view, but there are no other articles on apprenticeship training. Thus you must drop what seemed to be a promising and exciting topic and begin searching for another.

After perhaps one or two more false starts, suppose you finally find a category with a list of articles like this:

Electronics in Medicine

1. Expensive machines save lives
2. The electronystagmograph
3. A 200-mph surgical drill
4. Measuring blood pressures—a new machine
5. Relieving pain electronically
6. An electronic nurse (for 2¢ a day)
7. Electronics: a solution to the doctor shortage?
8. Engineers design medical devices

9. Medical devices: an unhealthy situation
10. Electronics aid the busy doctor

As your eyes move down the list of titles, you know that you have found enough material to support both a topic and a point of view. You are particularly interested in number 9, "Medical devices: an unhealthy situation." It indicates that there may be both positive and negative aspects to the use of medical devices. You may find that volumes of the *Readers' Guide* for other years reveal that there are more articles under the heading "Electronics in medicine." You have finally narrowed your subject effectively.

Find a Focus

To avoid making your paper a mere accumulation of facts, you must develop a genuine question and then use your facts to answer the question. Whether it can be definitively answered is unimportant. The important thing is to focus all your research on answering the broad question, so that your paper has direction and purpose.

Once you have narrowed your topic to medical electronics, your focus might be expressed with this question: "In what ways do electronic machines help a doctor in the practice of medicine?" Or, more pointedly: "Do electronic machines help or hinder a doctor in the practice of medicine?" The answer to the second question could make interesting reading. You may even discover, after you have done all your research, that you are willing to take a stand on the question. Then your facts could be organized around your point of view.

A word of caution about taking a stand on your subject: Don't become so biased that you consciously or unconsciously pick out the strongest arguments for the side that you want to win and ignore or minimize the evidence for the other side. Remember: You are not writing the research paper to win an argument. Your task is to inform both yourself and your readers. This does not mean that your guiding idea or point of view cannot be the essence of your organization. But be fair. Present both sides of the argument.

At this point, you have finally found a manageable topic, and you have found a focus by asking a good question about it. You do not yet know the answer to your question, but you are ready to start your research.

DOING RESEARCH

If you're writing a theme or a critical essay, you will be assigned the book or books to read. If you're writing a report, you will be reading about others' research or doing an experiment yourself and then writing the report. For these short papers, the assigned reading material will be quite specific. For a research paper, you need to do research in the library.

Start your research on the subject early. Books may be in great demand when the deadline for a paper is approaching. If you are going to choose one view and support it, don't decide definitely which one it's going to be until you've had a chance to do some preliminary research. Once you see what's available to support the different viewpoints, then you can decide which one you'll choose.

Your research will consist mainly of finding and reading published material that is relevant to your topic. For this, you will need to make full use of your school and neighborhood libraries. Libraries vary in resources, but the major sources you'll be concerned with are the reference section, the periodical section, and the card catalogue. Find out where each of them is. Get a map or a friendly librarian to help you at first.

The *reference section* is the place where reference books are kept—everything from encyclopedias to telephone directories. Most important for your research are the current indexes (lists) of articles in various magazines and journals. One index already mentioned is the *Readers' Guide to Periodical Literature.* Other useful indexes are the *New York Times Index,* the *Business Periodicals Index,* and the *Education Index.* They can all help you find pertinent articles.

The publications themselves will probably be located in the *periodical section.* There you will find magazines, newspapers, and other publications that come out periodically (weekly, monthly, etc.). Some libraries have microfilms of newspapers in a special location that is not part of the main periodical section. If you need them, a librarian will show you how to use the microfilm readers.

The *card catalogue* is your guide to the books and other materials in the library. It is usually located near the entrance. If you don't see it, ask. If you don't know how to use it, ask or read about it. This one resource is the indispensable key for finding all that the library has to offer you. (Note that many colleges now have card catalogues that are computerized. Chapter 21 presents specific information on how to use these systems.)

In the card catalogue, books are listed in two ways—under the author's name and under the subject (sometimes under the title, too). They're cross-referenced, and you'll find some helpful duplication in subject areas. If you should draw a complete blank, a librarian may be able to suggest some other categories that you can check. (If you have the names of authors of books that deal with your subject, look them up first to see if they're available in the library.) Look up your specific topic in the card catalogue; then try a more general subject area, to be sure you've found all that the library contains or the subject. For example, here are successive steps you could take to find information on the American winemaker James Smith:

1. Look up "James Smith" in the card catalogue.
2. Then look under "American winemakers"—information on Smith may be included in a book about a number of people in the field.
3. Then look under "wine."
4. Then look under "grape growing"—most winemakers grow their own grapes.

Once you have located all the available sources of information, you can begin taking notes for your paper. Don't forget that you can sometimes derive a wealth of information from experts on your campus or in your town, through personal interviews.

RECORDING INFORMATION

Take *two* sets of notes. The first set of notes will be your bibliography: one card for each book, magazine, or other source of information. The second set of notes should contain the detailed information that you gather from each source.

This system may sound time-consuming. "Why bother to write all that information down twice?" you may ask. But you won't be writing the same information twice. You'll be gathering *more* information with *less* writing. Here's how the system works.

Start with a Working Bibliography

A working bibliography is a list of the books and articles that you are going to consult. Not all of them will prove useful, but you have to check them all anyway. Be generous with your list. It's better to check out several references that do not help than to miss a good one because its title isn't appealing.

Instead of listing all these references on a large sheet of paper, use one 3 × 5 slip or card for each reference. Then, if a particular reference doesn't help you, you can simply throw away its slip.

An efficient format for a 3 × 5 working bibliography is shown in Figure 18.1. The different parts of each slip are used as follows:

A. On the front of the slip, record the name of the library where the reference is located. Later, if you should need the reference for additional material, you

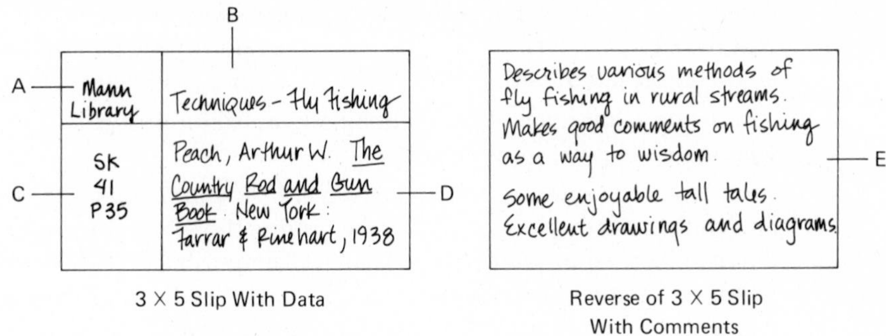

FIGURE 18.1 Working Bibliography: 3 × 5 Slip Method

will be able to find it directly, without going back to the card catalogue. (If your college has only one library, you can omit this step.)

B. Record the short title of your subject. This will be important when you are working on current and subsequent papers.

C. Record the library call number, so you will not have to refer to the card catalogue whenever you want to use the same book again.

D. Accurately record all the reference information, in exactly the form that you plan to use it in the bibliographical portion of your paper. This ensures that you will include all the essential parts of the reference; also, using the correct form now will make typing your paper much easier.

E. On the back of the 3 × 5 slip, briefly record your opinion of the reference. Write comments such as "Not useful—does not discuss principles" or "Excellent case studies of poor readers at the secondary-school level."

Take Detailed Notes

Taking detailed notes is time-consuming. However, if you take notes with painstaking care, you will be well repaid for your effort, because your paper will be half written by the time you have completed the note-taking step. Here are eleven suggestions that will help you take useful notes:

1. Use 3 × 5 paper slips because they are uniform in size and are less bulky and less expensive than note cards. Never make a running list of notes on large paper; such notes are almost impossible to organize.
2. Use only one side of each slip, and record only one topic on each slip.
3. Identify the reference on each slip by writing the author's last name or the title in the top left corner. Write the page number or numbers in

parentheses at the end of each item of information. Then you can quickly find the exact page again if further information is needed, and you have all the information you may need for a footnote (see Figure 18.2).

4. Just as in taking notes on a textbook, always skim the article or chapter you are reading before writing the notes.
5. Write notes in your own words. This will help you understand what you are reading. Furthermore, you will be putting the information into a form that can be used in your paper. Always distinguish clearly between your words and the author's. Failure to do so might lead you unwittingly into plagiarism.
6. Make your notes concise, yet sufficiently detailed to provide accurate meaning.
7. Take the time to write neatly, to avoid the frustration of having to decipher the notes later.
8. Use ink. Notes written in pencil will become blurred through handling and sorting.
9. If you need direct quotations, use only a few of the most outstanding phrases or sentences. Most students tend to quote too much and too often.
10. Abbreviate only the common words; otherwise, you will lose time figuring out an unfamiliar shorthand.

FIGURE 18.2 Detailed Note Written on One Side of a 3 × 5 Slip

11. When ideas and insights occur, write them on separate slips under the heading "my own."

Record all the pertinent information. If you find something you're not sure you'll need (remember that you need not decide exactly what approach your paper will defend or take until you've done the research), put it on a card anyway. It's easier to do this when you're in the library than to decide later that you need it. You may make a special trip to the library only to discover that the book isn't available because someone else is using it.

Be sure you have enough information. Too much is easier to work with than too little. If you haven't enough, you'll have to stop writing later to look up other references, or you'll be tempted to pad skimpy information with words that mean little.

Copy Quotations Carefully

When you quote exactly from a book or an article, place quotation marks on your slip, around the exact words copied from the reference. Then you'll know what is a direct quote and what you have put into your own words. To be sure you have copied it exactly, go back to the beginning and compare your quotation with the original. Be sure you have spelled all words exactly as they are in the original. If you note what seems to be an error or misspelling—some English spellings are different from those we use—retain the exact spelling, but use the parenthetical expression (*sic*) after the word. Here is an example:

> "They did research on the properties of chemical fertilisers (sic), and valuable research on animal nutrition."

If you leave a section or even one word out of the quoted material, use an ellipsis (a series of three periods . . .) to indicate that you omitted something. If the omitted material comes at the end of the sentence, add a period after the ellipses. Usually, what's omitted is left out because it doesn't relate to the point you're using the quote to support.

> *Original quote:* "Now that we know what has been the causative factor in this area of disaster we can, without further concern, move on to eliminate that cause."
>
> *Quote with ellipsis:* "Now that we know what has been the causative factor . . . we can . . . move on to eliminate that cause."

When you want to use the essence of what an author says but do not want to quote the exact words, you may paraphrase. Paraphrasing also allows you to condense the major thought. Even though you use mostly your own words, however, the material must be attributed to its source. In other words, in your paper you must give the author credit for having supplied the idea.

ORGANIZING THE PAPER

Choose Your Basic Premise

Look over the information in your notes; then ask yourself some hard questions. If there's a choice of viewpoint—for or against a question, for example—which view has the most evidence to support it? Or what should the basic theme or focus of your paper be? If you've done a good job of research, you should be able to decide now what you want to say in your paper, and you should have the evidence to support the view right at hand on your 3×5 slips.

Organize Your Paper Around the Basic Premise

Before you start to write, organize your material. You could use any of the organizational patterns listed under "The Organizational-Pattern Way" in Chapter 17. However, most college papers seem to work best with the time pattern or the process pattern.

Another organizational pattern that might work for you is that of development of an argument. You state a premise and then set out to support it with logical examples that build to a conclusion. More flexibility may be possible with this kind of organization than with the others.

The important thing is to decide what kind of organization is best for your basic premise. If you don't know how you want to proceed in your writing, your paper will probably appear haphazard and purposeless to the instructor.

Draw Up a Detailed Outline

Once you've decided what kind of organization fits the material you have, write down the points you want to cover in your paper—in any order. Don't worry at this time whether the points are major ones or less important ones. Just write them down briefly. Then go through them and decide which are the major points and which come under or support each major point (see Table 18.1). At this time you may decide that some point isn't important to your argument at all. Maybe it's interesting, but it won't help support any of the major points. Set the slip with this information aside.

You should now have your major points listed, with minor points under each major point. It is time to decide in which order you want to use the major points. Here's where your decision regarding the organizational pattern comes into play. Arrange the major points in the order that best fits the pattern you've chosen; then organize the slips with the information on them in

TABLE 18.1 How to Set Up an Outline

I. Introduction: Pertinent quote or striking statement if available
   a. Your purpose
   b. How you will accomplish it
II. Major point 1: State this point concisely
   a. Example of incident and supporting evidence
   b. Another example
III. Major point 2: State it as above
   a. Support for major point 2
IV. Major point 3: State it clearly
   a. Facts or quotes to support major point 3
   b. More examples to support major point 3
V. Major point 4: State the major point
   a. Supporting evidence for major point 4
   b. More examples
   c. Other supporting evidence
VI. Conclusion

the order of this organized outline. Number the slips in order from 1 to whatever. You're now ready to start writing. You will already have spent some time thinking through, or "digesting," your information.

WRITING THE RESEARCH PAPER

How Do You Start?

You start by writing. Whether you're typing or writing in longhand, just plunge in. Once your hands are going through the physical motions of writing, your brain will follow and then you can get into the meat of the paper. You already have most of it worked out—information, sources, organization. Now all you have to do is put it into sentences and paragraphs. Remember that you are planning to leave time for three drafts, so what you write on this first draft need not be perfect. You can always discard or rewrite the first part if you don't like it.

On your first draft, write as rapidly and spontaneously as possible. Record your thoughts on paper as they go through your mind, to help ensure continuity. Don't stop to ponder alternatives. Although this manner of writing often results in too much material, don't be concerned, because it is easier to cut than to add.

If your first sentence doesn't sound just as you would like it to, don't worry about it. No writer ever produces the perfect beginning sentence on the first try. What you read in books and magazines is always the result of revision and rewriting.

Writing the Body of the Paper

Begin with the introduction, which may end up as one or two paragraphs that state your purpose and perhaps catch the reader's interest. For now, just write out a general sentence of introduction, stating simply what you want to do in the paper. The introduction can be in very rough form right now. Forget it, and get into the main body of the paper.

Take each slip in order, and write. Start with major point 1. State what it is, and then use the supporting evidence to show why it is so or what happened. As you use a reference from the slip, note the slip number on your paper. You can put in the footnotes later, taking the exact information from the slip. Continue to write, following your organized and numbered slips.

Be Sure to Develop and Support the Important Points. Students often state a main point and then go on to something else without supporting it. The kinds of evidence you need to support a major point are statistics, quotations from other published works, facts, examples, comparisons and contrasts in views, expert opinion, and description. These are the specifics that will support your points. If you make statements and follow them up with generalities, you will not convince your reader that your main point is true. Use what you have collected on your slips to support your points. Here, with examples, are the steps you can take to develop a major point:

1. State your point clearly.

   Gardening is an enjoyable avocation.

2. Develop the point beyond a brief statement.

   Faced with the pressures of modern living, many people turn to working with plants to relax themselves and become absorbed in the living world around them. For some people, gardening may absorb every spare moment.

3. Support with quotes from authorities, statistics.

   Organizations that serve gardeners are growing rapidly. In the past two years garden clubs and other horticultural organizations report significant numbers of new members. An estimate of gardeners actively affiliated with these organizations numbers in the millions, according to James Jones, executive director of Gardeners, Inc.

4. Illustrate with examples.

One organization, the American Horticultural Society, has purchased an estate for its new headquarters to serve a membership that has tripled in the last 18 months.

5. Interrelate with other main points.

In addition to joining general gardening organizations, gardeners who specialize can join societies for those interested in growing irises, primroses, day lilies, African violets, orchids, and other garden favorites. Most of these groups have grown, too, as a result of the increased general interest in growing plants.

Be sure that all the main points are supported about equally with this kind of evidence. If you can't find enough evidence to support one point, perhaps it's not a major one. Then you need to reorganize the structure to include it under one of the other major points.

Avoid padding. You may be tempted to add extra words or to rephrase a point in several ways to make the paper seem longer. This sort of padding is very obvious to the reader, who's looking for logical arguments and good sense. It will not improve your grade. If you haven't enough evidence to support a statement, leave it out or get some more information.

Make a Clear Copy. The first draft is usually rough—full of deletions, additions, and directions that are understandable only to the writer (see Figure 18.3). If you leave it in this state for even a day, you may lose a lot of time trying to recall exactly what you meant by some of your notes. If you retype or rewrite the material while it is still very fresh, you may do some spontaneous revision. The result will be a clear copy that will be ready for revision after a cooling off period of a day or so.

Put the First Draft Aside for a While. What you now have is a first draft, organized in the order it will appear in the final paper, without a completed introduction and without a conclusion. You'll need both of these as well as a title. But they can come later, after you've set the paper aside for a day or so.

A cooling-off period is important. During the writing stage, your mind is so full of associations with the words you have written that you are likely to see clarity and step-by-step sequences where they do not exist, because your mind fills in and bridges gaps that you left. When you read your manuscript after your mind has dropped some of these associations, you will have to read the words themselves to gain the meaning. You will then easily spot errors.

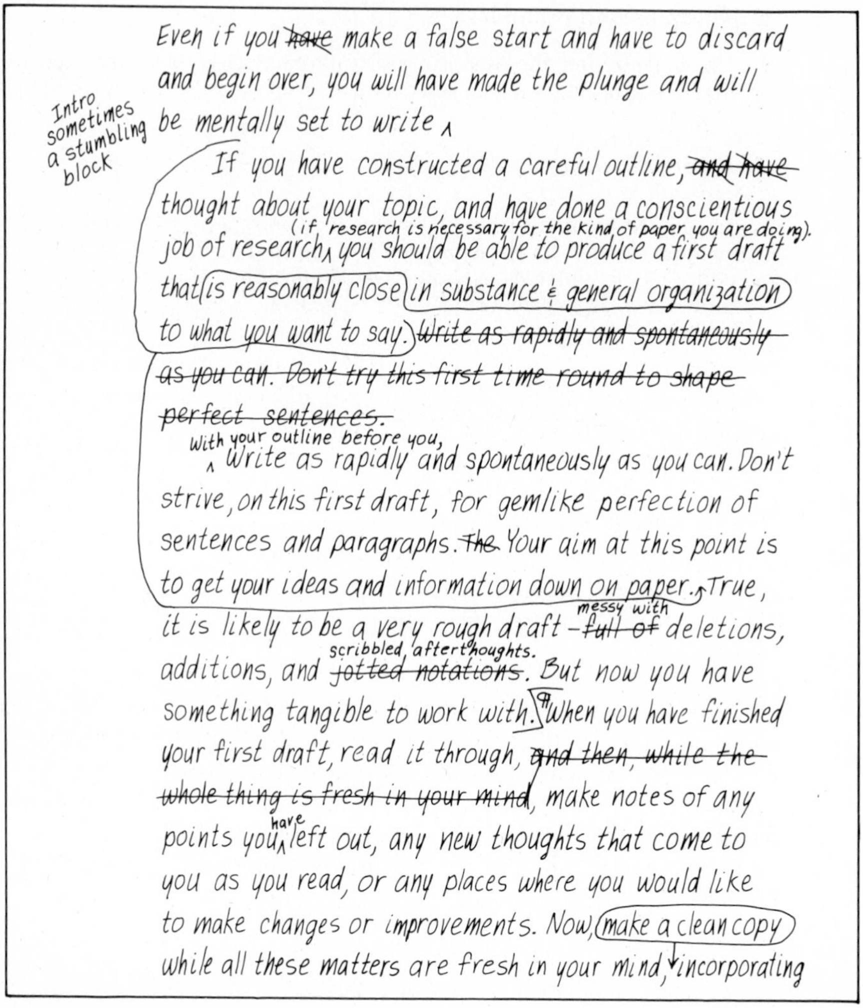

Intro sometimes a stumbling block

Even if you ~~have~~ make a false start and have to discard and begin over, you will have made the plunge and will be mentally set to write ^

If you have constructed a careful outline, ~~and have~~ thought about your topic, and have done a conscientious job of research ^ (if research is necessary for the kind of paper you are doing), you should be able to produce a first draft that (is reasonably close) in substance & general organization to what you want to say. ~~Write as rapidly and spontaneously as you can. Don't try this first time round to shape perfect sentences.~~

^ With your outline before you, Write as rapidly and spontaneously as you can. Don't strive, on this first draft, for gemlike perfection of sentences and paragraphs. ~~The~~ Your aim at this point is to get your ideas and information down on paper. True, it is likely to be a very rough draft – messy with ~~full of~~ deletions, additions, and scribbled afterthoughts ~~jotted notations~~. But now you have something tangible to work with. ¶ When you have finished your first draft, read it through, ~~and then, while the whole thing is fresh in your mind~~, make notes of any points you ^ have left out, any new thoughts that come to you as you read, or any places where you would like to make changes or improvements. Now, (make a clean copy) while all these matters are fresh in your mind, incorporating

FIGURE 18.3 Page from a First Draft

EDITING YOUR WORK

Editing your written work is one of the most important skills you can learn in college. It requires the ability to view your own production with enough courage to anticipate (and be concerned about) the potential reader's reaction. This means polishing and boiling down ideas, struggling to say things more clearly, tearing down and rebuilding sentences and paragraphs, and even, if necessary, writing three or four drafts.

Technical Details

There are some technical details that you must have under control if your paper is to make a good impression on the reader.

Transitions. In writing your paper, you need to consider how to help your readers move easily from one main point to the next. If they feel that there's no connection—that you jump from one point to another—they will find it hard to follow the logical sequence that you have established in your own mind. You must, therefore, use transitional words and phrases to make your paper easy to follow. Check carefully for transitions, and insert them where they are needed (see "The Pivotal-Words Way" in Chapter 17).

Grammar. Students who use the English language correctly get their ideas across to other people more clearly and forcibly than do those who fumble on every sentence. Moreover, students who apply the rules of grammar in their papers get better grades. If you are unsure about these rules or careless with them, your meaning may get lost. If you feel that you could use a review of grammar, there are good texts that give you the elements of English grammar by a programmed method. Some of them are even fun to read.

Spelling. If your spelling problems are not severe, you will find a dictionary helpful. If you spelling is poor, look for one of the paperback books that list the most commonly misspelled words. If you cannot recognize that you are spelling words incorrectly, have someone who is good at spelling read your paper and mark the words that are wrong. Have the person mark them, *not* correct them. Then you can look up the words and write them in correctly. If you do this conscientiously over a period of time, you will improve your spelling.

Plagiarism

Plagiarism is stealing other people's words and ideas and making them appear to be your own. It need not be as blatant as copying whole passages without giving credit. If you paraphrase something from already published material and do not cite your source, you're guilty of plagiarism even though you have no intention of stealing. Simply rearranging sentences or rephrasing a little without crediting is still plagiarism.

Those who grade papers are quick to notice a change
one of your papers to another or from one part of your pa
Your writing is like your fingerprints—individual. If you
work, his or her style will not match the rest of your pape
will be obvious. Instructors may give you the benefit

cannot prove where you got plagiarized material. But if they can—and doing so is usually not difficult—plagiarism is grounds for expulsion from college. In a world where the written word is a major product, stealing it from someone else is a serious offense.

ADDING THE MISSING ELEMENTS

Footnotes and Bibliography

Material quoted or paraphrased from other sources must be credited. You may include a credit right after the quoted material, within the body of the paper, in a format like this: (Jones, 1965, p. 264). This citation refers to page 264 of the work by Jones that was published in 1965 and is listed in your bibliography. (More about that later.) Or you can use a superscript ([1]) and cite the full source at the bottom of the page or in a complete listing at the end of the paper. Credits that appear at the bottom of the page are called *footnotes.* Figure 18.4 shows a format for footnotes and for listing credits at the end of the paper. References are numbered in the order in which they appear in your paper. Other forms are given in handbooks on English usage.

The *bibliography* includes the sources you cited in your credits and may include other books or published material that you read as background for the paper but did not quote. A bibliography is not "notes," "endnotes," or "sources." It is a listing of the books that you used in preparing the paper, and you should use the correct title for this listing. When you write the bibliography, use the 3 × 5 slips you prepared earlier. Each entry should include enough information so that a reader could identify the work and find it in a library.

Entries should be listed alphabetically by author. Different bibliographic forms are used in different fields. Either select a standard form from a handbook on English usage, or follow the form used in one of the journals that

1. Hunter Shirley, <u>Your Mind May Be Programmed Against You!</u> (Lafayette, La.: 21st Century Books, 1982), pp. 112-115.

2. Frank H. Winter, <u>Prelude to the Space Age</u> (Washington, D.C.: Smithsonian Institution Press, 1983), p. 18.

FIGURE 18.4 Format for Footnotes and End-of-Paper Credits

pertains to the subject you are writing about. No matter what form you use, follow it consistently in every entry in your bibliography (see Figure 18.5).

The Title

It's often a good idea to wait until you have written the paper before you decide on a final title. The title should reflect the content of the paper, but it can have an interesting twist or perhaps make use of part of a quote that you think is especially appropriate. A straightforward title is also fine. In some cases, a straightforward title telling what the paper is about is best.

The Introduction

You already have a general statement of the purpose of the paper—it is the basis of your introduction. Now, in revising the paper, you can write the introduction in its final form. It should briefly state your purpose for writing the paper and how you are going to carry out that purpose. It might include a quotation that is particularly suitable or an interesting example or anecdote. Choose any of these devices carefully; they must be right on target. If you're not sure they will add to the paper, then settle for a straightforward statement

Bibliography

Boyer, Ernest L., and Hechinger, Fred M. Higher Learning in the National Interest. Washington, D.C.: Carnegie Foundation, 1981.

Chaplin, James P., and Krawiec, T.S. Systems and Theories of Psychology. 4th ed. New York: Holt, Rinehart, and Winston, 1979.

Kleppner, Paul. Who Voted? New York: Praeger Publishers, 1982.

Shirley, Hunter. Your Mind May Be Programmed Against You! Lafayette, La.: 21st Century Books, 1982.

Uhler, Harry B. "Semicentennial: Baltimore-to-Venus Attempt," Science News, 114 (July 1978): 78-79.

Winter, Frank H. Prelude to the Space Age. Washington, D.C.: Smithsonian Institution Press, 1983.

FIGURE 18.5 Format for a Bibliography

of purpose and general method. The introduction, the title, and the conclusion should, however, have some continuity, something in common.

The Conclusion

Don't leave the paper without a concluding passage. If you do, your readers will be left dangling, wondering what happened to you and the rest of the paper. Let them know they have come to the end.

Usually the conclusion summarizes or restates the purpose described in the introduction. It can also state your opinion that something should be done about a situation. Or it can predict what is in store for the future, drawing on what you've written in the paper. The kind of conclusion you write depends on the kind of paper and the subject. It need not be long or involved. Just be sure you do have one.

MAKING THE FINAL COPY

All the time and energy you have spent on your research paper should be reflected in the appearance of the final copy. Make it neat, clean, and attractive.

1. Use only one side of white paper. Although few instructors specify what size paper to use, the most commonly used paper measures 8½ × 11 inches.
2. Type your paper or have it typed. Handwritten papers are difficult to read, and they may not be accepted in some courses.
3. Leave a generous margin at the top and bottom of each page and a margin of 1½ inches on both sides, to provide room for the instructor's comments.
4. Type your paper without any strikeovers. Erase errors thoroughly and neatly. Be sure to double-space.
5. Set up long, direct quotations (of five or more lines) in block style—that is, single-space and indent the lines from both sides about a half inch or five typewriter spaces. Omit the quotation marks when you block a quotation in this way—the block setup shows that you are quoting.
6. Proofread your final copy. Go over it carefully to catch spelling errors, typing errors, and other minor flaws. This is a very important step that is too often neglected.
7. Hand in the paper on time. It is not uncommon for instructors to deduct points for late papers.

THE COMPULSIVE READER

Linda Logan

Special Problems in Education

Education 207

January 18, 1984

Charles Fay,

Associate Professor of Education

FIGURE 18.6 Title Page of a Research Paper

L. Logan -1-
The Compulsive Reader
Education 207
January 18, 1984

Among the persons who people this planet there are some who have a yen for the printed word. They are the ones who watch television with a book in their laps. They are the visitors who riffle your magazines while pretending to converse. Their eyes have an unquenchable thirst for printer's ink which they devour whenever it is poured out in words. This addiction may vary in degree, and with age "matters of consequence" may alleviate it, but generally they remain a close friend of books for life.

From a fairly intensive search through the literature on "Reading" no mention of this type of reader could be found. Hildreth[1] has a section entitled "The Bookworm Problem" in which she states that "life in the modern school" which encourages many activities "will counteract the tendency toward excessive bookishness." Many articles deal with the "gifted" and the "able" reader. The gifted, and even the able reader, however, read with discrimination and purpose which is foreign to the wanton habits of the compulsive reader. An article in _Time_

---

[1]Hildreth, Gertrude. _Teaching Reading_ (New York: Holt, Rinehart, and Winston, 1961), pp. 596-597.

FIGURE 18.7 Format for Inside Pages of a Research Paper
Each inside page is identified and numbered at the top.

Figure 18.6 shows a typical format for a title page. The format for identifying and numbering an inside page is shown in Figure 18.7.

SUMMARY

What one thing is most important in writing a paper?	Actually, there are two most important things. First, give yourself plenty of time; don't put off the assignment until the night before it's due. Second, write about something that interests you; you'll work with enthusiasm, and your paper will show it.
What's the toughest part of writing a research paper?	Finding a topic. You'll need one that interests you, that suits the requirements of your instructor, and for which there are sufficient research sources. You can find out about research sources by checking the *Readers' Guide* and the library's card catalogue. To make sure the topic is not too broad, you'll have to narrow it down three or four times.
Once I've chosen my topic, can I start doing research?	Not yet. First give your topic a focus. Come up with an important question concerning your topic. This will give your paper direction and purpose. Then you can start.
What comes next?	Begin by accumulating references. Use listings in the card catalogue as well as in the *Readers' Guide.*
Why do I have to take research notes twice?	You don't. However, you should list your information in two different places. Use one set of 3 × 5 cards or slips for the detailed information from each article or book. Use a separate set as your working bibliography, or list of references.
Do I have to credit authors even when I paraphrase them?	Yes. Whether you use their exact words or not, the ideas are still those of the authors—not yours.
When all the notes are taken, what comes next?	Choose your paper's organizational pattern. (You will most likely use the time, process, or argument-development pattern.) Then list (in any order) all the points that you

want to cover. Next, pick out the major points, and arrange the minor and supporting points below each major point. Finally, organize your major points into an outline, according to your premise. Then organize your note slips in the same order, and number them.

May I skip the detailed outline?

No. The outline is the only control you have over your data. Outlining helps you to think through your paper, so that the writing comes naturally.

Now that the organizing is over, how do I begin writing?

Just start writing, as rapidly and spontaneously as possible. Begin with a sentence or two of introduction to set the mood, and then get straight to the body of the paper. Write from your slips, one at a time and in order—first a main point, then the supporting points. Then go on to the next main point, and so on.

Can I leave out the support for some of the main ideas?

No. All main points need support. If you can't find support for one of your main points, it shouldn't be a main point.

Would this be a good time to take a break?

Not quite. You've finished your first draft, but it's probably in very rough form. Make a clean copy of your paper by rewriting or retyping it. Then set it aside for at least a day before you edit or rewrite it.

What does editing my paper entail?

To edit your own paper well, you need the guts to tear down, rebuild, and rearrange sentences and paragraphs until they're just right. This can sometimes take three or four drafts. By the way, a good time to expand your purpose sentence into an introduction is while you're editing. The introduction should explain your purpose and method in writing the paper. Try to start it with a "grabber" like an anecdote or a quotation.

Should I determine my paper's title right from the start?

You may, but it's better to wait until you've finished writing. That way, you have a better feel for the paper's overall content and tone.

Can I skip the conclusion? I never know what to write.	Definitely not. A paper without a conclusion leaves the reader dangling. You should be able to draw some conclusion from your information, or state an opinion or prediction based on your information, or even summarize your main points. No matter what it contains, your paper should have a conclusion.
Why is a good final copy so important?	The final copy is the only draft that your instructor sees. It should reflect the time and energy that you have put into your paper. A sloppy final copy gives the impression that your paper contains sloppy work.

HAVE YOU MISSED SOMETHING?

1. *Sentence completion.* Complete the following sentences with one of the three words listed below each sentence.

a. Writing notes in your own words helps to avoid ________________.

plagiarism understanding confusion

b. A paper without a conclusion is likely to leave the reader ________.

interested dangling alone

2. *Matching.* In each blank space in the left column, write the number preceding the phrase in the right column that matches the left item best.

_____ a. Librarian	1. Orders and controls your information
_____ b. Theme	2. The "smoothing and improving" step in writing
_____ c. Editing	3. Helpful source for locating references
_____ d. Outline	4. Perhaps the most difficult writing task
_____ e. Choosing a topic	5. An often-overlooked reference source
_____ f. Interviews	6. Often based on personal experience

3. *True-false.* Write *T* beside the *true* statements and *F* beside the *false* statements.

_____ a. Ellipses are used to indicate left-out words and sentences in a quotation.

_____ b. You should use many quotations in a research paper.

_____ c. It's usually best to choose a title after the paper is written.

_____ d. Promising sources of information should be included in your working bibliography.

_____ e. You should never take a stand in a research paper.

4. *Multiple choice.* Choose the phrase that completes the following sentence most accurately, and circle the letter that precedes it.

In most libraries, you will find the *Readers' Guide to Periodical Literature* in the

a. reference section
b. card catalogue
c. periodical section
d. circulation area

CHAPTER 19

Studying Mathematics

Would you have a man reason well, you must . . . exercise his mind [and] nothing does this better than mathematics.

John Locke (1632–1704), English philosopher

Mathematics has always been a prerequisite for dozens of subjects. Now, it seems to be a prerequisite for simple survival. Whether you feel proficient at math or not, this chapter can be of help. It discusses

- How to remedy a weak background
- How to develop good study habits
- Practical suggestions for problem solving
- How to attack nonroutine problems

and finally

- Understanding and memory in mathematics

roblems are intriguing, and most people enjoy solving them. Try this one:

Problem:

> At exactly 2 o'clock, two bacteria are placed in a growing medium. One minute later there are four bacteria, in another minute eight bacteria, and so on. At exactly 3 o'clock, the growing mass of bacteria measures one gallon. At what time was there one pint of bacteria?

Is this a puzzle or a mathematical problem? It's like a mathematical problem because its solution requires some analysis and some computation. But it's really more of a puzzle. You have to see first that the number of bacteria doubles each minute and second that you must compute backward from one gallon at 3 o'clock to get one-half gallon (four pints) at 2:59; two pints at 2:58; and the required one pint at 2:57.

Doing mathematics is a form of problem solving that makes use of the most efficient methods—methods that have been developed over the centuries. That's why it is applicable to so many other subject areas. Once you see the usefulness of mathematics, you'll study and learn it more surely and enthusiastically.

HOW TO REMEDY A WEAK BACKGROUND

College work in mathematics is the continuation of a learning program that began in the elementary grades with the first operations of arithmetic and continued through junior and senior high school with algebra, geometry, trigonometry, and (perhaps) calculus. College courses expand and extend this sequence. Each subject builds on previous subjects, and at each stage in the program you must be prepared to use all the mathematics you have studied previously. If at some point you have difficulty with mathematics, it is almost always because you have not fully mastered some earlier principle or process.

What can you do about a shaky background in mathematics? One thing you *can't* do is start all over again—at least, not on top of your regular course load. Even a thorough review would likely take too much of your time. There are, however, two practical ways to identify and strengthen weak spots or fill in gaps: spot reviewing and self-diagnosis.

First, attack each difficulty as it arises. Whenever you come to a computation process or formula or principle that you don't recognize or don't understand, clear it up so that it won't bother you again. Because you have an immediate need for that material, you have an incentive to master it. This is a good way to get the exact math review that you personally need. It is also a very practical plan for someone who is experiencing only occasional difficulty with a college math course or with mathematics in other courses.

To do this kind of spot reviewing, you should have at hand textbooks covering all the mathematics you've had—from arithmetic on. The best review books are those you studied from, but they may be difficult to get. Your school library or bookstore might have some texts that are similar; otherwise, your best bet is standard review books. When you review, try to understand the underlying concept or principle as well as the mechanics. Make up a 3×5 card showing both (Figure 19.1); it will help you remember and will come in handy when you study for exams.

The second way to strengthen weak spots in your background is by diagnosing your mathematical competence. Get yourself a self-help review book, and work your way through it to discover what topics you need to study and practice. Your instructor can probably suggest a good one.[1] By

Given an isosceles right triangle with legs equal to 10". What is its hypotenuse?

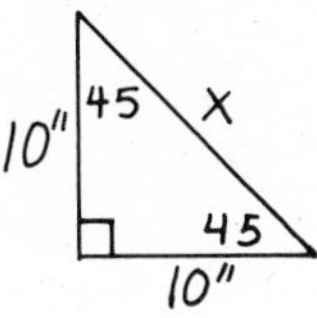

Isosceles right triangle has two 45° angles, equal legs.

$X^2 = 10^2 + 10^2 = 200$

$X^2 = \sqrt{200} = \sqrt{100}\sqrt{2} = 10\sqrt{2}$

Generalized:

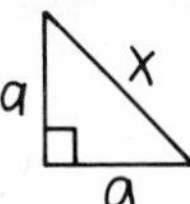

$X^2 = 2a^2$

$X = a\sqrt{2}$

FIGURE 19.1 Card for Background Review

[1]A good review workbook is M. Wiles Keller and James H. Zant, *Basic Mathematics*, Third Series (Boston: Houghton Mifflin, 1979). It covers arithmetic, algebra, and trigonometry and contains diagnostic tests from which you can determine your strengths and weaknesses.

doing drill problems in each area of difficulty, you will keep yourself from getting into trouble at more advanced levels. But you must follow through: Even minor weaknesses need to be attacked as soon as you discover them.

HOW TO DEVELOP GOOD STUDY HABITS

The change from secondary school to college is greater for mathematics than for any other area of study. In high school, you probably did most of your drill work in class, under supervision, or as homework to be passed in for correction and credit. In college, you'll have to get your drill by working exercises on your own, practicing operations and manipulations that are mastered only by doing them over and over. Most of this work will not be for credit; your reward will be your proficiency in working problems and in thinking your way to understanding.

There is good reason for learning to be self-propelled in mathematics. Unless you're a mathematics major, the mathematics you take is mainly to provide you with techniques that are applicable to what lies ahead; and in an advanced course or on the job, there may not be a teacher or a textbook at hand to tell you what process or formula to use. You have some powerful math tools at hand, but you must be able to apply them. To apply these tools requires that you learn to keep up-to-date, take notes in class, use your textbook, and study for exams.

Keeping Up-to-Date

Because mathematics is a cumulative subject in which you must be prepared at any point to use anything or everything you have previously learned, and because it is a subject in which drill and practice are required to master essential operations, it is absolutely necessary to keep your work up-to-date. If you fall behind, you'll be lacking some of the background on which the newest material is based. When you fall behind, you'll find it hard to catch up, because to do so you'll have to take time from your study of current material.

Taking Notes in Class

The general principles of note taking discussed in Part III apply to math lectures and class discussion. There is, however, a major difference: You should keep your notes to a minimum so that note taking doesn't prevent you from following the instructor's line of reasoning. Record main ideas, but do not try to list all the details and examples. Record how to attack particular kinds of problems, but do not record the individual steps in each solution. Note *how* a theorem is derived rather than its complete derivation. But do follow carefully as the instructor solves each problem and derives each theorem.

If the lectures are closely related to the textbook, you will usually find it helpful to read ahead before the lecture. You then can tell to what extent the lecture repeats and to what extent it supplements the text and can take notes accordingly. You might even want to keep your textbook open and write supplementary or clarifying information right on the book pages. If you do read ahead, expect to read again, more carefully, after the lecture.

If you lose the thread of a lecture or class discussion, or if you fail to understand a line of reasoning or a mathematical procedure, ask your instructor for clarification. Failure to clear up even a minor point may lead to major difficulties later. You'll have to do *your* part, though, by doing the required advance preparation and giving the instructor your full attention during the class period.

To provide maximum reinforcement for classroom learning, study your notes and the related text material and examples as soon after class as possible. Do the drill problems only when you are sure you understand the material. Working at an assignment before you are ready for it wastes time and—worse—can cause you to remember incorrect solution procedures.

Using Your Textbook

Your textbook is a very useful learning device—if you employ it correctly. You must read mathematics with great care. Mathematical terms and symbols are defined with great precision; each word has an exact meaning and only that meaning. Each term can also imply a number of other definitions and theorems that are part of its own definition.

Consider, for example, the square, a geometric figure. No doubt you can easily imagine a square and draw a reasonable representation of one. But what would the term *square* mean to you if you saw it in your textbook? A reasonable definition of a square is "a regular polygon of four sides." To a mathematician, "regular polygon" means that all the sides are equal in length and all the angles are equal in measure; it also implies, among other things, that the diagonals are equal in length. The expression "polygon of four sides" means that the sum of the interior angles is 360°. Because each angle is equal in measure, each angle measures 90° and is a right angle. There's more, but by now you get the point: Even a simple, everyday term like *square* can stand for a wealth of information. Math writers choose their terms with great care to state precisely what they mean. You, the reader of mathematics, must make sure—by reading carefully—that you understand precisely what the writer means.

Don't carry confusion along with you as you read. If you don't recall a term or concept that the author mentions, or if you can't easily define a term or concept for yourself, then stop reading. Go back, look up the term or concept, and make sure you understand it before you go on. Review it if you have to. Do the same for operations that you're unsure of, like adding fractions or taking a particular kind of derivative. If you can't follow the author's computation, look it up.

Read with a pen and plenty of paper at hand, and do all the computations along with the author of your textbook. Do every step in each computation—including all the worked-out examples as you come to them—so that you become comfortable with the process. You can't know what a computation process is like if you read it but don't *do* it.

When you understand the material and have a feel for the mechanics, do some problem solving. Do your homework assignment if you have one or the odd-numbered exercises if you are on your own. Look up the answers if they are available, and rework any exercises you got wrong the first time around (after trying to find where you went wrong). If you can't get the listed answer after two tries, stop and make a note to ask your instructor about the problem.

Studying for Examinations

The best way to study for an examination is to keep up with your daily work throughout the term. Then at examination time you can concentrate on polishing up what you already know.

Start early to review the problems you have had in assignments and previous tests, paying special attention to the more troublesome ones. This will give you a chance to ask your instructor for help if you are still unsure of some procedures. Review any 3 × 5 cards you made up as part of your background-repair effort.

You may also find 3 × 5 cards useful for memorizing important formulas and principles that you won't be able to look up during the examination (see Figures 19.2 and 19.3). Record one item to a card, and carry the cards around with you to study at odd moments. Be sure, however, that you understand the *meaning* of material you memorize in this way, so that you can still work the problem even if you forget the details. Consider a formula a convenience or a short cut, not an end in itself.

Whenever you get back a test or examination, rework the problems on which you made mistakes, and find out what you did wrong. Correcting your errors is one of the most valuable learning experiences you can have. You may want to make up review cards for these errors, to use in studying for later examinations.

IMPORTANT FORMULA:
$\cos^2\theta + \sin^2\theta = 1$
Derivation:
$x^2 + y^2 = r^2$
$\frac{x^2}{r^2} + \frac{y^2}{r^2} = 1$
Divide both sides by r^2
since $\cos\theta = \frac{x}{r}$
and $\sin\theta = \frac{y}{r}$
$\cos^2\theta + \sin^2\theta = 1$
r
y
θ
x

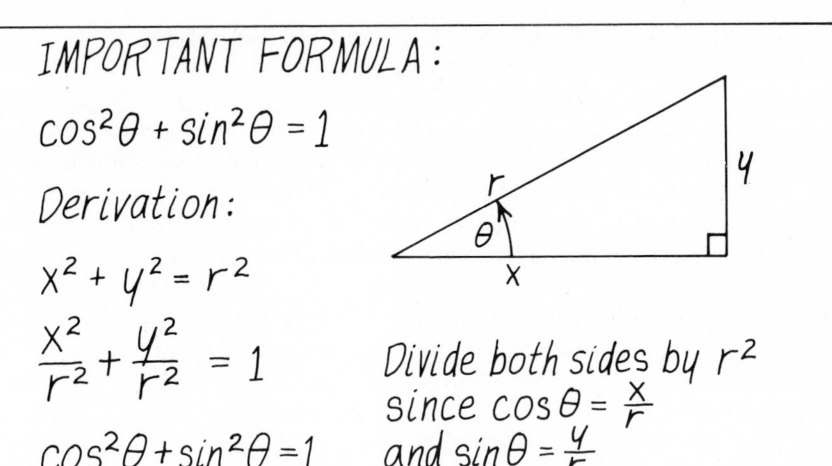

FIGURE 19.2 Card for Memorizing Formulas

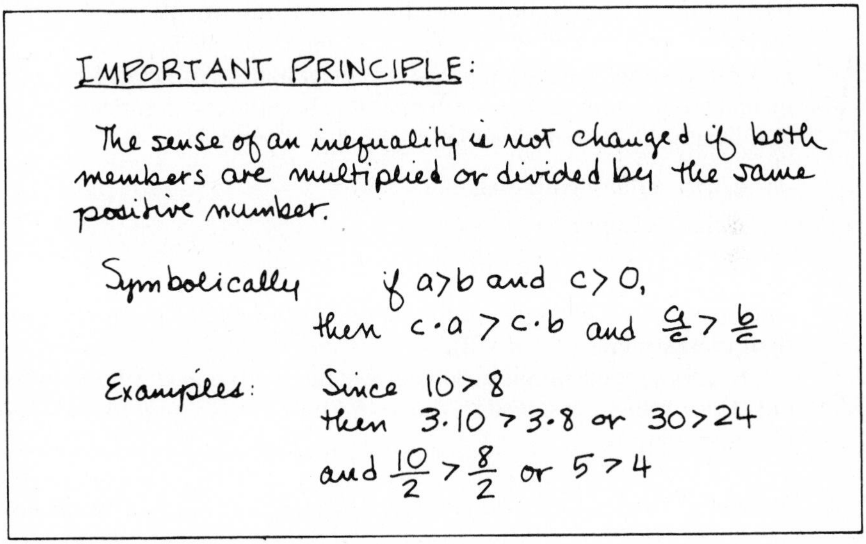

IMPORTANT PRINCIPLE:
The sense of an inequality is not changed if both members are multiplied or divided by the same positive number.
Symbolically if $a > b$ and $c > 0$,
then $c \cdot a > c \cdot b$ and $\frac{a}{c} > \frac{b}{c}$
Examples: Since $10 > 8$
then $3 \cdot 10 > 3 \cdot 8$ or $30 > 24$
and $\frac{10}{2} > \frac{8}{2}$ or $5 > 4$

FIGURE 19.3 Card for Memorizing Principles

PRACTICAL SUGGESTIONS FOR PROBLEM SOLVING

Solving a mathematical problem is basically a two-part operation. First you analyze, and then you compute. If you fail to size up the problem correctly, you can't compute your way to the correct solution. On the other hand, an error in calculation—whether from carelessness or from inadequate understanding of the basic operations—can cancel out even a brilliant piece of analysis.

As the first step in doing any problem, read it through twice—*carefully.* This will keep you from jumping into the problem too quickly.

Sort Out the Problem

Begin your analysis by noting what things are given, what relationships are stated or implied, and what is to be found or proved. Jot these things down for easy reference.

The next part of the analysis is to figure out how to get from what you have to what you need. (Don't do any real calculating yet—this is a planning step.) If necessary, jot down anything that is intermediary—what you have to find in order to find what is required. For example, you might be asked to find the perimeter of a square whose diagonal is 10 inches long. An intermediate step is to find the length of a side, because the perimeter is four times that length. Your analysis so far might look like this:

Given: Square with diagonal $d = 10''$

Find: Perimeter p

Need: Length S of a side; then $p = 4S$

Once you draw a diagram, you'll see how to complete the problem (isosceles right triangles give $S = d/\sqrt{2}$).

Here is a more complex problem together with one way it might be sorted out. This problem is solved to show you how easily computation follows an effective analysis.

Problem:

How many minutes will it take a pump delivering 2.75 gallons per stroke and making 88 strokes per minute to pump 500 barrels of oil? (One barrel = 42 gal)

Given: 2.75 gal/stroke

88 strokes/min

42 gal/barrel

Find: Minutes M for 500 barrels

Need: Barrels pumped per min, B

then $M = 500/B$

$$B = 2.75\frac{\text{gal}}{\text{stroke}} \times 88\,\frac{\text{strokes}}{\text{min}} \times \frac{1}{42}\,\frac{\text{barrel}}{\text{gal}} = 5.762\,\frac{\text{barrels}}{\text{min}}$$

$$M = 500 \text{ barrels} \times \frac{1}{5.762}\,\frac{\text{min}}{\text{barrel}} = 86.8 \text{ min}$$

Setting up the calculations in this way lets you follow the analysis as if it were a plan of action, which it can be. It also allows you to make a *dimensional check*: If you multiply and divide units along with numerical values, and then cancel similar units in the numerator and denominator, the result should be the unit of the required result. This is so in both of the calculations above.

Draw a Diagram

A carefully sketched diagram can highlight relationships and facts that are not very evident from statements alone. In the square-perimeter problem, for example, a drawing of the square and a diagonal immediately shows the relation between the diagonal and a side of the square.

A diagram can also give direction to your analysis and computation and serve to check that they are reasonable. Consider again the oil-pumping problem, and take a look at Figure 19.4. By drawing the "amounts of oil" pumped

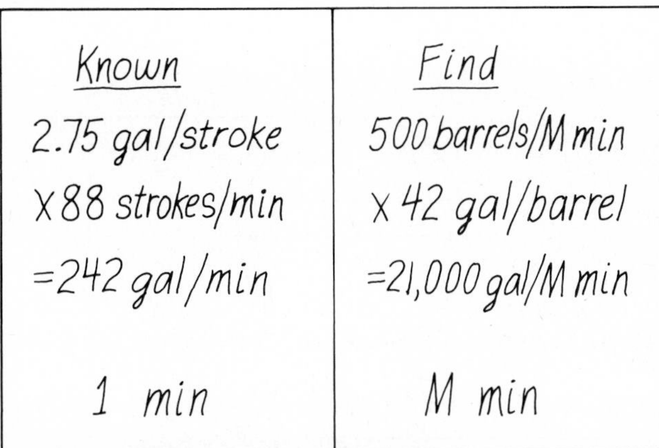

FIGURE 19.4 Diagram for the Oil-pumping Problem

in 1 minute and in M minutes, we see first that M must be nearly a hundred minutes (because 500 barrels comes out to nearly a hundred times the amount pumped in one minute). We also see from the diagram that we can find M by writing the proportion

$$\frac{242 \text{ gal}}{1 \text{ min}} = \frac{21{,}000 \text{ gal}}{M \text{ min}}$$

from which we find $M = 21{,}000/242 = 86.8$ min. Because this is somewhat less than a hundred minutes, it checks.

Diagrams are such an important part of problem analysis that most problem solvers draw them immediately. Here's a case in which the sketch almost does the entire analysis.

Problem:

> A pulley that is 7 inches in diameter is turning a belt and rotating at 60 revolutions per minute (rpm). How fast is the belt moving in feet per minute? (Assume no slippage between the belt and the pulley.)

Given: Pulley diam. $D = 7''$

Pulley speed $= 60$ rpm

Find: Belt speed B, ft/min

The diagram, shown in Figure 19.5, almost shouts that the pulley turns (and so the belt moves) one circumference in every revolution. Therefore,

Need: pulley circumference C, ft (ft/revolution)

$$\text{Then } B = 60\,\frac{\text{rev}}{\text{min}} \times C\,\frac{\text{ft}}{\text{rev}}$$

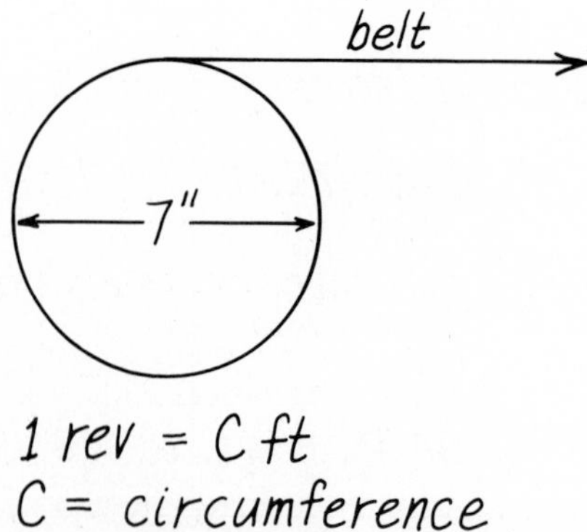

FIGURE 19.5 Diagram for the Pulley Problem

Then, being careful about the conversion from inches to feet, we write the computation as

$$B = 60\,\frac{\text{rev}}{\text{min}} \times C\,\frac{\text{ft}}{\text{rev}} = 60 \times \frac{\pi D}{12} = 60 \times \frac{22}{7} \times \frac{7}{12} = 110 \text{ ft/min}$$

Substitute Some Numbers

When the numbers involved in a problem are so large, so small, or so complicated that they interfere with your analysis of the problem, try substituting simpler numbers. This will often reveal the nature of the problem more clearly.

Problem:

> If the mass of an electron is about 9×10^{-28} grams, and the mass of a proton is about 1.62×10^{-24}(grams, approximately how many times the mass of an electron is the mass of a proton?

This problem can easily be sorted, but then what? If you're unsure about which operation to perform, substitute numbers that are easier to work with. Here, let the proton weigh 16 grams and the electron weigh 2 grams. Then the proton obviously weighs 16/2 = 8 times as much as the electron.

Our analysis tells us to divide proton weight by electron weight, so we calculate

$$\frac{\text{Proton weight}}{\text{Electron weight}} = \frac{1.62 \times 10^{-24}\text{ g}}{9 \times 10^{-28}\text{ g}} = 1.8 \times 10^{3}$$

Another effective technique, especially in word problems leading to equations, is to choose an answer *first* and use it to figure out what procedure is involved. It's best if your test answer is a reasonable one, but usually any answer will do.

Problem:

> An alloy of copper and zinc is 10% zinc. How many pounds of pure zinc should be added to 400 pounds of this alloy to make an alloy that is 20% zinc?

We choose a nice round number for our test answer—100 pounds of zinc. When we add that amount, we get 400 + 100 = 500 pounds of alloy and

$$0.1 \times 400 \text{ lb} + 100 \text{ lb} = 140 \text{ lb of zinc}$$

Then it is fairly obvious that the percentage of zinc now is

$$\text{Percent zinc} = \frac{140}{500} \times 100\%$$

Recalling that we substituted 100 pounds for the unknown in the numerator and denominator, we now go back and replace 100 pounds with X:

$$\text{Percent zinc} = \frac{40 + X}{400 + X} \times 100\%$$

We know the required percentage of zinc, so we have, after dividing both sides by 100%,

$$\frac{20\%}{100\%} = \frac{40 + X}{400 + X} \qquad \text{or} \qquad X = 50 \text{ lb}$$

A diagram showing the composition of the alloy before and after the zinc is added might bring us to the same result.

Make Use of Your Calculator

You will use your calculator to do most of the calculations for math problems. If you don't have a calculator, you're at a disadvantage. It removes the tedium from calculations, speeds them up, and thus gives you more time for analysis and for doing problems.

A calculator can also be useful in the analysis stage of problem solving. In particular, it can help you test a formula or identify one that you're not sure of. As an example, suppose you need the formula for $\cos 2\theta$ but can't remember whether it's $2 \cos^2 \theta - 1$ or $1 - 2 \cos^2 \theta$. To find out, all you have to do is pick a value for θ and then use your calculator to compute all three expressions. You find that the computed value for $2 \cos^2 \theta - 1$ is the same as that for $\cos 2\theta$, and you have your formula.

Naturally, to check trigonometric formulas you need a calculator that gives you the values of the trigonometric functions. But any calculator can be used to help you decide whether, for example, the following equations are true:

$$\sqrt{a^2 + b^2} \stackrel{?}{=} a + b \qquad \text{and} \qquad \frac{\sqrt{a}}{\sqrt{b}} \stackrel{?}{=} \sqrt{\frac{a}{b}}$$

By substituting pairs of numbers for a and b and calculating both sides of each equation, you would find that the equation on the left is generally false and the one on the right is generally true.

Implement Your Analysis

Your analysis of the problem is complete when you clearly understand how to proceed from what is given to what is required. Then do the calculations that implement the analysis as you developed it. Don't try a new idea once you've started calculating—a short cut, for example. Because you have not thought it through, it could lead you astray.

If you do want to try a different method—one that seems more elegant, perhaps, or that requires less work—do so. But do so only after you have made it part of a complete, start-to-finish analysis of the problem.

Check Your Results

Get in the habit of checking your answer every time you complete a problem. One or more of the following checks will usually apply to every type of problem:

1. Substitute your answer for the unknown in the problem, to make sure it satisfies the given conditions. This check is especially applicable to word problems and problems in the form of equations.
2. Rework the problem by an alternative method. (You've got to know another solution method before you can use this check.)
3. Do a dimensional check. Carry the units through your calculations, along with their values. Operate on the units exactly as you operate on the values. The resulting unit (after all computations are completed) should be the unit required by the problem. This method can be applied to all numerical problems and to many with letters replacing values. We used it above, in the oil-pumping example.
4. Estimate the answer before you do the computation. Then make sure the estimate and the answer are of about the same magnitude. This check too can be used for the majority of numerical problems.

Checking can help reveal errors in both analysis and computation. It will also help you understand what you are doing. Although checking might seem to be a duplication of effort, it really isn't. Rather, checking is a quality control operation that can enhance both your problem-solving ability and your examination grades.

HOW TO ATTACK A NONROUTINE PROBLEM

A nonroutine problem is somehow different from the problems you are used to solving; it can range from the slightly unusual to the unique. Math teachers often assign such problems to foster creative thinking and to test and extend your ability to apply what you have learned.

We shall use as an example the following problem, which may be nonroutine for you:

Problem:

> Find the length of the diagonal of a rectangular solid whose sides have lengths 3, 5, and 6 units.

Experienced problem solvers suggest a number of strategies for attacking nonroutine problems (or any problems whose solution is less than obvious):

1. Begin by reading the problem at least twice. Draw a diagram, labeling (for easy reference) the parts that might be used in the solution. When in doubt, label everything. Try to visualize the diagram from several viewpoints. Draw in any points, lines, or curves that might help your visualization or that might clarify relationships among the parts of your diagram (see Figure 19.6).

2. Sort out the facts of the problem. Note any implied facts.

Given: Rectangular solid; sides 3, 5, 6

Also: Angles all are 90°

Sides that look parallel are parallel

Diagonals are equal

Find: Length *d* of diagonal from A to C

What is needed now is a path to the solution—perhaps one or more intermediate steps.

3. Try to remember whether you've ever done a problem that was similar to this one or was related to it somehow or that involved the same kind of

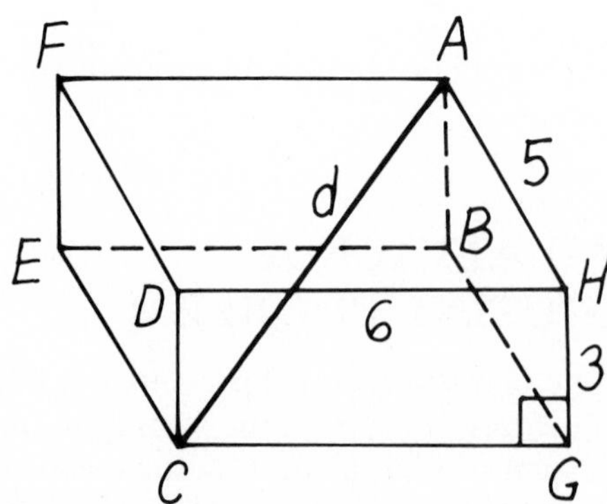

FIGURE 19.6 Diagram for the Diagonal Problem

unknown. Try to recall how you solved that problem, and apply the method here.

4. Try to restate the problem, perhaps more simply or in terms of a different unknown. Or see whether you can eliminate one of the conditions of the problem. Then solve the restated problem (if you can), as a step toward a full analysis and solution.

5. Try to solve part of the problem, to see whether that gets you any closer to the solution of the whole problem.

6. Make sure you are taking advantage of all the given and implied information in your analysis.

7. Start from the required result, and try to work backward to the given conditions.

For our example problem, the extra lines in Figure 19.6 do suggest a simpler but related problem—finding the length of the diagonal of a rectangle, in particular the upper or lower face of the solid. We can find the length of the diagonal in Figure 19.7 as $\sqrt{5^2 + 6^2} = \sqrt{61}$. But does that help?

It certainly does, because now we can draw right triangle ACD in plane ABCD (see Figure 19.8). That triangle has hypotenuse d and legs of lengths 3 and $a = \sqrt{61}$. Then

$$d = \sqrt{3^2 + a^2} = \sqrt{9 + 61} = \sqrt{70}$$

Successful problem solvers and those who have studied problem solving suggest one more strategy: Once you have solved a nonroutine problem and

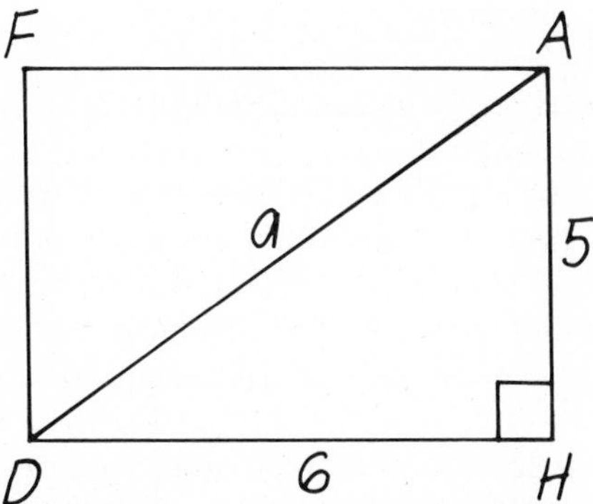

FIGURE 19.7 A Simpler Problem: Finding the Length of the Diagonal of a Face of the Solid

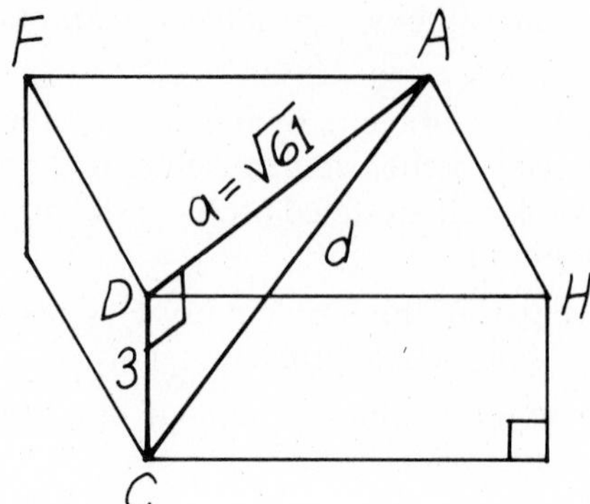

FIGURE 19.8 The Solution
Right triangle ACD can be solved for *d*.

checked your result, make it a part of your problem-solving tool kit. Apply the method and the result to other nonroutine problems whenever you can.

UNDERSTANDING AND MEMORY IN MATHEMATICS

Most students rely too much on memory in their study and use of mathematics. Competence in mathematics is not to any great extent a matter of remembering things. It is true that a child in the early grades is encouraged to memorize the multiplication tables. But he or she is also taught that, in concept, multiplication is really a form of addition. The memorization may help the child multiply more quickly, but when memory fails, the understanding that, for example, $5 \times 9 = 9 + 9 + 9 + 9 + 9$ will help the child out of difficulty.

Perhaps such early memorization builds up to a habit of memorizing in high school and college math courses. Having a needed formula memorized is certainly a convenience. But understanding the idea behind the formula and knowing how it comes about are much more important. This becomes especially true as soon as the student progresses beyond arithmetic.

An illustration is provided by the basic trigonometric identities. Students always seem to remember the formula $\sin^2 \theta + \cos^2 \theta = 1$; however, they are less successful in retaining similar formulas that relate the tangent and secant of an angle or its cotangent and cosecant. Actually, you don't have to memorize any of the identities if you understand the meanings of the trigonometric functions of angles. For example, to find the identity linking the tangent and secant of an angle, you need only draw a right triangle like that shown in Figure 19.9. Then, since $x^2 + y^2 = r^2$ (by the Pythagorean theorem), we have

$$\frac{x^2}{x^2} + \frac{y^2}{x^2} = \frac{r^2}{x^2}$$

Because $\tan \theta = y/x$ and $\sec \theta = r/x$, this becomes

$$1 + \tan^2 \theta = \sec^2 \theta$$

It's that simple, when you understand.

Of course, you do need skill to perform certain mathematical operations, but much of that skill comes from knowing what you are doing—from understanding what the operations are, what they produce, and what they mean. The remainder comes from practice, from doing those sometimes dreary but nonetheless useful routine problems. And you do need to memorize some facts in mathematics, as in every other subject. The proper mix of skill, memorization, and understanding, however, is one that leans heavily toward understanding.

Look at it this way: Most likely, you are studying mathematics so that later you will be able to apply it in science or engineering, business, economics, the social sciences, teaching, or some other area. You should know, then, that the usefulness of mathematics in these areas arises primarily from the application of its ideas, rather than from its formulas or processes (although all three have their uses). Memorizing and applying math formulas without understanding them is like repeating Russian words without knowing what they mean. You're not speaking the language; you're only imitating its noises.

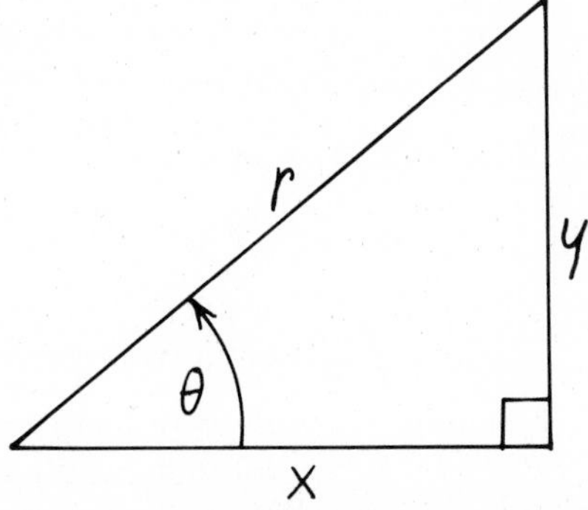

FIGURE 19.9 Right Triangle for Use in Deriving Trigonometric Identities

SUMMARY

What makes studying mathematics so different from studying other subjects?

Mathematics is one of the few subjects that is developed cumulatively through your school years, from grade school to college. What you learn this year depends on what you learned last year, and so on. What you didn't master years ago can keep you from progressing now.

What do I do if my background is weak?

You have two choices: First, you can attack each difficulty as you discover it. Your immediate need to understand the material will give you added incentive to master it. Second, if you're one of those people who can think ahead, you can diagnose your background to find your weak areas in advance. Then beef up those areas with self-help books. When a troublesome problem pops up on a test, you'll be ready.

How should note taking in math class differ from note taking in other classes?

Math notes should be taken sparingly—main ideas and clarifying remarks only—so that you can concentrate on the instructor's reasoning. You might want to keep your textbook open on your desk if the lecture seems to follow the book fairly closely. That way, you can place your notes where they will do the most good—close to the concepts or processes that they clarify.

What about reading my textbook?

Always read mathematics with great care, to make sure you extract the exact meaning of its precisely defined terms. Have pen and paper handy, and do all the examples and other computations along with the author, as you read. Clear up any confusion when it arises, before you read on. Finally, do the problems when you are sure you understand what you've read.

Any tips for preparing for math exams?

Be sure to keep up with your assignments throughout the term. When exam time rolls around, start studying early. That will give you plenty of time to correct any problems you might encounter during your review. You can use 3×5 cards, to make sure you have mastered all the important principles, processes, and formulas.

What's the plan of attack for a standard math problem?

First, analyze the problem. Sort out the given information, draw a diagram, and decide how you're going to find what is required. Only after you have completed the analysis are you ready for the second part, which is to compute the answer. Once you have an answer, check it to make sure it is *the* answer.

How do I attack nonstandard math problems?

The tough part of these problems is almost always the analysis. Begin them like standard problems, by sorting the information and drawing a diagram. Then try to find a link with a problem you've already solved or with a simpler problem. Restating the problem could help, as could working backward from what is required to what you are given. Manipulating the diagram could also show you a path to the solution.

Isn't memory important in studying math?

Memorizing should be done for convenience; it is not a necessity. If you use it as the foundation of your work, one brief lapse can bring your math knowledge crumbling to the ground. It is far better to base your study of mathematics on an understanding of the concepts that lie behind the processes and formulas. Then, if your memory fails, you won't be completely helpless.

HAVE YOU MISSED SOMETHING?

1. *Sentence completion.* Complete each of the following sentences with one of the three words listed below the sentence.

a. You should keep your old mathematics textbooks on hand for ______________________.

learning reviewing copying

b. A complicated problem can sometimes be analyzed by substituting simpler ______________________.

equations arithmetic numbers

2. *Matching.* In each blank space in the left column, write the number preceding the phrase in the right column that matches the left item best.

_____ a. Checking	1. Involves separating and listing the problem information
_____ b. Math note taking	2. Should not interfere with listening
_____ c. Open textbook	3. Can reveal errors in analysis and computation
_____ d. Diagrams	4. A firm basis for studying mathematics
_____ e. Sorting	5. Can reveal relationships in problems
_____ f. Understanding	6. Must be done carefully

3. *True-false.* Write *T* beside the *true* statements and *F* beside the *false* statements.

_____ a. Weak spots in your background should all be strengthened at the end of the semester.

_____ b. Mathematical terms are defined precisely to convey exact meanings.

_____ c. You can use your calculator to check formulas you're not quite sure of.

_____ d. Doing a problem backward can sometimes help your analysis.

_____ e. You should memorize any formula that you don't understand.

4. *Multiple choice.* Choose the word or phrase that completes the following sentence most accurately, and circle the letter that precedes it.

The most important part of your study of mathematics is

a. reading
b. formulas
c. note taking
d. understanding

CHAPTER 20

Studying Foreign Languages

The sum of human wisdom is not contained in any one language, and no single language is CAPABLE of expressing all forms and degrees of human comprehension.

Ezra Pound (1885–1972), poet, critic, translator, and editor

Knowing a foreign language gives you direct access to great thoughts, experiences, and cultures that would otherwise be out of reach. Getting someone to translate something for you, reading translations of literature, or watching a foreign film dubbed into English or with English subtitles is like shadowboxing. It is no way to get the full benefit of the experience.

This chapter gives you some information on learning foreign languages that should put the whole business into perspective. It discusses:

- The challenge of language study
- Learning to listen in a foreign language
- Learning to speak in a foreign language
- Learning to read in a foreign language
- Learning to write in a foreign language
- Getting the most from your textbook
- Getting the most out of class time

and finally

- Special notes on culture

If you find language courses easy, you may have a special, natural talent, or you may have greater motivation and enthusiasm than many. Even for you, however, learning a foreign language requires a lot of hard work.

THE CHALLENGE OF LANGUAGE STUDY

Language study is different from most other disciplines in that it entails learning both facts and skills. In addition to learning "facts" such as grammar rules and vocabulary, you must learn how to use those "facts" for listening, speaking, reading, and writing. There is a lot of overlap among these skills, but being good at one does not necessarily mean being good at the others (virtually no one is equally good at them all). Knowing this should help you understand why your language study goes better at some times than it does at others. Identifying the skills you are best at and determining how you learn best will go a long way toward helping you use your study time effectively.

Another peculiarity of language study is that learning to use a language well is partly a matter of habit—this is especially true of speaking. You speak your native language fluently, but you don't do so by thinking *about* the language. You didn't even learn it in the first place by "thinking." Instead, you listened to other people and imitated what they said. By doing this over and over again, you eventually developed the habits that allow you to speak with ease. You think not about *how* to use the language, but rather about *what* you are going to say. If your native language is English, for instance, you don't stop to think about saying "he works" (with an *-s* ending) and "they work" (with no *-s* ending). Nor do you have to stop to think about pronouncing the word *the* as "thee" in front of words that begin with a vowel ("the apple, the orange") but as "thuh" in front of words that begin with a consonant ("the peach, the banana"). You do things like that as matters of habit. Most of us don't realize that we do this kind of fancy footwork until someone points it out to us or makes an issue of teaching us a "rule."

In order to learn any language, you have to repeat a lot of what you learn over and over again until it becomes second nature to you. When you were learning your native language, you had essentially full-time practice without making any effort. When you try to learn a foreign language, you are handicapped in a couple of ways. First, you are unlikely to have enough time for practice. Second, you already have a set of language habits that are going to interfere with the new habits you are trying to develop. Don't be surprised if your brain has trouble coping at first. It is quite normal for people learning a new language to get their language habits mixed up a bit at first.

If learning a new language seems beyond your reach, remind yourself that every so-called foreign language is native to some people. Granted, the native learner had some advantages that you don't have when you approach a language as a second or other language. The chief advantage is age. Odd though it might seem, it is easiest to learn a language when you are very young. The critical thing to keep in mind, however, is that the language can be and is learned by lots of people—most of them no smarter than you.

Most of us take a very long time to learn our own language well, to use it with a reasonable amount of sophistication. All that listening and imitating takes years! At that rate, there is relatively little time to go through the process a second time, with another language. Besides, by the time you are in school, you are already past the "ideal" age for language learning, so it's too late to learn a new language in quite the way you learned your first. But don't worry, because there is another way to proceed.

You have some rational skills that you didn't have when you were a child, and those skills will help you learn a foreign language. It is true that just plain listening and imitating is harder for you now, but you can be told how the new language is put together, how it works, and how it differs from your native language. The information you are given, the set of instructions and directions on how the language works, can speed up the learning process considerably. When you were a child, you wouldn't have been able to cope with grammar rules at all. The adult's ability to reason, analyze, and systematize is a powerful asset. It is important to make use of your rational capacities, your ability to think about the language.

Thinking about the language and how it works is still not enough, however. Learning grammar is not an end in itself. Rather, mastering grammar is a way to make the imitation you still have to do more successful. If you understand the grammar as an adult and practice repeating and imitating in the way an uninhibited child would, you'll be able to overcome some of the disadvantages of not being a native learner.

LEARNING TO LISTEN IN A FOREIGN LANGUAGE

Although speaking might seem like the most interesting and important skill to learn in another language, proper listening really has to come first. Don't confuse listening with hearing (this distinction is discussed in Chapter 6). You are likely to understand what you hear only when you have learned to listen.

Most of us think when we hear people speaking a language we do not know that they are talking impossibly fast. Studies of recorded speech have shown, however, that speakers of most languages tend to utter very nearly the same number of syllables per minute when they speak at a normal rate. What makes them difficult to understand is not the speed of their speech, but rather our not knowing where the syllables (or even the words) break. Everything seems to run together. What we hear is like a torrent of sound.

Listening is really a matter of learning to discriminate sounds. In English, for instance, it matters a lot whether there is a *d* or a *t* sound at the end of a word. The word *had* is not at all the same as *hat,* and you need to listen closely to hear the difference so that you know which word is meant. That seems obvious and easy enough in a case like *had* and *hat,* when you already know the language. But when the language is unfamiliar, you have to pay extra close attention.

English has a lot of word pairs that won't seem similar to you at all, because you know the language, but that could easily be confusing to someone trying to learn the language. Think about *pin* and *pan, tin* and *thin, sin* and *fin, sheet* and *shoot, but* and *putt.* The trick in learning a new language is to train yourself to listen carefully to new sounds and sound combinations—and to new words. You need to concentrate especially hard in the beginning so that you can distinguish sounds, syllables, words, and intonation patterns that may turn out to be important in the new language.

Study Tips for Learning to Listen. Rule number one for learning to listen effectively is: Concentrate! Casual listening will result in mere hearing. Rule number two is: Do your listening practice in small doses. This means limiting the amount of time you engage in strict listening practice at any one sitting and limiting the amount you try to accomplish at any one sitting.

If you concentrate hard enough to be doing a good job of listening, you'll probably find it tiring. So give yourself a break by not overdoing it. Fifteen minutes of intensive listening work in a language lab—even when the practice includes repeating as well as listening—is enough for most people. (Thirty minutes of casual listening is nowhere nearly so helpful.) Going to the lab twice a day for fifteen minutes each time may not be efficient or even possible in your schedule, though. So go for a half hour, but at the end of each ten or fifteen minutes stand up and touch your toes three times or do something else to allow your brain to relax for a moment.

Try to concentrate on a small task. If you sing or play an instrument, you may have little trouble discriminating sounds. If you do find it difficult at first to make sense of the sounds and sound combinations in the new language, try breaking the task down. Instead of listening to a sentence with the aim of understanding the whole thing the first time through, listen just for a particular sound or a particular word. (How many times does it occur?) Then listen again, trying to pick up additional sounds or words.

Of course, in real life you can't play back a tape to listen to a sentence numerous times (though you can—and should—learn how to ask a conversational partner to repeat what he or she has said or to speak more slowly). But at the practice stage, it is both fair and sensible to play things back. Remember, you are trying initially to break down that torrent of sound into discrete elements that make sense to you.

Another strategy is to listen for the gist of what is being said—whether in a sentence, a dialogue, a paragraph, or a story. Even in your native language, you don't necessarily understand (or even hear) every single word. So why hold yourself to such an impossibly high standard in a new language? Eventually, you'll want to get to the point where you can and do get almost every word on the first pass, just as you do in your native language. At first, however, it's excellent practice to see whether you can at least get the drift of what is being said. This is called *global understanding,* meaning that you have a general (not a specific, local) idea of the topic even if you miss most of the details. Learning to get the drift is a critical part of listening comprehension and an important part of not trying to do too much at once.

Here's how to do it. Listen for familiar words. Try to pick out nouns and verbs. Learn to filter out the little words like articles and conjunctions, at first; even adjectives and adverbs are usually unimportant when you are after global understanding. Learn to watch out for powerful little words like *not,* however, which can significantly alter the meaning. Jot down words and ideas as you catch them (make your notes in the language you are studying). Then go back and listen again. Confirm what you heard by checking what you are listening to against what you jotted down. Try to fill in a few gaps.

For instance, on the first pass you may have understood that John did something, but you may not be sure what he did to whom or when or why. Before listening a second time, decide what additional information you would most like to have, which of your mental question marks it would be most helpful to eliminate. Then listen for that one thing. (What John did is likely to be more important than anything else.) It's possible that the information you are listening for is not in the passage. If you don't get it after a couple of tries, listen for something else. Go back and listen as many times as you need to, until you get all your questions answered.

When you are pretty sure that you understand the whole passage, put your notes aside and listen one more time. Try to let the rhythm and the sounds convey their message to you directly without thinking about the content in English. This is your chance to consolidate your learning (the principle of consolidation is discussed in Chapter 5).

LEARNING TO SPEAK IN A FOREIGN LANGUAGE

Because speaking is the most common, everyday way to communicate with language, it is probably the most useful of the language skills. If you can speak the language, you are almost certainly going to be able to read it, and you will have a solid base for writing as well. By mastering the speaking skill, you will get a leg up on two other skills.

The listening skill is crucial to learning to speak. Listening practice helps you understand others, and it is also important because it provides models for you to imitate in your own speaking.

Remember that language is a set of habits. Grammar rules explain some aspects of the way the language works, but thinking about those rules is not very helpful when you are trying to speak the language. The only way to learn the language is to learn the habits—by repetition, by lots of practice—not think about them. Instead of organizing, analyzing, and interpreting factual data, you must go home and practice the material you've heard in class over and over again until it becomes second nature. That means memorizing.

Children learn languages by imitating first the short phrases and expressions they hear frequently and need most. Those are the kinds of things you will learn first in your new language as well. The more complicated and abstract ideas you are used to being able to express in your native language are likely to be harder; you mustn't expect to be able to talk at the same level in the new language right away. You may feel you've been reduced to the intellectual level of a 10-year-old, for a while. But memorizing carefully what is modeled for you, and resisting the temptation to say things you haven't yet heard, will pay off. You'll end up making fewer mistakes, and you'll establish good foundations for your later language development.

One reason it is so important to limit yourself to the vocabulary and structures that have been modeled for you is that languages do not all work in the same way. Words that look and sometimes even sound alike in two languages do not necessarily mean the same thing. Also, in every language there are idiomatic expressions that cannot be constructed on the basis of rules.

An idiom is an expression with a peculiar, individual cast. It may mean something other than what the sum of its parts seems to imply. "It's raining cats and dogs" has nothing to do with animals, for instance, as every native speaker of English knows. Or an idiom may be the customary way of saying something. You could say "Happy Christmas" and "Merry Birthday," but you don't. The same ideas are frequently conveyed differently in any pair of languages. You and your friends would say in English, "We are hungry and thirsty." In many other languages, people say, "We have hunger and thirst."

You cannot know idioms ahead of time, and you cannot expect to figure them out. You have to hear the models and imitate them so often that you stop thinking about whether they are different from what you would say in your native language. Idioms have to become second nature through memorization.

Study Tips for Learning to Speak. One of the advantages children have in learning languages is that they tend to be amused by imitating new sounds. Adults, unfortunately, are likely to feel embarrassed by their attempts to say things in a new way. So rule number one in learning to speak a foreign language is: Throw caution to the wind! Try to get a kick out of the new sounds. Use exaggerated facial expressions—use those muscles!—to practice what you are saying. The odds are that the stranger you sound to yourself at first, the closer you are to imitating the new sounds correctly.

Rule number two is: Do all your practice out loud. Some people even say the louder the better—if you are going to make a mistake, make it boldly! Reading material silently is fine if all you are trying to do is understand the content. In doing that, however, you are learning only how the language is symbolized on paper, which doesn't have much to do with speaking. If you are going to develop new oral habits, you need oral practice (review the benefits of recitation discussed in Chapter 5).

There is another reason for practicing out loud. When you read silently, you are using only your visual memory. If you study out loud, you double your efficiency by adding auditory memory. You remember things you have heard *and* seen better than those you have merely seen. Beyond that, saying things out loud means you are adding motor memory, which generally quadruples efficiency. Motor memory is the memory of what you do with your muscles. One indication of its efficiency is that nobody ever forgets how to ride a bicycle.

Another way to put motor memory to work for you is to write out what you are trying to memorize. Read a passage (a sentence, a phrase, a word) out loud; then copy it, saying it again while you write. Now you've got eyes, ears, tongue, and hands all helping your brain. A side benefit of doing oral work this way is that so much of you is involved that you have to concentrate intensively.

Still another parallel exists between learning to listen and learning to speak, and that is the importance of not trying to take on too much at once. Most children are pretty good at memorizing. Adults, however, seem to be much less efficient at memorizing. That doesn't mean they can't do it, just that they have to work at it. The first crucial step in this work is to break material to be memorized into small units.

What counts as small? Some people seem to be able to memorize whole paragraphs easily. Most, however, find even a sentence too much if it is really new. They need to break sentences into phrases. And if they are tired or the passage is especially difficult, they may need to tackle smaller units than usual. How small depends in part on individuals' learning styles; there is no magic formula.

One trick that works well for most people is to tackle sentences backward. If you learn the end of a sentence first, you'll probably learn it best. Then when you've built up to saying the whole sentence, you'll always be working toward what you know best instead of struggling toward something new. Try it with this sample in English: "I'm going to Paris next summer with my whole family."

Start by figuring out what constitutes meaningful phrases or word clusters. "I'm going / to Paris / next summer / with my whole family." (If the words are especially difficult to say, you could break a sentence like this into even smaller units.) Now practice the last phrase—"with my whole family"—over and over until you can say it easily, without thinking about it. Then practice saying "next summer" until that phrase slips smoothly off your tongue, before you put the two together: "next summer with my whole family." Then work on "to Paris," "to Paris next summer," and "to Paris next summer with my whole family." Finally, you are ready to work on the last phrase (actually the first one in the sentence), "I'm going." Then you build that into the rest of the sentence.

This may sound awfully convoluted, but it takes less time to do than it does to explain. And it does work, if you are patient and systematic. You may want to reserve this technique for particularly long and complicated sentences; you probably won't need to do quite so much repetition with short ones.

Another aspect of breaking your memory work into small units has to do with the amount of time you spend at any one sitting. You should be able to work effectively on oral (speaking) work longer at one time than on aural (listening) exercises. One thing is virtually certain. If you spend two uninterrupted hours trying to memorize new material, you are unlikely to get the most out of your time.

How quickly any one person's powers of concentration diminish depends on lots of factors; you'll need to figure out for yourself how long your attention span is for different kinds of work, how much you can "take." Be honest! It won't help if you are too easy on yourself. You should be able to increase the amount of time you can concentrate as you get better at the language. For starters, try from twenty to thirty minutes at the most. Then do something else: Work on another subject, walk around the block, eat lunch, whatever. But then come back for another twenty- or thirty-minute stint. A couple of hours divided up in this way will produce better results than working straight through for two hours would.

Frequent small doses seem to work well for another reason. Learning a language is a cumulative process. Much of the new material you will be asked to learn as you go along—vocabulary and grammar as well as the conversational patterns you are memorizing—depends on what you have already learned. The new material either won't make sense or will be harder to learn if you have not mastered what went before or have allowed yourself to forget what you have learned. Language teachers sometimes talk about "frequent re-entry" of material, which means bringing old material (things you have already learned) back at frequent intervals. Most language textbooks are written in a way that tries to accomplish this, but you can help yourself by frequent reviewing and by doing assignments quickly, intensely, and more than once.

A final word must be said here about memory work, even though it has to do with aspects of language learning other than just the speaking skill. If you are going to learn to speak a new language as an adult, you have to do more than imitate what others say. Imitating takes too long to be an effective way for busy college students to learn languages. You have to do lots of memorizing of vocabulary, the rules of grammar, and so on. The principles and theories about forgetting discussed in Chapter 5 should be applied. Break your work—lists of words, for instance—into meaningful blocks. Organize words to be memorized in a way that makes sense to you, regardless of how they appear in your textbook. Group them by gender, by subject matter, by parts of speech, by length—whatever works for you.

Above all, try to fit rules of grammar into a context as you work on learning them. In this sense, you *do* need to think; memorizing is not sufficient for the adult language learner. You will help yourself enormously if, as you memorize, you think about the grammatical explanations that go with each bit of new material. The grammatical section of a new lesson may tell you, for example, about verb endings. After you have read the section and have spoken the examples out loud, start memorizing the new material. Every time you say a verb form, fit it mentally into the scheme that has just been explained to you. The ability to think about the structure of the language is the one big advantage you have over a child learning a new language. Make full use of it.

LEARNING TO READ IN A FOREIGN LANGUAGE

When you read something in your native language, you do not necessarily understand every word, and you certainly don't pronounce each word to yourself. That is worth keeping in mind, because there is a tendency to think you have to understand everything when you read a foreign language. Instead, the goal you should aim for is the ability to pick up a foreign language text (a book, a newspaper, a brochure) or look at a sign (directions, instructions, advertisements) and understand what it is about just as you would a similar document or bit of writing in your native language.

Just as you probably use different reading techniques in your native language, depending on the type of material and the situation, you need to develop different techniques for reading in a new language. First and foremost, this means thinking about the kind of material you are reading. Just because they are all course assignments does not mean you should look at them all in the same way. The precise meaning of each word is likely to matter more in poetry than in a novel. A close analysis of details is more important if you are going to discuss the relative merits of two proposals than if you are merely reading the minutes of some meeting. Directions on how to put something together need to be read differently from the words of a business letter. Learning to read is not just one kind of activity.

Although reading in a foreign language has a lot in common with reading in your own language, it presents some special challenges. The whole framework of what you are trying to read in another language may be foreign to you, so it's likely to be hard for you to get started. The percentage of unfamiliar words is likely to be uncomfortably high. These problems can be overcome, however. Keep in mind that reading in a foreign language should ultimately be like reading in your own language. It's a way to get information, to be exposed to new ideas, to pass the time pleasurably. These, not solving linguistic puzzles, are the legitimate goals for this activity.

One thing you will gradually discover is that reading is both easier and harder than listening and speaking. It is easier because when you read you can go back and reread, you can slow down or speed up, you can proceed at your own pace. Conversations don't work that way. On the other hand, when people take the trouble to write out ideas, the ideas tend to be expressed in a more complex way than they would have been in conversation. The ideas themselves may in fact be more complicated. This makes reading a bit of a challenge at times. Don't be surprised if you have to work at your foreign language reading, at least initially. The rewards of succeeding are high. You will be moving steadily toward the point where you can vastly increase the range of information directly available to you.

Study Tips for Learning to Read. Many of the tips given elsewhere in this book on how to read effectively (see especially Chapter 17) can and should be applied sensibly to reading in a foreign language. But since the single biggest hurdle in foreign language reading is usually the unfamiliar vocabulary, it merits special attention. Rule number one for learning to read in a foreign language is: Make sure you don't confuse *translating* with *reading*.

The whole point of learning to read in a foreign language is to avoid having to translate. Worrying about the exact meaning in your own language of each word and phrase you come to in a foreign language text is really undercutting the point of what you are doing. Your aim ought to be to learn to think in the new language, at least to the extent that you can understand what you are reading without translating it. In order to do this, you have to have worked hard at memorizing standard expressions, you have to have developed a good grasp of the grammar, and you have to be constantly expanding your vocabulary.

Fortunately, most foreign language courses are set up in such a way that you won't be asked to read things that really are too hard for you. What you read at first will often be made up mostly of things you have already heard and learned to say; you should get a nice "Aha!" sense of recognition from those parts of what you are reading. At the very least, reading selections are likely to be on topics you have already been exposed to, so the context and some of the vocabulary will be familiar.

As a result, some of the listening techniques previously discussed can be applied to learning to read as well. You don't have to and shouldn't try to get everything at once. Expect to go over any reading assignment several times. Three quick readings, done systematically, are almost always better than one slow, plodding one. Remember what has been said in Chapter 5 about study techniques for memory work, and about massed and distributed practice, as well.

Even before you start, look to see whether there are questions at the end of the passage. Studying the questions before you read can do a lot to help set the stage, give you a context, and tell you what to read for. Your first pass might then be just to get the gist of the selection. In a difficult assignment, you may want to tackle just one paragraph at a time.

You should make this first pass without looking up any words, even if there are a lot you do not know. Remember, you're just trying to get a general feel for what is under discussion, to get global understanding. Once you have done that, perhaps making notes for yourself of key words to help fix the basic topic in your mind, you're ready to begin a different, more precise kind of reading. But even then you should resist the temptation to check the meaning of each word.

Rule number two for reading in a foreign language is: Learn to make intelligent guesses. If you are going to learn how to read for content and pleasure, just about the most important skill for you to acquire is that of figuring out what a word means from the context in which it is used. You do this all the time in your native language; you read and understand a lot of words you never use in speaking or writing.

To deduce the meanings of words from their contexts—or to remember the meanings of words you have looked up—you will have to read them more than once. One rule of thumb that works well for many people is that you shouldn't look up a word until you have encountered it three times without being able to figure it out. This will save you a lot of time. You are also more likely to remember a word you've figured out from context than one you've looked up, especially if you looked up a great many words during that one reading session.

Sometimes it is not clear how far you have to read to get the context of something. Perhaps the best way to proceed is to read through the first sentence and then keep on reading until you get lost. You may be able to follow along for a paragraph, a page, or even a whole assignment. Once you begin to get lost, stop and go back to the beginning. Read along again until you come to the first word you still don't know. Underline the word so you can find it again quickly. Continue in this fashion to the point where you left off the first time, and then start over once more. If, on the third reading, you still cannot guess the meaning of a word you have underlined, look it up. Put a dot in the margin of the vocabulary or dictionary page beside the word to show you had to look it up. (Later, if you have to look the same word up again, add a dot. This will help you keep track of words that seem to be giving you extra trouble, so you can isolate and study them.) Find the English translation that best fits your sentence. Then, turning back to the text, reread the phrase in which the word occurs, trying to fix its meaning in your mind as you do so. Go through your whole first passage this way, looking up only the words you absolutely have to and making intelligent guesses at the others. Then tackle the next section in the same manner, until you have read about half of your assignment.

At that point, take a short break. Then reread the part you have already finished before you go on. Rereading while the section you have worked on is still fresh in your memory will really tie down the loose ends. If you wait until later on, much of it will have grown cold. Besides, seeing how easily you can read what you have worked so hard on should give you the courage to proceed with the second half of your assignment. Go through it in the same way, looking up only the words you cannot guess. When you've taken the second small break and reread the second half of your assignment, read quickly through the whole thing. Consolidate what you've learned, what you've worked so hard to achieve.

If you come to words, idioms, or grammatical constructions you cannot sort out, underline them. If after your second or third honest try you still cannot figure them out, put a vertical line in the margin to remind you to ask your instructor for an explanation. If you have been thorough about applying everything you know and systematic about making intelligent guesses, it will probably turn out that you are not the only one in the class who had difficulty in those spots.

This system of underlining phrases and making vertical lines in the margin should remind you of suggestions about marking your textbooks and writing questions in the margin discussed in Chapter 9. You might want to take the idea of making dots in the margins of the vocabulary pages a step further, and use 3 × 5 cards as discussed in Chapter 15. Remember, your aim is to read in the foreign language the way you do in your own, so it makes sense to apply some of the same techniques whenever you can.

LEARNING TO WRITE IN A FOREIGN LANGUAGE

Of the four language skills under discussion here, writing—at least writing on a sophisticated, adult level—is probably the most difficult. When you consider how hard it is for most people to write stylishly and clearly even in their native language, this is not surprising. Thus no one will expect you to produce very long or complicated written assignments in the early stages of your language study.

Nonetheless, the ability to put at least some ideas into writing is an important part of mastering another language. Learning to be accurate in the production of language as it is symbolized on paper is part of any foreign language course. Writing is a legitimate end in itself; it also involves motor memory, and it helps consolidate all aspects of what you are learning in the language.

Writing, too, has several different parts. The simplest aspect of this language skill is producing individual words and phrases on paper correctly. Essential to that is becoming a master of the language's sound-symbol correspondence. In other words, you have to learn to spell words, not just to recognize them. In fact, early assignments may include having you copy words, sentences, or dialogues from your textbook. Carrying out such simple tasks is the best way to get started on good writing habits. Accurately copying sentences that are known to be correct models keeps you from making mistakes. Writing is much more than putting words on paper, however. Even before you get to the point in your language courses where you are expected to do anything that might reasonably be called creative writing, some tips may be useful.

Study Tips for Learning to Write. Just as learning to speak correctly means learning to listen carefully to models and imitating them, learning to write correctly requires learning to observe written models closely enough to imitate them. Rule number one for writing is: Make sure you learn the spelling, gender and declension, or conjugation of each new word as it comes along. Just looking at a new word, or even saying it out loud, is not sufficient. Spell it out loud. Copy it out (think again about using 3 × 5 cards), spelling it aloud again as you write it.

The same applies to whole phrases, sentences, and paragraphs. Good oral and aural habits can help you in writing, just as writing things out can help your oral performance. Early assignments will almost certainly require you to put together in a sensible sequence sentences you already have read and know how to say. Take advantage of the existing models in your textbook to make sure you are reproducing such bits of language accurately when you write them.

Another of the suggestions made in connection with learning to speak is also useful when it comes to writing. Try to resist the temptation—at first—to express thoughts as complicated as those you are accustomed to writing in your native language. Build a solid base by getting the simple things right, often; the more complex matters will begin to fall into place later.

Rule number two for writing—especially as you move on to the point of creating original sentences and paragraphs—is: Follow the same procedures and steps you would for a written assignment in your native language (see Chapter 18). To be sure, the requirements with respect to length and complexity of topic will be very different. But you need to have exactly the same concerns: Define your topic precisely; organize your thoughts carefully; and make notes or an outline before you start to do the actual writing. You should follow these steps even on a very short assignment.

Above all, you will need to allow time to edit what you have written. If editing is an important part of writing in your native language, how much more so that will be in a language that is relatively new to you! Leave yourself time for a break between the initial writing and the editing (a day or more is ideal) so that you can look at what you have written with fresh eyes.

Remember, too, that editing is a complicated job. You should not expect to do an adequate job of editing simply by rereading what you have written. You'll need to go through your finished draft once to check mechanical details like spelling and punctuation; this is called copyediting, and it is only a small part of the editing process. Then you'll need to go through once to check the grammar and at least once more to make sure the ideas you tried to express are coming across clearly and correctly. Nothing less will do. This sounds time consuming, and it is. But it is also much more efficient than trying to tackle everything at once, and the results will be better than if you skip one or another of these tasks. If you break the task into its separate parts, you can be reasonably sure that the time you spend will be spent effectively.

You should read your paper out loud to test the sound. If you have been doing most of your homework orally, as has been recommended, you will gradually develop an ear for how things ought to sound. Does what you have written flow smoothly? Are the sentences too long and therefore hard to read? Are they too short and therefore choppy? Is it easy to follow the point of what you have written? Even better than just reading your work to yourself is to get a classmate to listen, to serve as a friendly critic. Offer to do the same for her or him. The practice of reading, listening, and criticizing will help both of you.

Finally, make a fair copy. You do not want the evidence of your hard work to get lost in a sloppy presentation. Give yourself plenty of time to copy the whole thing over carefully. This stage of the operation also gives you one last chance to make changes or corrections, if the need arises.

Writing well *is* hard work. Don't let the difficulty of the process surprise or discourage you. By following the models in your textbook, you are bound to do more right than wrong. You will get better as you go along, if you proceed cautiously.

GETTING THE MOST FROM YOUR TEXTBOOK

Look back at Chapters 8 and 9, "Learning from Your Textbooks" and "Making Notes in and from Your Textbooks." A lot of what is said there you will be able to apply to work with your foreign language textbook as well. On the other hand, your foreign language textbook will be different from others in some ways. This just means that surveying it is especially important. Language teachers are constantly working on new methods to help students learn foreign languages efficiently and thoroughly. Their efforts are reflected in the textbooks that get written. But because language learning is such a complex matter, the books differ; no one book can possibly be the best in every regard for every student. You need to become familiar with *your* book so that you can make it mesh with your learning style.

For example, some books give grammar explanations and rules first and only afterward give exercises for you to work on. Others provide a couple of models for you to follow in doing the exercises, giving you a chance to figure out the rules for yourself, before you come to any explanations. This is the difference, roughly, between a deductive and an inductive approach, from the student's point of view. Each method has much to be said in its favor. What you need to do is be sure you understand which your book is using; only then will you be able to work effectively with it.

If your book gives rules and explanations first (and encourages you to work deductively), you don't necessarily have to do every assignment in that way. You may discover that you learn better by doing the exercises first and trying to establish the rule on the basis of what you are doing (you may work better inductively) and then checking what you have figured out against what the book tells you. Most foreign language textbooks are deliberately written so that they can be used in a variety of ways. Feel free to experiment a bit until you find how your book works best for you.

Once you have become familiar with your book and have made any necessary adjustments in the way you approach assignments, to fit your learning style, stick with your system. Developing a systematic approach to your language study is an important part of building the new language habits.

Whatever system you develop, it should not entail short cuts. Don't leave things out. The people who write foreign language textbooks work very hard to include no extraneous material; everything in the book—every exercise, explanation, and example—is there for a reason. Furthermore, if a workbook or a lab manual and recorded materials accompany your textbook, be faithful about doing the work in them as well. Remember, learning a language is a complex task that is best aided by having frequent small doses repeated often. The various components of your foreign language program are designed to help strengthen the habits you are building.

One of the best ways to help yourself in this regard is to do exercises more than once. The second time will not take so long as the first, and you will have more than twice as good a chance of retaining what you've learned. Doing an exercise is one thing; learning the material well enough to retain it is quite different. Making new language material second nature requires extra effort.

To keep the repetition of exercises from being boring, adapt the exercises slightly the second time through. If the exercise is oral, write it out the second time. If it is written, do it out loud. Start at the end of an exercise and work backward the second time. Combine related exercises in your textbook and your workbook. And so on. Try to think of ways to put every kind of memory (visual, oral, auditory, motor) to work. With a little creative effort and extra time, you can make your textbook do double duty for you.

Remember, too, what has been suggested in Chapter 9 about marking your book up. Use the margins to ask yourself questions. Put vertical lines or dots in the margins to remind yourself of trouble spots. Figure out other ways to make the book yours. Make it help you. Eventually, however, you will want to be able to be independent of it.

Resist the temptation to write interlinear translations in your foreign language textbook. Such translations guarantee that you won't be learning to think in the other language, because your eye will keep going to the translation you have written in. They also prevent you from getting valuable additional practice with the foreign language material by going through it a second time or in class, again because your eye will go to the translation instead of to the original.

GETTING THE MOST OUT OF CLASS TIME

Any time you emerge from a foreign language class without being tired, you probably haven't been working hard enough. Your few hours of classes each week are a substitute for the countless hours you had for listening and imitating when you were learning your native language. You have to concentrate hard during those few hours; the effort of concentration should make you tired, even if you are having a good time.

If your instructor has decorated the classroom with pictures and artifacts from the country whose language you are studying, this was not done merely to make things look cheerful. Rather, it is part of an attempt to create an atmosphere where it will seem appropriate to speak a language other than English. You should do everything you can to add to and maintain the illusion that you are in a foreign language environment, because your hours in class are the closest you will come to it in most foreign language courses. Learn to greet your classmates and instructor in the new language. This will help set the mood and save you from switching back and forth between English and your new language—a sure way to interrupt the process of establishing new language habits.

Thus, even when material is presented in English in your textbook, you can endeavor to raise any questions you have and ask for clarifications in the foreign language. Try to think in your new language. It will help a lot if you seek out others in your class willing to make the same effort. Sit next to them, and arrange study sessions with them. Nothing will undermine your good intentions so quickly as sitting next to someone who maintains a steady undercurrent of English commentary on the work at hand.

Because of the cumulative nature of language learning, falling behind is an even more serious problem than in most courses. Because catching up is extremely difficult, be very disciplined about doing all your assignments completely and on time. If you have trouble, get help right away. There are several ways to get help. You can go over things again (after taking a break to clear your head). You can get a classmate who is doing well to help straighten you out. You can go to your instructor. If you know someone who has a different textbook for the same language, you may occasionally find it helps to see how another set of textbook authors presented the subject that is giving you difficulty. The different or additional explanation may do the trick for you.

Getting the most out of class time is closely related to getting the most out of your textbook. Look back at the previous section, and review the suggestions for learning effectively from your textbook that appear in Chapter 8. Pay special attention to the steps of reciting, reviewing, and reflecting when you are preparing for your foreign language class. The primary watchwords for making class time worthwhile are: Prepare before class. Attend every class. Work hard in class.

SPECIAL NOTES ON CULTURE

The skills discussed in this chapter are not the whole story when it comes to learning a foreign language. One reason for going to all this trouble is to learn about native speakers of the language you are studying—the places they live and the lives they lead. You are trying to gain access to a culture. Learning a language and learning a culture—by which we generally mean both highbrow culture (art, history, music, literature) and features of everyday living (people's customs, habits, likes and dislikes, food, clothing)—are integrally related. Those cultural matters are to a considerable extent the subject matter of foreign language courses, though it is easy to forget this when you are deeply involved in learning vocabulary and grammar. Because they do go hand in hand, everything you learn in the language opens avenues to the culture, and every exposure to the culture will help you in your understanding and eventual mastery of the language.

It is highly desirable for you to listen to music or go to movies in the language you are learning. If there are restaurants in your area that serve foods from the countries where your new language is spoken, go. If the waiters there can and will speak the foreign language, go with a friend who is willing to join you for a foreign language evening.

If your college or university has a foreign language house for your language, see what is involved in joining. If there is no foreign language table for your language on campus, see whether you can find an instructor willing to help you start one. If there is one already, go. Spending a mealtime even once a week speaking your new language and hearing it spoken will help, and you will find out which other students are as eager as you to press forward with their new language skills.

Try always to talk to your language instructors in the new language, even when you meet them outside of class. Try to get to know native speakers of the language, and use your new language skills to talk with them. Ask them to tell you something about the place they come from. You will get valuable practice in listening comprehension as well as interesting, firsthand cultural information.

Investigate possibilities for study abroad. If a year or semester program is not an option for you, perhaps a summer study trip is. Even an intensive summer school session at home or an "immersion" weekend is better than getting no exposure outside your regular classes. Talk to students in advanced courses about what they have done to supplement their regular class work; get recommendations from your instructor or other members of the language department.

The point is to find as many ways as possible to fill in the gaps that typically appear when adults try to learn a new language as well as to extend your knowledge of the language's culture. It may be harder in some ways for adults to learn languages, but they also have a greater variety of means to attack the task than children do. Exploring those means is an important part of your job as an adult learner of a foreign language.

SUMMARY

How is learning a foreign language different from learning other subjects?	Learning a language entails learning both knowledge and skills. You have to learn "facts," but you also have to become proficient at using those facts. Furthermore, learning a language is not just one task; four distinct skills are involved.
What are the four language skills?	Listening, speaking, reading, and writing. Although these skills require some differences in approach, they also have some things in common with each other. You must work on all four skills more or less simultaneously, throughout your language study.
Why do children often have an easier time learning languages than adults do?	Children are less inhibited about imitating what other people say; imitation is an essential part of building new language habits. Children also do not have an established set of language habits to interfere with the new ones they are trying to develop.
What advantages do adult learners have?	Adults have rational skills that children do not have. These skills enable adults to understand something about how language works and make it easy to learn a lot quickly. Adults can use knowledge about language to speed up the imitation process that takes so long when people learn their first language.
Why is thinking not the most important part of learning a language?	Language is largely a set of habits, and you have to *do* things rather than just think about them in order to build those habits. Furthermore, languages do not always work in a logical way. Some things—the meanings of certain idioms, for instance—you

simply have to memorize, repeating them until they become second nature. You cannot figure them out, no matter how hard you think about them.

Why is studying out loud important even on written assignments? Why is it a good idea to write out oral assignments?

Visual and auditory memory are enhanced dramatically when they are supplemented by motor memory. The more different kinds of memory you have working for you at once, the more likely you are to implant what you are learning in your long-term memory.

How are translating and reading different from each other?

Translating means reproducing in one language precisely what is said or written in another language. Reading entails thinking and understanding in the original language without using a second language as an aid. Hence translating necessarily involves at least two languages; reading involves only one.

Why is the time spent in class especially important in a language course?

In most language courses, the class hours are the closest you can get to an environment like the one in which the language you are learning is spoken. When part of what you are trying to do is learn by imitation, anything that helps create the right atmosphere is especially valuable. Your instructor and a well-run classroom come closer to creating the right illusion than your room or the library does.

How is culture connected to language study?

Language is in part a means of communicating culture. The ways people think and behave—their hopes and aspirations, their customs and habits, their literature and art—are all conveyed in part by language. When you learn the language, you are learning something about the culture. Conversely, learning something about the culture will probably make your language study more interesting, and it should help put what you are learning into perspective.

HAVE YOU MISSED SOMETHING?

1. *Sentence completion.* Complete the following sentences with one of the three words listed below each sentence.

a. Language study entails learning both knowledge and ________.

facts grammar skills

b. Language study is largely a set of ________________.

words habits rules

2. *Matching.* In each blank space in the left column, write the number preceding the phrase in the right column that matches the left item best.

____ a. Context
____ b. Culture
____ c. Motor
____ d. Imitation
____ e. Vocabulary
____ f. Idiom

1. Basic means of learning native language
2. Biggest challenge in reading a foreign language
3. Includes habits and customs as well as art
4. Expression peculiar to a particular language
5. Part of the best way to figure out what a word means
6. The most efficient kind of memory

3. *True-false.* Write *T* beside the *true* statements and *F* beside the *false* statements.

____ a. Adults learn languages better than children because they are more mature.

____ b. Language involves at least four skills.

____ c. The same language skills are equally easy or hard for everyone.

____ d. Translating is a necessary part of reading.

____ e. Memorization is a critical part of language learning.

4. *Multiple choice.* Choose the phrase that completes the following sentence most accurately, and circle the letter that precedes it.

One good way to improve your reading skill in a foreign language is to

a. look up every unfamiliar word as soon as you come to it
b. spend a long, uninterrupted block of time on one reading passage
c. look up unfamiliar words only if you still haven't figured out what they mean by the third time you encounter them
d. copy the whole passage into your notebook

CHAPTER 21

Learning with the Computer

I had rather dream of the future than read a history of the past.

Thomas Jefferson (1743–1826), third president of the United States

Does the thought of sitting down at a computer terminal leave you with high-tech anxiety? If so, you might be surprised to discover that you can learn many of the basics of computing within a few hours. Computers are not just easy to learn; they are useful. They can help you research and write papers, study, plan a schedule, and save time. This chapter covers some basic information about computing. It discusses

- Myths about computers
- Identifying your school's computer requirements
- Determining your computer needs
- Applications
- Using the computer in the library
- Computer-aided learning
- Graphics

and finally

- Continuing to learn

omputers are here to stay, and, over the course of your life, they are going to have a profound, direct impact on you. Microcomputers have become fundamental to the operation of most business and professional offices. If the current trend continues, computing is likely to become an essential component of virtually every profession and business in the United States. Learning to use a computer could be crucial to your success in college and later in the job market.

In response to this trend, colleges are bringing computers into the classroom and are providing courses on computer applications. Students who can use the computer successfully for these applications are said to be "computer literate." Computer literacy is a working understanding of the different ways in which computers can be used for word processing and for manipulating information.

MYTHS ABOUT COMPUTERS

Many schools require students to complete a course in computing as part of a general education requirement, and others strongly recommend such a course. The course is likely to teach word processing, spreadsheet accounting, and database management. Fields of study such as mathematics, sociology, statistics, and computer science require additional courses to develop computer skills.

If you have no firsthand computer experience, you may find the prospect of using computers distasteful for reasons that bear little relation to reality. Have you been letting one of the following myths prevent you from becoming computer literate?

1. *Everyone else knows about computers already. I'll just seem stupid.* The fact is that most people are familiar with only a few computer applications and they were just as apprehensive as you about facing a computer terminal for the first time. It's natural to be anxious about new learning situations. Research has shown that a healthy amount of anxiety makes you mentally alert for new learning situations. Combat overanxious feelings by remembering a successful, though stressful, learning experience of your own. Recall how your initial misgivings became feelings of interest and relief once you felt in control of the situation. After learning the basics of computing, you'll wonder why you were anxious at all.

2. *I'm not good with machines. I could damage the equipment or lose the data I'm working with.* The fact is that unless you pick up the computer and throw it against the wall, you're not likely to damage it. A computer will not be harmed if you accidentally press the wrong keys on the keyboard. Moreover, the computer software you will use is designed to tell you what key to press to perform a particular function. At worst, you may need to ask for assistance or refer to the manual that accompanies the software you're using.

3. *I'll have to take a computer programming course to understand computers.* The fact is that very few people need to know how to program a computer. The word *program* refers to the internal commands that the computer reads every time it performs a task, and *programming* refers to the writing of those commands into the computer's software. *Software* refers to the instructions, written onto a disk or tape, that direct the computer to perform a particular operation. To use the computer for word processing, spreadsheet accounting, or database management, you don't need to know anything about how the software you are using was programmed. An introductory programming course can help you appreciate how software programs are developed. It can also help you decide whether to take additional programming courses.

It's important to understand the difference between courses and workshops that teach *computer programming* and those that teach *computer applications* such as word processing, spreadsheet accounting, and database management. If you decide to take a course or workshop in applications, talk with friends who took the course or attended the workshop. Having a good first experience with computing is more important than taking a course just for the sake of taking it. If a friend has had a good experience, the chances are good that you will too.

4. *I'll need extensive skills before I'll be able to use the computer.* The fact is that you'll need to know only seven or eight of the most frequently used commands to begin to word-process a document. The same is true of learning to use a spreadsheet or working with a database management program. Many students can begin to use such programs within two or three hours. You'll find that after you've learned the introductory commands, you'll easily be able to learn more.

5. *It's a waste of time to learn on a particular computer, because they're always coming up with new models.* The fact is that the computer industry shows little sign of slowing down from its development boom, and there will always be a "next" model. Your best bet, therefore, is to identify your computer needs and learn to use a computer and software that suit those needs. Because new computer models are similar to the older models, you'll easily be able to transfer the skills you learn on one model to the next model.

6. *Maybe I shouldn't try to learn computing until I can afford to own a computer.* The fact is that if you buy a computer before you learn much about computers, you may end up with equipment not well suited to your needs. Because computers are expensive, it pays to know what you would get if you decided to buy. Use a friend's computer or learn in a workshop or computer lab until you have more experience.

IDENTIFYING YOUR SCHOOL'S COMPUTER REQUIREMENTS

Before the term begins, determine the type of computer and software that will be used in your major and in other courses you might take. The college catalogue is a good place to begin. Check also with your academic adviser or department secretary for additional information on departmental requirements. Once you've determined what you must take, it's important to plan how the course or courses will fit into your long-term plan of study. If your school requires that you take a computer course, find out whether you need to take it at a particular point in your college career. Some schools require or advise that you complete it during your freshman year. Others specify only that it be completed by graduation. Still others suggest that you complete a workshop in specific computer applications. The workshop usually takes place in a series of sessions over the course of several days.

Keep in mind as you plan your course of study that required computer courses and workshops often have limited enrollments. Computer labs have limited space and equipment, and you wouldn't want to be squeezed out simply because you didn't sign up on time. Find out whether you need to sign up early, or during the regular registration period.

Prepare for the course by familiarizing yourself with some of the texts that will be used. Knowing something about the basic terms and concepts can get you off to a faster start than approaching the subject cold. As soon as you can, purchase the required textbooks or manuals and read the introductory material, the headings, and the graphs and other illustrations. If you have time, begin to read the text itself. (You may want to review the techniques on surveying your textbooks presented in Chapter 8 and those on reading visually displayed material in Chapter 10.)

Locate the computer facilities on campus, and identify the person in charge. Sometimes the lab or workshop will be run by a computer specialist; more often its day-to-day operations are directed by a staff of students who have taken introductory courses themselves. Don't be shy about asking questions! The person answering them was at one time unfamiliar with computers, too. Besides, he or she is usually someone who enjoys computers and finds pleasure in teaching others. If you find it unsettling to be introduced to a lot of unfamiliar terminology in a single discussion, bring a notebook and take notes. They'll be useful when you later return to use a terminal. (If you receive instruction as you work at the terminal, you may want to take along a small, portable recorder for taping notes. When your hands are occupied, such a recorder can be invaluable.) Find out whether there is any introductory material available for reading on your own or whether a particular software manual is recommended.

Ask to be shown the computers, and have their capabilities described to you. A knowledgeable friend can be of help here. Sometimes the staff at the campus computer facilities run introductory workshops or sessions. Find out whether these are planned and how you can sign up for them. You may want to get the answers to some of the following questions when you check out the computer facilities:

1. *How many computer terminals are available?* Sometimes the terms *computer* and *computer terminal* are used interchangeably. A computer, however, is any electronic device that can accept (or *input*), process, store, display, and print (or *output*) information (or *data*). The term *computer* can refer to powerful mainframes, capable of supporting many terminals; it can also refer to smaller *microcomputers,* such as the *Apple MacIntosh* computer and the *IBM PC.* A terminal consists of a keyboard and a screen. You use the keyboard to input data and see it displayed on the screen. Sometimes, there is a printer near the terminal.

2. *What types of computers and computer software are available?* You are likely to have access to a number of different computers. Some computer labs use only one type of computer, but others contain two or more types. Initially, you may feel most comfortable by picking one type and learning on it. As you become experienced, you can experiment with other types.

Some software can be used on several different types of computers. For instance, "WordPerfect" software is available for IBM and Apple computers, although a different version is used for each computer. Knowing how to use different types of software will help you in the long run.

3. *How many and what kind of printers are available?* A printer is the device that gives you a printed version (the *hard copy*) of your work. Several kinds of printers are available, and each kind gives you a different quality of print on the page. The highest quality of print comes from a laser printer. Laser printers produce letter-quality results—the printed characters are good enough for professional correspondence and other documents. Dot matrix printers use a series of pins that strike the printer ribbon to produce characters. As the name implies, each character is composed of small dots, and the resulting effect may not be as strong or clear as letter-quality print. Some dot matrix printers, however, do produce letter-quality print, and most can produce at least a near-letter-quality result. Dot matrix printers are relatively cheap to buy and operate, and the computer lab is most likely to have more of them than other, more expensive, printers. They are excellent for printing drafts and final copy for college papers and projects.

4. *What are the general rules for using the computer lab?* In many computer labs, you will be assigned a *password*—a word or series of nonsense characters—that you type in as you *log in* or *log on* to the computer. Passwords protect the material in your files from being used by any other user. A *file* is the name given to any group or set of data stored in the computer.

Determine whether you need to sign up in advance to use a terminal. This may be necessary, especially during periods of heavy use such as the end of the term, when many students are completing term projects and research papers.

DETERMINING YOUR COMPUTER NEEDS

In addition to determining your school's computer requirements, think about how you personally can use the computer. This is worth doing even if your school has no required course or workshop, because the benefits to you of becoming computer literate are so great. For example, if you are an avid correspondent with family and friends, using a word-processing program can increase your speed. If, on the other hand, writing home is a time-consuming, laborious chore, you may find that word-processing improves your speed and efficiency.

Consider the kind of work you are likely to undertake in college. If you think you may become a humanities or a social sciences major, think about the benefits of word processing. If you are likely to study math, any of the sciences, or a technical field, think about how learning to store and retrieve data in a database will improve your ability to generate useful reports. In addition, some fields of study now endorse particular kinds of educational software. You may find such software useful in your field of study. (Educational software is discussed under "Computer-Aided Learning" later in this chapter.) Learning to use appropriate computer applications can allow you to perform tasks quickly and with great efficiency. As a result, you have more time for study and other day-to-day and long-term tasks. Overall, using a computer can enhance your creativity and help you save time.

APPLICATIONS

If you've ever labored over several drafts of a research paper, writing and rewriting until you've used reams of paper and feel as if you've permanently damaged your arm, you'll want to learn about word processing. If you've performed simple accounting, you know that to change a number in the middle of a spreadsheet can entail tedious recalculations of other numbers. If you've ever had to compile a large bibliography for research purposes, you know that searching for and copying the entries can gobble your time. Spreadsheet accounting and database management can make accounting, bibliographic, statistical, and other tasks quick and easy.

Word Processing

Word processing is nearly as simple as typing. You type text into the computer. The text is displayed on the screen. A simple command or short series of commands stores that information, probably on a floppy disk that you have inserted into the computer. At any time, you can print the text or retrieve it for further work. Table 21.1 lists common functions performed by word-processing programs.

Word-processing a document such as a research paper saves you time and energy. Even if you usually type the first drafts of your papers, you're still left with a fair amount of work revising, editing, and retyping. With word processing, however, once you've input the text, you can use a few simple commands to edit it quickly and efficiently. You can move a word, a line, or a large block of text from one place in the document to another. You can delete text from, or add text to, any place you like. In short, you can edit and rewrite with a few keystrokes, instead of retyping the entire paper.

Even if you've never learned to type or your typing is rusty, using a word processor to write and edit papers and other documents will save you time and energy. And remember, the more you practice at the terminal, the faster and more efficient your typing will become. Some software programs will even teach you how to keyboard on the computer.

TABLE 21.1 Common Functions Performed by Word-processing and Spreadsheet Programs

Function	Task
Create	Names a file and enters the document into it
Edit	Inserts and deletes information in a document already created
Format	Arranges page margins, line spacing, tabs, and other features
File management	Stores and retrieves the document
Print	Transfers the document to printed copy

Other features of word-processing software include spelling checkers, an electronic thesaurus, and style checkers. A *spelling checker,* activated with a couple simple commands, scans your manuscript, highlights the misspelled words it finds, and allows you to correct them. An *electronic thesaurus* provides on-screen lists of synonyms and antonyms, helpful if you're stuck trying to think of an interesting word. *Style checkers* look for awkward or grammatically incorrect phrases and sentences and punctuation errors. These features don't guarantee you'll write a great paper, but they'll help you check and edit your work, thus giving you more time for improving the quality of your work.

You can also use word-processing programs to help develop study outlines and study schedules, to keep lab notes, and to create study aids and note files. Special applications software that involve word processing include time management and scheduling software. These programs open an electronic datebook into which you can insert upcoming events and deadlines. Because your schedule is likely to change, you can modify the schedule by using a few keystrokes, instead of rewriting it entirely. You can also create a monthly calendar. Test dates, major assignments, and other notable events can be entered at the beginning of each semester or quarter.

You can also enter daily study schedules for routine class work. Taken together, this information can form a semester-long study plan, which can be reevaluated each week or so as needed. A "To-Do" electronic notepad lists immediate needs and target dates, thus allowing you to pinpoint crucial things that need to be started or finished. This is a perfect place to set times for completing projects and for making notes about the day's activities.

A major advantage of creating and using electronic schedules is that they can be edited without your having to redo the entire schedule. Planning your schedule at the beginning of each day provides you with a hard copy for reference.

Spreadsheet Accounting

An electronic spreadsheet takes the place of the conventional spreadsheet used by accountants and financial analysts. Like conventional spreadsheets, electronic spreadsheets are composed of horizontal rows and vertical columns that intersect and allow you to insert data at the cells. You can enter numbers, words, or formulas into each cell, store what you've entered, and then manipulate the stored information. The software is programmed so that you can perform a variety of calculations with the data, and the speed with which the program responds to your requests for these calculations makes it an invaluable tool.

Spreadsheets are used in business, economics, and accounting courses in which students are asked to work with case studies, problem sets, and statistical models. You can make personal use of spreadsheets as well. Spreadsheet accounting simplifies managing a personal budget or keeping financial records for an organization or social club. It also allows for quick and efficient personal tax planning.

The functions you are likely to encounter if you work with a spreadsheet are similar to those found in word-processing packages (see Table 21.1). That is an example of how becoming proficient with one type of software helps you with another type.

Database Management

You've probably called the telephone operator, asked for someone's phone number, and been given it by means of an electronic recording. This was accomplished by means of a database management program. A database management program allows you to enter data into a database (the place where it is stored) and retrieve it quickly and easily. You can retrieve and manipulate the information in a number of ways because of the cross-reference filing in the system.

Think of a database as you would think of a conventional filing cabinet. The item that holds the largest group of information in the filing cabinet is the file drawer. Each drawer is capable of holding several small manila file folders. Each manila folder holds numerous pieces of information, such as letters and numbers. In an electronic database, the file drawer is called the *file*; the manila folders they hold are called *records*; the pieces of information contained in the records are called *fields*. Individual numbers, letters, and symbols called *characters* are inserted into the fields. This system may seem unfamiliar, but consider its similarity to the hierarchical concept maps described in Chapter 10. In concept mapping, the largest, most inclusive item holds increasingly smaller, less inclusive items. In the context of database management, think of the largest files as the most inclusive, the smallest files as the least inclusive.

A database can be composed of one file, or it can contain numerous files, depending on the uses to which the database is being put and the characteristics of the software. One of the largest database files in the world is used by the Internal Revenue Service, which has access to the records of millions of taxpayers in the United States. Most databases are much smaller, holding only a few hundred or a few thousands pieces of information. Programs like "Filing Assistant" or "Reflex" can help you set up a database for further use, or they can be adapted to an existing database. These and other database management systems also allow you to store information, search for specific types of information, retrieve needed records, sort records alphabetically or numerically, update files, redesign files, and print.

USING THE COMPUTER IN THE LIBRARY

For years library specialists have used computers to track book purchases, monitor costs, and account for circulating books. Recently, computers have been introduced into the school library for students' use. Perhaps you've seen computer terminals in the library and wonder how they're used. If you have already used one, you know how much a computer can increase your efficiency during research projects.

In-Library Bibliographic Searches

Searching through the card catalogue can be a time-consuming task, particularly for a large research paper. Copying and tracking down all the sources in which you may be interested can send you shuttling between the floors of one library or between several libraries. Although the card catalogue still serves an immensely useful function, its days may be numbered because of the computer's ability to perform bibliographic searches.

Suppose you're interested in researching something about the work of T. S. Eliot (1888–1965), the American-born poet who lived most of his life in England. You are interested in finding out more about him or about some aspect of his work; you have not yet narrowed your search. First, you access the college's holdings on T. S. Eliot by typing his name into the terminal. (Your library's particular method of storing this data may be different from another's. Yours might require you to type "Eliot, Thomas Stearns," while another requires only "T. S. Eliot.") The computer screen will display the books, journal articles, and other items that pertain to T. S. Eliot. Let's say that 250 items are listed. That's too many items to investigate. The computer, however, will allow you to refine your search. If you are interested in Eliot's famous poem "The Waste Land," you can type in "T. S. Eliot; The Waste Land" and have displayed the holdings that directly pertain to the poem. Perhaps 25 items deal directly with it. Now let's say that you've seen some interesting article titles on the screen and decide to refine your search further by looking for information on allusions in the poem to fertility myths. You would then type in something like "T. S. Eliot; The Waste Land; fertility myths," and the computer would narrow its search accordingly. The computer may be attached to a printer, so that you can get a printout of the final list you decide on. Or you may have to copy the information shown on the screen. In either event, you've accessed the material and narrowed it for your specific purposes and can begin your research. (Note that this particular example points toward an author search. In some courses you may be assigned a subject search or a title search.)

Off-Campus Bibliographic Searches

Your library may be connected to a database service that provides bibliographic entries—often thousands more than can be stored in a single library's holdings. A significant difference between off-campus and in-library bibliographic searches is that the number of sources available to you is potentially much higher through an off-campus service. This can be quite important if you need to locate old or obscure books and articles.

The way in which you plug into the information may also be different. Because database services are not located at your school, you'll have to link your computer to the service and have the resulting information transmitted over the phone lines to your terminal. Such transmitting occurs by means of a *modem,* a device that allows one computer to "speak" with another. Check with the library resources specialist familiar with the system in your library; the service you use is likely to charge for the phone time, and you should know whether that cost is passed on to you.

Some in-library bibliographic services allow you to search for and print the abstract for an article or book, but many do not. Most off-campus services routinely provide you with a list of selected abstracts of articles in which you think you might be interested. These abstracts allow you to decide whether you want to track down a book or article.

COMPUTER-AIDED LEARNING

The term *computer-aided learning* refers to five general categories of software that can help you improve in specific subject areas, help you solve problems, and help you simulate real-life situations. The five basic types are drill and practice software, tutorial software, problem-solving software, simulation software, and educational games.

Drill and Practice Software

In its simplest form, drill and practice software, sometimes called *programmed instruction,* resembles flash cards on the screen. In the typical drill and practice program, a problem, accompanying question, and possible answers are simultaneously displayed on the screen. Drill and practice software allows you to choose the correct answer and immediately receive feedback about your response. Because the questions are usually matching or multiple choice questions, this kind of software is most useful for instruction in, and review of, basic concepts in math, the sciences, and languages. For instance, you could use a chemistry drill and practice program to review the elements in the Periodic Table. A math drill and practice program could display a problem and ask you to select the correct solution. Using this program and others like it requires only that you have simple word-processing skills.

The "Hypercard" program for the *Apple MacIntosh* computer is a useful program for creating stacks of cards that you can scan through, modify, and review whenever you like. This program requires minimal programming skills, and it allows you to create and modify your own drill and practice programs.

Tutorial Software

Tutorial programs are constructed so that all necessary instructions appear on the screen. No other supplemental instructions are required. Tutorial software can present information in different fields of study and can be adapted to a number of formats. Tutorial programs have even been written to teach students how to use the computer.

Problem-solving Software

Problem solving is an important part of many learning and decision-making situations. Problem-solving software can help teach you this skill, often with problems posed in the context of a particular discipline.

One kind of problem-solving software is based on a series of principles accepted for use in the sciences and social sciences. Problem-solving software teaching the procedural model typically asks you to recognize a problem, formulate a hypothesis or possible solution to that problem, gather information, test potential solutions, and arrive at a viable solution. Though the cognitive processes that are used for solving problems are complex and not well understood, recent research suggests that many kinds of thinking occur in a less than strictly linear fashion. With this in mind, more complex types of problem-solving software have been developed. Familiar examples of such software occur in spreadsheet accounting and database management programs. These programs are configured to require that you solve a problem through several nonsequential steps.

Simulation Software

Simulation software is a program that uses data to model a real-life event. The software allows you to vary certain conditions so that you can test various hypotheses and predict different outcomes. Like drill and practice software, simulation software allows you to get immediate feedback about situations that would otherwise take days or weeks to calculate using conventional methods. It also teaches and reinforces principles about complex phenomena that might otherwise exist only as abstractions. A simulation program could allow you to predict and then simulate certain chemical reactions, and it then would display the results of your simulation either in text or in graphics. Another type of simulation software allows you to forecast the economic results of certain stock-market transactions.

Educational Games

Educational games use a game format to teach strategizing, logical skills, and concept skills. Depending on the game, you can compete with yourself, against the computer, or against a friend. Using an educational game can lower your anxiety about using the computer in the first place, or it can sharpen your skills and relax you during a particularly intense studying session. Keep in mind that the level at which you learn is related to the demands of the game. Games in which you shoot aliens are not too likely to increase your problem-solving skills.

GRAPHICS

If you want to make the presentation of a research paper or other project more professional looking, consider using a graphics program to design figures, tables, and diagrams. Graphics add pizzazz to your presentation, and graphics programs, like the word-processing programs they often accompany, are easy to learn and use.

CONTINUING TO LEARN

One of the tremendous side effects of using a computer is that you will continue to want to learn. Learning simple applications encourages you to move on to more complex ones. As this occurs, you will find that you can teach yourself to a greater degree than you may have ever considered possible. As you progress through college and move into your job or career, you will find that using the computer encourages and rewards self-motivation.

As your abilities progress, you may find that you'll want to take more advanced workshops and courses that target particular skills. You can make those decisions at your own pace and with your own needs in mind. You can also increase your proficiency with the computer by regularly reading some of the computer journals on the market. Popular trade and specialized journals are available in your school library. If you become seriously interested in computing, you can always become a regular subscriber.

The ways in which we learn are changing at an increasingly fast pace. You will undoubtedly find yourself in the next few years being challenged to learn on the computer. And, because you will continue to learn in conventional ways, you'll be in a position to take advantage of both worlds, adapting the choices you have to your personal learning style and preferences. Thus learning can continue to be an invigorating and personally rewarding experience.

SUMMARY

Why is it important to learn to use a computer?	Computers are becoming a fixture in most professional and business offices. Computer literacy will enhance your learning skills and is now required for graduation in many schools. Using a computer brings many personal benefits as well.
What are the primary ways in which I should use the computer?	Word-processing, spreadsheet accounting, and database management programs are the computer applications from which you are most likely to benefit. Educational software, written for a specific class or field of study, is another likely use. Learning these applications can save you time and energy on numerous projects you are likely to undertake in college and in the workplace.
How should I start to learn about computers at college?	First determine your college's computer requirements. Find out what courses you must take and whether you need to take them at any particular point in your college career. Prepare for required courses by familiarizing yourself with the texts that will be used. Locate the computer facilities on campus, and identify the student or students in charge. Ask to have the computers and their capabilities described to you.

What should I specifically ask about as I check out my college's computer facilities?	(1) How many computer terminals are available? (2) What types of computers and computer software are available? (3) How many and what type of printers are available? (4) What are the general rules for using the computer lab? Find out whether you need to sign up in advance to use the facilities.
What should I consider as I try to determine my personal computer needs?	In general, think about the ways in which learning to use a word processor can help you with correspondence, with keeping note files, and with making schedules for yourself. More specifically, try to determine how using a computer can help you in your proposed course of study. If you think you will major in the humanities or social sciences, think of the benefits of word processing. If you are likely to major in mathematics, any of the sciences, or a technical field, think about how you might benefit from learning to use a database management program.
What are the specific benefits of learning to use word-processing software?	Word processing a paper can save you considerable time in the editing and revising stages. After you have entered the text of your paper onto the computer, you can edit your work directly on the screen without having to redo the entire paper.
What about spreadsheet accounting and database management programs?	Spreadsheet accounting software allows you to enter, store, retrieve, and manipulate data for accounting and other purposes. You can perform a variety of calculations with speed and accuracy, which makes these programs invaluable for business, economics, and accounting courses. Database management software allows you to retrieve and manipulate data that has been entered into a database.
How can I use the computer in the library?	Computers in the library allow you to perform in-library bibliographic searches, which increase your speed and efficiency on

research projects because they allow you to find a large number of potentially useful sources quickly. Once you have accessed a large group of potential sources you can quickly and easily narrow your search for those that pertain to your interests.

What are some other uses to which I can put the computer?

Several types of computer software have been developed to aid in learning. Often described as computer-aided learning programs, these are drill and practice software, tutorial software, problem-solving software; simulation software, and educational games. Each of these has specific purposes and uses.

How can I continue to learn on the computer?

Once you have learned the general applications on the computer, you may find that your interests focus specifically on a more complex application. If you are interested, you can always take an advanced course in computer applications or in computer programming. The more you learn on the computer, the more you'll be able to learn, since many skills are transferable. Take advantage of computer publications. If you find one that is particularly well-suited to your needs, you may want to become a regular subscriber. By becoming a computer user, you will be in a good position to adapt to changes in the ways in which you will learn in the future.

HAVE YOU MISSED SOMETHING?

1. *Sentence completion.* Complete each of the following sentences with one of the three words listed below the sentence.

   a. Using a word-processing program is likely to increase your ______________________.

      productivity   labor   activity

   b. Hard copy refers to a ______________________.

      printout   disk   mainframe

2. *Matching.* In each blank space in the left column, write the number preceding the phrase in the right column that matches the left-hand item best.

_____ a. Dot matrix printer	1. A keyboard and a screen
_____ b. Computer applications	2. Provides sources for research
_____ c. Computer software	3. Programmed instruction
_____ d. Word processing	4. Word processing, spreadsheet accounting, and database management
_____ e. Terminal	5. Uses pins to strike the printer ribbon
_____ f. Bibliographic searches	6. Instructions written on disk or tape
_____ g. Drill and practice software	7. Allows you to revise documents easily

3. *True-false.* Write *T* beside the *true* statements and *F* beside the *false* statements.

_____ a. You can learn to use simple computer software by mastering six or seven basic steps.

_____ b. Files, fields, and characters are used in database management programs.

_____ c. Spreadsheet accounting software is useful for performing off-campus bibliographic searches.

_____ d. Learning to use one kind of computer software makes it more difficult to learn to use a different kind.

_____ e. I need to learn to use a computer only if I am going to major in a technical field.

4. *Multiple choice.* Choose the word or phrase that completes the following sentence most accurately, and circle the letter that precedes it.

Probably the biggest advantage to becoming computer literate is that you

a. understand programming languages.
b. can take advantage of new ways of learning.
c. know complex terminology.
d. know which computer to buy for yourself.

Appendix A

Answers to "Have You Missed Something?"

Chapter 1 Preparing for Academic Success

1. a. abilities b. responsibility
2. a. 4 b. 8 c. 3 d. 1 e. 5 f. 6 g. 2 h. 7
3. a. T b. F c. F d. T e. T f. T
4. a. Yes b. Yes c. Yes d. No e. No f. No
5. c

Chapter 2 Understanding Your Emotional and Physical Needs

1. a. tension b. failure c. assertive
2. a. 8 b. 7 c. 2 d. 6 e. 5 f. 4 g. 1 h. 3
3. a. T b. F c. F d. F e. T f. F
4. a. Yes b. No c. Yes d. No e. No f. Yes g. Yes
5. c

Chapter 3 Controlling Your Time

1. a. time b. habit
2. a. 3 b. 4 c. 6 d. 2 e. 1 f. 5
3. a. F b. T c. T d. F e. T f. F
4. a. Yes b. No c. Yes d. No e. Yes f. Yes
5. c

Chapter 4 Concentrating to Learn

1. a. problem b. cumulative c. boredom
2. a. 2 b. 7 c. 5 d. 1 e. 4 f. 8 g. 3 h. 6

3. a. T b. F c. F d. T e. F f. T
4. a. Yes b. No c. Yes d. No e. No f. Yes
5. a

Chapter 5 Forgetting and Remembering

1. a. 6 b. middle c. disliked
2. a. 6 b. 1 c. 5 d. 4 e. 8 f. 7 g. 3 h. 2
3. a. F b. T c. T d. F e. F
4. a. Yes b. Yes c. No d. Yes e. Yes f. No
5. d

Chapter 6 Listening to Take Good Notes

1. a. absorbed b. themes c. sympathetic
2. a. 2 b. 5 c. 8 d. 4 e. 3 f. 7 g. 1 h. 6
3. a. T b. F c. F d. T e. T
4. a. No b. Yes c. No d. Yes e. Yes f. Yes
5. c

Chapter 7 Notetaking

1. a. minutes b. forgetting
2. a. 4 b. 3 c. 7 d. 2 e. 6 f. 8 g. 5 h. 1
3. a. F b. T c. F d. T e. T f. T
4. a. Yes b. No c. Yes d. Yes e. No f. Yes g. Yes h. No
5. c

Chapter 8 Learning From Your Textbook

1. a. cramming b. sparingly c. high
2. a. 4 b. 6 c. 7 d. 5 e. 3 f. 1 g. 2 h. 8
3. a. F b. T c. T d. F e. T
4. a. Yes b. No c. Yes d. No e. Yes f. Yes
5. a

Chapter 9 Marking and Noting Textbooks

1. a. sentence b. telegraphic c. difficult
2. a. 5 b. 8 c. 2 d. 6 e. 7 f. 3 g. 1 h. 4

3. a. F b. T c. T d. T e. F f. T
4. a. Yes b. No c. Yes d. No e. Yes f. Yes
5. b

Chapter 10 Thinking Visually

1. a. brainpower b. logical c. oriented
2. a. 2 b. 3 c. 4 d. 5 e. 1 f. 8 g. 7 h. 6
3. a. F b. T c. T d. F e. T f. T
4. a. No b. Yes c. Yes d. No e. Yes f. Yes
5. d

Chapter 11 Preparing for Exams

1. a. success b. crisis c. first
2. a. 3 b. 8 c. 7 d. 1 e. 5 f. 4 g. 6 h. 2
3. a. T b. F c. T d. T e. T f. F
4. a. No b. Yes c. Yes d. No e. Yes f. Yes
5. d

Chapter 12 Answering True-False, Multiple-Choice, and Matching Questions

1. a. circled b. correct
2. a. 3 b. 5 c. 6 d. 1 e. 4 f. 2
3. a. F b. T c. F d. F e. T f. F
4. d

Chapter 13 Answering Sentence-Completion and Short-Answer Questions

1. a. context b. telegraphic
2. a. 4 b. 1 c. 5 d. 3 e. 6 f. 2
3. a. T b. F c. T d. T e. F f. T
4. b

Chapter 14 Answering Essay Questions

1. a. reasoning b. facts
2. a. 3 b. 6 c. 2 d. 5 e. 1 f. 4
3. a. F b. T c. T d. T e. F
4. b

Chapter 15 Improving Your Vocabulary

1. a. success b. context c. synonyms
2. a. 2 b. 3 c. 7 d. 6 e. 1 f. 4 g. 5 h. 8
3. a. F b. T c. T d. F e. T f. T
4. a. Yes b. No c. No d. Yes e. Yes f. Yes
5. b

Chapter 16 Improving Your Reading Speed

1. a. speed b. naturally
2. a. 2 b. 5 c. 3 d. 1 e. 4
3. a. F b. F c. T d. T e. F f. T
4. a

Chapter 17 Ten More Techniques for Improving Your Reading

1. a. magnets b. information
2. a. 3 b. 5 c. 4 d. 7 e. 1 f. 2 g. 6
3. a. F b. T c. T d. T e. T f. F
4. d

Chapter 18 Researching and Writing Papers

1. a. plagiarism b. dangling
2. a. 3 b. 6 c. 2 d. 1 e. 4 f. 5
3. a. T b. F c. T d. T e. F
4. a

Chapter 19 Studying Mathematics

1. a. reviewing b. numbers
2. a. 3 b. 2 c. 6 d. 5 e. 1 f. 4
3. a. F b. T c. T d. T e. F
4. d

Chapter 20 Studying Foreign Languages

1. a. facts b. habits
2. a. 5 b. 3 c. 6 d. 1 e. 2 f. 4

3. a. F b. T c. F d. T e. T
4. c

Chapter 21 Learning with the Computer

1. a. productivity b. printout
2. a. 5 b. 4 c. 6 d. 7 e. 1 f. 2 g. 3
3. a. T b. T c. F d. F e. F
4. b

Appendix B

Answers to PSAT and SAT Tests

TABLE 15.1 Answers to PSAT Vocabulary Test

Question Number	Correct Answer	Grade Level*	Percentage of Students Answering the Question Correctly†
1	D	6	68%
2	B	12	30
3	E	8	87
4	C	6	69
5	E	6	73
6	A	10	70
7	B	10	72
8	D	12	79
9	B	13	64
10	E	16	63
11	E	10	75
12	C	16	79
13	A	16	79
14	D	16	23
15	E	12	47
16	D	16	40
17	A	16	50
18	D	16	71
19	B	16	59
20	A	16	59

*Grade levels of students who attained the listed percentages.

†Percentage scores of students in specified grade levels as determined by Edgar Dale and Joseph O'Rourke in *The Living Word Vocabulary* (Chicago: Field Enterprises Educational Corporation, 1976).

TABLE 15.2 Answers to SAT Vocabulary Test

Question Number	Correct Answer	Percentage of Students Answering the Question Correctly
1	E	96%
2	C	95
3	B	90
4	B	87
5	A	85
6	D	80
7	E	80
8	A	71
9	B	75
10	C	69
11	C	66
12	B	68
13	D	55
14	D	35
15	E	32
16	A	24
17	A	22
18	A	20
19	B	19
20	A	18
21	A	16
22	E	15
23	C	13
24	A	18
25	B	10

Index